T0367066

QUINTILIAN

I

LCL 124

QUINTILIAN

THE ORATOR'S EDUCATION

BOOKS 1–2

EDITED AND TRANSLATED BY

DONALD A. RUSSELL

HARVARD UNIVERSITY PRESS
CAMBRIDGE, MASSACHUSETTS
LONDON, ENGLAND
2001

Copyright © 2001 by the President and Fellows
of Harvard College
All rights reserved

First published 2001

LOEB CLASSICAL LIBRARY® is a registered trademark
of the President and Fellows of Harvard College

Library of Congress Control Number 2001016920
CIP data available from the Library of Congress

ISBN 978-0-674-99591-8

*Composed in ZephGreek and ZephText by
Technologies 'N Typography, Merrimac, Massachusetts.
Printed on acid-free paper and bound by
The Maple-Vail Book Manufacturing Group*

CONTENTS

PREFACE

This is essentially a new translation of Quintilian, though I have felt free to use the elegant Loeb version of H. E. Butler (1920–1922) wherever I wanted. My aim has been to make the *Institutio* more intelligible and usable both to students of classics and to others interested in the general history of rhetoric, which is a much more popular subject than it was in Butler's day. Hence all the analyses, subheadings, introductions, footnotes, and indexes.

I could not have made the attempt at all without the generous help of many friends. Professor Michael Winterbottom has put his unique knowledge of Quintilian unreservedly at my disposal. Professor J. N. Adams and Dr. Philomen Probert have helped me enormously, especially in the grammatical parts of Book One. Dr. Doreen Innes has read the whole, and done it a great deal of good. She and Professor Winterbottom have also been kind enough to share the proofreading with me. Tobias and Eva Reinhardt have undertaken a lot of work on the Indexes, and Tobias has helped me also in Book Five. My St John's colleagues Nicholas Purcell and Gordon Baker have also come to my aid, as indeed have all the friends I have had occasion to consult. Rachel Chapman has turned the manuscript into an acceptable collection of disks and printouts, and also had a sharp and kind eye for the many problems of consistency that such a long work involves. I am immensely grateful to all these, and also to the editors and all connected with the production, and especially to Philippa Goold.

But it will of course be wholly my responsibility if the words of the publisher in George Borrow's *Lavengro* should prove prophetic: "I am not prepared, sir, to say that Quintilian is a drug, never having seen him; but I am prepared to say that man's translation is a drug, judging from the heap of rubbish on the floor." (See below, p. 28.)

St John's College   D. A. Russell
Oxford

INSTITUTIO ORATORIA
THE ORATOR'S EDUCATION

GENERAL INTRODUCTION

Life of Quintilian

Marcus Fabius Quintilianus was born at Calagurris (Calahorra) in the upper valley of the Ebro, probably around AD
35. His father was skilled in rhetoric (9.3.73), and the "old
Quintilian" named as a declaimer by the elder Seneca
(*Controversiae* 10 *praef.* 2) is probably a member of the
same family. Like the Annaei at Corduba, they were hop-
ing to rise in the world with the help of rhetoric and advocacy. Our Quintilian went to Rome as a young man. He
knew and admired Domitius Afer, orator and informer,
and witnessed his declining years; Afer died in 59. He re-
calls also (8.3.31) a literary dispute between Seneca and
Pomponius Secundus about the language of tragedy. Pomponius seems to have died in the early fifties.

We do not know when, or why, Quintilian returned to
Spain. But he was there, ready to join Galba, when the
latter set out for Rome to become emperor in 68. When
Vespasian, early in his reign, offered salaries to some
teachers in Greek and Latin rhetoric (Suetonius, *Vespasian* 18; Zonaras 11.17), Quintilian was a beneficiary. He
then (by his own statement) taught and practised as an
advocate for the next twenty years. His court work was important to him; he was thereby able to distance himself

from the mere scholastic declaimers, and offer a more "relevant" course to the ambitious young. We hear of four cases in which he was involved (4.1.19; 6.1.39; 7.2.24; 9.2.73). The most prestigious of these (4.1.19) was that involving Queen Berenice, the Jewish princess with whom Titus had fallen in love in Judaea: the case presumably happened during her stay in Rome between 75 and 79. By 85/6, Quintilian was a notable establishment figure: Martial's poem of that year (2.90) addresses him as "supreme controller of the wayward youth" and "glory of the Roman gown." It is easy, and perhaps not wrong, to see irony here, when the poet contrasts the successful advocate and teacher with his own modest wishes for "a night that brings sleep and a day without litigation." To Juvenal too (6.75, 280; 7.186), Quintilian is a type of the rich and successful careerist. His position improved further under Domitian, and he was ultimately (4 prooem. 2) made tutor to the two children of Flavius Clemens, who were destined to be the emperor's heirs. Late in life, too, he received *ornamenta consularia* (Ausonius, *Gratiarum actio* 7.31). By this time however he had retired from public teaching (2.12.12 perhaps implies that his retirement from practice was a bit later) and was engaged on the *Institutio Oratoria, The Orator's Education*. The chronology of these latter years, when his books were written, is of interest, and not altogether easy to sort out.

Our main evidence comes from the Prooemium to Book Six, his emotional introduction to his book on emotions, in which he grieves eloquently and lavishly for his elder son, the great hope of his life. (Fathers' hopes for their sons are central to Quintilian's views of education: "When the child is born," he says (1.1.1) "let the father

2

form good hopes of him.") It appears that Quintilian, in middle age, had married a very young wife of good family. Two sons were born (we do not hear of daughters, but that does not mean there were none) and the wife then died, still under nineteen. The younger son died a few months after his mother at the age of five, when Quintilian was composing his essay "on the reasons for the decadence of eloquence." The elder survived for a while, but died while the *Institutio* was being written. From the marriage to this last bereavement must have been ten or eleven years, perhaps a little more; but we cannot give an absolute date for the marriage. That the *Institutio* was completed before the disgrace and death of Flavius Clemens (who was accused of "atheism," apparently Judaism, or, according to later tradition, Christianity, at the end of his consulship in the summer of 95) seems to follow from the fact that the reference to Quintilian's tutorship of the two boys (4 *praef.* 2) was not removed when the work was handed over to the bookseller Trypho, who had long been complaining of delay. We may guess that Quintilian died soon after the completion of the book; if this is so, he did not live to see Domitian's murder or have to adapt himself to the new regime, as so many of his pupils did.

Among these pupils was the younger Pliny, who acknowledges Quintilian as a teacher (*Epist.* 2.14.9, 6.6.3), and perhaps also Tacitus. At any rate, Tacitus' *Dialogus de oratoribus,* composed under the new regime but having a dramatic date of 73, appears to challenge Quintilian's educational ideals, and certainly does not endorse them (see esp. C. O. Brink, *CQ* 39 (1984) 472–503). Of its three main characters, Messala takes a very Quintilianic line about education, but does not share Quintilian's optimism about future progress. He remains a simple *laudator temporis acti*. Aper is a modernist of whom Quintilian would not have approved; and Maternus advances political arguments to explain "decline" which are alien to Quintilian as we know him from the *Institutio*.

"Decadence of Eloquence"

But what about the lost, and much discussed, *De causis corruptae eloquentiae*, "Decadence of Eloquence"? There are a number of passages in the *Institutio* from which its tendency can be inferred: 2.4.41, 2.10.3, 5.12.17–23 (?), 8.3.50–58, 8.6.76, 10.1.125 (?). As we have seen, 6 *praef.* 3 gives an indication of its date. Like the *Institutio*, it is a work of retirement, a reflection of a lifetime's teaching and advocacy, not the programmatic polemic of a younger man. It is the professor's valedictory lecture, not his inaugural. From the references to it, it would seem to have been largely concerned with style (or at least with what Quintilian puts under *elocutio*), including tropes (8.6.76), and with the extravagances and mistakes of declaimers who have lost touch with the real world (2.10.3). It evidently dealt also with the origins of declamation itself in the fourth century BC (2.4.41). That it contained a critique of Seneca is less certain (see 10.1.125), and Quintilian's well-advertised dislike of the greatest prose writer of the century may well date from an earlier period, maybe even from some antipathy between two groups of Spanish *literati* on the make. To judge from Quintilian's inclusion of *decorum* (11.1) under *ornatus,* and so under *elocutio,* and from his discussion of *cacozelia* (8.3.56–58), it would be surprising if *De causis* did not have a strong moral ten-

4

dency (*vir bonus dicendi peritus,* "the good man skilled in speaking," is a key idea with him) and an insistence on the connection between morals and manners of writing and speaking. No doubt Tacitus knew this book; but his veiled response to Quintilian in the *Dialogus* seems to be to Quintilian's attitudes as a whole, without distinguishing between the shorter work and the long synthesis.

The Institutio: Sources and General Structure

It is the comprehensiveness of this synthesis that makes the *Institutio* unique among extant ancient works on rhetoric. It is this which made Richard Volkmann (1885, vi), himself the great nineteenth-century synthesizer of classical rhetoric, speak of Quintilian as offering an "Ariadne's thread" in the confused tangle *(in dem krausen Gewirre)* of rhetorical concepts and technical terms. The Elder Pliny's *Studiosus,* lost but apparently comparable in purpose (Pliny, *Epist.* 3.5.5), since it traced the whole education of the orator "from the cradle," can hardly have been more than half as long. Quintilian regarded his work as a piece of scholarship, involving not only the fruit of his own teaching experience, but a study of a large amount of the "literature" of the subject, even if some of this seemed to him unprofitable. Much of this technical writing is lost and unknown to us, but it is clear that he read very widely. It would be unfair to think that his reports of the views of others—his "doxographies" of "parts of speech," "status theory" and so on—are all based on pre-existing compilations. He often refers to the classics of early rhetorical theory—Plato, Aristotle, and Isocrates—but the extent of his direct knowledge of these is doubtful. His interpreta-

5

tions of the *Gorgias,* however (2.15, 2.21), imply a fairly detailed study of this text, which was indeed central to the "rhetoric v. philosophy" debate in Roman times (on this see D. Karadimas, *Sextus Empiricus against Aelius Aristides* (Lund 1996) 1–12). He also knew many Greek treatises of Hellenistic and later times, especially Hermagoras of Temnos and Dionysius of Halicarnassus; his dependence on the latter's *On Imitation* is such that one is tempted to question his first-hand knowledge of many of the Greek authors he recommends in 10.1. He also certainly made use of Greek writers on Figures and Tropes, such as the younger Gorgias (9.2.102, 106) and Caecilius of Caleacte, Longinus' "opponent" (9.1.22, 9.3.38). His most frequently used sources however were Latin. First among them was Cicero, the almost unassailable master both as an orator and as a theorist. Quintilian once adopts the unique procedure (9.1.26–45) of quoting long passages of *De oratore* and *Orator* to provide a framework for his own discussion of Tropes and Figures, a text, as it were, on which he offers a gloss.

There has been much dispute as to whether Quintilian used the book we know as *Rhetorica ad Herennium.* In a number of places (3.1.21, 5.10.2, 9.2.27, 9.3.64–71, 9.3.98) he quotes "Cornificius," and we notice that "Cornificius" says the same things as *Ad Herennium* IV. H. Caplan, in the excellent Loeb *Ad Herennium* (ix–xiv), takes a sceptical line. He stresses the point that "Cornificius" is usually cited after Cicero or among the Augustan authors (9.3.89), whereas *Ad Herennium* is usually (but not universally) believed to date from c. 80 BC, when Cicero was a young man. Others are more positive, and it is difficult to escape the conclusion that "Cornificius" is identical with, at any rate, the last part of *Ad Herennium* IV on Figures and Tropes, whether or not Quintilian knew the text which we have directly or only through an intermediary.

Celsus, Pliny, and Valgius, authors of the first century AD, are also often quoted, usually to be criticized. Celsus in particular (known to us from the surviving part of his "encyclopedia," the elegant *De medicina* (ed. W. G. Spencer in LCL)), appears to have been uncongenial to Quintilian because he did not take a high enough moral line about the purposes and qualifications of the orator, and was unduly concerned to appear original (9.1.18). As to contemporaries, Quintilian resolutely declines to name them, for good or ill, just as he names no living authors in his list of recommended reading: "some will be heard of one day" (10.1.94).

In compiling such a comprehensive synthesis, Quintilian needed a scheme which would cover everything. He chose a traditional one (3.3.1): the Five Parts of Rhetoric, nowadays sometimes called "Canons." This organization goes back in its essentials to Aristotle, and was the framework of Cicero's rhetorical works (cf. *De inventione* 1.9) and of *Ad Herennium* (1.3). It even structures the specialist treatise of "Longinus" *On Sublimity* (8). The whole later corpus of Greek rhetoric centring on the work of Hermogenes is based on the same principle. In Quintilian, it works out as follows: Books III–VII, *inventio,* including *dispositio* as a subordinate item (VII); VIII–XI *elocutio,* with "memory" and "delivery" (XI.2–3) as ancillaries. The whole is prefaced (I-II) by a discussion of the primary education to be given before the boy goes to his rhetor, and also of various general topics regarding the nature of rhetoric—whether it is an art, or a virtue, and so on. These

7

topics were important in the defence of rhetoric against philosophy, and they naturally formed part of any curriculum which offered some sort of general education and did not confine itself to the purely practical. The later Greek *Prolegomena* (*Prolegomenon Sylloge*, ed. H. Rabe, 1921) are full of these arguments, and offer many parallels to Quintilian's discussion. Book XII stands outside this scheme. It constitutes in fact the second and third sections in another way of dividing the subject: Art, Artist, Work. This division is also in Quintilian's mind; he regards it indeed as "the best" (2.14.5). But his work is of course overwhelmingly concerned with Art, not with the other two, and this demands the "five-part" scheme, which therefore articulates most of the work.

There is no problem here. "Art, Artist, Work" will stand as a scheme, even if "Art" fills immensely more space than the rest. But there are other ways of breaking up the subject which do not sit so easily with the Five Parts.

(1) Forensic (some prefer the term Judicial), Deliberative, Epideictic. These traditional categories are set out in 3.4–11. Both in Invention and in Elocution (not to speak of Gestures), these three types (*genera*) of oratory have some common demands, and some which are peculiar to each. Quintilian has to bring in the special needs of each from time to time, as the context requires.

(2) Parts of a speech: Prooemium, Narrative, Argument and Refutation, Epilogue. This division of the subject is found in early rhetoric (e.g. Aristotle, *Rhet.* 1414a30ff.) under the head of "Disposition" (*taxis, oikonomia*); but in the Hellenistic tradition reflected in Cicero's *De inventione* and in the *Ad Herennium*, it has been transferred to Invention, as in Quintilian. It is set out in 4 *praef.* 6, and

then in detail in Books IV–VI. It is the basic plan of many elementary treatises (e.g. Anonymus Seguierianus and Apsines), and was at all periods a natural basis for practical instruction. If it is used in this way, it does of course demand discussion of Invention, Elocution, and Gesture for each Part separately. In Quintilian's general scheme, however, these have their own place; and we therefore find the "Five Parts" (like the three *genera*) recurring where required, e.g. in 11.3.161–174, where recommendations are made for Gesture and Delivery in each of the Parts.

(3) The characterization of the orator's duties (*officia*) as "to inform, to please, and to move" (3.5) constitutes another possible way of organizing much of the subject, though it does not seem to have been used as the structural principle of any work. The three *officia* correspond to the three types of style (12.10.59; compare Cicero, *Orator* 69) and the relative importance of one or the other varies as the speech progresses—"information," for example, is crucial to the Narrative, emotional effect to the Epilogue.

None of these plans gives a curriculum. Teaching was practical, with many exercises and commented readings. So Invention, Disposition, Elocution, and Gesture were all involved at every stage. If *memoria artificiosa* was to be used (though Quintilian did not think much of it, 11.2), it would surely have to start very early, when the boy could master the system more easily and make it "second nature." In short, as Quintilian often makes clear (e.g. 1.4.17), the *Institutio* is a handbook for teachers and parents, and contains far more than it is wise to tell the average student. Looked at from this point of view, some features of its organization which at first sight seem surprising cease to matter very much. A striking example is

9

the split discussion of the Theory of Issues (*status*): the basic principles are in Book III under Invention, the detailed *divisiones* in Book VII, as the sole topic to be considered under Disposition. Practical teaching must always have combined these, and may have been more like what we see in the much later *Diaireseis* of Sopater, where cases are arranged according to their *status*, and one can conceive a course of lessons which would develop progressively.

Consider also the treatment of *decorum* in 11.1. Quintilian has already observed (1.5.1) that most people regard "appropriate" language as part of *ornatus*; and the traditional account of the "virtues" of style, coming down from Theophrastus, included this (as *to prepon*). It comes therefore under *elocutio*; but it is really too important in Quintilian's thinking to be comfortable here. It is both a moral and an aesthetic concept; the only orator who will grasp it properly is the man of sound moral principles, the *vir bonus dicendi peritus* (for the phrase, see e.g. 1 *praef.* 8, 2.15.1, 2.16.1, 12.1.1).

Again, the elaborate list of recommended reading (10.1) strictly comes under *elocutio,* its professed object being only to supply verbal facility and fluency. But of course its educational value is far greater than this; it provides a store of ideas and thoughts (10.2.1) conducive to virtue. Quintilian's teaching, as is clear from Book I, involved study of historians and poets at all stages, from the boy in the grammarian's class to the nearly adult student of rhetoric—and indeed beyond. He envisages his pupil not only as a future orator, but, in certain circumstances, as writer or historian—for example, in old age (12.11.4), or if he lacks memory or talent for improvisation (11.2.49).

Finally, why does the famous theory of Three Styles—grand, slight, and smooth or intermediate—appear not under *elocutio* at all, but in the account of the finished Work (12.10)? In *Ad Herennium* IV, by contrast, these styles are brilliantly illustrated (and their excesses parodied) as part of the author's discussion of *elocutio,* other parts of which Quintilian seems to have treated as authoritative. The answer is not simple. On the one hand, Quintilian plainly does not regard the categorization as particularly important: he reports it (12.10.58) as essentially the view of others, and he criticizes it (12.10.66–68) as not allowing for the innumerable shades and tones that lie between the three principal "styles." On the other hand, he recognizes that all these manners have their uses, in different contexts or parts of a speech. It is important that the orator should control them all. What matters most to Quintilian is the difference between style which he can approve and style which is "corrupt" or decadent; and this difference goes much deeper than the contrast between the "grand" and the "turgid," or between the "plain" and the "low," contrasts which are so well defined in the *Ad Herennium.* Once again, it is a matter of the whole personality of the orator, as it has been trained and developed by Art; the Work which emerges at the end is the expression of all this. Nature *alone*—as Quintilian quite often urges, with depreciators of education in his sights—will not do; yet no amount of professional training can fill the gap if the basic ability and good character are not there. "Nature," in fact, remains a key concept in Quintilian's thinking: she is, as Elaine Fantham puts it (*Rhetorica* 13 (1995) 136), "the efficient cause of artistic eloquence and the patroness of

11

the *Institutio*." The effort to attain the ideal—and we must always remember that Quintilian (like Cicero) is delineating an ideal, not describing the common practice of his day—involves working with her, not against her, and having a rather lofty view of the "nature" of man as a rational, moral, and political being.

Analysis

The chapter headings in the MSS (not reproduced in this edition) are not Quintilian's, neither are the chapter divisions, but these generally represent fairly coherent pieces of the argument. The headings and subheadings given in the translation are mine.

A.   Prefatory material: 1.1–3.5

(i)   The educational preliminaries

1.1   Early childhood: learning to read and write letters, syllables and complete words.

1.2   Home teaching or school?

1.3   Advice to teachers on diagnosing abilities and handling young children. Against corporal punishment.

1.4–7   Linguistic teaching from the *grammaticus* (*ratio loquendi*).

1.8–9   Reading texts under the *grammaticus*. Writing elementary exercises (fable, *gnōmē, chria,* simple narrative) under the *grammaticus.*

1.10   Other disciplines: logic, music, geometry.

1.11   Other teachers: actors, gymnastic trainers.

14

Text

The text of this edition is based on that of M. Winterbottom (Oxford 1970) and follows it in matters of orthography and the treatment of Greek words (see Winterbottom, *Problems in Quintilian* (1970) 35–60). It does however differ in many places in choice of readings. The textual apparatus is of course very basic, but it does show all substantial divergences from the Oxford text.

The medieval transmission of Quintilian has led to a tradition which is less reliable in some parts of the work than in others: details in Winterbottom, *Problems* 3–32, summary also in *Texts and Transmission*, ed. L. D. Reynolds (Oxford 1983) 332–334. The primary sources are the following:

A, Ambrosianus E 153 sup., a ninth-century MS, now mutilated, and containing contemporary corrections (*a*).
B, Bernensis 351, also ninth century, incomplete and taken from a mutilated original; where available, our best guide.
Bg, Bambergensis M.4.14, tenth century; derived from *B,* but having corrections (*b*) which come from *A.*
G, the later (but not much later) part of this Bamberg manuscript, also derived from *A.*

Our text depends on these primary sources as follows:

On *AB:* 1.2.5–5.14.12; 8.3.64–8.6.17; 8.6.67–9.3.2.
On *Bb:* 10.1.107–11.1.71; 11.2.33–12.10.43.
On *AG:* 5.14.12–8.3.64; 8.6.17–67; 9.3.2–9.4.135; 12.11.22–31.

On *G:* 9.4.135–10.1.107; 11.1.71–11.2.33; 12.10.43–12.11.22.

We are on surest ground where *AB* are available; *Bb* offer the next best thing. The beginning of the work (down to 1.2.5) is best known from *H* (Harleianus 2664), and for 10.1.46–131 and 12.10.10–15 *G* is supplemented by *X* and *Y* (Parisinus lat. 7696, 7231, eleventh century). For these, and other medieval manuscripts occasionally referred to, see Sigla.

Renaissance manuscripts also provide good readings, generally to be regarded as good conjectures. I have not specified these, but indicate them by the general symbol *recc.* For details, and for further information about the corrections in *A* and *B,* see Winterbottom's edition and his *Problems in Quintilian* (1970). Similarly, *edd.* indicates a reading found in one or more of the early editions listed below. For Regius, see M. Winterbottom, "In Praise of Raphael Regius" in *Antike Rhetorik und ihre Rezeption. Symposion zu Ehren von Prof. C. J. Classen,* ed. S. Döpp (Stuttgart, 1999) 99–116. Many minor uncontroversial corrections from these sources have been tacitly accepted.

The most famous episode in the history of Quintilian's text is the discovery by Poggio in 1416 of a complete manuscript at St. Gallen. Poggio and some others went over from Constance (where they were attending the Council), looking for books. They found Quintilian, among many others, dirty and dusty—not in the library, but in the basement of a tower, "not fit for condemned prisoners." The manuscript he found (*T*) is a descendant of *A;* it was with its discovery that a process of restoring Quintilian to fame and favour may be said to have begun.

Quintilian's Influence

Quintilian's influence on European culture has hardly ever been surveyed as a whole. Two old editions of Book I (Fierville 1890, and more usefully Colson 1924) provide the nearest approaches to a complete view. More recently, the nineteenth centenary of the *Institutio,* supposed to have fallen in 1995, has given rise to two collections of essays: one in *Rhetorica* 13.3 (1995), and one in the third volume of the proceedings of an international congress held at Madrid and Calahorra, and published as *Quintiliano: historia y actualidad de la retórica,* ed. T. Alabadejo, E. del Rio, J. A. Caballero (1998) (hereafter *QHAR).*

Quintilian's influence is to be seen in the history of rhetoric, of education, and of literary criticism. It is often of course inextricably linked with that of other ancient writers, especially Cicero and Plutarch, in a way that makes it impossible to isolate the truly "Quintilianic" elements. And the three areas are by no means distinct. Rhetoric has always been a school discipline, and it has always had a tendency (shown in Quintilian in 10.1 and in much of the discussion of Figures and Tropes) to use poetry and other forms of literature as examples, and so to develop into a kind of literary criticism. With these provisos, I offer here a brief chronological sketch of a very large subject.

In late antiquity, Quintilian's views on primary education were certainly known. It is intriguing to observe how they are adapted by Jerome (*Letter* 107, pp. 338–370 Wright, LCL) to fit the case of a little Christian girl destined to be a nun. He may also have been known as an orator. At least, Sidonius Apollinaris speaks of his "thunderbolt" (*fulmen*) and of his pungency (*acrimonia*); but those

21

passages (*Carmina* 2.191 and *Epistles* 5.10) may, as W. B. Anderson (LCL Sidonius, vol. I, 23) suggests, refer only to the declamations attributed to Quintilian. However, he did allow a speech or two to be published, and something may have survived. At the same time, the rhetorical treatises of late antiquity show comparatively little dependence on Quintilian, with the single exception of Julius Victor, who copies him out extensively and is often a valuable witness to the text.

We should not exaggerate the incompleteness of the texts of Quintilian known in the Middle Ages. More than half the book could be read, though Books VI and VII, and large parts of VIII, IX, and X, were among the missing items. He certainly played a considerable part both in suggesting methods of teaching (M. C. Woods, *QHAR* 3. 1531–1540) and in the actual content of rhetorical doctrine. But he was not the primary text for this: that was *Ad Herennium*, believed to be by Cicero, and made the subject of voluminous commentaries (much as Hermogenes was in the Greek-speaking East at the same time), to the enrichment of which Quintilian made a large contribution (J. O. Ward, *Rhetorica* 13 (1995) 231–284). We should therefore not make too much of the impact of Poggio's discovery: it caught the imagination of the times precisely because Quintilian was already well known, just as newly found speeches of Cicero were acclaimed because they added something to the works of an acknowledged master. Nevertheless, it is very important that Quintilian was complete when the enthusiasms of the Renaissance multiplied manuscripts, and even more so when printing began. The sections on imagination, emotion, Figures, and Tropes, much of which mainly depended on the new discovery, were among the most eagerly studied parts of the whole work.

Cicero and Quintilian were indissolubly associated in men's minds both before and after 1416. Petrarch had a manuscript which he corrected (= K, Parisinus Latinus 7720), and in 1374 he wrote an autobiographical letter to Luca de Penna (*Epist. de rebus senilibus* XVI.1 = *Epistolae selectae* ed. A. F. Johnson (1923), 198) in which he says that his study of Quintilian has confirmed him in the opinion that Cicero is the one supreme master: he quotes with approval 10.1.112, to the effect that "anyone who takes great pleasure in Cicero can have good hopes of himself." (The same sentence is quoted also by Racine in a letter to his son (4 October 1692): *souvenez-vous toute votre vie de ce passage de Quintilien, qui étoit lui-même un grand personnage.*)

This was certainly the attitude of Renaissance humanism in the fifteenth and early sixteenth centuries. Quintilian was important, not only for his Latinity and his judiciousness, but as an interpreter of Cicero. Being himself both a theorist and a practitioner of *imitatio,* he was a natural model for an educational ideal founded on the attempt to revive the literary, social, and political qualities seen in the classical authors. Thus Lorenzo Valla (1407–1457), who began his career with a (lost) "comparison of Cicero and Quintilian," and who had a bad relationship with Quintilian's "discoverer" Poggio, was none the less an enthusiast, taught and commented on Quintilian, and accepted both the moral dimension of the *Institutio* and its integration of dialectic (i.e. the subject of Book V) into the rhetorical curriculum (Kennedy (1980) 207–208; Grafton and Jardine (1986) 66–82). As for Erasmus, one only has to

23

look through the various educational works translated in the Toronto *Complete Works of Erasmus* (*CWE*), vols. 24–25, to see how pervasive the Quintilianic ingredient is in all of them. It is impertinent, Erasmus says in *De ratione studii ac legendi* (*CWE* 24. 672), to write about teaching after Quintilian; and if Quintilian had only gone into more detail, *De copia* (*CWE* 24. 297) would never have been needed. In *De conscribendis epistulis,* Quintilian is referred to about 80 times, and in *De pronuntiatione* about 50. *De pueris instituendis* rests mainly on Quintilian and on the book on the education of children attributed to Plutarch (*Moralia* 1–13), the other principal ancient treatment of the subject which survives.

Thus the two main areas in which Erasmus sees himself as a follower of Quintilian are (1) Latinity and the principles of composition, and (2) the education of children. In the latter area, he is following a tradition well established in the fifteenth century by Aeneas Sylvius, later Pope Pius II, in his *De liberorum educatione* (1450), and by Guarino's *De ordine docendi et studendi* (1458). It was a tradition to be seen also in the educational works of Juan Luis Vives (*De ratione studii puerilis* 1523, *De tradendis disciplinis* 1531) which, next to Erasmus, were the main channel for Quintilian's ideas on this subject, especially in England and northern Europe. It emerges again in the earliest English treatise of this kind, Sir Thomas Elyot's *Boke called the Governour* (1531), which adopts the unusual view (presumably suggested by the priority given to Greek by Quintilian, 1.1.12) that Greek should be begun as soon as Latin.

In the latter part of the sixteenth century, however, there were changes which affected the value accorded to Quintilian's rhetoric, and thus to his book as a whole. In the

Rhetoric of Bartolomeo Cavalcante (published 1559, but the fruit of many years' work) Quintilian is often criticized, and his organization of the subject regarded as inferior to Aristotle's, whom Cavalcante wishes to restore to the chief place. More significantly, the French school of Ramus (Pierre de la Ramée, 1515–1572) and Talaeus (Omer Talon, c. 1510–1562) treated Invention and Disposition, the first two of the "parts" of rhetoric in Quintilian's system, as parts of *dialectic,* and so confined rhetoric proper to Quintilian's *elocutio* and *pronuntiatio.* At the same time, they parted company with Quintilian's ideals by not putting moral and civic duties at the centre of the education they offered. For Ramus, "the good man skilled in speaking" was a faulty and misleading definition of the orator: *qua* orator, he had nothing to do with goodness (Kennedy (1980) 210–213; Grafton and Jardine (1986) 161–170). In any case, for some reason, Quintilian fell somewhat out of fashion as the century wore on. Muretus (1526–1588) complained that the *Institutio* was no longer the basic textbook that it had been when he was a boy. This decline, partly at least due to the influence of Ramus, can be seen, for example, in the rhetorical teaching of Gabriel Harvey (Grafton and Jardine (1986) 184–196). It can also be seen reflected in the English treatises on education which followed Elyot: Ascham's *Schoolmaster* (1571), Mulcaster's *Positions* and *The Elementarie* (1581–1582), and Milton's *Tractate on Education* (1644). In this last, rhetoric is given a late place in the curriculum, following many other studies; there is here a marked contrast with Quintilian, for whom the other studies are ancillary to the acquisition of oratorical skill. The most famous reference to Quintilian in English literature comes of course from Milton: his "words that would make Quintilian stare and gasp" (*Sonnet* XI) carries the implication that Quintilian was an authority on euphony.

Nevertheless, Quintilian was not yet eclipsed. The use made of him in Ben Jonson's *Discoveries* (1640; ed. Herford and Simpson, 8. 561–649) is enough to show this. In the advice he gives the Earl of Newcastle on bringing up children, Jonson draws very heavily on Quintilian, not only on Book I, and not only through Vives. And in the formal teaching of school and university rhetoric Quintilian remained always a central authority. It should be remembered that this kind of teaching continued well into the nineteenth century, especially in France and countries under French influence: Heinrich Heine, at school in French-occupied Düsseldorf around 1810, was subjected to the *Art oratoire* of the Abbé Daulnoy, rules taken from Quintilian, illustrations from the masterpieces of French pulpit oratory (*Memoiren;* see W. Wülfing, *QHAR* 3. 1542). It continued also in America, but with different emphases, and with less and less direct relationship to the classical authorities. And it persisted even through periods when "rhetorical" came to be a synonym of "insincere" or "mechanical," and rhetoric came to be thought of not as a normative system which should aid and control literary composition, but as an object of historical scholarship, to be studied in the light of the social circumstances which gave rise to it.

These changes of course had hardly begun in the seventeenth century. French schools, not only Port Royal, where Racine was taught, but all the Jesuit *collèges* (such as that where Voltaire went to school) taught a thoroughly Quintilianic form of the subject. Jouvency's *De ratione discendi et docendi* bases reading recommendations and written exercises largely on Quintilian (E. Flamarion, *QHAR* 3. 1275–1287), and the Jansenist Charles Rollin abridged Quintilian for schools and paid him a great tribute in his influential *Traité des études* (1726). Much the same happened all over Europe, more especially in Catholic countries. A striking example is the *Instituzioni oratorie* of Ignazio Falconieri, published at Naples in 1789, which follows Quintilian's order almost precisely: an Introduction on the definition, usefulness, nobility, and history of rhetoric: separate books on Invention, Disposition, and Elocution; and an appendix on the presentation of a speech (see Luigi Spina, in *La cultura classica a Napoli dell' Ottocento,* with preface by M. Gigante (Naples 1987) 129–133).

What in Falconieri is a matter for an appendix, the actual delivery of a speech, is of course a subject on which Quintilian (11.3) gives instructions far more elaborate than can be found in any other ancient source. It is no wonder that he was the basis (if not much more) of some very learned and ingenious works in this field: John Bulwer's *Chirologia* and *Chironomia* (1644), and the Jesuit Louis de Crésolles' (Cresollius) *Vacationes Autumnales* (on this, see S. Conte in *QHAR* 3. 1219–1228).

In the English-speaking world, a series of famous lectures on rhetoric tell a story which is not very different. Adam Smith's Glasgow lectures on "Rhetoric and Belles Lettres" were first given in 1748, but were not published till our own time, when a student's notes were discovered (Quintilian would have sympathized: see 1 *prooem.* 7) and edited (best by J. C. Bryce, Oxford 1983). *Belles lettres* in the title is significant: the lectures contain much that is directed more towards the private study of literature in general than towards the practical oratory of the pulpit or the bar. The same is true of a more famous work with the same title, said by some to plagiarize Adam Smith, namely the Edinburgh lectures of Hugh Blair, first given in 1754, and published in 1783, and in many subsequent editions. Blair's admiration for Quintilian is practically unbounded; he even cautiously recommends the "dry and tedious" technical parts (i.e. Books V and VII) as useful to "pleaders of the bar." But, like Smith, he is primarily concerned to instil good literary taste, on principles applicable to modern as well as to classical literature (Kennedy (1980) 234–240; G. L. Hatch, *QHAR* 3. 1336–1345 gives a useful brief account). John Quincy Adams's famous Harvard lectures of 1806 are more Quintilianic, more practical, and less aesthetic; but his example was not followed, and the chair which he held was later converted into a professorship of poetry. Rhetoric, divorced from classical scholarship, went its own way (Kennedy (1980) 240).

I conclude with a passage from George Borrow's autobiographical novel *Lavengro* (1851), in which he relates a conversation with the prospective editor of a Review. The dramatic date is 1824.

> The conversation consisted entirely of compliments till just before we separated, when the future editor inquired of me whether I had ever read Quintilian, and, on my replying in the negative, expressed his surprise that any gentleman should aspire to become a critic who had never read Quintilian, with the comfortable information, however, that he could supply me with a Quintilian at half-price, that

is, a translation made by himself some years previously, of which he had, pointing to the heap on the floor, still a few copies remaining unsold. For some reason or other, perhaps a poor one, I did not purchase the editor's translation of Quintilian.

Fact or fiction? The only complete English Quintilian produced in the nineteenth century was the (still very useful) version of J. S. Watson (1856), who himself comments on the inadequacy of his eighteenth-century predecessors, W. Guthrie (1756), and J. Patsall (1774). If Patsall is meant, "some years" means fifty.

BIBLIOGRAPHY AND
ABBREVIATIONS

Select Editions of Quintilian

(a) Not separately specified (= edd.)
Campanus, Rome 1470
Jenson, Venice 1471
Aldus, Venice 1514
Ascensius, Paris 1516, 1531

(b)
P. Burman, Leyden 1720
G. L. Spalding, Leipzig 1798–1816
C. Halm, Leipzig 1868–1869
L. Radermacher, Leipzig 1907, 1935
H. E. Butler, LCL, 1920–1922
M. Winterbottom, Oxford 1970
H. Rahn, Darmstadt (with German trans.) 1972, 1988
J. Cousin, Paris (with French trans.) 1975–1980
S. Corsi and C. M. Calcante, Milan (with Italian trans.)
    1997

(c)
Book I: F. H. Colson, Cambridge 1924
Book II: M. Winterbottom, Oxford D.Phil. thesis 1962
Book III: J. Adamietz, Munich 1966

Book X: W. Peterson, Oxford 1891
Book XII: R. G. Austin, Oxford 1954

Select Editions of Other Classical Authors

Anonymus Seguierianus, and Apsines of Gadara, ed. M. R. Dilts and G. A. Kennedy. Leiden, 1997. (= D–K)

Caecilius of Caleacte, ed. E. Ofenloch. Leipzig, 1907.

Callimachus, ed. R. Pfeiffer. Oxford, 1949–1953.

Calpurnius Flaccus, *Declamationes,* ed. L. Håkanson, Stuttgart, 1978; ed. L. A. Sussman, Leiden, 1994.

Cicero, *De oratore,* ed. (comm. only) A. D. Leeman and others. Heidelberg, 1981–.

Cicero, *Orationum deperditarum fragmenta,* ed. F. Schoell. Leipzig, 1917. (See also General Bibliography, s.v. Crawford.)

Demetrius, *On Style,* ed. D. C. Innes (LCL), 1995.

Dionysius of Halicarnassus, *Critical Essays,* ed. S. Usher (LCL), 1974–1985; *Opuscula,* ed. H. Usener and L. Radermacher, vol. 2, Leipzig, 1904.

Doxographi Graeci, ed. H. Diels. Berlin, 1879 (1958).

Ennius, ed. E. H. Warmington (in *ROL*); ed. J. Vahlen (ed. 2, 1903); O. Skutsch, *Annales,* 1985.

Epicurea, ed. H. Usener. Leipzig, 1887 (1966).

Fragmenta Poetarum Latinorum, ed. W. Morel. Leipzig, 1927. (See also General Bibliography, s.v. Courtney.)

Fronto, *Epistulae,* ed. P. P. J. van den Hout (ed. 2, 1988); ed. C. R. Haines (LCL), 1928–1929.

Hermagoras, ed. D. Matthes. Leipzig, 1962.

Hermogenes, ed. H. Rabe. Leipzig, 1913.

Imperatoris Augusti Fragmenta, ed. H. Malcovati. Turin, 1947.

Julius Victor, ed. R. Giomini and M. S. Celentano. Leipzig, 1980. (= G–C)

"Longinus" *On the Sublime,* ed. D. A. Russell, Oxford, 1964 (also LCL 1995); ed. L. M. Mazzucchi, Milan, 1992.

Menander Rhetor, ed. D. A. Russell and N. G. Wilson. Oxford, 1981 (cited also by pages of Spengel, *Rhetores Graeci*).

Minor Latin Poets, ed. J. W. and A. M. Duff (LCL), 1935.

Prolegomenon Sylloge, ed. H. Rabe. Leipzig, 1931.

[Quintilian] *Declamationes Maiores,* ed. L. Håkanson. Stuttgart, 1982.

[Quintilian] *Declamationes Minores,* ed. M. Winterbottom. Berlin, 1984.

Rutilius Lupus, ed. E. Brooks. Leiden, 1970.

Seneca, *Controversiae and Suasoriae,* ed. M. Winterbottom (LCL), 1974.

Theon, *Progymnasmata,* ed. M. Patillon and G. Bolognesi. Paris, 1997. (English translation in G. A. Kennedy, *Progymnasmata,* privately published (Fort Collins, Colorado; second edition, 2000).)

General Bibliography

(See also the *Index Editorum et Virorum Doctorum* in M. Winterbottom's edition, pp. xvii–xxii.)

Adamietz, J. (1966). *M. Fabi Quintiliani Institutio Oratoria, Liber III.* Munich.

    (1988). "Quintilians Institutio Oratoria." *ANRW* 2.32.4.2226–2271.

BIBLIOGRAPHY AND ABBREVIATIONS

Adams, J. N. (1982). *The Latin Sexual Vocabulary*. London.

Adams, J. N., and R. G. Mayer, edd. (1999). *Aspects of the Language of Latin Poetry*. Oxford. (= Proceedings of the British Academy 93.)

Allen, W. S. (1965). *Vox Latina*. Cambridge.

Atherton, C. (1988). "Hand over fist: the failure of Stoic rhetoric." *CQ* 38: 392–427.

(1993). *The Stoics on Ambiguity*. Cambridge.

Axelson, B. (1945). *Unpoetische Wörter*. Lund.

Barwick, K. (1957). *Probleme der stoischen Sprachlehre und Rhetorik*. Berlin. (*Abh. Sachs. Ak., phil.–hist. Kl.*, 49.3.)

(1963). *Das rednerische Bildungsideal Ciceros*. Berlin. (ibid. 54.3.)

Beare, W. (1950). *The Roman Stage*. London.

Bellaira, G. (1968). *Tiberii de figuris Demosthenicis liber*. Rome.

Bernabé, A. (1987). *Poetae Epici Graeci* 1. Leipzig.

Bieber, M. (1961). *The History of the Greek and Roman Theater*. Princeton.

Birkett, N. (Lord) (1961). *Six Great Advocates*. London.

Biville, F. (1990). *Les emprunts du latin au grec: approche phonétique*. 2 vols. Louvain–Paris.

Blank, D. L. (1998). *Sextus Empiricus "Against the Grammarians."* Oxford.

Blum, H. (1969). *Die antike Mnemotechnik*. Hildesheim.

Bonner, S. F. (1949). *Roman Declamation*. Cambridge.

(1977). *Education in Ancient Rome*. London.

Bornecque, H. (1902). *Les déclamations et les déclamateurs d'après Sénèque le père*. Lille.

(1907). *Les clausules métriques latines*. Lille.

Bremmer, J., and H. Roodenburg (1991). *A Cultural History of Gesture.* Polity Press, Cambridge.

Brink, C. O. (1989). "Quintilian's *de causis corruptae eloquentiae* and Tacitus' *Dialogus de oratoribus.*" *CQ* 39: 472–503.

Buchheit, V. (1960). *Untersuchungen zur Theorie des Genos Epideiktikon.* Munich.

Buck, C. D. (1955). *The Greek Dialects.* Chicago.

Burgess, T. C. (1902). *Epideictic Speeches.* Chicago.

Calboli Montofusco, L. (1986). *La dottrina degli status nella retorica greca e romana.* Hildesheim.

Clark, D. L. (1957). *Rhetoric in Greco-Roman Education.* Columbia U. P.

Classen, C. J. (1965). "Die Aufbau des zwölften Buches . . ." *Museum Helveticum* 22: 181–190.

Coleman, K. (1988). *Statius, Silvae IV.* Oxford.

Courtney, E. (1980). *A Commentary on the Satires of Juvenal.* London.

(1993). *The Fragmentary Latin Poets.* Oxford.

(1995). *Musa Lapidaria, A Selection of Latin Verse Inscriptions.* Atlanta.

Cousin, J. (1936). *Etudes sur Quintilien.* Paris.

Crawford, J. (1994). *M. Tullius Cicero: the fragmentary speeches.* Ed. 2, Atlanta.

Crook, J. A. (1967). *Law and Life of Rome.* Ithaca.

(1995). *Legal Advocacy in the Roman World.* London.

Cupaiolo, F. (1966). *Tra Poesia e Poetica.* Naples.

de Decker, J. (1913). *Juvenalis Declamans.* Ghent.

Dyck, A. R. (1996). *Cicero, De officiis.* Ann Arbor.

Edelstein, E. L., and I. G. Kidd (1972–1988). *Posidonius: fragments.* Cambridge.

Fairweather, J. (1981). *Seneca the Elder.* Cambridge.

Fortenbaugh, W. W. (and others) (1992). *Theophrastus of Eresus: Sources.* Leiden.

Giannantoni, G. (1990). *Socratis et Socraticorum Reliquiae* (= *Elenchos* XVIII). Naples.

Gleason, M. (1994). *Making Men.* Princeton.

Grafton, A., and Jardine, L. (1986). *From Humanism to the Humanities.* London.

Grant, M. A. (1924). *The Ancient Rhetorical Theories of the Laughable.* Madison.

Green, R. D. H. (1991). *The Works of Ausonius.* Oxford.

Gudeman, A. (1894). *Tacitus: Dialogus de Oratoribus.* Boston.

Guthrie, W. K. C. (1962–1981). *History of Greek Philosophy.* Cambridge.

Hadot, I. (1984). *Arts libéraux et philosophie dans la pensée antique.* Paris.

Heath, M. (1995). *Hermogenes On Issues.* Oxford.

Heldemann, K. (1982). *Antike Theorien über Entwicklung und Verfall der Redekunst* (*Zetemata* 77). Munich.

Hillgruber, M. *Die pseudoplutarchische Schriften de Homero, Beiträge zur Altertumskunde* 57 (1994) and 58 (1999). Stuttgart and Leipzig.

Innes, D. C., and M. Winterbottom (1988). *Sopater the Rhetor.* London. (*BICS* 48.)

Jocelyn, H. D. (1969). *The Tragedies of Ennius.* Cambridge.

Kaster, R. A. (1988). *Guardians of Language.* Berkeley. (1993). *Suetonius de grammaticis et rhetoribus.* Oxford.

Kennedy, G. A. (1963). *The Art of Persuasion in Greece.* London. (1969). *Quintilian.* New York.

(1972). *The Art of Rhetoric in the Roman World.* Princeton.

(1980). *Classical Rhetoric and its Christian and Secular Tradition.* London.

Kindstrand, J. F. (1982). *The Stylistic Evaluation of Aeschines in Antiquity.* Uppsala.

Kohl, R. (1915). *De scholasticarum declamationum argumentis ex historia petitis.* Paderborn.

Lausberg, H. (1963). *Elemente der literarischen Rhetorik.* Munich.

Lindsay, W. M. (1894). *The Latin Language.* Oxford.

Leeman, A. D. (1963). *Orationis Ratio.* Amsterdam.

Löfstedt, E. (1933, 1942). *Syntactica.* Lund and Leipzig.

Long, A. A., and D. N. Sedley (1987). *The Hellenistic Philosophers.* Cambridge.

Lunderstedt, P. (1911). *De C. Maecenatis fragmentis* (*Comm. Phil. Ien.* 9.1). Leipzig.

McCall, M. H. (1969). *Ancient Rhetorical Theories of Simile and Comparison.* Cambridge, Mass.

Maier-Eichhorn, U. (1989). *Die Gestikulation in Quintilians Rhetorik.* Frankfurt.

Maltby, R. (1991). *A Lexicon of Ancient Latin Etymologies.* Francis Cairns, Leeds.

Mariotti, I. (1967). *Marii Victorini Ars Grammatica.* Florence.

Marrou, H. I. (1950). *Histoire de l'éducation dans l'antiquité.* Paris.

Martin, J. (1974). *Antike Rhetorik.* Munich.

Marx, F. (1915). *A. Corneli Celsi quae supersunt* (= *Corp. med. Lat.* 1). Leipzig.

Morgan, T. (1998). *Literate Education in the Hellenistic and Roman Worlds.* Cambridge.

Morrow, G. R. (1960). *Plato's Cretan City*. Princeton.

Murgia, C. E. (1990). "Notes on Quintilian." *CQ* 41: 183–212.

Nicolai, R. (1992). *La storiografia nell' educazione antica*. Pisa.

Norden, G. (1958). *Antike Kunstprosa*. Ed. 5, Stuttgart.

Otto, A. (1890, 1962). *Die Sprichwörter und sprichwörtlichen Redensarten der Römer*. Leipzig.

Palmer, L. R. (1954). *The Latin Language*. London.

Pernot, L. (1993). *La rhétorique de l'éloge dans le monde gréco-romain*. Paris.

Platnauer, M. (1951). *Latin Elegiac Verse*. Cambridge.

Pollitt, J. J. (1974). *The Ancient View of Greek Art*. New Haven and London.

Reynolds, L. D., and N. G. Wilson (1991). *Scribes and Scholars*. Ed. 3. Oxford.

Rhys Roberts, W. (1902). *Demetrius on Style*. Cambridge.

Riginos, A. S. (1976). *Platonica*. Leiden.

Russell, D. A. (ed., 1990). *Antonine Literature*. Oxford.
   (1992). *Dio Chrysostom, Orations 7, 12, 36*. Cambridge.
   (1993). *Plutarch: Selected Essays and Dialogues*. Oxford (World's Classics).
   (1996). *Libanius: Imaginary Speeches*. London.
   (See also Abbreviations.)

Rutherford, I. C. (1998). *Canons of Style in the Antonine Age*. Oxford.

Rutherford, W. G. (1905). *A Chapter in the History of Annotation*. London.

Salomies, O. H. (1982). "Quintilian and Vitorius Marcellus." *Arctos* 16: 153–158.

Schenkeveld, D. M. (1964). *Studies in Demetrius On Style*. Amsterdam.

Schindel, U. C. (1974). "Textkritisches zu lateinischen Figurenlehren." *Glotta* 52: 95–114.

(1993). *Glotta* 71:112–119.

Shackleton Bailey, D. R. (1983). "Notes on Quintilian." *HSCP* 87: 217–240.

Sherwin-White, A. N. (1960). *The Letters of Pliny*. Oxford.

Sihler, A. L. (1995). *New Comparative Grammar of Greek and Latin*. Oxford.

Sittl, K. (1890). *Die Gebärden der Griechen und Römer.*

Solmsen, F. (1941). "The Aristotelian tradition in ancient rhetoric." *AJP* 62: 35–50; 169–190 (reprinted in Stark 1968).

Speyer, W. (1971). *Die literarische Fälschung im heidnischen und Christlichen Altertum.* Munich.

Stark, R. (ed., 1968). *Rhetorica: Schriften zur aristotelischen und hellenistischen Rhetorik.* Hildesheim.

Steinmetz, P. (1964). "Gattungen und Epochen der griechischen Literatur in der Sicht Quintilians." *Hermes* 92: 454–466 (reprinted in Stark 1968).

Stroh, W. (1975). *Taxis und Taktik.* Stuttgart.

Syme, R. (1964). *Sallust.* Berkeley.

(1978). *History in Ovid.* Oxford.

(1979–1991). *Roman Papers.* 7 vols. Oxford.

Thesleff, H. (1965). *The Pythagorean Texts of the Hellenistic Period.* Åbo.

Treggiari, S. (1991). *Roman Marriage.* Oxford.

Trimpi, W. (1983). *Muses of One Mind.* Princeton.

Volkmann, R. (1885). *Die Rhetorik der Griechen und Römer.* Leipzig.

Wackernagel, J. (1950). *Vorlesungen über Syntax.* Basel.

Watt, W. S. Notes on Quintilian, in:
  (1982). *Liverpool Classical Monthly* 7.9.
  (1988). *Grazer Beiträge* 15: 139–160.
  (1993). *Tria Lustra, Essays presented to John Pinsent.*
    Liverpool: 315–320.
  (1998). *ZPE* 121: 68–71.
Wehrli, F. (1944–1953). *Die Schule des Aristoteles.* Basel.
Wilkinson, L. P. (1963). *Golden Latin Artistry.* Cambridge.
Wilson, L. M. (1938). *The Clothing of the Ancient Romans.*
Winterbottom, M. (1970). *Problems in Quintilian.* London. (*BICS* Supplement 25.)
  (1998). "Quintilian the Moralist." *QHAR* 1: 317–334.
Wooten, C. W. (1987). *Hermogenes On Types of Style.* Chapel Hill.
Wyss, B. (1936). *Antimachi Colophonii Reliquiae.* Berlin.
Yates, F. A. (1966). *The Art of Memory.* Oxford.
Ziebarth, E. (1913). *Aus der antiken Schule* (Kleine Texte 65). Bonn.
Zundel, E. (1989). *Clavis Quintilianea.* Darmstadt.

Abbreviations

(Abbreviations used for journals are generally those given in the Oxford Classical Dictionary.)

Anon. Seg.   Anonymus Seguierianus, ed. M. Dilts and
              G. A. Kennedy, in *Two Rhetorical Treatises
              from the Roman Empire.* Leiden, 1997.
ANRW   *Aufstieg und Niedergang der römischen
              Welt,* ed. W. Haase and H. Temporini.
              Berlin, 1974–.

AP	G. A. Kennedy, *The Art of Persuasion in Greece*. London, 1963.
ARRW	G. A. Kennedy, *Art of Rhetoric in the Roman World*. Princeton, 1972.
AS	*Artium Scriptores*, ed. L. Radermacher. Vienna, 1951.
CA	D. A. Russell, *Criticism in Antiquity*. London, 1981 (ed. 2, 1995).
CHLC	*The Cambridge History of Literary Criticism*, vol. 1, *Classical Criticism*, ed. G. A. Kennedy. Cambridge, 1989.
CRHP	*Handbook of Classical Rhetoric in the Hellenistic Period 330 BC–AD 400*, ed. S. E. Porter. Leiden, 1997.
F Gr Hist	F. Jacoby, *Fragmente der griechischen Historiker.*
FOR	H. Meyer, *Oratorum Romanorum Fragmenta*, ed. 2. 1842.
FPL	*Fragmenta Poetarum Latinorum*, ed. W. Morel. Leipzig, 1927 (1963).
GD	D. A. Russell, *Greek Declamation*. Cambridge, 1983.
GL	*Grammatici Latini*, ed. H. Keil, 7 vols. Leipzig, 1855–1880.
HRR	*Historicorum Romanorum Reliquiae*, ed. H. Peter. Leipzig, 1906.
Lampe	G. W. H. Lampe, *A Patristic Greek Lexicon*. Oxford, 1961.
Lausberg	H. Lausberg, *Handbook of Literary Rhetoric*, ed. and trans. D. E. Orton and R. Dean Anderson. Leiden, 1998.
LCL	Loeb Classical Library.

L–H–S   Leumann–Hofmann–Szantyr, *Lateinische Grammatik* (*Handbuch der Altertumswissenschaft* 2.2.2). Munich, 1965.

OCD[3]   *Oxford Classical Dictionary*, ed. 3, edd. S. Hornblower and A. Spawforth. Oxford, 1996.

OLD   *Oxford Latin Dictionary*, ed. P. G. W. Glare. Oxford, 1968–1982.

ORF   *Oratorum Romanorum Fragmenta liberae rei publicae*, ed. H. Malcovati. Ed. 2, Turin, 1955.

PMG   *Poetae Melici Graeci*, ed. D. L. Page, Oxford, 1962.

QHAR   *Quintiliano: historia y actualidad de la retórica*, edd. T. Abaladejo, E. del Rio, J. A. Caballero. Calahorra, 1998.

RAC   *Reallexikon für Antike und Christentum.* Stuttgart, 1941–.

RD   S. F. Bonner, *Roman Declamation.* Liverpool, 1949.

RE   G. Wissowa, etc., *Paulys Realenzyklopädie der klassischen Altertumswissenschaft.* 1893–1980.

RLM   *Rhetores Latini Minores*, ed. C. Halm. Leipzig, 1863.

ROL   *Remains of Old Latin*, ed. E. H. Warmington, 4 vols. LCL, 1935–1940.

RP   R. Syme, *Roman Papers*, 7 vols. Oxford, 1979–1988.

Spengel   *Rhetores Graeci*, ed. L. Spengel, 3 vols. Leipzig, 1853–1856.

41

Spengel–Hammer	*Rhetores Graeci* 1.2, ed. L. Spengel and C. Hammer. 1894.
SVF	*Stoicorum Veterum Fragmenta,* ed. H. von Arnim. 1905 (reprint Stuttgart, 1964).
VPH	[Plutarch] *De vita et poesi Homeri,* ed. J. F. Kindstrand. 1990. Commentary: M. Hillgruber, 1994–1999.
Walz	*Rhetores Graeci,* ed. C. Walz. 1832–1836 (reprint Osnabruck, 1968).

Sigla

A	Ambrosianus E 153 sup.
a	Its contemporary corrections
B	Bernensis 351
Bg	The older part of Bambergensis M.4.14
b	Its corrections
G	The later part of Bambergensis M.4.14
N	Parisinus lat. 18527
J	Cantabrigiensis Ioannensis 91
E	Parisinus lat. 14146 (Breviarium of Stephen of Rouen)
D	Parisinus lat. 7719
K	Parisinus lat. 7720 (corrected by Petrarch)
H	Harleianus 2664
T	Turicensis 288 (corrected $(= t)$ by Ekkehard IV of St. Gall, c. 1050)
X	Parisinus lat. 7696
Y	Parisinus lat. 7231
recc.	One or more of the later MSS listed in Winterbottom (1970), v–vii

edd.   One or more of the editions listed under (a) above (p. 30)

Regius   R. Regius, in ed. Ven. 1493, or in *Ducenta problemata in totidem Institutionis Oratoriae Quintiliani depravationes* (1492)

D.A.R.   Suggestions by the present editor

M.W.   Suggestions made in discussion with the editor by M. Winterbottom. See also *More Problems in Quintilian, BICS* 44 (2000) 167–177

BOOK ONE

INTRODUCTION

Book One has been quite well served by editions: Fierville 1890, Colson 1924, Niedermann 1947 (partial).

The general Preface, presumably written last of all because it closely echoes the challenging but optimistic tone of Book Twelve and summarizes that book (§ 22), consists of three parts: §§ 1–8 give the occasion (Quintilian's retirement and Vitorius Marcellus' need), and explain that the book was written in haste, because some unauthorized versions of his teaching have been published; §§ 9–20 stress that the theme is the ideal orator, who needs philosophical understanding, which ought not to be the monopoly of professional philosophers; in §§ 21–27 we have a synopsis of the proposed work; teaching advice is to be included at each stage; but of course teaching can do little without natural endowments.

The book as a whole deals with the early education of the orator, whose adult career will be seen in Book Twelve. Morgan (1998) contains much useful comment on many passages of it.

1.1. Quintilian begins with the hopes of the proud father and the choice of nurses, paedagogi, and child companions. He goes into some detail about learning the alphabet, syllables, and words, and always has it in mind that the child is to be an *orator*—hence the emphasis on pronunciation, and the early introduction of scraps of learning which will be useful later. The only other extant ancient text which deals with early education on this scale is [Plutarch] *On the education of children* (= *Moralia* 1–14), and this is much more moral and philosophical in outlook. Papyri and ostraca however provide ample evidence for school exercises (Marrou (1950) 2.6 (210–222); Morgan (1998) esp. 152–189 and 198–225).

2. Quintilian prefers school to home education, despite possible moral and social problems, because the future orator has to be a competitive person and should start early.

3. Differences of temperament and talent must determine the handling of the child. Flogging is to be avoided (on this, see [Plutarch], op. cit., ch. 12).

4–9. *Grammaticē* (Quintilian habitually uses the Greek form)—"the study of correct speech and the interpretation of the poets"—is the responsibility of a specialist teacher, the *grammaticus,* whose relationship to the rhetor is not easily defined. It is a wide-ranging subject, involving both what we should call grammar, and interpretation of poetical texts. It leads to the study of music, science, and philosophy, and will give lifelong pleasure (4.1–5). It is, of course, not Quintilian's business to give a systematic account of Latin grammar (see 1.4.17), but he nevertheless explains in some detail what is to be taught at this stage: it includes questions about the necessity and adequacy of the letters of the alphabet (4.7–17); syllables (4.17, also 7); parts of speech (4.17–21); inflections (gender, voice, etc., 4.22–29). In 5 and 6 we learn about "correct speech," the avoidance of "barbarism" and "solecism," proper pronunciation and accentuation, and the principles (Reason (including Analogy), Antiquity, Authority, and Usage) which underpin "correctness." In 7, Quintilian moves on to correct *writing* (orthography). In all this, he shows his profound knowledge of the Latin grammarians: many of his facts and ideas are to be found already in Varro's *De lingua Latina.* The tradition of this kind of linguistic study, based on Greek models, was vigorous, and was an important cultural resource for Cicero and Caesar as well as for Quintilian and his contemporaries and successors. Much background information is in Kaster (1991 and 1995), and in D. L. Blank's commentary (1998) on the sceptical critique of *grammatici* in Sextus Empiricus. In 8, Quintilian passes to the second part of the *grammaticus'* work, the reading and interpretation of the classics. He approves most poetry (with some reservations, 8.6, and a general insistence on good moral tone) and gives a cautious welcome to explanations of myth and history, so long as there is no pedantry; it is a good point in a *grammaticus* "not to know some things" (8.2). Finally (9) he allows the *grammaticus* to teach some of the elementary exercises (*progymnasmata:* the term is late; earlier Greek writers use *gymnasmata,* and Quintilian has *exercitationes*) which originally belonged to the rhetor's sphere; but the rhetor must keep the more advanced of these exercises in his own hands. This addresses what was clearly a thorny demarcation dispute.

As well as *grammaticē,* other parts of the general course of education (*enkyklios paideia*: see especially I. Hadot (1984)) are useful for the budding orator: music (10.9–33), geometry (which includes mathematics generally, 10.34–49: on this see D. A. Russell, "Arts and Sciences in Ancient Education," *Greece and Rome* 36 (1989) 210–225), and the techniques of acting (11.1–14) and gymnastics (11.15–19). Quintilian's positive attitude to these studies, in which he sees some broadly practical use, contrasts with Seneca's (*Epistles* 88), who views them as ancillary to philosophy, and in themselves valueless. The contrast with Seneca helps to define Quintilian's educational aims and ideals; he is primarily concerned with success and respectability in public life, not with private virtue and happiness.

In the concluding chapter (12) he takes up the practical question whether these subjects can all be taught at the same time. He has an optimistic view of what boys can do in the years before they have to specialize; and he concludes by a defence of his ambitious ideal, a defence which he takes up again, even more emphatically, at the very end of his great work (12.11).

M. Fabius Quintilianus Tryphoni suo salutem.

1   Efflagitasti cotidiano convicio ut libros quos ad Marcellum meum de institutione oratoria scripseram iam emittere inciperem. Nam ipse eos nondum opinabar satis maturuisse, quibus componendis, ut scis, paulo plus quam biennium tot alioqui negotiis districtus inpendi: quod tempus non tam stilo quam inquisitioni operis prope infiniti et legendis
2   auctoribus, qui sunt innumerabiles, datum est. Usus deinde Horati consilio, qui in arte poetica suadet ne praecipitetur editio 'nonumque prematur in annum', dabam his otium, ut refrigerato inventionis amore diligentius
3   repetitos tamquam lector perpenderem. Sed si tantopere efflagitantur quam tu adfirmas, permittamus vela ventis et oram solventibus bene precemur. Multum autem in tua quoque fide ac diligentia positum est, ut in manus hominum quam emendatissimi veniant. Vale.

Marcus Fabius Quintilianus to his friend Trypho[1]: greeting

You have been pressing me every day, with great insistence, to start publishing the books on "the orator's education" which I had written for my friend Marcellus.[2] My own view was that they had not yet matured enough. As you know, I spent little more than two years on composing them, at a time when I was anyway distracted by much business. The time has been spent not so much on the actual writing as on the research required by a work of almost infinite scope, and on reading the countless authorities. Since then, following the advice of Horace, who, in the *Ars Poetica*,[3] urges that publication should not be hurried but "kept in store till the ninth year comes round," I have been giving them a rest, to let my satisfaction in my own productions cool, so as to go over them again more carefully, with a reader's eyes. But if they are called for as urgently as you allege, let us spread our sails before the wind and pray for a good voyage as we cast off. But it depends very much on your own loyal care also to see that they come into people's hands in as correct a form as possible. Farewell.

[1] A bookseller known also from Martial 4.72, 13.3.

[2] M. Vitorius Marcellus, addressee of Statius, *Silvae* 4, was praetor 95, suffect consul September–December 105. His son Geta (1 *prooem.* 6) is probably the C. Vitorius Hosidius Geta co-opted by the *fratres Arvales* in 118 (*CIL* vi. 2078). See K. Coleman (1988) xix, 135–137.

[3] 388.

LIBER PRIMUS

PROHOEMIUM

1   Post impetratam studiis meis quietem, quae per viginti annos erudiendis iuvenibus inpenderam, cum a me quidam
familiariter postularent ut aliquid de ratione dicendi com-
ponerem, diu sum equidem reluctatus, quod auctores
utriusque linguae clarissimos non ignorabam multa quae
ad hoc opus pertinerent diligentissime scripta posteris
2   reliquisse. Sed qua ego ex causa faciliorem mihi veniam
meae deprecationis arbitrabar fore, hac accendebantur illi
magis, quod inter diversas opiniones priorum et quasdam
etiam inter se contrarias difficilis esset electio, ut mihi si
non inveniendi nova, at certe iudicandi de veteribus iniun-
3   gere laborem non iniuste viderentur. Quamvis autem non
tam me vinceret praestandi quod exigebatur fiducia quam
negandi verecundia, latius se tamen aperiente materia
plus quam imponebatur oneris sponte suscepi, simul ut
pleniore obsequio demererer amantissimos mei, simul ne
vulgarem viam ingressus alienis demum vestigiis insiste-
4   rem. Nam ceteri fere qui artem orandi litteris tradiderunt

BOOK ONE

PROOEMIUM

When at last I won leisure for my studies, which for twenty years I had devoted to the training of the young, some friends asked me to write something on the theory of oratory. I resisted for a long time, because I knew that some very famous authors, in both Greek and Latin, had left to posterity many very carefully composed works relevant to this subject. But the reason that made me think I should have an easier excuse for saying no served only to inflame their enthusiasm. They urged that there was a difficulty in choosing between the different and in some instances contradictory opinions of my predecessors. They seemed therefore to be justified in imposing upon me the task of passing judgement on old ideas, if not of discovering new ones. I was moved to comply not so much because I felt confident that I could meet their requirements, but because I was ashamed to refuse. However, as the subject opened up more widely, I voluntarily undertook a heavier load than was being imposed upon me, partly to oblige my loving friends by fuller compliance, and partly to avoid going along the beaten track and finding myself merely treading in others' footsteps. For almost all others who have committed their teaching on the art of oratory to writ-

ita sunt exorsi quasi perfectis omni alio genere doctrinae
summam [in eloquentiae][1] manum imponerent, sive
contemnentes tamquam parva quae prius discimus studia,
sive non ad suum pertinere officium opinati, quando
divisae professionum vices essent, seu, quod proximum
vero, nullam ingenii sperantes gratiam circa res etiamsi
necessarias, procul tamen ab ostentatione positas, ut ope-
5   rum fastigia spectantur, latent fundamenta. Ego cum exis-
timem nihil arti oratoriae alienum sine quo fieri non posse
oratorem fatendum est, nec ad ullius rei summam nisi
praecedentibus initiis perveniri, ad minora illa, sed quae si
neglegas non sit maioribus locus, demittere me non recu-
sabo, nec aliter quam si mihi tradatur educandus orator
studia eius formare ab infantia incipiam.

6   Quod opus, Marce[2] Vitori, tibi dicamus, quem cum
amicissimum nobis tum eximio litterarum amore flagran-
tem non propter haec modo, quamquam sint magna, dignissimum hoc mutuae inter nos caritatis pignore iudicaba-
mus, sed quod erudiendo Getae tuo, cuius prima aetas
manifestum iam ingenii lumen ostendit, non inutiles fore
libri videbantur quos ab ipsis dicendi velut incunabulis per
omnes quae modo aliquid oratori futuro conferant artis ad
7   summam eius operis perducere festinabimus, atque eo
magis quod duo iam sub nomine meo libri ferebantur artis

1 *del. Schoell*
2 Marcelle *edd. See Salomies* 1982

1 So Pliny, *Epistulae* 3.5.5, describes his uncle's *Studiosus* as
educating the orator *ab incunabulis.*

ing have started with the assumption that their pupils were perfect in every other branch of learning, and that they simply had to add the finishing touch; this was either because they despised the earlier stages of education as trivial, or because they thought they were not their concern (the roles of the professions being distinct), or, most probably, because they had no hope of winning favour for their talents by dealing with subjects which, however necessary, are very far from being showy—just as, in buildings, the rooftops are seen, but the foundations are hidden. For my part, however—holding as I do that nothing is foreign to the art of oratory which must be admitted to be essential for the making of an orator, and that one cannot reach the top in any subject without going through the elementary stages—I shall certainly not refuse to stoop to those matters which, though minor, cannot be neglected without blocking the way to greater things. I shall proceed exactly as if a child were put into my hands to be educated as an orator, and shall plan his studies from his infancy.

I dedicate this work to you, Marcus Vitorius. You are a very good friend of mine, and you have a burning enthusiasm for literature; but these are not the only reasons (strong as they are) why I regard you as particularly worthy of this pledge of our mutual affection. It is also because I think that these books will be useful for the education of your son Geta, whose early years already show such clear promise of talent. To carry the work through from the very cradle of eloquence,[1] as it were, through all the skills that may be of some service to the future orator, right to the conclusion of the whole matter, shall be my urgent task—all the more urgent because two books on the Art of Rhetoric are already circulating in my name, though they were

rhetoricae neque editi a me neque in hoc comparati. Namque alterum sermonem per biduum habitum pueri quibus
id praestabatur exceperant, alterum pluribus sane diebus,
quantum notando consequi potuerant, interceptum boni
iuvenes sed nimium amantes mei temerario editionis ho-
8   nore vulgaverant. Quare in his quoque libris erunt eadem
aliqua, multa mutata, plurima adiecta, omnia vero com-
positiora et quantum nos poterimus elaborata.

9   Oratorem autem instituimus illum perfectum, qui esse
nisi vir bonus non potest, ideoque non dicendi modo exi-
miam in eo facultatem sed omnis animi virtutes exigimus.
10 Neque enim hoc concesserim, rationem rectae honestae-
que vitae, ut quidam putaverunt, ad philosophos relegan-
dam, cum vir ille vere civilis et publicarum privatarumque
rerum administrationi accommodatus, qui regere consiliis
urbes, fundare legibus, emendare iudiciis possit, non alius
11 sit profecto quam orator. Quare, tametsi me fateor usurum
quibusdam quae philosophorum libris continentur, tamen
ea iure vereque contenderim esse operis nostri proprieque
12 ad artem oratoriam pertinere. An si frequentissime de
iustitia fortitudine temperantia ceterisque similibus disse-
rendum est, adeo ut vix ulla possit causa reperiri in quam
non aliqua ex his incidat quaestio, eaque omnia inventione
atque elocutione sunt explicanda, dubitabitur, ubicumque
vis ingenii et copia dicendi postulatur, ibi partes oratoris
13 esse praecipuas? Fueruntque haec, ut Cicero apertissime

never published by me nor prepared for this purpose. One is a two days' lecture course which was taken down by the slaves to whom the responsibility was given. The other lecture course, which spread over several days, was taken down by shorthand (as best they could) by some excellent young men who were nevertheless too fond of me, and therefore rashly honoured it with publication and wide circulation. In the present work, therefore, there will be some things the same, many things changed, and very many things added, and the whole will be better written and worked up to the best of my ability.

I am proposing to educate the perfect orator, who cannot exist except in the person of a good man. We therefore demand of him not only exceptional powers of speech, but all the virtues of character as well. I cannot agree that the principles of upright and honourable living should, as some have held, be left to the philosophers. The man who can really play his part as a citizen, who is fit for the management of public and private business, and who can guide cities by his counsel, give them a firm basis by his laws, and put them right by his judgements, is surely no other than our orator. And so, although I admit that I shall use some ideas found in philosophical books, I would contend that these truly and rightfully belong to our work, and are strictly relevant to the art of oratory. We are often obliged to speak of justice, courage, temperance, and the like—indeed, scarcely a Cause can be found in which some question relating to these is not involved—and all these topics have to be developed by Invention and Elocution: how then can there be any doubt that wherever intellectual power and fullness of diction are required, the orator has the leading role? These two disciplines, as Cicero very

colligit, quemadmodum iuncta natura, sic officio quoque
copulata, ut idem sapientes atque eloquentes haberentur.
Scidit deinde se studium, atque inertia factum est ut artes
esse plures viderentur. Nam ut primum lingua esse coepit
in quaestu institutumque eloquentiae bonis male uti,
14 curam morum qui diserti habebantur reliquerunt, ea vero
destituta infirmioribus ingeniis velut praedae fuit. Inde
quidam contempto bene dicendi labore ad formandos
animos statuendasque vitae leges regressi partem quidem
potiorem, si dividi posset, retinuerunt, nomen tamen sibi
insolentissimum adrogaverunt, ut soli studiosi sapientiae
vocarentur; quod neque summi imperatores neque in
consiliis rerum maximarum ac totius administratione rei
publicae clarissime versati sibi umquam vindicare sunt
15 ausi: facere enim optima quam promittere maluerunt. Ac
veterum quidem sapientiae professorum multos et honesta praecepisse et ut praeceperint etiam vixisse facile
concesserim: nostris vero temporibus sub hoc nomine
maxima in plerisque vitia latuerunt. Non enim virtute ac
studiis ut haberentur philosophi laborabant, sed vultum et
tristitiam et dissentientem a ceteris habitum pessimis
16 moribus praetendebant. Haec autem quae velut propria

---

2 *De inventione* 1.3.4, *De oratore* 3.56–81.

3 Dionysius of Halicarnassus (*On ancient orators,* Preface =
1.4 Usher LCL) also develops the concept of "philosophical rhetoric" to characterize the good old days of oratory before the Hellenistic decline.

4 *Inertia* (from *in* + *ars*) is the contrary of *ars*.

5 The word *philosophos,* "lover of wisdom," was thought to
have been invented by Pythagoras (e.g. Cicero, *Tusculanae Disputationes* 5.3.8). Domitian expelled philosophers from Rome in

clearly argues,[2] were once so closely joined by nature and united in function, that philosophers and orators were taken to be the same.[3] The subject then split into two, and it came about, through failure of art,[4] that there were thought to be more arts than one. For as soon as the tongue began to offer a way of making a living, and the practice developed of making a bad use of the good gifts of eloquence, those who were counted able speakers abandoned moral concerns, and these, left to themselves, became, as it were, the prey of weaker minds. At this point, some, disdaining the effort of speaking well, returned to the business of forming character and establishing rules of life, and kept for themselves what would be, if the division were possible, the more important part; they laid claim, however, to a very presumptuous name, wishing to be regarded as the only "students of wisdom"[5]—a distinction which neither the greatest generals nor the most famous statesmen and administrators have ever dared claim for themselves, because they have always preferred to do right rather than to profess it. I am very ready to admit that many of the old philosophers taught honourable principles and lived in accordance with their teaching; but in our day, very great vices have been concealed under this name in many persons. They did not try by virtue or learning to be regarded as philosophers; instead, they put on a gloomy face and an eccentric form of dress as a cover for their immorality.[6] In fact, we all regularly handle the themes which philosophy

94 (Suetonius, *Domitianus* 10), and this political fact may have influenced Q.'s tone here and elsewhere (see 11.1.33–35) despite his generally positive (Ciceronian) view (see 12.2).

[6] See 12.3.12; in general, Juvenal 2, with Courtney (1980) 120.

philosophiae adseruntur, passim tractamus omnes. Quis enim non de iusto, aequo ac bono, modo non et vir pessimus, loquitur? Quis non etiam rusticorum aliqua de causis naturalibus quaerit? Nam verborum proprietas ac differentia omnibus qui sermonem curae habent debet esse
17 communis. Sed ea et sciet optime et eloquetur orator; qui si fuisset aliquando perfectus, non a philosophorum scholis virtutis praecepta peterentur. Nunc necesse est ad eos [aliquando][3] auctores recurrere, qui desertam, ut dixi, partem oratoriae artis, meliorem praesertim, occupaverunt, et velut nostrum reposcere, non ut illorum nos utamur
18 inventis, sed ut illos alienis usos esse doceamus. Sit igitur orator vir talis qualis vere sapiens appellari possit, nec moribus modo perfectus (nam id mea quidem opinione, quamquam sunt qui dissentiant, satis non est), sed etiam
19 scientia et omni facultate dicendi; qualis fortasse nemo adhuc fuerit, sed non ideo minus nobis ad summa tendendum est: quod fecerunt plerique veterum, qui, etsi nondum quemquam sapientem repertum putabant, praecepta
20 tamen sapientiae tradiderunt. Nam est certe aliquid consummata eloquentia neque ad eam pervenire natura humani ingenii prohibet. Quod si non contingat, altius tamen ibunt qui ad summa nitentur quam qui praesumpta desperatione quo velint evadendi protinus circa ima substiterint.
21   Quo magis impetranda erit venia si ne minora quidem illa, verum operi quod instituimus necessaria, praeteribo. Nam liber primus ea quae sunt ante officium rhetoris

---

[3] *del. Radermacher*

---

[7] See Cicero, *De oratore* 3.108, 123; and below, 2.21.13.

claims for its own. Who—if not an utter villain—does not speak about justice and equity and goodness? Who—even among country folk—does not ask some questions about the causes of natural phenomena? As for verbal precision and distinctions, this should be a study common to all who care for language. But it is the orator who will both know these things best and best express them in words; and if the perfect orator had existed at some epoch, there would be no need to apply to the schools of the philosophers for the precepts of virtue. As things are, we must return to those authors who, as I said, took possession of the better part of rhetoric when it was unoccupied, and demand its return—as ours by right—not appropriate their discoveries but show them that they have appropriated what was not theirs.[7] So let our orator be the sort of man who can truly be called "wise," not only perfect in morals (for in my view that is not enough, though some people think otherwise) but also in knowledge and in his general capacity for speaking. Such a person has perhaps never yet existed; but that is no reason for relaxing our efforts to attain the ideal. Many of the ancients indeed acted on this principle, and handed down precepts of wisdom, despite their belief that no "wise" man had yet been found. Consummate eloquence is surely a real thing, and the nature of human abilities does not debar us from attaining it. But even if we fail, those who make an effort to get to the top will climb higher than those who from the start despair of emerging where they want to be, and stop right at the foot of the hill.

This will be a further reason for forgiving me if I do not pass over even minor details, which are nevertheless essential to the work. Book One will deal with what comes

continebit. Secundo prima apud rhetorem elementa et
quae de ipsa rhetorices substantia quaeruntur tractabi-
22 mus. Quinque deinceps inventioni (nam huic et dispositio
subiungitur), quattuor elocutioni, in cuius partem memoria ac pronuntiatio veniunt, dabuntur. Unus accedet in quo
nobis orator ipse informandus est: ubi qui mores eius, quae
in suscipiendis discendis agendis causis ratio, quod eloquentiae genus, quis agendi debeat esse finis, quae post
finem studia, quantum nostra valebit infirmitas dissere-
23 mus. His omnibus admiscebitur, ut quisque locus postula-
bit, docendi ratio quae non eorum modo scientia quibus
solis quidam nomen artis dederunt studiosos instruat et, ut
sic dixerim, ius ipsum rhetorices interpretetur, sed alere
24 facundiam, vires augere eloquentiae possit. Nam plerumque nudae illae artes nimiae subtilitatis adfectatione fran-
gunt atque concidunt quidquid est in oratione generosius,
et omnem sucum ingenii bibunt et ossa detegunt, quae ut
esse et adstringi nervis suis debent, sic corpore operienda
25 sunt. Ideoque nos non particulam illam, sicuti plerique,
sed quidquid utile ad instituendum oratorem putabamus
in hos duodecim libros contulimus, breviter omnia de-
monstraturi; nam si quantum de quaque re dici potest
persequamur, finis operis non reperietur.
26   Illud tamen in primis testandum est, nihil praecepta
atque artes valere nisi adiuvante natura. Quapropter ei cui

---

8 Q.'s phrase is ambiguous: it may mean rather that Memory
and Delivery "come to the aid of," are ancillary to, *elocutio*.

before the rhetor begins his duties. In Book Two, I shall handle the first elements taught by the rhetor, and problems connected with the nature of rhetoric itself. The next five books will be given over to Invention (Disposition forms an appendix to this), and the following four to Elocution, with which are associated Memory and Delivery.[8] There will be one further book, in which the orator himself is to be portrayed: I shall there discuss (as well as my poor powers allow) his character, the principles of undertaking, preparing, and pleading cases, his style, the end of his active career, and the studies he may undertake thereafter. With all these discussions, I shall combine, as appropriate at each point, a method of teaching which is not only intended to instruct students in the topics to which some teachers confine the name of "the art," and thus, as it were, interpret the law of rhetoric, but which can also nourish their powers of speech and develop their eloquence. The familiar dry textbooks, with their striving for excessive subtlety, merely weaken and cripple any generous stylistic tendencies there may be, drain off all the juice of the mind, and expose the bones—which must of course be there, and be bound together by the proper sinews, but which also need to be covered by the flesh. This is why I have not (like most writers) confined myself to this small part of the subject, but have gathered together in these twelve books everything that I think useful for the orator's education. I shall set it all out briefly, for if I were to go into everything that can be said on each subject, the work would have no end.

There is one point which I must emphasize at the start: without the help of nature, precepts and techniques are powerless. This work, therefore, must not be thought of as

63

deerit ingenium non magis haec scripta sint quam de agro-
27   rum cultu sterilibus terris. Sunt et alia ingenita cuique
adiumenta, vox, latus patiens laboris, valetudo, constantia,
decor, quae si modica optigerunt, possunt ratione am-
pliari, sed nonnumquam ita desunt ut bona etiam ingenii
studiique corrumpant: sicut haec ipsa sine doctore perito,
studio pertinaci, scribendi legendi dicendi multa et continua exercitatione per se nihil prosunt.

1

1   Igitur nato filio pater spem de illo primum quam optimam
capiat: ita diligentior a principiis fiet. Falsa enim est quere-
la, paucissimis hominibus vim percipiendi quae tradantur
esse concessam, plerosque vero laborem ac tempora tardi-
tate ingenii perdere. Nam contra plures reperias et faciles
in excogitando et ad discendum promptos. Quippe id est
homini naturale, ac sicut aves ad volatum, equi ad cursum,
ad saevitiam ferae gignuntur, ita nobis propria est mentis
agitatio atque sollertia: unde origo animi caelestis creditur.
2   Hebetes vero et indociles non magis secundum naturam
hominis eduntur quam prodigiosa corpora et monstris in-
signia [sed hi pauci admodum fuerunt].[1] Argumentum,
quod in pueris elucet spes plurimorum: quae cum emori-
tur aetate, manifestum est non naturam defecisse sed

---

[1] *del. Winterbottom*

---

[1] Q. seems to echo the famous first sentence of Sallust's
Iugurtha: *falso queritur de natura sua genus humanum.*
[2] Compare 12.2.28.

written for persons without talent, any more than treatises on agriculture are meant for barren soils. And there are other aids also, with which individuals have to be born: voice, strong lungs, good health, stamina, good looks. A modest supply of these can be further developed by methodical training; but sometimes they are so completely lacking as to destroy any advantages of talent and study, just as these themselves are of no profit without a skilled teacher, persistence in study, and much continuous practice in writing, reading, and speaking.

CHAPTER 1

Elementary education

As soon as his son is born, the father should form the highest expectations of him. He will then be more careful about him from the start. There is no foundation for the complaint[1] that only a small minority of human beings have been given the power to understand what is taught them, the majority being so slow-witted that they waste time and labour. On the contrary, you will find the greater number quick to reason and prompt to learn. This is natural to man: as birds are born for flying, horses for speed, beasts of prey for ferocity, so are we for mental activity and resourcefulness. This is why the soul is believed to have its origin in heaven.[2] Dull and unteachable persons are no more normal products of human nature than prodigious and monstrous births [but these have been very few]. The proof of this is that the promise of many accomplishments appears in children, and when it fades with age, this is plainly due to the failure not of nature but of care. "But some have

3   curam. 'Praestat tamen ingenio alius alium.' Concedo; sed
plus efficiet aut minus: nemo reperitur qui sit studio nihil
consecutus. Hoc qui perviderit, protinus ut erit parens fac-
tus, acrem quam maxime datur curam spei futuri oratoris
inpendat.
4   Ante omnia ne sit vitiosus sermo nutricibus: quas, si
fieri posset, sapientes Chrysippus optavit, certe quantum
res pateretur optimas eligi voluit. Et morum quidem in his
haud dubie prior ratio est, recte tamen etiam loquantur.
5   Has primum audiet puer, harum verba effingere imitando
conabitur, et natura tenacissimi sumus eorum quae rudibus animis percepimus: ut sapor quo nova ⟨vasa⟩[2] inbuas
durat, nec lanarum colores quibus simplex ille candor mu-
tatus est elui possunt. Et haec ipsa magis pertinaciter
haerent quo deteriora sunt. Nam bona facile mutantur in
peius: quando in bonum verteris vitia? Non adsuescat
ergo, ne dum infans quidem est, sermoni qui dediscendus
sit.
6   In parentibus vero quam plurimum esse eruditionis op-
taverim. Nec de patribus tantum loquor: nam Gracchorum
eloquentiae multum contulisse accepimus Corneliam ma-
trem, cuius doctissimus sermo in posteros quoque est epistulis traditus, et Laelia C. filia reddidisse in loquendo
paternam elegantiam dicitur, et Hortensiae Q. filiae oratio

_____

[2] add. D.A.R. after Hagenbuch

_____

[3] SVF iii. 734. [Plutarch] On the education of children 3D
also insists on the importance of the nurse's character. Tacitus
(Dialogus 29) complains that "nowadays" children are exposed to
the influence of Greek female slaves who do not care what they
say coram infante domino "in front of the infant master."

more talent than others." I agree: then some will achieve more and some less, but we never find one who has not achieved something by his efforts. A parent who grasps this must devote the keenest possible care, from the moment he becomes a parent, to fostering the promise of the orator to be.

First of all, make sure the nurses speak properly. Chrysippus[3] wished them, had it been possible, to be philosophers; failing that, he would have us choose the best that our circumstances allowed. No doubt the more important point is their character; but they should also speak correctly. These are the first people the child will hear, theirs are the words he will try to copy and pronounce. We naturally retain most tenaciously what we learned when our minds were fresh: a flavour lasts a long time when the jar that absorbs it is new, and the dyes that change wool's pristine whiteness cannot be washed out.[4] Indeed, the worse these impressions are, the more persistent they are. Good is easily changed to worse: can you ever hope to change bad to good? So do not let the child become accustomed, even in infancy, to a type of speech which he will have to unlearn.

As to the parents, I should wish them to be as highly educated as possible. (I do not mean only the fathers. We are told that the eloquence of the Gracchi owed much to their mother Cornelia, whose highly cultivated style is known also to posterity from her letters; Laelia, Gaius Laelius' daughter, is said to have echoed her father's elegance in her own conversation;[5] and the speech delivered before

---

[4] See Horace, *Epistulae* 1.2.69, and *Carmina* 3.5.27.

[5] Cicero, *Brutus* 210, *De oratore* 3.45.

apud triumviros habita legitur non tantum in sexus hono-
7   rem. Nec tamen ii quibus discere ipsis non contigit minorem curam docendi liberos habeant, sed sint propter hoc
ipsum ad cetera magis diligentes.

8   De pueris inter quos educabitur ille huic spei destina-
tus idem quod de nutricibus dictum sit. De paedagogis hoc
amplius, ut aut sint eruditi plane, quam primam esse curam velim, aut se non esse eruditos sciant. Nihil est peius
iis qui paulum aliquid ultra primas litteras progressi falsam
sibi scientiae persuasionem induerunt. Nam et cedere
praecipiendi partibus indignantur et velut iure quodam
potestatis, qua[3] fere hoc hominum genus intumescit, im-
periosi atque interim saevientes stultitiam suam perdo-
9   cent. Nec minus error eorum nocet moribus, si quidem
Leonides Alexandri paedagogus, ut a Babylonio Diogene
traditur, quibusdam eum vitiis inbuit quae robustum quoque et iam maximum regem ab illa institutione puerili sunt
persecuta.

---

[3] *B*: quo *A*

---

[6] Appian, *Civil Wars* 4.32–33, gives a Greek version of this
speech (delivered in 42 BC) in which she objected to the triumvirs'
demand for wealthy women to give up their valuables for war
expenses. See also Valerius Maximus 8.3.3.

[7] [Plutarch], op. cit. 3F; Bonner (1977) 35–37. Close and
enduring connections could be formed between free and slave
children in the household, as in that in which Aelius Aristides was
brought up (C. A. Behr, *Aelius Aristides and the Sacred Tales*
(Amsterdam, 1968) 8–9).

[8] These were the slaves who attended the child to school,

the triumvirs by Hortensia, the daughter of Quintus Hortensius, is still read—and not just because it is by a woman.)[6] However, those who have not been lucky enough to learn themselves should not for that reason take less trouble about their sons' teaching; on the contrary, it should make them all the more careful in other matters.

As to the slave boys with whom the child born to such high hopes is to be brought up,[7] I would repeat what I said about the nurses. Regarding his *paedagogi*,[8] I would add that they should either be thoroughly educated (this is the first priority) or know themselves to be uneducated. Nothing can be worse than those who, having got just beyond the alphabet, delude themselves that they have acquired some knowledge. They both scorn to give up the role of instructor and, conceiving that they have a certain title to authority (a frequent source of vanity in this class of persons), become imperious and sometimes even brutal teachers of their own foolishness. Their failings have an equally bad moral effect: Alexander's *paedogogus,* Leonides, according to Diogenes of Babylon,[9] infected him with some faults which clung to him as a result of his childhood education even when he was a grown man and had become a mighty king.

and took responsibility for his early training and behaviour: [Plutarch], op. cit. 4A–F.

[9] *SVF* iii, p. 220. Plutarch (*Alexander* 5–7, 22.7, 25.6) tells stories about this Leonidas, a relative of Alexander's mother Olympias, who "did not refuse the title of *paidagōgos,*" though the nominal *paidagōgos* was another person, presumably a slave. Jerome (*Epistulae* 107.4 (= 348 Wright, LCL) also mentions Leonidas' failings.

10   Si cui multa videor exigere, cogitet oratorem institui, rem arduam etiam cum ei formando nihil defuerit, praeterea plura ac difficiliora superesse: nam et studio perpetuo et praestantissimis praeceptoribus et plurimis disciplinis opus est. Quapropter praecipienda sunt optima: quae si quis gravabitur, non rationi defuerint sed homini. Si tamen non continget quales maxime velim nutrices pueros paedagogos habere, at unus certe sit adsiduus loquendi non imperitus, qui, si qua erunt ab iis praesente alumno dicta vitiose, corrigat protinus nec insidere illi sinat, dum tamen intellegatur id quod prius dixi bonum esse, hoc remedium.

12   A sermone Graeco puerum incipere malo, quia Latinum, qui pluribus in usu est, vel nobis nolentibus perbibet, simul quia disciplinis quoque Graecis prius instituendus est, unde et nostrae fluxerunt. Non tamen hoc adeo superstitiose fieri velim ut diu tantum Graece loquatur aut discat, sicut plerisque moris est. Hoc enim accidunt et oris plurima vitia in peregrinum sonum corrupti et sermonis, cui cum Graecae figurae adsidua consuetudine haeserunt, in diversa quoque loquendi ratione pertinacissime durant.

14   Non longe itaque Latina subsequi debent et cito pariter ire. Ita fiet ut, cum aequali cura linguam utramque tueri coeperimus, neutra alteri officiat.

15   Quidam litteris instituendos qui minores septem annis

---

10 So also Jerome, *Epistulae* 107.9.

70

If anyone thinks I am asking too much, let him reflect that we are educating an orator, which is a hard enough business even if there is nothing lacking for his education, and that more and greater difficulties are still to come. He needs continuous application, first-class teachers, and many different branches of study. We must therefore recommend the optimum procedure: if anyone finds this too hard, the fault will lie with the individual, not with the principle. But if it is not possible to secure the sort of nurses, young companions, and *paedagogi* that I should most prefer, let there be anyway one person always at hand who knows the right ways of speaking, and who can correct on the spot any faulty expression used by the others in the pupil's presence, and so stop it becoming a habit. But it must be understood that this is only a remedy: what I said above is the ideal course.

I prefer a boy to begin by speaking Greek, because he will imbibe Latin, which more people speak, whether we will or no; and also because he will need to be taught Greek learning first, it being the source of ours too. However, I do not want a fetish to be made of this, so that he spends a long time speaking and learning nothing but Greek, as is commonly done. This gives rise to many faults both of pronunciation (owing to the distortion of the mouth produced by forming foreign sounds) and of language, because the Greek idioms stick in the mind through continual usage and persist obstinately even in speaking the other tongue.[10] So Latin ought to follow not far behind, and soon proceed side by side with Greek. The result will be that, once we begin to pay equal attention to both languages, neither will get in the way of the other.

Some have held that children should not be taught to

essent non putaverunt, quod illa primum aetas et intellectum disciplinarum capere et laborem pati posset. In qua
sententia Hesiodum esse plurimi tradunt qui ante gram-
maticum Aristophanen fuerunt (nam is primus ὑποθήκας,
in quo libro scriptum hoc invenitur, negavit esse huius
16 poetae); sed alii quoque auctores, inter quos Eratosthenes,
idem praeceperunt. Melius autem qui nullum tempus va-
care cura volunt, ut Chrysippus. Nam is, quamvis nutricibus triennium dederit, tamen ab illis quoque iam formandam quam optimis institutis mentem infantium iudicat.
17 Cur autem non pertineat ad litteras aetas quae ad mores
iam pertinet? Neque ignoro toto illo de quo loquor tempore vix tantum effici quantum conferre unus postea possit
annus; sed tamen mihi qui id senserunt videntur non tam
discentibus in hac parte quam docentibus pepercisse.
18 Quid melius alioqui facient ex quo loqui poterunt? Faciant
enim aliquid necesse est. Aut cur hoc quantulumcumque
est usque ad septem annos lucrum fastidiamus? Nam certe
quamlibet parvum sit quod contulerit aetas prior, maiora
tamen aliqua discet puer ipso illo anno quo minora didicis-
19 set. Hoc per singulos prorogatum in summam proficit, et
quantum in infantia praesumptum est temporis adules-
centiae adquiritur. Idem etiam de sequentibus annis praeceptum sit, ne quod cuique discendum est sero discere
incipiat. Non ergo perdamus primum statim tempus,
atque eo minus quod initia litterarum sola memoria
constant, quae non modo iam est in parvis sed tum etiam
tenacissima est.

---

11 Hesiod fr. 285 Merkelbach–West. The poem contained the
"advice" of the centaur Chiron to his pupil Achilles.
12 *SVF* iii. 733.

read under the age of seven, on the ground that this is the earliest age which can grasp the subjects taught and sustain the effort. This view is attributed to Hesiod by most writers who lived before Aristophanes the grammarian, who was the first to deny that the *Hypothecae,* in which this can be found, was by that poet.[11] Other authorities also, including Eratosthenes, have given the same advice. But one finds better advice in those who believe that no age should be without some interest, like Chrysippus,[12] who gives the nurses the first three years, but holds that they too should already have a part in forming the mind on the best possible principles. But why should an age already capable of moral instruction not be capable of learning its letters? I know of course that in all this period one can hardly get the results that a single year later on can achieve; still, those who have taken this line seem to me to have spared the teachers rather than the pupils. What better thing can they be doing anyway, from the moment they are able to speak? Something at least they must be doing! Or why should we despise the gains to be made before the age of seven, however small they are? For though the knowledge contributed by the early years may be small, still the boy will be learning some more important things in the year in which he would otherwise have been learning more elementary matters. Carried forward year by year, this all adds up, and the time saved in childhood is a gain for the period of adolescence. The same advice may be taken to apply to the subsequent years: let the child not begin too late to learn what he has to learn. Let us therefore not waste the earliest years, especially as the elements of reading and writing are entirely a matter of memory, which not only already exists in little children, but is then at its most retentive.

20   Nec sum adeo aetatium inprudens ut instandum protinus teneris acerbe putem exigendamque plane operam.
Nam id in primis cavere oportebit, ne studia qui amare
nondum potest oderit et amaritudinem semel perceptam
etiam ultra rudes annos reformidet. Lusus hic sit, et roge-
tur et laudetur et numquam non fecisse[4] se gaudeat, aliquando ipso nolente doceatur alius cui invideat, contendat
interim et saepius vincere se putet: praemiis etiam, quae
capit illa aetas, evocetur.

21   Parva docemus oratorem instituendum professi, sed est
sua etiam studiis infantia, et ut corporum mox fortissimo-
rum educatio a lacte cunisque initium ducit, ita futurus
eloquentissimus edidit aliquando vagitum et loqui primum incerta voce temptavit et haesit circa formas litterarum: nec, si quid discere satis non est, ideo nec necesse est.

22   Quodsi nemo reprehendit patrem qui haec non neglegen-
da in suo filio putet, cur improbetur si quis ea quae domi
suae recte faceret in publicum promit? Atque eo magis
quod minora etiam facilius minores percipiunt, et ut corpora ad quosdam membrorum flexus formari nisi tenera
non possunt, sic animos quoque ad pleraque duriores ro-

23   bur ipsum facit. An Philippus Macedonum rex Alexandro
filio suo prima litterarum elementa tradi ab Aristotele

---

[4] profecisse *Andresen*

---

[13] Isocrates is supposed to have said, "the root of education is
bitter, but the fruit is sweet." Discussion of this as a *chreia* was a
stock exercise: Aphthonius, *Progymnasmata* 4 Rabe.

[14] This advice is adapted by Jerome (*Epistulae* 107.4) for the
young Paula.

I am not so careless of age differences as to think that the very young should be forced on prematurely, and that set tasks should be demanded of them. For one of the first things to take care of is that the child, who is not yet able to love study, should not come to hate it and retain his fear of the bitter taste[13] he has experienced even beyond his first years. Let it be a game; let him be questioned and praised and always feel glad that he has done something; sometimes, when he refuses a lesson, it should be given to another child, of whom he can be jealous; sometimes he should compete, and more often than not think he is the winner; and finally, he should be encouraged by rewards suitable to his age.[14]

These are trivial recommendations for one who claims to be educating an orator; but study also has its infancy, and, as the rearing of what will one day be the strongest bodies begins with breast feeding and the cradle, so the great speaker of the future once cried as a baby, tried to speak with an uncertain voice, and was puzzled by the shapes of letters. If learning something is not sufficient in itself, it does not follow that it is not necessary. If no one blames a father for thinking these things should not be neglected in his son, why should a person be criticized for bringing into public view what he would rightly do in his own home? All the more so, because little children grasp little things more easily, and, just as the body can only be trained to flex the limbs in certain ways when it is young and tender, so the acquisition of strength itself makes the mind also more resistant to many kinds of learning. Would King Philip of Macedon have chosen that his son Alexander be taught his letters by Aristotle, the greatest philoso-

summo eius aetatis philosopho voluisset, aut ille suscepis-
set hoc officium, si non studiorum initia et a perfectissimo
quoque optime tractari et pertinere ad summam credidis-
24 sent?[25] Fingamus igitur Alexandrum dari nobis, impositum
gremio dignum tanta cura infantem (quamquam suus cuique dignus est): pudeatne me in ipsis statim elementis
etiam brevia docendi monstrare compendia?

Neque enim mihi illud saltem placet, quod fieri in plurimis video, ut litterarum nomina et contextum prius quam
25 formas parvoli discant. Obstat hoc agnitioni earum, non
intendentibus mox animum ad ipsos ductus dum ante-
cedentem memoriam secuntur. Quae causa est praecipientibus ut, etiam cum satis adfixisse eas pueris recto illo
quo primum scribi solent contextu videntur, retro agant
rursus et varia permutatione turbent, donec litteras qui
instituuntur facie norint, non ordine: quapropter optime
sicut hominum pariter et habitus et nomina edocebuntur.

26 Sed quod in litteris obest in syllabis non nocebit. Non
excludo autem (id quod est notum) irritandae ad discendum infantiae gratia eburneas etiam litterarum formas in
lusum offerre, vel si quid aliud quo magis illa aetas gaudeat
inveniri potest quod tractare intueri nominare iucundum
sit.

27 Cum vero iam ductus sequi coeperit, non inutile erit
eos tabellae quam optime insculpi, ut per illos velut sulcos

---

5 *Anon. in Spalding*: credidisset *AB*

---

15 Plutarch's account (*Alexander* 7) is consistent with Q.'s,
since he indicates that Philip was dissatisfied with the ordinary
teachers of elementary subjects. Aulus Gellius (9.3) quotes what
he claims to be Philip's letter to Aristotle.

pher of the age,[15] or would Aristotle have accepted the commission, if they had not believed that elementary instruction is best given by the most accomplished teacher and that it is important for the ultimate outcome? So let us imagine that an Alexander is entrusted to our care, that the child placed in our lap deserves as much attention (though of course every father thinks this of his son): ought I to be ashamed to point out a short way of teaching even for the first elements?

At any rate, I do not like the procedure (which I see is very common) by which children learn the names and sequence of the letters before their shapes. This is an obstacle to the recognition of the letters, since they do not when the time comes pay attention to the actual outlines, because they follow the promptings of their memory, which runs ahead of their observation. This is why teachers, even when they think they have sufficiently fixed the letters in a child's mind in the order in which they are commonly first written, next reverse this, or muddle it up in various ways, until the pupils come to recognize the letters by their shape and not by the order in which they come. It will be best therefore for them to be taught the appearance and the name side by side: it is like recognizing people.

But what is an obstacle in learning letters will do no harm when we come to syllables. Nor do I rule out the well-known practice of giving ivory letter-shapes to play with, so as to stimulate little children to learn—or indeed anything else one can think of to give them more pleasure, and which they enjoy handling, looking at, or naming.

Once the child has begun to trace the outlines, it will be useful to have these inscribed as neatly as possible on a

ducatur stilus. Nam neque errabit quemadmodum in ceris (continebitur enim utrimque marginibus neque extra praescriptum egredi poterit) et celerius ac saepius sequendo certa vestigia firmabit articulos neque egebit adiutorio

28 manum suam manu super imposita regentis. Non est aliena res, quae fere ab honestis neglegi solet, cura bene ac velociter scribendi. Nam cum sit in studiis praecipuum, quoque solo verus ille profectus et altis radicibus nixus paretur, scribere ipsum, tardior stilus cogitationem moratur, rudis et confusus intellectu caret: unde sequitur alter dic-

29 tandi quae transferenda sunt labor. Quare cum semper et ubique, tum praecipue in epistulis secretis et familiaribus delectabit ne hoc quidem neglectum reliquisse.

30 Syllabis nullum compendium est: perdiscendae omnes nec, ut fit plerumque, difficillima quaeque earum diffe-

31 renda ut in nominibus scribendis deprehendantur. Quin immo ne primae quidem memoriae temere credendum: repetere et diu inculcare fuerit utilius, et in lectione quoque non properare ad continuandam eam vel adcelerandam, nisi cum inoffensa atque indubitata litterarum inter se coniunctio suppeditare sine ulla cogitandi saltem mora poterit. Tunc ipsis syllabis verba complecti et his sermonem conectere incipiat: incredibile est quantum morae

32 lectioni festinatione adiciatur. Hinc enim accidit dubitatio intermissio repetitio plus quam possunt audentibus, deinde cum errarunt etiam iis quae iam sciunt diffidentibus.

---

16 See Marrou (1950) II. 5–6, III. 4; Morgan (1998) 163; also texts in E. Ziebarth (1913) p. 3; and (again) Jerome, *Epistulae* 107.4.

tablet, so that the stilus is guided by the grooves.[16] In this way, the child will not make mistakes as on wax (for he will be constrained by the edges on both sides, and will not be able to stray beyond the marks), and, by following these well-defined traces so quickly and often, he will strengthen his fingers, and not need the help of a guiding hand placed over his own. Practice in writing well and quickly, which people of standing tend to neglect, is not an irrelevance. Writing in one's own hand is important in our studies, and is the only way of ensuring real, deep-rooted progress; slow writing delays thought, ill-formed or confused writing is unintelligible, and this produces a second laborious stage of dictating what needs to be copied out. So, at all times and in all places, and especially in confidential and familiar letters, one will find pleasure in not having neglected this skill either.

With syllables, there is no short cut. They must all be learned; there is no point in the common practice of postponing the most difficult questions relating to them, to be discovered only when we come to write words. We must beware also of trusting the first memory too readily: it is better to have repeated syllable-drill over a long period, and not be in a hurry to achieve continuity or speed in reading either, unless the sequences of letters are produced without hesitation or doubt, and anyway without the child having to stop and think. Only then let him begin to construct words with the syllables themselves and form connected sentences with the words. It is unbelievable how much further delay in reading is produced by haste. The result is hesitation, interruption, and repetition, because they are venturing beyond their powers, and then, when they make mistakes, losing confidence also in what

QUINTILIAN

33 Certa sit ergo in primis lectio, deinde coniuncta et diu len-
tior, donec exercitatione contingat emendata 'velocitas.
34 Nam prospicere in dextrum, quod omnes praecipiunt, et
providere non rationis modo sed usus quoque est, quoniam sequentia intuenti priora dicenda sunt, et, quod dif-
ficillimum est, dividenda intentio animi ut aliud voce aliud
oculis agatur.

Illud non paenitebit curasse, cum scribere nomina puer
quemadmodum moris est coeperit, ne hanc operam in vo-
35 cabulis vulgaribus et forte occurrentibus perdat. Protinus
enim potest interpretationem linguae secretioris, id est
quas Graeci glossas vocant, dum aliud agitur ediscere, et
inter prima elementa consequi rem postea proprium tempus desideraturam. Et quoniam circa res adhuc tenues
moramur, ii quoque versus qui ad imitationem scribendi
proponentur non otiosas velim sententias habeant, sed ho-
36 nestum aliquid monentis. Prosequitur haec memoria in senectutem et inpressa animo rudi usque ad mores proficiet.
Etiam dicta clarorum virorum et electos ex poetis maxime
(namque eorum cognitio parvis gratior est) locos ediscere
inter lusum licet. Nam et maxime necessaria est oratori,
sicut suo loco dicam, memoria; et ea praecipue firmatur
atque·alitur exercitatione et in his de quibus nunc loquimur aetatibus, quae nihildum ipsae generare ex se queunt,
prope sola est quae iuvari cura docentium possit.
37 Non alienum fuerit exigere ab his aetatibus, quo sit
absolutius os et expressior sermo, ut nomina quaedam

---

17 *Glōssai*, lit. "tongues," first found in this sense in Aristotle
(*Poetics* 1457b4, *Rhetoric* 1410b12).
18 In 11.2.

they already know. Reading must therefore first be sure, then connected, and for a long time quite slow, until practice enables correctness to be combined with speed. For to look forward to the right (as is universally taught), and so foresee what is coming, is a matter not only of theory but of practice, since we have to keep our eyes on what follows while reading out what precedes, and (most difficult of all) divide the attention of the mind, the voice doing one thing and the eyes another.

One will never regret making sure that, when the child (according to the usual practice) begins to write names, he does not waste his time on common words that occur all the time. Right from the start, he can, incidentally, learn the explanations of obscure words (what the Greeks call "glosses"),[17] and so, at this elementary stage, acquire knowledge which would need time for itself later on. And, as we are still dealing with minor matters, I should like to suggest that the lines set for copying should not be meaningless sentences, but should convey some moral lesson. The memory of such things stays with us till we are old, and the impression thus made on the unformed mind will be good for the character also. The child may also be allowed to learn, as a game, the sayings of famous men and especially selected passages from the poets (which children particularly like to know). Memory (as I shall show in due time[18]) is very necessary to the orator; there is nothing like practice for nourishing and strengthening it, and, since the age-group of which we are now speaking cannot as yet produce anything on its own, it is almost the only faculty which the teacher's attention can help to develop.

It would be a good idea, at this age, in order to develop the vocal organs and make the speech more distinct, to get

versusque adfectatae difficultatis ex pluribus et asperrime
coeuntibus inter se syllabis catenatos et veluti confragosos
quam citatissime volvant (χαλινοί Graece vocantur): res
modica dictu, qua tamen omissa multa linguae vitia, nisi
primis eximuntur annis, inemendabili in posterum pravitate durantur.

2

1   Sed nobis iam paulatim adcrescere puer et exire de gremio
et discere serio incipiat. Hoc igitur potissimum loco tractanda quaestio est, utiliusne sit domi atque intra privatos
parietes studentem continere, an frequentiae scholarum
2   et velut publicatis[1] praeceptoribus tradere. Quod quidem
cum iis a quibus clarissimarum civitatium mores sunt instituti, tum eminentissimis auctoribus video placuisse. Non
est tamen dissimulandum esse nonnullos qui ab hoc prope
publico more privata quadam persuasione dissentiant. Hi
duas praecipue rationes sequi videntur: unam, quod moribus magis consulant fugiendo turbam hominum eius aetatis quae sit ad vitia maxime prona, unde causas turpium
factorum saepe extitisse utinam falso iactaretur: alteram,
quod, quisquis futurus est ille praeceptor, liberalius tempora sua inpensurus uni videtur quam si eadem in pluris
partiatur.
3   Prior causa prorsus gravis: nam si studiis quidem scho-

---

[1] publicitus *("at public expense") Radermacher*

---

[19] Lit. "bit" or "curb" for a horse (Latin *freni*, Martianus
Capella 5.518). Examples are known (Ziebarth, op. cit. p. 5):
knaxzbikh, phlegmodrōps, beduzaps, khthōm, plēktron, sphinx.

the child to rattle off, as fast as he can, words and verses designed to be difficult, formed of strings of syllables which clash with one another, and are really rocky, as it were: the Greeks call them *chalinoi* (tongue twisters).[19] This sounds no great matter; but its omission leads to many faults of pronunciation which, unless removed in early years, persist through life as an incurable bad habit.

CHAPTER 2

Home or school?

But now our boy is to grow up little by little, leave the nursery, and begin his education seriously. This is therefore the best place to discuss the question whether it is better to keep him studying at home, within one's own walls, or hand him over to the general society of the schools and teachers who, as it were, are available to the public. I know this has been the favoured course of those who have established the customs of the most famous cities, and of other very eminent authorities besides. But we must not conceal the fact that there are some who disagree with this publicly approved custom because of private convictions of their own. They seem to have two main reasons. First, they are making (they think) better provision for morality by avoiding the crowd of persons of an age which is particularly liable to vice; and I only wish that the view that this has often been a cause of shameful behaviour were false! Secondly, the future teacher, whoever he is, seems likely to give a single pupil more of his time than if he had to divide it among several.

The first point is certainly serious. If it were agreed that

las prodesse, moribus autem nocere constaret, potior mihi ratio vivendi honeste quam vel optime dicendi videretur. Sed mea quidem sententia iuncta ista atque indiscreta sunt: neque enim esse oratorem nisi bonum virum iudico et fieri, etiam si potest, nolo. De hac igitur prius.

4   Corrumpi mores in scholis putant: nam et corrumpuntur interim, sed domi quoque, et sunt multa eius rei exempla, tam hercule quam conservatae sanctissime utrubique opinionis. Natura cuiusque ‹in ›[2] totum curaque distat. Da mentem ad peiora facilem, da neglegentiam formandi custodiendique in aetate prima pudoris, non minorem flagitiis occasionem secreta praebuerint. Nam et potest turpis esse domesticus ille praeceptor, nec tutior inter servos malos quam ingenuos parum modestos conversatio

5   est. At si bona ipsius indoles, si non caeca ac sopita parentium socordia est, et praeceptorem eligere sanctissimum quemque (cuius rei praecipua prudentibus cura est) et disciplinam quae maxime severa fuerit licet, et nihilo minus amicum gravem virum aut fidelem libertum lateri filii sui adiungere, cuius adsiduus comitatus etiam illos meliores faciat qui timebantur.

6   Facile erat huius metus remedium. Utinam liberorum nostrorum mores non ipsi perderemus! Infantiam statim deliciis solvimus. Mollis illa educatio, quam indulgentiam vocamus, nervos omnis mentis et corporis frangit. Quid non adultus concupiscet qui in purpuris repit? Nondum prima verba exprimit, iam coccum intellegit, iam conchy-

---

[2] *add. Watt* 1998

---

[1] A common complaint: Juvenal 10.224, Suetonius, *De grammaticis* 23 (on the notorious Remmius Palaemon).

schools were good for study, but bad for morals, I should put a higher value on respectability of life than on any excellence as a speaker. In my view, however, the two are inseparably connected. I hold that no one can be an orator unless he is a good man; and even if it *is* possible, I do not want it to happen. So I take this question first.

People think that morals are corrupted in schools.[1] Sometimes indeed they are, but so they are at home, and there are numerous instances of this, and also of course of the most scrupulous preservation of good repute in both situations. The whole difference lies in the nature of the individual and the attention he receives. Given a natural bent towards evil, and some carelessness in developing and guarding modesty in early years, privacy will give just as much opportunity for sin. The teacher employed at home may be of bad character, and the company of bad slaves is no safer than that of immodest companions of good birth. On the other hand, if the boy's natural bent is good, and the parents are not sunk in blind indifference, it is possible to choose a teacher of unexceptionable character (this is the wise parent's prime concern) and the strictest system of education conceivable, and at the same time to attach some respectable man or loyal freedman to one's son as a friend, whose regular companionship may even improve those who gave rise to our fears.

The remedy for these anxieties should be easy enough. If only we did not ourselves damage our children's characters! We ruin their infancy by spoiling them from the start. That soft upbringing which we call indulgence destroys all the sinews of mind and body. If a toddler crawls around in purple, what will he not want when he grows up? He cannot articulate a word yet, but he already understands what

85

7 lium poscit. Ante palatum eorum quam os instituimus. In
lecticis crescunt: si terram attigerunt, e manibus utrimque
sustinentium pendent. Gaudemus si quid licentius dixerint: verba ne Alexandrinis quidem permittenda deliciis
risu et osculo excipimus. Nec mirum: nos docuimus, ex no-
8 bis audierunt; nostras amicas, nostros concubinos vident;
omne convivium obscenis canticis strepit, pudenda dictu
spectantur. Fit ex his consuetudo, inde natura. Discunt
haec miseri antequam sciant vitia esse: inde soluti ac flu-
entes non accipiunt ex scholis mala ista, sed in scholas
adferunt.
9 'Verum in studiis magis vacabit unus uni.' Ante omnia
nihil prohibet esse illum nescio quem unum etiam cum eo
qui in scholis eruditur. Sed etiamsi iungi utrumque non
posset, lumen tamen illud conventus honestissimi tenebris
ac solitudini praetulissem: nam optimus quisque praeceptor frequentia gaudet ac maiore se theatro dignum putat.
10 At fere minores ex conscientia suae infirmitatis haerere
singulis et officio fungi quodam modo paedagogorum non
indignantur.
11 Sed praestet alicui vel gratia vel pecunia vel amicitia ut
doctissimum atque incomparabilem magistrum domi habeat, num tamen ille totum in uno diem consumpturus est
aut potest esse ulla tam perpetua discentis intentio quae
non ut visus oculorum optutu continuo fatigetur, cum
praesertim multo plus secreti temporis studia desiderent?
12 Neque enim scribenti ediscenti cogitanti praeceptor adsis-

---

2 Alexandria had a bad reputation: Caesar, *De bello civili*
3.110, Dio Chrysostom, *Oration* 32. Colson, ad loc., draws attention to Ben Jonson's use of this passage in *Every man in his hu-
mour,* II.v.   3 I.e. than it requires contact with a teacher.

scarlet is, and demands the best purple. We train their palate before we teach their lips to speak. They grow up in litters; if they put a foot on the ground, they are held up by helping hands on either side. We like it if they say something outrageous; we reward with a smile and a kiss words that would be objectionable in an Alexandrian fancy boy.[2] No wonder: it was we who taught them, they heard it all from us. They see our mistresses, our boy lovers; every dinner party echoes with obscene songs; things are to be seen which it is shameful to name. Hence comes first habit, then nature. The wretched children learn these things before they know they are wrong. This is what makes them dissolute and spineless: they do not get these vices from the schools, they import them into them.

"The teacher will be able to give more time, one to one." In the first place, there is nothing to prevent the "one" teacher being also with the boy who is being taught at school. And even if the two things were incompatible, I should still have preferred the broad daylight of honest company to darkness and solitude. All good teachers like a large class, and think they deserve a bigger stage. It is the weaker teachers, conscious of their own defects, who cling to individual pupils and seem content with something like the job of the *paedagogi*.

But let us suppose that influence or money or friendship provides a very learned and incomparable teacher at home: is he going to spend the whole day on his one pupil? Or can the learner's attention be kept up so continuously without getting tired, as the eye tires with continual looking, especially as learning requires much more private time?[3] The teacher does not stand over the pupil when he

87

tit: quorum aliquid agentibus cuiuscumque interventus
impedimento est. Lectio quoque non omnis nec semper
praeeunte vel interpretante eget: quando enim tot aucto-
13   rum notitia contingeret? Modicum ergo tempus est quo in
totum diem velut opus ordinetur, ideoque per plures ire
possunt etiam quae singulis tradenda sunt. Pleraque vero
hanc condicionem habent, ut eadem voce ad omnis simul
perferantur. Taceo de partitionibus et declamationibus
rhetorum, quibus certe quantuscumque numerus adhi-
14   beatur, tamen unusquisque totum feret: non enim vox illa
praeceptoris ut cena minus pluribus sufficit, sed ut sol uni-
versis idem lucis calorisque largitur. Grammaticus quoque
si de loquendi ratione disserat, si quaestiones explicet,
historias exponat, poemata enarret, tot illa discent quot
audient.
15   'At enim emendationi praelectionique numerus obstat.' Sit incommodum (nam quid fere undique placet?):
mox illud comparabimus commodis.
'Nec ego tamen eo mitti puerum volo ubi neglegatur.'
Sed neque praeceptor bonus maiore se turba quam ut sus-
tinere eam possit oneraverit, et in primis ea habenda cura
est ut is omni modo fiat nobis familiariter amicus, nec
officium in docendo spectet sed adfectum. Ita numquam
16   erimus in turba. Nec sane quisquam litteris saltem leviter

is writing, learning by heart, or thinking something over; indeed the intervention of another person is a hindrance to any of these activities. Reading also does not always and in every case need a model rendering or an interpretation by the teacher. If it did, how could one ever get to know so many authors? Quite a short time is needed for assigning the work for the whole day, and so even teaching that needs to be given individually can be given to a number of pupils in turn. There are also many things which require to be imparted to all the pupils at once. I say nothing of the analyses and declamations of the rhetors. For them, the audience can be as large as you like, yet each individual can get the full benefit; the voice of the lecturer is not like a dinner which is insufficient for a large company, but like the sun that dispenses light and heat equally to all. Similarly, if a *grammaticus* is lecturing on correct speech, or explaining problems, or giving the historical background, or paraphrasing poems, all who hear him will profit by the lesson.

"But a large class is unsuitable for the correction of mistakes and for reading and expounding a text." It may indeed be inconvenient (what gives satisfaction in every respect?); but we shall later balance the inconvenience against the advantages.

"But I do not want my boy to be sent where he will be neglected." But, firstly, a good teacher will not burden himself with a bigger crowd of pupils than he can manage; and secondly it is very important to ensure that he becomes in every way on terms of friendship with us, and looks at his teaching as a matter not of duty but of affection. In that way we shall never be part of a crowd. Again, any teacher who has the least tincture of literary cul-

inbutus eum in quo studium ingeniumque perspexerit
non in suam quoque gloriam peculiariter fovebit. Et ut
fugiendae sint magnae scholae (cui ne ipsi quidem rei adsentior, si ad aliquem merito concurritur), non tamen hoc
eo valet ut fugiendae sint omnino scholae. Aliud est enim
vitare eas, aliud eligere.

17   Et si refutavimus quae contra dicuntur, iam explicemus
18 quid ipsi sequamur. Ante omnia futurus orator, cui in maxima celebritate et in media rei publicae luce vivendum est,
adsuescat iam a tenero non reformidare homines neque
illa solitaria et velut umbratili[3] vita pallescere. Excitanda
mens et attollenda semper est, quae in eius modi secretis
aut languescit et quendam velut in opaco situm ducit, aut
contra tumescit inani persuasione: necesse est enim ni-
19 mium tribuat sibi qui se nemini comparat. Deinde cum
proferenda sunt studia, caligat in sole et omnia nova offen-
dit, ut qui solus didicerit quod inter multos faciendum est.
20 Mitto amicitias, quae ad senectutem usque firmissime durant religiosa quadam necessitudine inbutae: neque enim
est sanctius sacris isdem quam studiis initiari. Sensum ipsum, qui communis dicitur, ubi discet cum se a congressu,
qui non hominibus solum sed mutis quoque animalibus
21 naturalis est, segregarit? Adde quod domi ea sola discere

[3] umbratica A

---

[4] Shade characterizes the quiet life of the private and inactive,
contrasted with the heat of the sun which soldiers and workers
endure. For the form *umbratilis* (rather than *umbratica*), see
Cicero, *De oratore* 1.157, *Orator* 64.

[5] An old and favourite metaphor for education, underlining

ture will not fail to take a particular interest in any boy in whom he sees industry and talent, because this will advance his own reputation too. But even if big schools are to be avoided (though I cannot agree even with this proposition, if a teacher is deservedly popular), it does not follow that schools in general are to be avoided. It is one thing to avoid them, quite another to choose among them.

If I have succeeded in refuting these objections, let me now explain my own practice. First of all, let the future orator, who has to live in the crowd and in the full glare of public life, become accustomed from childhood not to be frightened of people or acquire the pallor that comes from that solitary life that is lived in the shade.[4] The mind needs constant stimulus and challenge; and, in that kind of privacy, it either languishes and gathers mold, as it were, in the dark, or else swells up with vain conceit, because any person who has no one with whom to compare himself is bound to rate himself too highly. Later, when the fruits of his study have to be made public, he is dazzled by the sun and stumbles over everything new, because he has learned as a solitary something which can only be practised among many. I say nothing of the friendships which endure firm and unbroken to old age, imbued with almost religious feelings of attachment. Initiation in the same studies is no less binding than initiation in the same mysteries.[5] And where will he learn what we call common feeling if he shuts himself off from society, which is natural not only to humans but to the dumb animals? And again, at home he

the elite status of the educated: Aristophanes, *Frogs* 354, Aulus Gellius, *Praefatio* 20–21; Kaster (1988) 15–16. See also on 5.13.60.

potest quae ipsi praecipientur, in schola etiam quae aliis.
Audiet multa cotidie probari, multa corrigi, proderit ali-
22 cuius obiurgata desidia, proderit laudata industria, excita-
bitur laude aemulatio, turpe ducet cedere pari, pulchrum
superasse maiores. Accendunt omnia haec animos, et licet
ipsa vitium sit ambitio, frequenter tamen causa virtutum
23 est. Non inutilem scio servatum esse a praeceptoribus
meis morem, qui, cum pueros in classis distribuerant,
ordinem dicendi secundum vires ingenii dabant, et ita
superiore loco quisque declamabat ut praecedere profectu
24 videbatur: huius rei iudicia praebebantur. Ea nobis ingens
palma, ducere vero classem multo pulcherrimum. Nec de
hoc semel decretum erat: tricesimus dies reddebat victo
certaminis potestatem. Ita nec superior successu curam
remittebat et dolor victum ad depellendam ignominiam
25 concitabat. Id nobis acriores ad studia dicendi faces sub-
didisse quam exhortationem docentium, paedagogorum
custodiam, vota parentium, quantum animi mei coniectu-
ra colligere possum, contenderim.
26   Sed sicut firmiores in litteris profectus alit aemulatio,
ita incipientibus atque adhuc teneris condiscipulorum
quam praeceptoris iucundior hoc ipso quod facilior imitatio est. Vix enim se prima elementa ad spem tollere ef-
fingendae quam summam putant eloquentiae audebunt:
proxima amplectentur magis, ut vites arboribus adplicitae

---

6 The precise procedure is unclear: does Q. mean that it was
an honour to be moved up in the class as a result of the teacher's
assessment (and to be top was of course very special), or that the
class itself made the "judgements"?

7 When the teacher was paid (compare Herodas, *Mimiambi*
3.9) and would naturally want to display his pupils' progress.

can only learn what is taught to him personally, while at school he will also learn what is taught to others. He will hear many things praised and many things corrected every day; he will profit from hearing indolence rebuked or industry commended. His emulation will be excited by praise; he will think it a disgrace to be outdone by a contemporary, and a fine thing to do better than his seniors. All these things stimulate the mind, and though ambition may be a fault in itself, it is often the cause of virtues. I remember that my own masters maintained a practice which was not without its uses. Having distributed the boys in classes, they made the order of speaking depend on ability, so that the place in which each of them declaimed was a consequence of the progress which they thought he had made. Judgements were made public;[6] that itself was a tremendous honour, but to be top of the class was most wonderful. The decision was not permanent; the end of the month[7] brought the defeated pupil the chance to compete again, and so success did not encourage the victor to relax, while the vexation of it goaded the unsuccessful into wiping out his disgrace. I am prepared to argue that to the best of my recollection this did more to kindle our oratorical ambitions than all the exhortations of our teachers, the watchfulness of our *paedagogi,* and the hopes of our parents.

But, while rivalry nurtures literary progress when it is more firmly established, beginners and the very young find imitation of their fellow pupils more agreeable than imitation of their masters, because it is easier. Elementary students will scarcely dare raise themselves to any hope of reproducing what they believe to be a crowning achievement of eloquence; they will prefer to embrace what is

inferiores prius adprendendo ramos in cacumina evadunt.
27 Quod adeo verum est ut ipsius etiam magistri, si tamen
ambitiosis utilia praeferet, hoc opus sit, cum adhuc rudia
tractabit ingenia, non statim onerare infirmitatem discentium, sed temperare vires suas et ad intellectum audientis
28 descendere. Nam ut vascula oris angusti superfusam umoris copiam respuunt, sensim autem influentibus vel etiam
instillatis complentur, sic animi puerorum quantum exci-
pere possint videndum est: nam maiora intellectu velut pa-
29 rum apertos ad percipiendum animos non subibunt. Utile
igitur habere quos imitari primum, mox vincere velis: ita
paulatim et superiorum spes erit. His adicio praeceptores
ipsos non idem mentis ac spiritus in dicendo posse concipere singulis tantum praesentibus quod illa celebritate
30 audientium instinctos. Maxima enim pars eloquentiae
constat animo: hunc adfici, hunc concipere imagines rerum et transformari quodam modo ad naturam eorum de
quibus loquitur necesse est. Is porro quo generosior cel-
siorque est, hoc maioribus velut organis commovetur,
ideoque et laude crescit et impetu augetur et aliquid
31 magnum agere gaudet. Est quaedam tacita dedignatio vim
dicendi tantis comparatam laboribus ad unum auditorem
demittere: pudet supra modum sermonis attolli. Et sane
concipiat quis mente vel declamantis habitum vel orantis
vocem incessum pronuntiationem, illum denique animi et
corporis motum, sudorem, ut alia praeteream, et fatigatio-

---

8 Elms were the usual tree used to support vines: Vergil, *Georgics* 2.367. For agriculture as a metaphor for education, compare 1.3.5, 2.4.11.

closest to them, just as vines trained on trees climb to the
top by first taking hold of the lower branches.[8] So true is
this that it is the master's own duty too, if (that is) he prefers the serviceable to the showy, not to begin by overload-
ing his pupils' limited strength when he is dealing with unformed minds, but to keep his own powers under control
and come down to his hearer's intellectual level. Vessels
with narrow mouths reject liquid if too much is poured in
at once, but can be filled if it flows in gradually or a drop at
a time; likewise, we have to consider how much the children's minds can take: what is too big for their understanding will not get into minds which have not been opened
enough to accept it. It is useful to have people whom you
would like first to imitate and then to surpass; this will
gradually lead to hope of even higher things. I add the further point that the teachers themselves cannot develop the
same intelligence and energy in speaking to an audience of
one as when inspired by the more numerous gathering of
which we were speaking. Why? Because eloquence is
mainly a psychological matter: it is the mind which must be
emotionally stirred and must conceive images and somehow be itself adapted to the subject of the speech. The
nobler and more elevated the mind, the more powerful the
mechanism, as it were, that it needs to stir it up. This is why
it grows with praise, develops with effort, and finds joy
in doing something big. There is a certain unexpressed
feeling that it is unworthy to deploy a power of speech so
laboriously acquired on an audience of one: the speaker is
embarrassed to raise his voice above the ordinary conver-
sational level. Just imagine the attitude of a declaimer, or
the voice, gait, and delivery of an orator—the motions of
mind and body, the sweat (to say nothing of anything else),

nem audiente uno: nonne quiddam pati furori simile
videatur? Non esset in rebus humanis eloquentia si tantum
cum singulis loqueremur.

3

1 Tradito sibi puero docendi peritus ingenium eius in primis
naturamque perspiciet. Ingenii signum in parvis praecipuum memoria est: eius duplex virtus, facile percipere et
fideliter continere. Proximum imitatio: nam id quoque est
docilis naturae, sic tamen ut ea quae discit effingat, non habitum forte et ingressum et si quid in peius notabile est.
2 Non dabit mihi spem bonae indolis qui hoc imitandi studio
petet ut rideatur; nam probus quoque in primis erit ille
vere ingeniosus. Alioqui non peius duxerim tardi esse
ingeni quam mali:[1] probus autem ab illo segni et iacente
3 plurimum aberit. Hic meus quae tradentur non difficulter
accipiet, quaedam etiam interrogabit: sequetur tamen magis quam praecurret. Illud ingeniorum velut praecox ge-
4 nus non temere umquam pervenit ad frugem. Hi sunt qui
parva facile faciunt et audacia provecti quidquid illud possunt statim ostendunt, possunt autem id demum quod in
proximo est: verba continuant, haec vultu interrito, nulla
tardati verecundia proferunt: non multum praestant, sed
5 cito; non subest vera vis nec penitus inmissis radicibus

[1] cati (*"clever"*) Colson

and the fatigue—all for a single listener! Would it not seem
a bit like madness? If we only talked to one person at a
time, there would be no such thing as eloquence in human
life.

CHAPTER 3

The different gifts of children
and how to handle them

As soon as a boy is entrusted to him, the skilled teacher will
first spy out his ability and his nature. In children, the principal sign of talent is memory. There are two virtues of
memory: quickness of grasp, and accurate retention. Next
comes imitation; this also is a mark of a teachable nature,
provided that it is exercised on what he is learning, not on
someone's bearing or walk or some observable defect. I
shall not form any expectation of good qualities, if the
object of those efforts at imitation is to raise a laugh. The
really gifted will also be a good boy. In any case, I cannot
think it worse to be stupid than to be bad; but the good boy
will be anything but a dullard or a lazybones. My ideal
pupil anyway will absorb instruction without difficulty and
even ask some questions; but he will follow rather than
anticipate the teacher. Those precocious intellects do not
readily come to fruition. They are the boys who do small
things easily and then, emboldened by this, quickly show
what it is that they can do—and this is just what lies nearest
at hand: they string words together and bring them out
with a bold face, uninhibited by any feelings of modesty.
They have little to offer, but what there is comes quickly.
There is no real underlying force that has any deep roots: it

nititur, ut quae summo solo sparsa sunt semina celerius se
effundunt et imitatae spicas herbulae inanibus aristis ante
messem flavescunt. Placent haec annis comparata; deinde
stat profectus, admiratio decrescit.

6   Haec cum animadverterit, perspiciat deinceps quonam
modo tractandus sit discentis animus. Sunt quidam, nisi
institeris, remissi, quidam imperia indignantur; quosdam
continet metus, quosdam debilitat; alios continuatio ex-
tundit, in aliis plus impetus facit. Mihi ille detur puer
7 quem laus excitet, quem gloria iuvet, qui victus fleat. Hic
erit alendus ambitu, hunc mordebit obiurgatio, hunc
honor excitabit, in hoc desidiam numquam verebor.

8   Danda est tamen omnibus aliqua remissio, non solum
quia nulla res est quae perferre possit continuum laborem,
atque ea quoque quae sensu et anima carent ut servare
vim suam possint velut quiete alterna retenduntur, sed
quod studium discendi voluntate, quae cogi non potest,
9 constat. Itaque et virium plus adferunt ad discendum re-
novati ac recentes et acriorem animum, qui fere necessita-
10 tibus repugnat. Nec me offenderit lusus in pueris (est et
hoc signum alacritatis), neque illum tristem semperque
demissum sperare possim erectae circa studia mentis fore,
cum in hoc quoque maxime naturali aetatibus illis impetu
11 iaceat. Modus tamen sit remissionibus, ne aut odium studiorum faciant negatae aut otii consuetudinem nimiae.
Sunt etiam nonnulli acuendis puerorum ingeniis non inutiles lusus, cum positis invicem cuiusque generis quaes-

---

1 A familiar idea: Otto, *Sprichwörter* 36, Horace, *Carmina*
2.10.19, with Nisbet–Hubbard ad loc. The bow and the lyre are
types of inanimate things which need to be slackened or relaxed at
times.

is like seed scattered on the surface of the soil; it comes up too quickly, the blade looks like a full ear, but it turns yellow before the harvest, and there is no substance in the crop. These things give pleasure, taking the age into account; but then progress stops, and admiration declines.

Having noticed all this, the teacher must next consider how the pupil's mind should be handled. Some are idle unless you press them; others are impatient of discipline. Fear restrains some and paralyses others. Some need continuous effort to knock them into shape; with others, the sudden attack is more effective. Give me a boy who is encouraged by praise, pleased by success, and who cries when he has lost. He is the one who will be nourished by ambition, hurt by reproof, and excited by honour. In him I shall never have to fear laziness.

However, everyone must be given some relaxation, not only because there is nothing that can stand perpetual strain[1]—even things which are without sense or life need to be relaxed by periods of rest in order to preserve their strength—but also because study depends on the will to learn, and this cannot be forced. Thus renewed and refreshed, they will bring to their learning both more energy and that keener spirit which so often resists compulsion. I am not bothered by playfulness in the young (it too is a sign of a lively mind), nor would I ever expect a gloomy and perpetually depressed boy to show alertness in his work, lacking as he is also in the energy which is particularly natural at his age. But there must be moderation in holidays: if we refuse them, the boys will hate their work; if there are too many, they will get used to being idle. There are even some games which are useful for sharpening the wits, for example competitions in which they ask one another all sorts of

QUINTILIAN

12 tiunculis aemulantur. Mores quoque se inter ludendum
simplicius detegunt: modo nulla videatur aetas tam infirma quae non protinus quid rectum pravumque sit discat,
tum vel maxime formanda cum simulandi nescia est et
praecipientibus facillime cedit; frangas enim citius quam
13 corrigas quae in pravum induruerunt. Protinus ergo ne
quid cupide, ne quid improbe, ne quid inpotenter faciat
monendus est puer, habendumque in animo semper illud
Vergilianum:

adeo in teneris consuescere multum est.

14 Caedi vero discentis, quamlibet id receptum sit et
Chrysippus non improbet, minime velim, primum quia
deforme atque servile est et certe (quod convenit si aetatem mutes) iniuria: deinde quod, si cui tam est mens in-
liberalis ut obiurgatione non corrigatur, is etiam ad plagas
ut pessima quaeque mancipia durabitur: postremo quod
ne opus erit quidem hac castigatione si adsiduus studio-
15 rum exactor adstiterit. Nunc fere neglegentia paedagogorum sic emendari videtur ut pueri non facere quae recta
sunt cogantur, sed cur non fecerint puniantur. Denique
cum parvolum verberibus coegeris, quid iuveni facias, cui
nec adhiberi potest hic metus et maiora discenda sunt?
16 Adde quod multa vapulantibus dictu deformia et mox

---

2 *Georgics* 2.272.

3 *SVF* iii. 738. Q. is unusually liberal: Horace's "flogging" master, *plagosus Orbilius* (*Epistulae* 2.1.71), is more typical. Compare also Seneca, *De clementia* 1.16, and the mother in Herodas,
Mimiambi 3.1, who asks the teacher to flog her son till his "soul is
hanging on his lips."

100

little questions. Character reveals itself too more naturally in games—but bear in mind that no age is too immature to learn straight away what is right and what is wrong, and that the best age for forming character is when they do not know how to pretend, but obey their teachers most readily. It is easier to break than to straighten anything which has hardened into a bad shape. There must be no delay, then, in warning the boy that he must not behave greedily, dishonestly, or without controlling himself. Let us always keep in mind the words of Vergil:

So strong is habit in the tender plant.[2]

Flogging a pupil is something I do not at all like, though it is an accepted practice and Chrysippus approves.[3] In the first place, it is humiliating and proper only for slaves; and certainly it is an infringement of rights (as it is agreed to be at a later age).[4] Secondly, if a boy is so lacking in self-respect that reproof is powerless to put him right, he will even become hardened to blows, like the worst type of slave. And finally, there will be no need for this form of punishment if there is always someone there to make sure the work gets done. As it is, we try to make amends for the negligence of the *paedagogi* not by forcing boys to do the right thing but by punishing them for not having done it. Moreover, though you may compel a child with blows, what can you do with a young man who cannot be threatened like this and who has more important lessons to learn? And again, when children are beaten, the pain and fear often have results which it is not pleasant to speak of

---

[4] I.e. there would be an action for *iniuria* if a free adult were struck or beaten.

verecundiae futura saepe dolore vel metu acciderunt, qui
pudor frangit animum et abicit atque ipsius lucis fugam et
taedium dictat.

17   Iam si minor in eligendis custodum et praeceptorum
moribus fuit cura, pudet dicere in quae probra nefandi homines isto caedendi iure abutantur, quam det aliis quoque
nonnumquam occasionem hic miserorum metus. Non mo-
rabor in parte hac: nimium est quod intellegitur. Quare
hoc dixisse satis est: in aetatem infirmam et iniuriae ob-
noxiam nemini debet nimium licere.

18   Nunc quibus instituendus sit artibus qui sic formabitur
ut fieri possit orator, et quae in quaque aetate inchoanda,
dicere ingrediar.

4

1   Primus in eo qui scribendi legendique adeptus erit facultatem grammaticis est locus. Nec refert de Graeco an de
Latino loquar, quamquam Graecum esse priorem placet:
utrique eadem via est.

2   Haec igitur professio, cum brevissime in duas partis
dividatur, recte loquendi scientiam et poetarum enarratio-

3 nem, plus habet in recessu quam fronte promittit. Nam et
scribendi ratio coniuncta cum loquendi[1] est et enarratio-
nem praecedit emendata lectio et mixtum his omnibus
iudicium est; quo quidem ita severe sunt usi veteres gram-

---

[1] *Madvig*: loquendo *AB*

and which will later be a source of embarrassment. This shame breaks and depresses the spirits, and leads the child to shun and loathe the light of day.

If not enough care has been taken about the character of the supervisors or teachers, I blush to mention the shameful purposes for which evil men abuse their right to flog, and what opportunities the terror felt by these poor children sometimes gives to other persons also. I will not dwell on this subject: what I am hinting at is already too much. It is enough to observe that no one ought to be allowed too much power over helpless and easily victimized young people.

I shall now proceed to name the subjects in which the boy who is being trained to be an orator should be educated, and the age at which each subject should be begun.

CHAPTER 4

Grammaticē. (1) Some linguistic observations

When the child has acquired a facility in writing and reading, the first turn belongs to the *grammatici*. What I say applies indifferently to the Greek teacher and to the Latin, though I prefer the Greek to come first. Both use the same methods.

Although (to put it in a word) this subject comprises two parts—the study of correct speech and the interpretation of the poets—there is more of it behind the scenes than meets the eye. The principles of writing are closely connected with those of speaking, correct reading is a prerequisite of interpretation, and judgement is involved in all these. The old *grammatici* indeed were so severe in their

QUINTILIAN

matici ut non versus modo censoria quadam virgula notare
et libros qui falso viderentur inscripti tamquam subditos
summovere familia permiserint sibi, sed auctores alios in
ordinem redegerint alios omnino exemerint numero.

4   Nec poetas legisse satis est: excutiendum omne scripto-
rum genus, non propter historias modo, sed verba, quae
frequenter ius ab auctoribus sumunt. Tum neque citra
musicen grammatice potest esse perfecta, cum ei de me-
tris rhythmisque dicendum sit, nec si rationem siderum
ignoret poetas intellegat, qui, ut alia mittam, totiens ortu
occasuque signorum in declarandis temporibus utuntur,
nec ignara philosophiae, cum propter plurimos in omnibus
fere carminibus locos ex intima naturalium quaestionum
subtilitate repetitos, tum vel propter Empedoclea in Graecis, Varronem ac Lucretium in Latinis, qui praecepta sa-
5   pientiae versibus tradiderunt. Eloquentia quoque non
mediocri est opus, ut de unaquaque earum quas demon-
stravimus rerum dicat proprie et copiose. Quo minus sunt
ferendi qui hanc artem ut tenuem atque ieiunam cavillan-
tur. Quae nisi oratoris futuri fundamenta fideliter iecit,
quidquid superstruxeris corruet: necessaria pueris, iucun-

---

1 Obelizing lines (see Reynolds and Wilson (1991) 10), discussion of authenticity, and the establishment of "canons" (see 10.1,
54, 59, 61) were characteristic achievements of Alexandrian scholarship.

2 *Historiae* covers historical, geographical, mythological, or
even scientific information.

3 Empedocles was evidently well-known in the Roman period:
Cicero (*Ad Quintum fratrem* 2.9.3) knows of a Latin adaptation by
one "Sallustius," which he thinks unreadable, and Lucretius both

104

judgements that they not only allowed themselves to mark lines with a sign of disapproval[1] and disinherit, as it were, as bastards any books which seemed to be wrongly attributed, but also listed some authors in a recognized canon, and excluded others altogether.

It is not enough just to read the poets. Every type of literature must be thoroughly combed, and not only for learned information[2] but for words, which often get their legitimacy from the great authors. Again, *grammaticē* cannot be complete without music, because it has to discuss metre and rhythm; nor can it understand the poets without a knowledge of astronomy, since (to mention nothing else) they so often use the risings and settings of constellations as indications of time; nor again should it be ignorant of philosophy, both because of the numerous passages in practically every poem that depend on intricate points of natural science, and indeed because of Empedocles[3] among the Greeks, and Varro[4] and Lucretius among the Latins, all of whom have expounded philosophical doctrines in verse. Eloquence too is needed, and in no small measure, to give a proper and fluent explanation of the various matters I have just mentioned. This should make us even less tolerant of people who criticize *grammaticē* as trivial and jejune. Unless it has faithfully laid the future orator's foundations, whatever you build on them will collapse. It is a necessity for children, and a pleasure to the

admired and imitated the great Greek poet (*De rerum natura* 1.716ff.).

[4] This is Varro Atacinus, and the reference is to his *Ephemeris* (which adapted Aratus' *Phaenomena*) and perhaps his *Chorographia* (Courtney (1993) 237). Q. gives him faint praise, 10.1.87.

da senibus, dulcis secretorum comes, et quae vel sola in
omni studiorum genere plus habeat operis quam ostenta-
tionis.

6   Ne quis igitur tamquam parva fastidiat grammatices
elementa, non quia magnae sit operae consonantes a vocalibus discernere ipsasque eas in semivocalium numerum
mutarumque partiri, sed quia interiora velut sacri huius
adeuntibus apparebit multa rerum subtilitas, quae non
modo acuere ingenia puerilia, sed exercere altissimam
7   quoque eruditionem ac scientiam possit. An cuiuslibet
auris est exigere litterarum sonos? Non hercule magis
quam nervorum. At[2] grammatici saltem omnes in hanc
descendent rerum tenuitatem, desintne aliquae nobis
necessariae litterae, non cum Graeca scribimus (tum enim
8   ab isdem duas mutuamur), sed proprie in Latinis: ut in his
'servus' et 'vulgus' Aeolicum digammon desideratur, et
medius est quidam U et I litterae sonus (non enim sic 'optimum' dicimus ut 'opimum'), et in 'here' neque E plane
9   neque I auditur; an rursus aliae redundent, praeter illam
adspirationis ⟨notam⟩,[3] quae si necessaria est etiam contrariam sibi poscit, ut[4] K, quae et ipsa quorundam nominum nota est, et Q, cuius similis effectu specieque, nisi

---

² *recc.*: aut *AB*   ³ *add. edd.*   ⁴ *Capperonnier*: et *AB*

---

⁵ Compare Cicero, *Pro Archia* 16.   ⁶ Y and z. See also
12.10.27–28.   ⁷ The digamma (ϝ) had a w-sound.

⁸ *Optumus* came to be spelled *optimus* in Caesar's time (see
1.7.21) and it is generally supposed that the sound of the second
vowel was distinct both from *u* and from *i:* the emperor Claudius
(see 1.7.26) is said to have felt the need for a new letter to represent it. See W. S. Allen (1965) 56–59; Sihler (1995) 64. Q. also

old,[5] the delightful companion of our privacy and perhaps the only branch of study that has more substance than show.

So no one should despise the elements of *grammaticē*, as though they were of little importance. It is not that it is a major task to distinguish consonants from vowels, and to subdivide the former into semivowels and mutes. But as we draw near to the inner shrine of this mystery, the great intricacy of the subject will be apparent, for it is capable not only of sharpening childish minds but of exercising the most profound knowledge and erudition. It is not given to every ear to appreciate the sounds of the letters properly, any more than to distinguish the different musical notes. Yet every *grammaticus* will surely go into minute questions like the following. (1) Are we lacking some necessary letters, not indeed when we are writing Greek words (for then we borrow two from them),[6] but strictly in Latin? For example, we feel the lack of the Aeolic digamma[7] in *servus* and *vulgus*, and there is also a sound between *u* and *i* (we do not pronounce *optimus* and *opimus* in the same way),[8] while in *here* the sound heard is neither precisely *e* nor *i*. (2) Are some letters redundant (apart from the mark of the aspirate,[9] and if this is necessary, so is its opposite), such as *k*, which is also an abbreviation for some names,[10] and *q*, which (though with us somewhat more slanting) looks and

(compare 1.7.22) assumes a distinct sound for the second syllable of *heri/here*.   [9] Latin used *h* for the aspirate, but (unlike Greek) had no sign for a smooth breathing.

[10] *Kaeso, Kalendae*; but also *calumnia, caput* in some legal contexts. The grammarians' rule was that *k* should be written before *a*, *q* before *u* (W. S. Allen (1965) 15). See also 1.7.10.

quod paulum a nostris obliquatur, coppa apud Graecos
nunc tantum in numero manet, et nostrarum ultima, qua
tam carere potuimus quam psi non quaerimus.

10   Atque etiam in ipsis vocalibus grammatici est videre an
aliquas pro consonantibus usus acceperit, quia 'iam' sicut
'etiam'⁵ scribitur et 'quos'⁶ ut 'tuos.'⁷ At quae ut vocales
iunguntur aut unam longam faciunt, ut veteres scripserunt, qui geminatione earum velut apice utebantur, aut
duas: nisi quis putat etiam ex tribus vocalibus syllabam fieri
11   si non aliquae officio consonantium fungantur. Quaeret
hoc etiam, quo modo duabus demum vocalibus in se ipsas
coeundi natura sit, cum consonantium nulla nisi alteram
frangat: atqui littera I sibi insidit ('coniicit' enim est ab illo
'iacit') et V, quo modo nunc scribitur 'vulgus' et 'servus'.
Sciat etiam Ciceroni placuisse 'aiio' 'Maiiam'que geminata
I scribere: quod si est, etiam iungetur ut consonans.
12   Quare discat puer quid in litteris proprium, quid commune, quae cum quibus cognatio; nec miretur cur ex

⁵ Ritschl: tam AB   ⁶ vos edd.   ⁷ Ritschl: cos AB

---

11 ϙ as a numeral = 90.

12 X, which could be replaced by ks or cs.

13 Ritschl's emendation etiam . . . tuos makes the point that i
and u have both consonantal and non-consonantal values (i is a
vowel in etiam and u is a vowel in tuos). This fits what follows.

14 See also 1.7.14. The use of double vowels (e.g. aa) for long
vowels is said to have been recommended by the tragic poet
Accius, and is found also in Lucilius (ROL 3. 368–372). The apex,
a mark over a letter ("a lopsided circumflex, sometimes little more
than an acute accent," Sihler (1995) 21) was a commoner way of

acts like the Greek *koppa,* which they use now only as a
numeral;[11] and also our last letter,[12] which we could have
done without as easily as we do without *psi?*

With regard to the vowels themselves too, it is for the
grammaticus to inquire whether usage has accepted some
as consonants: we write *iam* like *etiam* and *quos* like *tuos.*[13]
When joined together as vowels, however, they either
make one long vowel (as in the old writers who used double vowels instead of an *apex*)[14] or two vowels—unless one
supposes that a syllable can consist of three vowels, none of
which has the function of a consonant! He will also inquire
how it is that two vowels can coalesce with themselves,
while a consonant can "fracture"[15] only a different consonant.[16] But *i* can follow itself (*coniicit* comes from *iacit*)
and so can *u,* as in the modern spelling[17] of *vulgus* and
servus. He should also know that Cicero preferred to write
aiio and *Maiiam* with a double *i*; if that is done, one will
again be joined to the other as a consonant.

The child should therefore learn the special properties
of the letters, their common properties, and how they are
related to one another. He is not to be surprised that

indicating a long vowel (see 1.7.2) or a doubled consonant. On the
apex, see J. N. Adams, *Journal of Roman Studies* 85 (1995) 97.

[15] See also 12.10.29: the sound of a second consonant is modified by the first, but the two do not coalesce (as vowels do in diphthongs). *OLD* s.v. *frango* 6.

[16] Double consonants (*pp, rr, ff, ss*) are never within the same
syllable; combinations such as *pl, br, sc, fr* can occur both initially
and medially. On this passage, see R. G. G. Coleman, *Classical
Quarterly* 13 (1963) 1–10.

[17] As against *volgus* ("crowd") and *servos* ("slave"), the older
spelling (Sihler (1995) 66).

'scamno' fiat 'scabillum' aut a 'pinno', quod est acutum,
securis utrimque habens aciem 'bipennis', ne illorum sequatur errorem qui, quia a pennis duabus hoc esse nomen
13 existimant, pennas avium dici volunt. Neque has modo no-
verit mutationes, quas adferunt declinatio aut praepositio,
ut 'secat secuit', 'cadit excidit', 'caedit excidit', 'calcat exculcat' (et fit a 'lavando' 'lotus' et inde rursus 'inlutus', et
mille alia), sed et quae rectis quoque casibus aetate trans-
ierunt. Nam ut 'Valesii' 'Fusii' in 'Valerios' 'Furios'que
venerunt, ita 'arbos', 'labos', 'vapos' etiam et 'clamos' ac
14 'lases' fuerunt: atque haec ipsa S littera ab his nominibus
exclusa in quibusdam ipsa alteri successit: nam 'mertare'
atque 'pultare' dicebant, quin 'fordeum' 'faedos'que pro
adspiratione velut simili littera utentes: nam contra Graeci
adspirare ei solent, ut pro Fundanio Cicero testem qui primam eius litteram dicere non possit inridet.
15   Sed B quoque in locum aliarum dedimus aliquando,

---

18 "Stool, bench."

19 See Isidore, *Etymologiae* 19.19.11: *pinnum autem antiqui
acutum dicebant.* But *pinnus* is perhaps a grammarians' invention
(so Ernout–Meillet, *Dictionnaire étymologique du latin,* s.v. *penna;* see also Maltby (1991) 80).

20 The examples mean: cuts, cut; falls, falls out; cuts, cuts out;
stamps, stamps down; washing, wash, unwashed.

21 I.e. *Lares,* as in the *Carmen Arvale* (Courtney (1995) p. 34).
Intervocalic *s* became *r* in Latin in many words, and nominatives
like *arbor* ("tree"), *labor* ("work") were then formed from the
oblique cases *arboris, laboris.* Sihler (1995) 172.

22 *Mertare* ("drown") is known from Accius, *pultare* ("knock")
is common in Plautus and Terence; the common later frequenta-

scabillum is formed from *scamnus*[18] or that a double-edged axe is called a *bipennis* from *pinnus*, which means "sharp"; he must not fall into the error of those who suppose that the word is derived from "two *pennae*," and so think that birds' wings are meant.[19] He must know also not only the changes due to inflexion and composition (*secat secuit, cadit excidit, caedit excīdit, calcat exculcat*—and also *lotus* from *lavare* and hence *inlotus*, and countless other examples)[20] but also changes that time has brought about even in nominatives. As *Valesius* and *Fusius* have become *Valerius* and *Furius*, so at one time we had *arbos, labos,* and even *vapos, clamos,* and *Lases*,[21] while the letter *s* itself, which has disappeared from these words, has replaced another letter in some others: people used to say *mertare* and *pultare*; indeed they also said *fordeum* and *faedi,* using *f* (as being somewhat similar) in place of the aspirate.[22] The Greeks on the other hand commonly aspirate this letter; Cicero in his defence of Fundanius makes fun of a witness who cannot pronounce the first letter of that name.[23]

We have also sometimes replaced other letters by *b*:

tives are *mersare, pulsare.* Sihler (1995) 510, 528. Q. is the earliest witness for *fordeum* (= *hordeum,* "barley"; same example in Scaurus, 7.11.4 *GLK*), though Varro (*De lingua Latina* 5.97) says *fedus* is Sabine for *haedus,* "kid," and later grammarians cite *folus* = *holus* ("cabbage"), *fostis* = *hostis* ("enemy").

23 Cicero, *Fr. orat.* V. 7 Schoell (Crawford (1994) 57–64); hardly anything is known of this case. The Greek witness could not pronounce *f,* but only Greek ϕ (= *p* aspirate); ϕ is not transliterated as *f* until well after Cicero's time.

unde 'Burrus' et 'Bruges' et 'balaena'.[8] Nec non eadem
fecit ex 'duello' 'bellum', unde 'Duellios' quidam dicere

16 'Bellios' ausi. Quid 'stlocum' 'stlites'que? Quid T litterae
cum D quaedam cognatio? Quare minus mirum si in ve-
tustis operibus urbis nostrae et celebribus templis legantur
'Alexanter' et 'Cassantra'. Quid O atque U permutata invicem? ut 'Hecoba' et 'nutrix Culchidis' et 'Pulixena' scribe-
rentur, ac, ne in Graecis id tantum notetur, 'dederont' et
'probaveront'. Sic Ὀδυσσεύς, quem Ὀλισσέα, fecerant

17 Aeolis, ad 'Ulixem' deductus est. Quid? non E quoque I
loco fuit ⟨ut⟩[9] 'Menerva' et 'leber' et 'magester' et 'Diiove
Victore', non 'Diiovi Victori'?

Sed mihi locum signare satis est: non enim doceo, sed
admoneo docturos.

---

[8] *edd.*: belena *AB*
[9] *add. recc.*

---

[24] Cicero, *Orator* 160: "Ennius always has *Burrus,* never *Pyrrhus; vi patefecerunt Bruges,* not *Phryges*" ("the Phrygians by
force have opened up . . . "): Ennius, trag. fr. 183 Warmington
(*ROL* 1. 282) = 334 Jocelyn). See Lindsay (1894) 48, 75; Biville
(1990) 1. 179, 181: she suggests that Ennius is influenced by a
south Italian pronunciation.

[25] Greek φάλαινα ("whale"). Lindsay, op. cit. 48. But Biville
(1990) 1. 88 retains *belena,* as a form of *Helena,* and compares
Velena, attested by late grammarians.

[26] See Cicero, *Orator* 153.

[27] Archaic form of *locus* ("place") and *lites* ("lawsuits"): Lindsay, op. cit. 307.

[28] Ibid. 73. Forms with *-t-* are found on mirrors from Praeneste (*CIL* 14, 4099, 4107), and are of Etruscan origin (Biville
(1990) 1. 217).

Burrus, Bruges,[24] *balaena.*[25] B also turns *duellum* into *bellum,* and some have ventured on *Bellii* for *Duellii.*[26] And what about *stlocus* and *stlites?*[27] What is the relation between *t* and *d,* which makes it less surprising to find *Alexanter* and *Cassantra*[28] in old buildings in Rome and some famous temples? And what of the interchange of *o* and *u,* as in *Hecoba,*[29] *nutrix Culchidis,*[30] *Pulixena,*[31] or (to take examples which are not Greek) *dederont* and *probaveront?*[32] So too *Odusseús* (which the Aeolians made *Olisseus*) came to be *Ulixes.*[33] And was not *e* used for *i,* as in *Menerva, leber, magester,*[34] and *Diiove victore* for *Diiovi victori?*[35]

I only need to indicate this topic; I am not the teacher, but only the teachers' adviser.

[29] Classical Latin *Hecuba,* from Greek Ἑκάβη: ibid. 197.

[30] "The Colchian woman's (i.e. Medea's) nurse."

[31] Classical Latin *Polyxena,* Greek Πολυξένη.

[32] For the "raising" of the vowel from *o* to *u* see Palmer, *Latin Language* 219–220: *-ont* is the older ending of the third person plural of present and perfect. This change from *o* to *u* before *l* or two consonants was established by 200 BC (Sihler (1995) 62).

[33] Greek vase inscriptions of the archaic period show forms like Ὀλυξεύς, Ὠλίξης, and it may be from this tradition that the Latin form derives, rather than from direct change of *d* to *l* in the normal epic form Ὀδυσσεύς: Sihler (1995) 151. (Q.'s *Aeolis* transliterates the Greek nominative plural Αἰολεῖς.)

[34] This spelling, indicating a more open pronunciation of short *i,* is attested elsewhere (e.g. *CIL* 1. 34); the analogous *leber* ("book") and *magester* ("master") apparently not.

[35] *ei* and *i* originally represented different sounds, and *-ei* is the earlier dative ending, sometimes written *-e.* See also 1.7.15; and *OLD* s.v. Iuppiter.

Inde in syllabas cura transibit, de quibus in orthographia pauca adnotabo.

18 Tum videbit, ad quem hoc pertinet, quot et quae partes orationis, quamquam de numero parum convenit. Veteres enim, quorum fuerunt Aristoteles quoque atque Theodectes, verba modo et nomina et convinctiones tradiderunt, videlicet quod in verbis vim sermonis, in nominibus materiam (quia alterum est quod loquimur, alterum de quo loquimur), in convinctionibus autem complexum eorum esse iudicaverunt: quas coniunctiones a plerisque dici scio,

19 sed haec videtur ex syndesmo magis propria tralatio. Paulatim a philosophis ac maxime Stoicis auctus est numerus, ac primum convinctionibus articuli adiecti, post praepositiones: nominibus appellatio, deinde pronomen, deinde mixtum verbo participium, ipsis verbis adverbia. Noster sermo articulos non desiderat ideoque in alias partes orationis sparguntur, sed accedit superioribus interiectio.

20 Alii tamen ex idoneis dumtaxat auctoribus octo partes secuti sunt, ut Aristarchus et aetate nostra Palaemon, qui vocabulum sive appellationem nomini subiecerunt tamquam speciem eius, at ii qui aliud nomen, aliud vocabulum faciunt, novem. Nihilominus fuerunt qui ipsum adhuc vocabulum ab appellatione diducerent, ut esset vocabu-

---

36 See 1.7.7.

37 Q.'s account depends on Dionysius of Halicarnassus, *On Literary Composition* 2 (2.20–21 Usher), who also attributes the three basic "parts" to Theodectes' work. See J. Vahlen, *Beiträge zu Aristoteles' Poetik* (1914) 114.

38 I.e. "binding" or "bond," the regular Greek term, from Aristotle onwards.

Attention will next turn to syllables, on which I shall make a few remarks under the heading of orthography.[36]

The teacher responsible will then need to consider how many parts of speech there are, and what they are, although there is little agreement about the number. Earlier writers,[37] including even Aristotle and Theodectes, listed only verbs, nouns, and "convinctions"; they took the active element in language to be in the verbs, and the material element in the nouns, because the one is what we say, the other is what we say it about, while the "convinctions" provided the connections between them. (I know most people say "conjunctions," but "convinctions" seems the better translation of *syndesmos*.)[38] The philosophers, particularly the Stoics, gradually increased the number: articles were first added to "convinctions," and then "prepositions"; to nouns were added "appellations" and "pronouns," and the quasi-verbal "participle"; to verbs were added "adverbs." Our language does not feel its lack of articles, and these are therefore distributed among other parts of speech. In addition, however, there is the "interjection."

Some, with good authorities to back them, have gone as far as eight parts of speech: so Aristarchus[39] and, in our own day, Palaemon,[40] who both put "vocable" or "appellative" under "noun," as species of that genus. Those who distinguished "vocable" from "noun" make the total nine. Yet some have also separated "vocable" itself from "appellation," making "vocable" indicate visible and tangible

---

[39] Most famous as a Homeric scholar and editor, but also a theorist, and a defender of "analogy."

[40] Probably known to Q.: Suetonius (*De grammaticis* 23, with Kaster (1995) 228–241) gives an unfriendly account of his morals.

lum corpus visu tactuque manifestum: 'domus' 'lectus',
appellatio cui vel alterum deesset vel utrumque: 'ventus'
'caelum' 'deus' 'virtus'. Adiciebant et adseverationem, ut
'eu',[10] et tractionem, ut 'fasciatim'; quae mihi non adpro-
bantur.

21   Vocabulum an appellatio dicenda sit προσηγορία et
subicienda nomini necne, quia parvi refert, liberum opina-
turis relinquo.

22   Nomina declinare et verba in primis pueri sciant:
neque enim aliter pervenire ad intellectum sequentium
possunt. Quod etiam monere supervacuum erat nisi ambi-
tiosa festinatione plerique a posterioribus inciperent, et
dum ostentare discipulos circa speciosiora malunt, com-
23   pendio morarentur. Atqui si quis et didicerit satis et (quod
non minus deesse interim solet) voluerit docere quae didicit, non erit contentus tradere in nominibus tria genera et
24   quae sunt duobus omnibusve communia. Nec statim dili-
gentem putabo qui promiscua, quae epicoena dicuntur,
ostenderit, in quibus sexus uterque per alterum apparet,
aut quae feminina positione mares aut neutrali feminas
25   significant, qualia sunt 'Murena' et 'Glycerium'. Scrutabi-

<hr/>

[10] *Niedermann*: eheu *AB*: euhoe *Colson*

<hr/>

[41] "Bravo" seems a more convincing example of *asseveratio*
than *eheu* ("alas!").   [42] The adverb is "derived" from the noun
fascia ("bandage, bundle").   [43] A difficult term: sometimes
meaning "common noun" (Dionysius of Halicarnassus, *Letter to
Ammaeus* 2.11 (2. 418 Usher)), it may also cover participles and
adjectives (Dionysius Thrax, 23 Uhlig).

[44] "Common to all three genders" is an odd concept; the grammarians gave the adjective *felix* ("happy") as an example.

objects—"house" or "bed"—and "appellation" things in which either or both of these characteristics were absent, like "wind," "heaven," "God," or "virtue." They have also added "asseveration" (like *eu*)[41] and "derivative" (like *fasciatim*).[42] I do not approve of these.

Whether we should translate *prosēgoria*[43] as "vocable" or as "appellation," and whether it should be regarded as a subclass of the noun, is an unimportant question, and I leave it open to personal opinions.

Children should first know how to inflect nouns and verbs, for they cannot otherwise come to understand the following stages. It would be unnecessary to give this warning, were it not that many teachers, ambitious to get on quickly, begin with what should come later, and so, in their anxiety to display their students' progress in the showier parts of the subject, actually hold them up by their "short cuts." And yet a teacher who has both learned enough and is ready to teach what he has learned—a qualification no less likely to be absent from time to time!—will not be content with explaining the three genders of nouns and saying which forms are common to two or three of these.[44] Nor shall I immediately see real scholarship in the man who points out that there are "promiscuous" nouns— what are called *epikoina*—in which both sexes are indicated by a single form, or words which have a feminine ending but a masculine sense, or a neuter ending but a feminine sense, like "Murena" or "Glycerium."[45] No: the

---

[45] Many Greek women's names (especially of slaves or *hetairai*) are neuter diminutives (diminutives are often neuter, whatever the gender of the basic noun), and many Roman *cognomina* end in -*a* (some at least will be of Etruscan origin).

tur ille praeceptor acer atque subtilis origines nominum:
quae ex habitu corporis 'Rufos' 'Longos'que fecerunt (ubi
erit aliquid secretius ⟨ut⟩[11] 'Sullae' 'Burri' 'Galbae' 'Plauti'
'Pansae' 'Scauri' taliaque) et ex casu nascentium (hic
Agrippa et Opiter et Cordus et Postumus erunt) et ex iis
quae post natos eveniunt, unde 'Vopiscus'. Iam 'Cottae'
26 'Scipiones' 'Laenates' 'Serani' sunt ex variis causis. Gentes
quoque ac loca et alia multa reperias inter nominum causas. In servis iam intercidit illud genus quod ducebatur a
domino, unde 'Marcipores' 'Publipores'que.

Quaerat etiam sitne apud Graecos vis quaedam sexti
casus et apud nos quoque septimi. Nam cum dico 'hasta
percussi', non utor ablativi natura, nec si idem Graece
dicam, dativi.

27 Sed in verbis quoque quis est adeo imperitus ut ignoret
genera et qualitates et personas et numeros? Litterarii
paene ista sunt ludi et trivialis scientiae. Iam quosdam illa
turbabunt quae declinationibus non cernuntur.[12] Nam et
quaedam participia an [verba an][13] appellationes sint dubi-

---

[11] *add. Burman*   [12] *Halm*: teruntur *AB*
[13] *del. Claussen*

---

[46] "Red-haired," "Lanky," "Blotchy" (see Plutarch, *Sulla* 2),
"Fatty" (but see various explanations in Suetonius, *Galba* 3),
"Flatfoot," "Broadfoot," "Clubfoot" (Horace, *Sermones* 1.3.48).
Colson rightly refers also to Plutarch, *Coriolanus* 11, which con-
tains a discussion of a number of such names.

[47] "Born feet first" (Aulus Gellius 16.16.2, from Varro), "late-
born" (i.e. after an unusually long pregnancy, Varro, *De re rustica*
2.1.19), "born after father's death but in grandfather's lifetime,"
"posthumous."

really sharp and subtle teacher will look at the origins
of names, derived either from bodily characteristics
("Rufus," "Longus": there will be some more obscure
examples, like "Sulla," "Burrus," "Galba," "Plautus,"
"Pansa," "Scaurus,"[46] and the like) or from the chances
of birth ("Agrippa," "Opiter," "Cordus," "Postumus")[47] or
again from accidents after birth ("Vopiscus").[48] Cotta,
Scipio, Laenas, Seranus also have various origins.[49] One
could find nations, places, and many other things also giving rise to names. In slave names, the type derived from
the master's name (Marcipor, Publipor) is now obsolete.[50]

He should also ask whether the Greeks have what is virtually a sixth case, and we a seventh.[51] When I say *hasta
percussi*,[52] I do not use the natural sense of the ablative;
nor, if I say the same in Greek, do I use the natural sense of
the dative.

Turning to verbs, who is so ignorant as not to know their
voices, moods, persons, and numbers? These matters almost belong to the elementary school and to everyday
knowledge. At this stage, some may be confused by words
which are not distinguished by their inflections. It is possible to question whether certain participles are "appella-

---

[48] "Surviving twin," the other having been aborted: Pliny, *Nat.
Hist.* 7.47.   [49] "Angry" (?), "wand" (*scipio*), "woollen" (*laena*),
"sawman" (*serra*: *Serrani* may be the better reading).

[50] Usually taken to mean *Marci puer, Publi puer*, i.e. Marcus'
or Publius' "boy."   [51] Q. is making a distinction in Greek between the true dative and the instrumental, and in Latin between
true ablative and instrumental.

[52] For "I struck *with a spear*," Latin uses its ablative and Greek
its dative in an instrumental sense.

tari potest, quia aliud alio loco valent, ut 'tectum'[14] et 'sa-
28 piens': quaedam verba appellationibus similia, ut 'fraudator' 'nutritor'. Iam

> itur in antiquam silvam

nonne propriae cuiusdam rationis est? Nam quod initium
eius invenias? Cui simile 'fletur'. <'Tur'>[15] accipimus aliter
ut

> panditur interea domus omnipotentis Olympi,

aliter ut 'totis usque adeo turbatur agris'. Est etiam quidam
tertius modus, ut 'urbs habitatur', unde et 'campus curri-
29 tur' et 'mare navigatur'. 'Pransus' quoque ac 'potus' diversum valet quam indicat. Quid quod multa verba non totum
declinationis ordinem ferunt? Quaedam etiam mutantur,
ut 'fero' in praeterito, quaedam tertiae demum personae
figura dicuntur, ut 'licet' 'piget'. Quaedam simile quiddam
patiuntur vocabulis in adverbium transeuntibus. Nam ut
'noctu' et 'diu', ita 'dictu' 'factu'; sunt enim haec quoque verba, participalia quidem, non tamen qualia 'dicto'
'facto'que.

---

[14] *Faber*: lectum *AB*
[15] *add. Colson*

---

[53] "Roof" or "covered"; "wise" or "tasting."

[54] Agent nouns or passive "future" imperatives.

[55] Q. contrasts the impersonal passives seen in *itur, Aeneid*
6.179 ("their way leads into an ancient wood") and *fletur*, Terence,
Andria 129 ("there is weeping") with (1) *turbatur, Eclogues* 1.11
("such confusion reigns over the whole countryside"), (2) the personal passive *panditur* in *Aeneid* 10.1 ("meanwhile the house of

tions," because they have different meanings in different contexts (such are *tectum* and *sapiens*),[53] while some verbs are also like "appellations" (*fraudator, nutritor*).[54] Is not *itur in antiquam silvam* a peculiar usage? Where is the subject to be found? *Fletur* is similar; *-tur* is taken in one way in *panditur interea domus omnipotentis Olympi* and in another in *totis usque adeo turbatur agris.* There is yet a third variant, as in *urbs habitatur,* whence come *campus curritur, mare navigatur.*[55] *Pransus* and *potus*[56] also have a different meaning from that which they suggest. And what about the fact that many verbs do not have a complete set of inflexions? Some are entirely changed, like *fero* in its past tense;[57] others are used only in the third person, like *licet* ("it is allowed") and *piget* ("it irks"); some again are examples of the process we see in "vocables" passing over into adverbs: *dictu* and *factu* are like *noctu* and *diu.*[58] These are indeed participial forms, but they are not like *dicto* and *facto.*

all-powerful Olympus is opened"), and (3) a third type ("a city is inhabited," "a plain is traversed," "a sea is sailed"), where the subject of the passive verb would be an internal object of the corresponding active. These abstruse distinctions were discussed by the Latin grammarians; see, e.g., Diomedes, *GL* 1. 337.34 Keil.

[56] "Having dined" and "having drunk," with active not passive sense.

[57] I.e. the perfect *tuli.*

[58] These forms are all originally ablatives or locatives; the examples from verbs are of what is called "the supine in *-u*"; *noctu* ("by night") and *diu* ("by day," but more usually "for a long time") are from *nox* and (*perhaps* by analogy) *dies* (but see Sihler (1995) 339).

5

1 Iam cum oratio tris habeat virtutes, ut emendata, ut diluci-
da, ut ornata sit (quia dicere apte, quod est praecipuum,
plerique ornatui subiciunt), totidem vitia, quae sunt supra
dictis contraria: emendate loquendi regulam, quae grammatices prior pars est, examinet.

2   Haec exigitur verbis aut singulis aut pluribus. Verba
nunc generaliter accipi volo: nam duplex eorum intellectus
est, alter qui omnia per quae sermo nectitur significat, ut
apud Horatium:

        verbaque provisam rem non invita sequentur;

alter in quo est una pars orationis: 'lego' 'scribo'; quam
vitantes ambiguitatem quidam dicere maluerunt voces, lo-
3 cutiones, dictiones. Singula sunt aut nostra aut peregrina,
aut simplicia aut composita, aut propria aut tralata, aut
usitata aut ficta.

       Uni verbo vitium saepius quam virtus inest. Licet enim
dicamus aliquod proprium speciosum sublime, nihil tamen horum nisi in complexu loquendi serieque contingit:
4 laudamus enim verba rebus bene accommodata. Sola est
quae notari possit velut vocalitas, quae εὐφωνία dicitur;

---

1 This list of the virtues (ἀρεταί) of style goes back to Aristotle
(see *CHLC* 1. 190–195) and forms the basis of most later theory:
Lausberg §§458–461, and below, Introduction to Book Eight.
Theophrastus separated τὸ πρέπον (*decorum*) as a fourth "virtue." Q. will discuss Correctness in 8.1, Clarity in 8.2, *ornatus* in
general in 8.3, and *decorum* in 11.1.

CHAPTER 5

Grammaticē. (2) Some rules of correct language:
Barbarism and Solecism

Style in general has three virtues: correctness, clarity, and
ornament (appropriateness, which is of prime importance,
is commonly put under "ornament"),[1] and the same number of faults, these being the opposites of the virtues. Thus
the teacher should next attend to the principles of correct
speech, which form the first part of *grammaticē*.

These principles apply either to individual words (*ver-*
ba) or to groups. (I mean *verba* to be taken here in a general sense, for the term has two meanings: one in which it
covers all the parts of which language is made up, as in
Horace's line "The words (*verba*) will follow willingly, once
the matter has been provided";[2] and another in which it is a
particular part of speech: "I read," "I write." To avoid this
ambiguity, some have preferred to say *voces, locutiones,* or
dictiones.) Individual words are (1) either Latin or foreign,
(2) either simple or compound, (3) either literal or metaphorical, (4) either in current use or made up.

An individual word contains a fault more often than a
virtue. We can say that some word is appropriate, beautiful, or sublime, but none of these qualities belongs to it except in so far as it is part of a complex or context of speech:
we praise words when they are well adapted to the matter.
The only detectable virtue is "vocality,"[3] what is called in

[2] *Ars poetica* 311, based on Cato's saying *rem tene, verba*
sequentur, "grasp the thing and the words will follow."

[3] Probably Q.'s coinage to represent εὐφωνία.

QUINTILIAN

cuius in eo dilectus est ut inter duo quae idem significant
ac tantundem valent quod melius sonet malis.

5   Prima barbarismi ac soloecismi foeditas absit. Sed quia
interim excusantur haec vitia aut consuetudine aut auctoritate aut vetustate aut denique vicinitate virtutum (nam
saepe a figuris ea separare difficile est): ne qua tam lubrica
observatio fallat, acriter se in illud tenue discrimen grammaticus intendat, de quo nos latius ibi loquemur ubi de
6 figuris orationis tractandum erit. Interim vitium quod fit in
singulis verbis sit barbarismus. Occurrat mihi forsan aliquis: quid hic promisso tanti operis dignum? aut quis hoc
nescit, alios barbarismos scribendo fieri, alios loquendo
(quia quod male scribitur male etiam dici necesse est,
quae vitiose dixeris non utique et scripto peccant), illud
prius adiectione detractione inmutatione transmutatione,
hoc secundum divisione complexione adspiratione sono
7 contineri? Sed ut parva sint haec, pueri docentur adhuc et
grammaticos officii sui commonemus. Ex quibus si quis
erit plane inpolitus et vestibulum modo artis huius ingressus, intra haec, quae profitentium commentariolis vulgata
sunt, consistet; doctiores multa adicient: vel hoc primum,
8 quod barbarum pluribus modis accipimus. Unum gente,

---

⁴ See also 9.3.3, 11.1.28. The relationship between Barbarism,
Solecism, Tropes, and Figures is set out in Alexander Numeniu
(Spengel, *Rhetores Graeci* 3.9): Barbarism and Solecism are *vi-
cious,* Tropes and Figures *virtuous* variations from normality respectively in individual words and in groups of words. Lausberg
§§475–527.

⁵ See Lausberg §462 for this type of classification, which Q.
will use again for Figures (and for Solecism, below, §38).

124

Greek "euphony"; this is the basis of the choice by which
the better-sounding word is preferred when there are two
which mean the same and have the same connotations.

Barbarisms

The first disfigurement to be avoided is that of Barbarism and Solecism. But as these faults are sometimes excused on grounds of Usage or Authority or Antiquity or
(finally) closeness to some Virtue[4] (for it is often difficult to
distinguish them from Figures), the teacher, to avoid being mistaken in so ticklish a decision, must pay close attention to this fine distinction, on which I shall say more when
I come to Figures of Speech. For the time being, let us define Barbarism as a fault in individual words. Someone
may object: "What is there here worthy of the claims of
your great work? Surely everybody knows that some Barbarisms are found in writing and others in the spoken
word—because bad writing is bound to be bad speaking,
but bad speaking is not necessarily wrong writing—and
those that are found in writing arise out of Additions,
Omissions, Substitutions, and Transpositions,[5] whereas
the other type comes from wrong division or combination
of syllables, breathings, or pronunciation." Of course this
is all trivial; but we are still teaching children, and we are
advising the *grammatici* on their duties. If a teacher is
quite uneducated, and has barely crossed the threshold of
his profession, he will confine himself to the rules commonly known from teachers' manuals; a more learned man
will be able to add many more: for example, in the first
place, the fact that we understand Barbarism in several
senses. (1) One type is the ethnic word, as when an African

quale sit si quis Afrum vel Hispanum Latinae orationi nomen inserat: ut ferrum quo rotae vinciuntur dici solet 'cantus', quamquam eo tamquam recepto utitur Persius, sicut
Catullus 'ploxenum' circa Padum invenit, et in oratione
Labieni (sive illa Corneli Galli est) in Pollionem 'casamo'
[adsectator][1] e Gallia ductum est: nam 'mastrucam', quod
est Sardum, inridens Cicero ex industria dixit.

9   Alterum genus barbari accipimus quod fit animi natura,
ut is a quo insolenter quid aut minaciter aut crudeliter dictum sit barbare locutus existimatur.

10   Tertium est illud vitium barbarismi, cuius exempla vulgo sunt plurima, sibi etiam quisque fingere potest, ut verbo
cui libebit adiciat litteram syllabamve vel detrahat aut
aliam pro alia aut eandem alio quam rectum est loco ponat.

11   Sed quidam fere in iactationem eruditionis sumere illa
ex poetis solent, et auctores quos praelegunt criminantur.
Scire autem debet puer haec apud scriptores carminum
aut venia digna aut etiam laude duci, potiusque illa docen-

12   di erunt minus vulgata. Nam duos in uno nomine faciebat
barbarismos Tinga Placentinus, si reprehendenti Horten-

---

[1] del. D.A.R.: affectate Colson

[6] Compare Greek κανθός, but probably a Gaulish word, like
so many connected with horses and vehicles: Ernout–Meillet,
Dictionnaire étymologique, s.v.   [7] 5.71.

[8] Catullus 97.6 ("carriage body").

[9] Perhaps the case of the heirs of Urbinia (see also 4.1.11,
9.3.13, Tacitus, Dialogus 3.8; ORF p. 522), an Augustan cause
célèbre. For T. Labienus, see Seneca, Controversiae 10, praefatio
5. Cornelius Gallus, however, was disgraced and driven to suicide

or Spanish expression is used in a Latin text: for example, the iron tyre of a wheel is called *cantus*,[6] though Persius[7] actually uses it as a received term; similarly, Catullus found *ploxenum*[8] in the Po valley, and in Labienus' (or is it Cornelius Gallus'?) speech against Pollio,[9] the word *casamo* [("follower")][10] comes from Gaul, while Cicero used the Sardinian *mastruca* deliberately, simply to ridicule it.[11]

(2) A second type of Barbarism comes from a state of mind: anyone who uses insolent, threatening, or cruel language is thought to have spoken "barbarically."

(3) A third type of Barbarism, of which there are many examples in common use (and anyone can also invent others for himself), consists in adding or omitting a letter or syllable in any word you please, substituting one for another, or putting one in the wrong place.

Some, however, in order to show off their learning, tend to take examples from the poets and find fault with the authors whom they are expounding. The child should realize that, in verse writers, these things are pardonable or even praiseworthy; it is more important that they should be taught the less hackneyed instances. Tinga of Placentia[12] (if we are to believe Hortensius' criticisms) made two

in 26 BC, and so dead long before this case, which Tacitus dates to the middle period of Augustus' reign *(mediis divi Augusti temporibus)*, which perhaps means c.10 BC.   [10] We do not know if the gloss *adsectator* (not, I think, Q.'s, because he does not explain the other words in this sentence) is correct or not.

[11] *Pro Scauro* 20. The word means a heavy cloak (of skins, according to Isidore, *Etymologiae* 19.23.5).

[12] Cicero, *Brutus* 172 (Tinca). The context of Q.'s quotation from Hortensius is not known (*ORF* p. 330).

sio credimus, 'preculam' pro 'pergula' dicens, et inmutatione, cum C pro G uteretur, et transmutatione, cum R
praeponeret antecedenti. At in eadem vitii geminatione
'Mettoeo[2] Fufetioeo' dicens Ennius poetico iure defendi-
13 tur. Sed in prorsa quoque est quaedam iam recepta inmutatio (nam Cicero 'Canopitarum exercitum' dicit, ipsi
Canobon vocant), et 'Trasumennum' pro 'Tarsumenno'
multi auctores, etiamsi est in eo transmutatio, vindicave-
runt. Similiter alia: nam sive est 'adsentior', Sisenna dixit
'adsentio' multique et hunc et analogian secuti, sive illud
14 verum est, haec quoque pars consensu defenditur: at ille
pexus pinguisque doctor aut illic detractionem aut hic
adiectionem putabit.

Quid quod quaedam, quae singula procul dubio vitiosa
15 sunt, iuncta sine reprehensione dicuntur? Nam et 'dua'
et 'tre' [pondo][3] diversorum generum sunt barbarismi, at
'dua pondo' et 'tre pondo' usque ad nostram aetatem ab
omnibus dictum est, et recte dici Messala confirmat.

16 Absurdum forsitan videatur dicere barbarismum, quod
est unius verbi vitium, fieri per numeros aut genera sicut
soloecismum: 'scala' tamen et 'scopa' contraque 'hordea'

[2] *Ritschl*: mettieo *A*: ettieo *B*
[3] *del. Halm, after Spalding*

---

[13] Lindsay (1894) 76 (*c* and *g*), 97 (metathesis).

[14] *Annales* 126 Vahlen = 139 Warmington = 120 Skutsch: a
Grecism, copying the Homeric genitive ending in *-oio*. See
Skutsch ad loc. for Q.'s omission of *-que*, which Ritschl would
insert.

[15] Clearly from a speech about Egypt; so perhaps *De rege
Alexandrino,* 65 BC; fr. XVI. 11 Schoell, Crawford (1994) 44–56.

Barbarisms in one word, saying *precula* instead of *pergula* ("market-stall"), substituting *c* for *g* and transposing *r* and *e*.[13] But when Ennius writes *Mettoeo Fufetioeo*,[14] again with a double Barbarism, he is defended by poetic licence. Some substitutions are even admitted in prose: Cicero[15] says "the army of the Canopitans," though they themselves say "Canobos," and many authors have given support to *Trasumennus* for *Tarsumennus*, despite the metathesis.[16] There are similar examples. If *adsentior* is right, Sisenna nevertheless said *adsentio* and many have followed him (and analogy);[17] if *adsentio* is right, the other form can be defended by general usage. But our smug, well-groomed teacher will say that one involves an omission and the other an addition.

Again, some words which are undoubtedly faulty in isolation escape criticism when combined. *Dua* and *tre* are Barbarisms of various kinds: but *duapondo* and *trepondo*[18] have been universally used down to our own days, and Messala[19] confirms that they are quite correct.

It may perhaps seem absurd to say that Barbarism, which is a fault of a single word, is produced by number and gender, like a Solecism. But *scala* and *scopa*, and on

[16] Q. appears to be our only authority for *Tars-*; the name is very variously spelt in texts of historians and poets.

[17] Gellius (2.25.9) also attests Sisenna's use of the active form *adsentio*, on the authority of Varro (from whom Q. too draws much of his material).

[18] I.e. "*two* by weight," "*three* by weight." *Dua* (seen in Pompeian inscriptions) is a morphological barbarism, *tre* is perhaps a phonetic spelling (but it also occurs in *trecenti*, "300").

[19] See 1.5.61, 1.7.35, 10.1.113.

QUINTILIAN

et 'mulsa', licet litterarum mutationem detractionem adiectionem habeant, non alio vitiosa sunt quam quod pluralia singulariter et singularia pluraliter efferuntur: et

17 'gladia' qui dixerunt genere exciderunt. Sed hoc quoque notare contentus sum, ne arti culpa quorundam pervicacium perplexae videar et ipse quaestionem addidisse.

Plus exigunt subtilitatis quae accidunt in dicendo vitia, quia exempla eorum tradi scripto non possunt, nisi cum in versus inciderunt, ut divisio 'Europai' 'Asiai', et ei contrarium vitium, quod συναίρεσιν et ἐπισυναλοιφήν Graeci vocant, nos complexionem dicamus,[4] qualis est apud P. Varronem:

tum te flagranti deiectum fulmine Phaethon.

18 Nam si esset prorsa oratio, easdem litteras enuntiare veris syllabis licebat.

Praeterea quae fiunt spatio, sive cum syllaba correpta producitur, ut

[4] *B*: dicimus *A*

20 *Scala,* "ladder"; *scopa,* "broom." The plurals are said to be more correct because a ladder has a number of steps and a broom many twigs: Varro, *De lingua Latina* 8.7, 9.69, 10.24. See J. Wackernagel (1950) 1. 88; E. Löfstedt, *Syntactica* 1 (Lund, 1942) 31–32. For *hordea* ("barley"), note Vergil, *Eclogues* 5.36, *Georgics* 1.210, 317. *Mulsum* is a drink made with wine and honey. The neuter *gladium* ("sword") is quoted from Lucilius and is in Varro (*De lingua Latina* 5.116, 8.45), who also accepts *gladius* (ibid. 9.81).

the other hand *hordea* and *mulsa,* though they involve substitution, omission, and addition of letters, are incorrect
only because plurals are expressed in singular form and
singulars in plural form, while those who say *gladia*
are guilty of an error of gender.[20] I just mention this, not
wishing to be thought myself to have added a problem to
a subject which has been complicated by the deplorable
obstinacy of certain persons.

Barbarisms in speaking

Faults which arise in speaking need a finer appreciation, because examples cannot be given in writing, unless
they occur in verse, like the divided diphthong in *Europai*
and *Asiai,*[21] and the opposite fault, which the Greeks call
synairesis or *episynaloiphē* (let us call it *complexio*) and
which is seen in Publius Varro's *tum te flagranti deiectum
fulmine, Phaethon.*[22] If this were prose, one could pronounce the letters with the proper syllable division.

Faults of length also, whether due to the lengthening of

---

[21] The archaic genitive in *-āī* (two syllables) persisted as an oc-
casional ornament in poetry: 4 examples in Vergil, but 166 in
Lucretius (almost all nouns): C. Bailey, *Lucretius* (Oxford, 1947)
1. 75–77; O. Skutsch, *The Annals of Q. Ennius* (Oxford, 1985) 61;
Coleman in Adams and Mayer (1999) 41. See also below, 1.7.18.

[22] "Then, Phaethon, thee, by flaming bolt thrown down":
Varro Atacinus, fr. 10 Morel = fr. 11 Courtney, from *Argonautica,*
translating Apollonius Rhodius 4.597–598. On *Phaethon* as a di-
syllable, see Housman on Manilius 1.736, with *addenda.* The correct scansion is Phăĕthōn. For *episynaloiphē,* see Lausberg §492.

Italiam fato profugus,

seu longa corripitur, ut

   unius ob noxam et furias,

extra carmen non deprendas, sed nec in carmine vitia
dicenda sunt.

19   Illa vero non nisi aure exiguntur quae fiunt per sonos:
quamquam per adspirationem, sive adicitur vitiose sive
detrahitur, apud nos potest quaeri an in scripto sit vitium,
20 si H littera est, non nota. Cuius quidem ratio mutata cum
temporibus est saepius. Parcissime ea veteres usi etiam in
vocalibus, cum 'aedos' 'ircos'que dicebant. Diu deinde
servatum ne consonantibus adspirarent, ut in 'Graccis'
et 'triumpis'. Erupit brevi tempore nimius usus, ut 'cho-
ronae' 'chenturiones' 'praechones' adhuc quibusdam
inscriptionibus maneant, qua de re Catulli nobile epi-
21 gramma est. Inde durat ad nos usque 'vehementer' et
'comprehendere' et 'mihi': nam 'mehe' quoque pro 'me'
apud antiquos tragoediarum praecipue scriptores in veteribus libris invenimus.

---

23 *Aeneid* 1.6: "exiled by Fate to Italy." The first syllable of
Italia, which is really short, is lengthened by both Greek and
Roman poets when metre demands it.

24 *Aeneid* 1.41; "because of the guilt and madness of one man."
Unīus is normal, but *unĭus* common in poetry.

25 See 1.4.9.

26 For *haedus,* "kid," and *hircus,* "goat."

27 Cicero, *Orator* 160 concedes that current usage is acceptable, and that *pulcer, Cetegus, triumpus,* and *Cartago* are old-

a short syllable (as in *Ītaliam fato profugus*)[23] or the short-ening of a long one (as in *unĭus ob noxam et furias*),[24] cannot be detected outside poetry; but in poetry they are not to be regarded as faults.

Errors in sound, on the other hand, cannot be detected except by the ear—though as regards the faulty addition or omission of the aspirate, one may ask whether this is a fault detectable in writing in Latin, if *h* is a letter and not just a mark of breathing.[25] Practice has often varied with the times. Early writers used it rarely even with vowels, and said *aedus* and *ircus;*[26] the practice of not aspirating conso-nants was long maintained *(Graccus, triumpus);* then for a little while there was an outbreak of aspirating too much *(chorona, chenturio, praecho* ("crown," "centurion," "her-ald") still survive in some inscriptions),[27] and there is a well-known epigram of Catullus about this.[28] Hence the survival down to our own time of *vehementer, compre-hendere*[29] and *mihi;* we actually find *mehe* for *me* in old texts, especially of the early tragic poets.[30]

---

fashioned; but he will not tolerate *chorona*. This aspiration in Latin words, which was a temporary phenomenon, is quite differ-ent from that found at all periods in loan-words from Greek. See Lindsay (1894) 59; Sihler (1995) 142.

[28] 84 *(chommoda, hinsidias)*.

[29] For Q.'s remarks on *vehemens*, see C. O. Brink, *Horace: Epistles II* (Cambridge, 1983) 436; for *comprehendere*, Winter-bottom (1970) 58.

[30] We have no evidence to corroborate this last statement; but the dative *mihi* was pronounced, and often spelt, *mī*, and *mehe* is presumably an analogous form for the ablative.

QUINTILIAN

22   Adhuc difficilior observatio est per tenores (quos quidem ab antiquis dictos tonores comperi, videlicet declina-
to a Graecis verbo, qui τόνους dicunt) vel adcentus, quas
Graeci προσῳδίας vocant, cum acuta et gravis alia pro alia
23   ponuntur, ut in hoc 'Camillus', si acuitur prima, aut gravis
pro flexa, ut 'Cethegus' (et hic prima acuta; nam sic media
mutatur), aut flexa pro gravi, ut 'alvei'[5] circumducta
sequenti, quam ex duabus syllabis in unam cogentes et
24   deinde flectentes dupliciter peccant. Sed id saepius in
Graecis nominibus accidit, ut 'Atreus', quem nobis iuvenibus doctissimi senes acuta prima dicere solebant, ut necessario secunda gravis esset, item 'Nerei' 'Terei'que.
25   Haec de accentibus tradita.[6] Ceterum scio iam quosdam eruditos, nonnullos etiam grammaticos sic docere
ac loqui ut propter quaedam vocum discrimina verbum
interim acuto sono finiant, ut in illis

                quae circum litora, circum
piscosos scopulos,

[5] *Kiderlin*: apice A: *om. B*
[6] Haec . . . tradita *suspected by Colson as interpolation*

---

[31] Q. states below (1.5.30) the basic rule of Latin accentuation
in his time, viz. that the accent is generally recessive and falls as far
back as the antepenultimate, unless the penultimate is long, in
which case it falls on this. See Lindsay (1894) 148–170; Allen
(1965) 83–88; Sihler (1995) 239–242. The use of Greek terminol-
ogy gave rise to considerable confusion and difficulty for the Latin
grammarians, who have to use *gravis* for unaccented syllables,
and *acutus* both for the tonic acute accent of Greek and for the
stressed syllables of Latin.

BOOK 1.5

Accentuation[31]

It is even harder to observe errors in tones (*tenores:* I note that old writers have *tonores,* presumably from the Greek term *tonos*) or accents (which the Greeks call *prosodiai*), when an acute accent is substituted for a grave or a grave for an acute: for instance, an acute on the first syllable of *Camillus,* or grave for circumflex in *Cethegus,*[32] with the first syllable here also acute (for in this way the quantity of the middle syllable is changed); or again, circumflex for grave, as when the second syllable of *alvei* is made circumflex: this actually involves two mistakes, the conflation of two syllables into one, and the use of the circumflex accent.[33] This happens more often in Greek names, as in *Atrei,* which old scholars, when I was young, used to pronounce with an acute on the first syllable, so that the second was necessarily grave: similarly *Nérei* and *Térei.*

This is the traditional doctrine of accents. But I am aware that some learned writers (and even some *grammatici*), anxious to preserve certain distinctions between words, sometimes, both in teaching and in speaking, put an acute accent on a closing syllable, as in *quae circum litora,*

---

[32] Greek accents Κέθηγος, not Κεθῆγος. Q. sees that this is abnormal in Latin, where a long penultimate always carries the accent; to accent the first syllable therefore implies that the second is short. Perhaps this reflects how the family pronounced their name.

[33] I.e. the word should be pronounced *álveī* not *alveī.* It is the genitive of *alveus,* "river-bed."

QUINTILIAN

26 ne, si gravem posuerint secundam, 'circus' dici videatur, non 'circumitus':[7] itemque cum 'quale' interrogantes gravi, comparantes acuto tenore concludunt; quod tamen in adverbiis fere solis ac pronominibus vindicant, in ceteris
27 veterem legem secuntur. Mihi videtur condicionem mutare quod his locis verba coniungimus. Nam cum dico 'circum litora', tamquam unum enuntio dissimulata distinctione, itaque tamquam in una voce una est acuta: quod idem accidit in illo

Troiae qui primus ab oris.

28 Evenit ut metri quoque condicio mutet accentum:

pecudes pictaeque volucres.

Nam 'volucres' media acuta legam, quia, etsi natura brevis, tamen positione longa est, ne faciat iambum, quem
29 non recipit versus herous. Separata vero haec a praecepto nostro non recedent, aut si consuetudo vicerit vetus lex

[7] circum *Corsi*

[34] *Aeneid* 4.254–255, "which round the shores, round rocks where fish abound." The *grammatici* whom Q. criticizes would accent *circúm lítora, circúm piscósos scópulos:* his response (§27) is the correct one. Latin grammarians (Donatus 4.391 Keil, Priscian 3. 27 Keil) also hold that prepositions combined with cases of nouns may lose their acute accent.

circum piscosos scopulos,[34] lest by making the last syllable
of *circum* grave they give the impression that the poet
means a "circus" and not "going round." Similarly, when
quale is interrogative they end it with a grave accent, when
it is comparative, with an acute.[35] However, they claim this
rule only for adverbs[36] and pronouns; in other words, they
follow the old law. Personally, I feel that the situation is
changed by the fact that, in these passages, we join the
words together. When I say *circum lítora*, I pronounce it as
one word and conceal the break, so that there is only one
acute, just as in a single word. The case is the same in
Troiae qui primus ab óris.[37] Metrical circumstances may
also affect the accent, as in *pecudes pictaeque volucres*.[38]
Here, I read *volúcres* with an acute on the middle syllable,
which, though short by nature, is long by position, so as not
to make an iambus, which the heroic metre does not allow.
Regarded as a special case, however, these will not be
deviations from our rule; otherwise, if the usage described

---

[35] Perhaps in imitation of Greek distinctions, as between τίνες
"who?" and τινες "some persons," ποῖος "of what kind?" and
ποιός "of a certain kind." Latin grammarians (e.g. Priscian 2. 61,
3. 9 Keil) adapt this distinction by saying that two-syllable prepositions and relatives are in themselves oxytone (this too is perhaps
based on Greek περί, ἀνά, κατά, etc.), but lose this accent "in
reading," i.e. when another word follows.

[36] Q. should say "prepositions" instead of, or as well as, "adverbs."

[37] *Aeneid* 1.1: "who first from shores of Troy." The word group
(preposition + noun) carries only one accent *(ab óris)*.

[38] *Georgics* 3.243, *Aeneid* 4.525: "flocks and bright-coloured
birds."

137

sermonis abolebitur.

Cuius difficilior apud Graecos observatio est, quia plura illis loquendi genera, quas dialectus vocant, et quod alias vitiosum, interim alias rectum est. Apud nos vero bre-
30 vissima ratio: namque in omni voce acuta intra numerum trium syllabarum continetur, sive eae sunt in verbo solae sive ultimae, et in iis aut proxima extremae aut ab ea tertia. Trium porro de quibus loquor media longa aut acuta aut flexa erit, eodem loco brevis utique gravem habebit sonum ideoque positam ante se, id est ab ultima tertiam, acuet.
31 Est autem in omni voce utique acuta, sed numquam plus una nec umquam ultima, ideoque in disyllabis prior. Praeterea numquam in eadem flexa et acuta, quia in flexa est acuta;[8] itaque neutra cludet vocem Latinam. Ea vero quae

---

[8] quia . . . acuta *Winterbottom, after Spalding*: qui in eadem flexa et acuta *B*: *om. A*

---

[39] A difficult passage. I have followed the suggestion of J. N. Adams and taken *separata* as "special cases": compare 8.4.29, 11.1.36. Most translators however take it as meaning "in isolation," i.e. words standing on their own and not *coniuncta* (compare, e.g., 1.5.35). I have seriously considered two other possibilities: (1) following Spalding, to take §28 as parenthetical, so that *haec* in §29 does not include the case illustrated by *volucres*. Q. is then saying that words like *circum,* if proclitic, have no accent of their own (this, on this view, is his *praeceptum*); but if taken in isolation (e.g. in *stant circum*) are accented in accordance with the *vetus lex* (which is formulated below, §29, to show the uniformity of Latin accentuation compared with Greek) on the first syllable (*círcum*). This would translate: "If these words occur in isolation, they will not be a deviation from our rule [i.e. the proclitic rule stated in §27, which will not apply now]; otherwise, if the usage [i.e. that recommended by the people he is opposing] prevails, the

prevails, the old linguistic law will be annulled.[39]

This law is more difficult to formulate for the Greeks, because they have several varieties of speech, which they call dialects, and what is wrong in one is sometimes correct in another.[40] But with us the principle can be stated very shortly. In every word, the acute falls within three syllables, whether these are the only syllables in the word or the last three, and in these it is either on the penultimate or on the antepenultimate. Moreover, of the three syllables of which I speak, the middle, if long, will be either acute or circumflex; a short syllable in this place will invariably have a grave accent, and so will make the syllable which precedes it (the antepenultimate) acute. Now there must be an acute accent in every word, but never more than one; it is never on the last syllable, and therefore in disyllabic words it must be on the first. Moreover, an acute and a circumflex are never found in the same word, because the circumflex includes an acute; neither of them can therefore occur at the end of a Latin word. Monosyllables how-

old linguistic law will be annulled"; (2) to take *non . . . aut* as *non . . . neque* (a possible parallel is Lucan 2.360–362) and translate: "In isolation, however, these will not be a deviation from our rule [i.e. the proclitic rule, which no longer applies] nor, if *consuetudo* [i.e. normal educated usage, which has *círcum* whether it means "around" or "a circus"] prevails, will the old linguistic law [i.e. the general law to be formulated as in §29] be annulled." This too means taking §28 as a parenthesis. Both these interpretations make *praeceptum nostrum* and *vetus lex* distinct; Adams's view, which I adopt, identifies them, and gives better coherence to the whole passage.   [40] Aeolic was characterized by recessive accent, and Doric accentuation is also said to have differed from Attic–Ionic in some respects (Buck (1955) §103).

sunt syllabae unius erunt acuta aut flexa, ne sit aliqua vox
sine acuta.

32   Et illa per sonos accidunt, quae demonstrari scripto
non possunt, vitia oris et linguae: iotacismus[9] et labdacismus et ischnotetas et plateasmus feliciores fingendis nominibus Graeci vocant, sicut coelostomian, cum vox quasi in
33 recessu oris auditur. Sunt etiam proprii quidam et inenar-
rabiles soni, quibus nonnumquam nationes deprehendi-
mus.[10]

    Remotis igitur omnibus de quibus supra diximus vitiis
erit illa quae vocatur ὀρθοέπεια, id est emendata cum
suavitate vocum explanatio: nam sic accipi potest recta.

34   Cetera vitia omnia ex pluribus vocibus sunt, quorum
est soloecismus. Quamquam circa hoc quoque disputatum
est; nam etiam qui complexu orationis accidere eum con-
fitentur, quia tamen unius emendatione verbi corrigi pos-
35 sit, in verbo esse vitium, non in sermone contendunt, cum,
sive 'amarae corticis' seu 'medio cortice' per genus facit
soloecismum (quorum neutrum quidem reprehendo, cum

---

[9] miotacismus *A*   [10] *Burman*: reprehendimus *A* (repren-
dimus *B*) *("find fault with")*

---

[41] "Iotacism" is obscure: it may mean an excessive lengthening
of *i,* or the double pronunciation of *i* in, e.g., *Maia* (1.4.11). In any
case, it is a fault, and presumably a fault in *Latin. Mutacismus,*
which Claussen proposed to add, is some feature of the pronunciation of final *m. Labdacismus* is also obscure, and Latin grammarians give no clear account. One would suppose it to be a faulty
pronunciation of *l,* or the lisping replacement of *r* by *l (trau-
lismos),* satirized by Aristophanes (*Wasps* 44). The other terms—
"thinnesses," "broadnesses," "hollow mouth"—are more easily

ever will be either acute or circumflex, so that no word is without an acute.

There are accidental features of pronunciation, which cannot be shown in writing, being faults of the mouth and the tongue. The Greeks, who are more fertile than we are in inventing names, call them iotacisms, lambdacisms, *ischnotētes* and *plateiasmoi,* and also *koilostomia,* when the voice seems to come from the back of the mouth.[41] There are also certain special, indescribable sounds, by which we sometimes recognize particular nations.[42]

If all these faults which I have described have been removed, we have what is called Orthoepy, "rightness of speech," that is to say, a correct and agreeable articulation of words: this is what "right" pronunciation can be taken to mean.

Solecism

All other faults involve more words than one, including Solecism, though there has been some controversy on this point too. Even those who admit that it occurs in connected speech contend that the fault is in a word and not in the context, on the ground that it can be put right by correcting a single word. Whether *amarae corticis* or *medio cortice* is a solecism in gender (personally I object to nei-

---

understood. As often, the use of Greek terms in a Latin context produces difficulties.   [42] Here however we seem to have a comment on local and provincial types of Latin, though Greek may still be in mind.

sit utriusque Vergilius auctor: sed fingamus utrumlibet
non recte dictum), mutatio vocis alterius, in qua vitium
erat, rectam loquendi rationem sit redditura, ut 'amari corticis' fiat vel 'media cortice'. Quod manifestae calumniae
est: neutrum enim vitiosum est separatum, sed compositione peccatur, quae iam sermonis est.

36   Illud eruditius quaeritur, an in singulis quoque verbis
possit fieri soloecismus, ut si unum quis ad se vocans dicat
'venite', aut si pluris a se dimittens ita loquatur: 'abi' aut
'discede'. Nec non cum responsum ab interrogante dissentit, ut si dicenti 'quem video?' ita occurras: 'ego'. In gestu
etiam nonnulli putant idem vitium inesse, cum aliud voce,
37 aliud nutu vel manu demonstratur. Huic opinioni neque
omnino accedo neque plane dissentio; nam id fateor accidere voce una, non tamen aliter quam si sit aliquid, quod
vim alterius vocis optineat, ad quod vox illa referatur: ut
soloecismus ex complexu fiat eorum quibus res signi-
38 ficantur et voluntas ostenditur. Atque ut omnem effugiam
cavillationem, sit aliquando in uno verbo, numquam in
solo verbo.

        Per quot autem et quas accidat species, non satis con-
venit. Qui plenissime, quadripertitam volunt esse rationem nec aliam quam barbarismi, ut fiat adiectione 'nam
enim', 'de susum', 'in Alexandriam', detractione 'ambulo
39 viam', 'Aegypto venio', 'ne hoc fecit', transmutatione, qua
ordo turbatur, 'quoque ego', 'enim hoc voluit', 'autem non
habuit': ex quo genere an sit 'igitur' initio sermonis posi-

<hr/>

43 *Eclogues* 6.62 ("of bitter bark"), *Georgics* 2.74 ("from the
middle of the bark").

44 "Come" (plural); "go" (singular).

45 The correct answer would be *me* ("me").

ther, for Vergil after all is our authority for both:[43] but let us
suppose that one or other is wrong), the change of one
word, in which the fault lay, will restore correctness, either
as *amari corticis* or as *media cortice.* This is a plain misrep-
resentation; neither is faulty in isolation, but the error
arises in the combination, and this is a matter of connected
speech.

A more learned question is whether a Solecism can also
occur in a single word, if (for example) one summons a single person with the word *venite,* or dismisses a group of
people by saying *abi* or *discede,*[44] or again when the answer
does not agree with the questioner's intention, as when
someone asks "Whom do I see?" and you answer "I."[45]
Some believe that the same fault can be detected in gesture, when the message conveyed by the nod or the hand is
different from that conveyed by the voice. I neither sub-
scribe completely to this view nor totally disagree with it. I
admit that a Solecism may occur in a single word, but only
if there is something else, tantamount to another word, to
which the single word can be referred, so that the Solecism
arises from the combination of the different means by
which the facts are expressed and the intention displayed.
To avoid any quibbling, let us assume that it can sometimes
occur in one word, but never in a word quite by itself.

The number and nature of the kinds of Solecism are
not entirely agreed. Those who have discussed it most
fully make a fourfold classification, as with Barbarism:
(1) by addition (*nam enim, de susum, in Alexandriam*);
(2) by omission (*ambulo viam, Aegypto venio, ne hoc fecit*);
(3) by transposition (*quoque ego, enim hoc voluit, autem
non habuit*). Whether *igitur* at the beginning of a sentence

tum dubitari potest, quia maximos auctores in diversa
fuisse opinione video, cum apud alios sit etiam frequens,
40   apud alios numquam reperiatur. Haec tria genera quidam
diducunt a soloecismo, et adiectionis vitium πλεονασμόν,
detractionis ἔλλειψιν, inversionis ἀναστροφήν vocant:
quae si in speciem soloecismi cadat, ὑπερβατόν quoque
41   eodem appellari modo posse. Inmutatio sine controversia
est, cum aliud pro alio ponitur. Id per omnis orationis partis deprendimus, frequentissime in verbo, quia plurima
huic accidunt, ideoque in eo fiunt soloecismi per genera
tempora personas modos (sive cui 'status' eos dici seu 'qualitates' placet) vel sex vel ut alii volunt octo (nam totidem
vitiorum erunt formae in quot species eorum quidque de
42   quibus supra dictum est diviseris): praeterea numeros, in
quibus nos singularem ac pluralem habemus, Graeci et
δυϊκόν. Quamquam fuerunt qui nobis quoque adicerent
dualem 'scripsere' 'legere' (quod evitandae asperitatis gratia mollitum est, ut apud veteres pro 'male mereris' 'male
merere'), ideoque quod vocant duale in illo solo genere

---

46 Of Q.'s examples, *nam enim* duplicates words meaning
"for"; *de susum* "from above" illustrates a later Latin tendency
to combine *de* with adverbs (L–H–S §160 (b)); *in Alexandriam*
shows the incorrect use of a preposition with the name of a town
(but *Declamationes minores* 333 has *in Athenas,* and Vitruvius has
several examples of this usage); *ambulo viam,* "I walk the road," is
taken to show the omission of *per*; *Aegypto venio,* "I come from
Egypt," lacks the preposition usual with names of countries (but
see, e.g., Plautus, *Mostellaria* 440); *ne hoc fecit,* "he did not even
do this," for *ne hoc quidem fecit,* is found in the Vindolanda tablets
(J. N. Adams, *Journal of Roman Studies* 1995, 131–132); *quoque*
("also"), *enim* ("for") and *autem* ("but") are all postpositives and
cannot come first in their clauses. Q. is right to be doubtful about

is an instance of this may be doubted; I note that the best
authors disagree, some frequently putting it first, others
never.[46] Some separate these three types from Solecism,
and call the fault of addition Pleonasm, that of omission
Ellipse, and that of transposition Anastrophe; they argue
that if this is a species of Solecism, then Hyperbaton may
also be so described. (4) Substitution (one word put instead of another) is not controversial. It is found in all parts
of speech, but more often in verbs, because these have
most variety of form, so that we get Solecisms of voice,
tense, person, mood (or "state" or "quality," if you prefer,
whether there are six of these or, as some say, eight:[47] there
will be as many types of fault as there are subdivisions of
the various things we have mentioned), and finally number, in which we have only singular and plural whereas the
Greeks have also the dual.[48] Some have given us a dual
also, in *scripsere* ("they wrote") and *legere* ("they read"):
but this is just a softened form to avoid some harshness,
like *male merere* ("you deserve ill") for *male mereris*[49] in
old writers. What they call "dual," then, is found only in

igitur, which he uses in first place himself in nearly 10% of cases.

[47] The six seem to be: indicative, imperative, subjunctive, optative (though not distinct in Latin), infinitive, and perhaps impersonal (Donatus, *GL* 4. 359.19 Keil). To get up to eight, we should
add future and gerund, as Probus and others do.

[48] *Ambo* and *duo* (and perhaps *octo,* if it really means the two
sets of four fingers: Lindsay (1894) 415) are traces of a dual inflection. The attempt to see *-ēre* as a dual ending is, as Q. shows, easy
to refute. See J. Wackernagel (1950) 1. 76.

[49] Sihler (1995) 475: the *-re* ending is original, and *-ris* is based
on it with the addition of *-s,* taken from the active ending. If this is
right, Q.'s reconstruction is mistaken.

consistit, cum apud Graecos et verbi tota fere ratione et in
nominibus deprendatur (et sic quoque rarissimus sit eius

43   usus), apud nostrorum vero neminem haec observatio reperiatur, quin e contrario 'devenere locos' et 'conticuere
omnes' et 'consedere duces' aperte nos doceant nil horum
ad duos pertinere, 'dixere' quoque, quamquam id Antonius Rufus ex diverso ponit exemplum, de pluribus patro-

44   nis praeco pronuntiet. Quid? non Livius circa initia statim
primi libri 'tenuere' inquit 'arcem Sabini' et mox: 'in
adversum Romani subiere'? Sed quem potius ego quam
M. Tullium sequar? Qui in Oratore 'non reprendo' inquit
'scripsere; scripserunt esse verius sentio'.

45   Similiter in vocabulis et nominibus fit soloecismus
genere, numero, proprie autem casibus, quidquid horum
alteri succedet. Huic parti subiungantur licet per com-
parationes et superlationes, itemque in quibus patrium
pro possessivo dicitur vel contra.

46   Nam vitium quod fit per quantitatem, ut 'magnum peculiolum', erunt qui soloecismum putent, quia pro nomine
integro positum sit deminutum: ego dubito an id inpro-
prium potius appellem; significatione enim deerrat: soloecismi porro vitium non est in sensu, sed in complexu.

47   In participio per genus et casum ut in vocabulo, per
tempora ut in verbo, per numerum ut in utroque peccatur.

---

50 "They came to the place" (*Aeneid* 1.365), "all fell silent"
(*Aeneid* 2.1), "the leaders sat down" (Ovid, *Metamorphoses* 13.1).

51 Unknown: he evidently argued that the formula *dixere,*
"they have spoken," referred specifically to the two parties to a
case.   52 "The Sabines held the citadel," "the Romans advanced uphill" (Livy 1.12.1).   53 157.

54 E.g. *Agamemnonius* for "son of Agamemnon." However,

this one form, whereas in Greek it is found through almost the whole inflexion of the verb, and also in nouns; and even so the use of it is very rare. We find no trace of this usage in any of our writers; on the contrary *devenere locos* and *conticuere omnes* and *consedere duces*[50] make it clear that these forms have nothing to do with a dual subject; even *dixere,* though Antonius Rufus[51] gives it as an example to prove the contrary, is spoken by the court official to denote more than two advocates. Again, does not Livy say, near the beginning of his first book, *tenuere arcem Sabini,* and then *in adversum Romani subiere*?[52] But whom should I follow rather than Cicero? "I do not object to *scripsere,*" he writes in the *Orator,*[53] "but I feel *scripserunt* is more correct."

In substantives and names, Solecisms may occur (as in verbs) in gender and number, but specifically also in cases, whenever one of these replaces another. One can add here Solecisms in comparatives and superlatives, or when a patronymic is put for a possessive, or the reverse.[54]

As for faults involving quantity, like *magnum peculiolum,*[55] some will take this as a Solecism, because the diminutive is used instead of the complete noun. I think I should rather call it an improper use, because it is a mistake in meaning, whereas the wrongness of a Solecism lies not in the sense but in the relations between words.

As regards participles, the fault occurs in respect of gender and case (as with substantives), of tense (as with verbs), and of number (as in both).

patrius can also denote the genitive (*OLD* s.v. 5), and Q. may therefore be denouncing the use, e.g., of *mei* for *meus* ("of me" for "my").   55 "A big little sum of money."

Pronomen quoque genus numerum casus habet, quae
omnia recipiunt huius modi errorem.

48   Fiunt soloecismi et quidem plurimi per partis orationis:
sed id tradere satis non est, ne ita demum vitium esse credat puer si pro alia ponatur alia, ut verbum ubi nomen esse

49   debuerit, vel adverbium ubi pronomen, ac similia. Nam
sunt quaedam cognata, ut dicunt, id est eiusdem generis,
in quibus qui alia specie quam oportet utetur, non minus

50   quam ipso genere permutato deliquerit. Nam et 'an' et
'aut' coniunctiones sunt, male tamen interroges 'hic aut
ille sit'; et 'ne' ac 'non' adverbia: qui tamen dicat pro illo 'ne
feceris' 'non feceris', in idem incidat vitium, quia alterum
negandi est, alterum vetandi. Hoc amplius 'intro' et 'intus'
loci adverbia, 'eo' tamen 'intus' et 'intro sum' soloecismi

51   sunt. Eadem in diversitate pronominum interiectionum
praepositionum accident.

Est enim soloecismus in oratione comprensionis unius
sequentium ac priorum inter se inconveniens positio.

52   Quaedam tamen et faciem soloecismi habent et dici vitiosa non possunt, ut 'tragoedia Thyestes', ut 'ludi Floralia
ac Megalesia'—quamquam haec sequentia tempore inter-
ciderunt numquam aliter a veteribus dicta. Schemata igitur nominabuntur, frequentiora quidem apud poetas, sed

53   oratoribus quoque permissa. Verum schema fere habebit

---

56 "Is it *he* or *he*?" The use of *aut* for *an* in alternative questions
is late, and would seem incorrect to Q.; but it apparently occurs in
Varro, *De lingua Latina* 7.32.

57 "Do not do."

58 *Intus*, "inside," does not combine with verbs of motion, nor
intro with verbs of rest. But Q.'s *pollice intus inclinato,* "with the
thumb bent inwards" (11.3.99), comes near to breaking the rule.

The pronoun also possesses gender, number, and case, all of which admit this type of error.

Solecisms—and in great numbers—arise in respect of the parts of speech; but it is not enough simply to teach this, lest the boy should think that the only fault is to put one part of speech for another, verb where noun should be, or adverb where pronoun should be, and the like. For there are some words which are, as they say, "cognate," that is belonging to the same genus, and anyone who uses the wrong species is no less at fault than if he had made a change of genus. Thus *an* and *aut* are both conjunctions: but it is wrong to ask a question in the form *hic aut ille sit*;[56] *ne* and *non* are adverbs, but to say *non feceris* for *ne feceris*[57] is to fall into the same fault, because *non* negates and *ne* forbids. Again, *intro* and *intus* are adverbs of place, but *eo intus* and *intro sum* are Solecisms.[58] Similar things can happen with different pronouns, interjections, and prepositions.

A Solecism in speech, in fact, is the internally inconsistent disposition of the preceding and following elements of a single syntactical structure.

However, there are expressions which have the appearance of Solecism but cannot be treated as faults: *tragoedia Thyestes, ludi Floralia ac Megalesia;* these last are universal in the older writers, but later became obsolete.[59] They can therefore be called Figures, frequent in the poets but not forbidden to orators. A Figure, however, will normally

---

[59] "The tragedy *Thyestes*," "the games Floralia and Megalesia." The alternative usage, *ludi Florales,* etc., was still recent in Q.'s time: our earliest evidence for it appears to be Valerius Maximus 2.10.8.

QUINTILIAN

aliquam rationem, ut docebimus eo quem paulo ante pro-
misimus loco, sed id[11] quoque quod schema vocatur, si ab
aliquo per inprudentiam factum erit, soloecismi vitio non
carebit.

54   In eadem specie sunt, sed schemate carent, ut supra
dixi, nomina feminina quibus mares utuntur, et neutralia
quibus feminae.

Hactenus de soloecismo: neque enim artem grammati-
cam componere adgressi sumus, sed cum in ordinem in-
curreret, inhonoratum[12] transire noluimus.

55   Hoc amplius, ut institutum ordinem sequar, verba aut
Latina aut peregrina sunt. Peregrina porro ex omnibus
prope dixerim gentibus ut homines, ut instituta etiam mul-
56 ta venerunt. Taceo de Tuscis et Sabinis et Praenestinis
quoque (nam ut eorum sermone utentem Vettium Lucilius insectatur, quem ad modum Pollio reprendit in Livio
Patavinitatem): licet omnia Italica pro Romanis habeam.
57   Plurima Gallica evaluerunt, ut 'raeda' ac 'petorritum',
quorum altero tamen Cicero, altero Horatius utitur. Et

11 hic B   12 *Kiderlin*: inhonoratam AB

60 Above, §5, looking forward to 9.3.   61 Not said in 4.24;
Colson suggested *quae* for *ut*: i.e. "the feminine nouns which I
mentioned . . . "   62 See 1.4.24.   63 As in §3 above.

64 1322 Marx, cf. 1138–1141 Warmington (*ROL* 3. 370). Vettius may be Vettius Philocomus, younger friend of Lucilius:
Suetonius, *De grammaticis* 2, with Kaster (1995) 66–67.

65 Many interpretations have been proposed. Likeliest is linguistic provincialism (compare Cicero, *Brutus* 171 on a speaker
from Cisalpine Gaul); but Q.'s version (8.1.3) of the story of
Theophrastus, who was perceived to be a foreigner because his

have some rational grounds, as I shall show in the future discussion to which I have already alluded.[60] And even what is called a Figure, if it is uttered by a speaker accidentally, will not escape the charge of Solecism.

Of the same species, though not involving Figure, are (as already mentioned)[61] feminine nouns with masculine application, and neuter nouns with feminine application.[62]

So much for Solecism. I did not set out to write a treatise on *grammaticē,* but when this topic presented itself I was unwilling to let it pass without due honour.

Latin and foreign words

Furthermore—to resume my original plan[63]—words are either Latin or foreign. Foreign words, just like people and indeed many institutions, have come to us from almost every nation. I say nothing of Tuscan, Sabine, and even Praenestine elements (Lucilius[64] attacks Vettius for using Praenestine words, as Pollio criticizes "Patavinity"[65] in Livy); I can surely treat all Italian words as Roman. Many Gaulish words have become established (*raeda, petorritum*:[66] one used by Cicero, the other by Horace). *Mappa*

Attic was too good, suggests that some sort of pedantic precision may be meant. As the context is all about language, R. Syme's odd notion (*Roman Revolution* 486) of a provincial moral tone cannot be right.   [66] *Raeda* ("carriage") is in *Pro Milone* 54, *Philippics* 2.58; *petorritum* ("open carriage") in Horace, *Sermones* 1.6.104 (Gellius 15.30 defends the Gaulish origin against attempts to give a Greek derivation). For the Gaulish contribution to Latin horse and carriage vocabulary in general, see Palmer, *The Latin Language* 53.

'mappam' circo quoque usitatum nomen Poeni sibi vindicant, et 'gurdos', quos pro stolidis accipit vulgus, ex His-
58 pania duxisse originem audivi. Sed haec divisio mea ad
Graecum sermonem praecipue pertinet; nam et maxima
ex parte Romanus inde conversus est, et confessis quoque
Graecis utimur verbis ubi nostra desunt, sicut illi a nobis
nonnumquam mutuantur.

Inde illa quaestio exoritur, an eadem ratione per casus
59 duci externa qua nostra conveniat. Ac si reperias gramma-
ticum veterum amatorem, neget quicquam ex Latina
ratione mutandum, quia, cum sit apud nos casus ablativus,
quem illi non habent, parum conveniat uno casu nostro,
60 quinque Graecis uti: quin etiam laudet virtutem eorum
qui potentiorem facere linguam Latinam studebant nec
alienis egere institutis fatebantur. Inde 'Castorem' media
syllaba producta pronuntiarunt, quia hoc omnibus nostris
nominibus accidebat quorum prima positio in easdem
quas 'Castor' litteras exit, et ut 'Palaemo' ac 'Telamo' et
'Plato' (nam sic eum Cicero quoque appellat) dicerentur
retinuerunt, quia Latinum quod O et N litteris finiretur
61 non reperiebant. Ne in A quidem atque S litteras exire temere masculina Graeca nomina recto casu patiebantur,
ideoque et apud Caelium legimus 'Pelia cincinnatus' et
apud Messalam 'bene fecit Euthia' et apud Ciceronem

---

67 The "cloth" or "towel" used to give the starting signal: Martial 12.28(29).9.

68 Cf. 1.6.31; the view that Latin was a variety of Greek, particularly close to Aeolic (Priscian 3. 467 K.), was common: cf. Dionysius of Halicarnassus, *Roman Antiquities* 1.90. The idea survived
into the nineteenth century: see M. Mühmelt, *Griechische Grammatik in der Vergilerklärung* (Munich, 1965) 70.

(familiar in the circus)[67] is claimed as Punic; and I have heard that *gurdus,* the vulgar word for "fool," comes from Spain. But "foreign," in my classification, mainly means Greek, because Latin is largely derived from that language[68] and we also openly use Greek words where we have none of our own, just as they sometimes borrow from us.

The question then arises whether foreign words should be declined in the same way as ours. If you come across a *grammaticus* who loves the old writers, he would probably say that there must be no change from the Latin rule, because, since we have an ablative and they do not, it would be irrational to use one Latin case and five Greek;[69] he would also praise the patriotism of those who tried to make Latin a more authoritative language and did not allow that it needed foreign rules. They therefore pronounced *Castorem* with the middle syllable long,[70] because this is the form in which all our nouns are declined whose nominative ending is the same as in *Castor.* They also maintained the use of *Palaemo, Telamo,* and *Plato* (Cicero too calls him by this name), because they did not find any Latin name ending in *ōn.* They did not even tolerate masculine Greek nouns ending in *as* in the nominative: we read *Pelia cincinnatus* in Caelius,[71] *bene fecit Euthia* in Messala,[72] and *Hermagora* in Cicero:[73] no wonder then

[69] The *grammaticus* is arguing against declining Greek words in a Greek manner (e.g. *Platona,* not *Platonem*).

[70] See Varro, *De lingua Latina* 10.70.

[71] *ORF* p. 488: "a curly-haired Pelias."

[72] *ORF* p. 533: "Euthias did well."

[73] Our MSS of *De inventione* 1.8 have *Hermagoras.*

'Hermagora', ne miremur quod ab antiquorum plerisque
62 'Aenea' ut 'Anchisa' sit dictus. Nam si ut 'Maecenas' 'Sufenas' 'Asprenas' dicerentur, genetivo casu non E littera sed
TIS syllaba terminarentur. Inde Olympo et tyranno acu-
tam syllabam mediam dederunt, quia [duabus longis
sequentibus][13] primam [brevem][13] acui noster sermo non
63 patitur. Sic genetivus 'Ulixi' et 'Achilli' fecit, sic alia plurima. Nunc recentiores instituerunt Graecis nominibus
Graecas declinationes potius dare, quod tamen ipsum non
semper fieri potest. Mihi autem placet rationem Latinam
sequi, quousque patitur decor. Neque enim iam 'Calypsonem' dixerim ut 'Iunonem', quamquam secutus antiquos
C. Caesar utitur hac ratione declinandi; sed auctoritatem
64 consuetudo superavit. In ceteris quae poterunt utroque
modo non indecenter efferri, qui Graecam figuram sequi
malet non Latine quidem sed tamen citra reprehensionem
loquetur.
65 Simplices voces prima positione, id est natura sua,
constant, compositae aut praepositionibus subiunguntur,
ut 'innocens' (dum ne pugnantibus inter se duabus, quale

[13] *del. Hermann*

[74] See Naevius fr. 2 Warmington (*ROL* 2.48).
[75] *Inde* refers back to the discussion of *Castorem* in §60. We
must take *Olympo* and *tyranno* as datives dependent on *dederunt*.
The words Q. is discussing are *Olympus* and *tyrannus*. In these,
it is only the length of the middle syllable that determines the
accent. We should accept Hermann's deletion of the bracketed
words as a false interpretation based on the assumption that the
datives *Olympo* and *tyranno* were being discussed. In fact, Q. is
pointing out (as Colson saw) that Latin accented these words on

that most ancient writers said *Aenea* and *Anchisa*.[74] If such words were formed like *Maecenas, Sufenas, Asprenas,* the genitive would not be in -*e* but in -*tis*. Similarly, they placed an acute accent on the middle syllable of *Olympus* and *tyrannus,* because Latin does not allow the first syllable to be acute [if it is short and two longs follow].[75] So also the genitive made *Ulixi* and *Achilli* and many others. More recent scholars however have started to give Greek names Greek declensions, though this is sometimes impossible. My preference is for following the Latin rule as far as elegance allows. I should not care to say *Calypsonem* on the analogy of *Iunonem,* though Caesar, following ancient precedents, uses this form.[76] Usage has now prevailed over Authority. In other instances, where words can be declined in either way without loss of elegance, anyone who prefers to follow the Greek form will not be speaking Latin, but he can hardly be blamed.

Simple and compound words

Simple words consist of their primary, i.e. natural, form: compounds either (1) are formed by adding a prefix, as in *innocens* (with the proviso that two mutually incompatible prefixes must not be used, as in *imperterritus*;[77]

the middle syllable in all cases, whereas in Greek the accent depends on the length of the final syllable (Ὄλυμπος, but Ὀλύμπου). [76] Caesar's *De analogia* (written in Gaul) was famous: Suetonius, *Divus Iulius* 56. Fragments in H. Funaioli, *Grammaticae Romanae Fragmenta* (1907) 145–147.

[77] "Unterrified": but Vergil uses the word, *Aeneid* 10.770, as does Silius Italicus (11.207, 14.187).

est 'inperterritus': alioqui possunt aliquando continuari
duae, ut 'incompositus' 'reconditus' et quo Cicero utitur
'subabsurdum'), aut e duobus quasi corporibus coales-
66 cunt, ut 'maleficus'. Nam ex tribus nostrae utique linguae
non concesserim, quamvis 'capsis' Cicero dicat compositum esse ex 'cape si vis', et inveniantur qui 'Lupercalia'
aeque tris partes orationis esse contendant quasi 'luere
67 per caprum'; nam 'Solitaurilia' iam persuasum est esse
'Suovetaurilia', et sane ita se habet sacrum, quale apud
Homerum quoque est. Sed haec non tam ex tribus quam
ex particulis trium coeunt. Ceterum etiam ex praeposi-
tione et duobus vocabulis dure videtur struxisse Pacuvius:

    Nerei repandirostrum incurvicervicum pecus.

68 Iunguntur autem aut ex duobus Latinis integris, ut 'superfui' 'supterfugi', quamquam ex integris an composita sint
quaeritur, aut ex integro et corrupto, ut 'malevolus', aut ex
corrupto et integro, ut 'noctivagus', aut duobus corruptis,
ut 'pedisecus', aut ex nostro et peregrino, ut 'biclinium',
aut contra, ut 'epitogium' et 'Anticato', aliquando et ex

---

78 *Orator* 154. Compare 6.3.23.

79 Ibid. In fact *capsis* and *capsis* are distinct forms, both archaic in Q.'s time, the first serving as a future, and the second (presumably intended by Cicero) as an optative.

80 "To purify by means of a goat." The same (improbable) explanation of the famous February festival of the Lupercalia is
given by Servius on *Aeneid* 8.343: the *luperci,* "wolf men," were
the *sodales* who conducted it. See *OCD*3 s.v.   81 I.e. the sacrifice of a pig, a sheep, and a bull. The Homeric parallel is probably *Odyssey* 11.131. *Solitaurilia* may be different; this word was
variously explained as meaning a sacrifice of only (*soli*) male animals or of "complete" animals (*solidus,* Oscan *sollus*).

BOOK 1.5

otherwise two can sometimes be combined, as in *in-compositus, reconditus,* or Cicero's *subabsurdum*),[78] or (2) arise from the coalescence of two separate elements, as in *maleficus.* I cannot allow our language triple compounds, though Cicero[79] says that *capsis* is made up of *cape si vis,* and some can be found to contend that *Lupercalia* also has three parts, and comes from *luere per caprum.*[80] *Solitaurilia* is now universally believed to stand for *suovetaurilia,*[81] and certainly that is what the ritual is, as it is also in Homer. But these are formed not so much from three words as from parts of three words. Pacuvius however seems to have made some very awkward compounds out of a preposition and two vocables: *Nerei repandirostrum incurvicervicum pecus.*[82] However, compounds are formed either (1) from two complete Latin words, as in *superfui* and *supterfugi*[83] (though one may ask whether we can speak of a "compound" when each part is a complete word); or (2) from a complete word and a modified one (as *malevolus*); or (3) from a modified word and a complete one (*noctivagus*);[84] or (4) from two modified words (*pedisecus*);[85] or (5) from a Latin word and a foreign one (*biclinium*); or (6) the reverse (as in *epitogium* and *Anticato*);[86] or (7) sometimes from two foreign words

[82] Pacuvius 352 Warmington (*ROL* 2. 292): "Nereus' upturn-snouted and roundcrooknecked flock"—dolphins, apparently.

[83] "I survived," "I slipped away."

[84] "Night-wandering."   [85] "Foot-follower, footman."

[86] In *biclinium* ("a dining couch for two persons"), *bi-* is Latin, *clin-* is Greek; in *epitogium* ("over-toga") *epi-* is Greek, *toga* Latin; in *Anticato* (the title of a book by Caesar), *anti-* is Greek, *-cato* the Roman name.

157

QUINTILIAN

duobus peregrinis, ut 'epiraedium'; nam cum sit 'epi' praepositio Graeca, 'raeda' Gallicum (neque Graecus tamen
neque Gallus utitur composito), Romani suum ex alieno
utroque fecerunt.

69 Frequenter autem praepositiones quoque copulatio
ista corrumpit: inde 'abstulit' 'aufugit' 'amisit', cum praepositio sit 'ab' sola, et 'coit', cum sit praepositio 'con'. Sic
70 'ignavi' et 'erepublica' et similia. Sed res tota magis Graecos decet, nobis minus succedit: nec id fieri natura puto,
sed alienis favemus, ideoque cum κυρταύχενα[14] mirati
simus, 'incurvicervicum' vix a risu defendimus.

71 Propria sunt verba cum id significant in quod primo
denominata sunt, tralata cum alium natura intellectum,
alium loco praebent.

Usitatis tutius utimur, nova non sine quodam periculo
fingimus. Nam si recepta sunt, modicam laudem adferunt
orationi, repudiata etiam in iocos exeunt. Audendum ta-
72 men: namque, ut Cicero ait, etiam quae primo dura visa

[14] *edd.*: συραύχενα AB

---

[87] Q. is wrong here: *eporaedium* or *epiraedium* is a word of
Gaulish origin meaning "horse carriage": but Juvenal 8.66 (see
Courtney ad loc.) seems to have accepted Q.'s etymology.
[88] "Took away," "fled away," "lost." Compare Cicero, *Orator*
158.   [89] "Comes together."
[90] "Inactive" (*in* + *navus*), "in the public interest" (*e* for *ex*):
Cicero, *Orator* loc. cit.
[91] "With arching neck": this generally accepted emendation,
equivalent in sense to Pacuvius' *incurvicervicum,* is admitted as a
tragic fragment (*Trag. Adesp.* 438a Kannicht), but the word is not
otherwise known. The manuscript reading συραύχην would

158

(*epiraedium: epi* is a Greek preposition, *raeda* is a Gaulish word;[87] no Greek or Gaul uses the compound, but the Romans have made their own word out of the two strangers).

Prefixes are also often modified by this joining: thus we have *abstulit, aufugit, amisit,*[88] though the preposition is only *ab; coit,*[89] though the preposition is *con*; and so *ignavi* and *erepublica*[90] and the like. But all this suits the Greeks better. It is not very successful with us—not I think because of any innate weakness, but we favour foreign imports, and so admire *kurtauchen,*[91] but can hardly protect *incurvicervicum* from ridicule.

"Proper" and metaphorical words

Words are "proper" when they signify that which they were first designed to name; metaphorical, when they have one meaning by nature and another in the context.

Words in current use or made up

It is safer to use current words; there is a certain danger in making words up.[92] If they are accepted, they do not give our style much credit; if they are rejected, they may even end up as a joke. Still, we have to take risks; for, as Cicero says,[93] use softens even words which at first seemed

mean "with trailing neck": a possible description of a creature (even a man) being dragged backwards along the ground.

[92] Compare Caesar's famous remark (Aulus Gellius 1.10.4) that we should "steer clear of any unheard-of and unusual word like a rock." [93] Compare *De natura deorum* 1.95.

sunt, usu molliuntur. Sed minime nobis concessa est ὀνο-
ματοποιία. Quis enim ferat si quid simile illis merito lau-
datis λίγξε βιός et σίζ’ ὀφθαλμός fingere audeamus?
Iam ne 'balare' quidem aut 'hinnire' fortiter diceremus nisi
iudicio vetustatis niterentur.

6

1 Est etiam sua loquentibus observatio, sua scribentibus.
Sermo constat ratione vetustate auctoritate consuetudine.

Rationem praestat praecipue analogia, nonnumquam
etymologia.

Vetera maiestas quaedam et, ut sic dixerim, religio
commendat.

2 Auctoritas ab oratoribus vel historicis peti solet (nam
poetas metri necessitas excusat, nisi si quando nihil impe-
diente in utroque modulatione pedum alterum malunt,
qualia sunt 'imo de stirpe recisum' et 'aëriae quo congessere palumbes' et 'silice in nuda' et similia): cum sum-
morum in eloquentia virorum iudicium pro ratione, et vel
error honestus sit[1] magnos duces sequentibus.

1 *Halm*: est *AB*

---

94 See 8.6.31.
95 "Bow twanged" (Homer, *Iliad* 4.25), "eye hissed" (*Odyssey*
9.394: the Cyclops' eye when Odysseus thrusts in the red-hot
stake). Such things, Q. says, are not suitable in Latin.
96 "Baa" and "whinny." Varro (*Saturarum Menippearum Reliquiae* fr. 1 Riese) lists these words for animal sounds: *mugit* (cow),
balat (sheep), *hinniunt* (horses), *pipat* (hen).

harsh. On the other hand, onomatopoeia[94] is not for us. Who would tolerate anything like the deservedly praised *linxe bios* or *siz' ophthalmos*?[95] Indeed, we should not feel confident even about using *balare* or *hinnire*,[96] if we had not the judgement of antiquity to support us.

CHAPTER 6

Principles of correct speech: Reason, Antiquity, Authority, and Usage

Speaking and writing both have their own rules. Language is based on Reason, Antiquity, Authority, and Usage.[1]

Reason is grounded principally on Analogy, but sometimes also on Etymology.

Antiquity is commended to us by a certain majesty and, I might almost say, religious awe.

Authority is generally sought from orators and historians. (Poets are excused from doing us this service, because of their metrical constraints, except on the occasions when they choose one of two alternatives, though the metre is not an objection to either, as in *imo de stirpe recisum* and *aeriae quo congessere palumbes* and *silice in nuda* and the like).[2] This is because the judgement of the supreme orators replaces Reason, and even error is honourable if it comes from following such great guides.

---

[1] For these "guidelines" see Lausberg §§465–469.

[2] All from Vergil: "cut from the lowest stem," *Aeneid* 12.208; "where airborne doves collected," *Eclogues* 3.69; "on the bare flint," *Eclogues* 1.15. These are all choices of gender: *stirps* is usually feminine, *palumbes* and *silex* usually masculine.

QUINTILIAN

3   Consuetudo vero certissima loquendi magistra, uten-
dumque plane sermone, ut nummo, cui publica forma est.
     Omnia tamen haec exigunt acre iudicium, analogia
praecipue: quam proxime ex Graeco transferentes in Lati-
4 num proportionem vocaverunt. Eius haec vis est, ut id
quod dubium est ad aliquid simile de quo non quaeritur
referat, et incerta certis probet. Quod efficitur duplici
via: comparatione similium in extremis maxime syllabis,
propter quod ea quae sunt e singulis negantur debere
5 rationem, et deminutione. Comparatio in nominibus aut
genus deprendit aut declinationem: genus, ut, si quaeratur
'funis' masculinum sit an femininum, simile illi sit 'panis':
declinationem, ut, si veniat in dubium 'hac domu' dicendum sit an 'hac domo', et 'domuum' an 'domorum', similia
6 sint [domus]² 'anus' 'manus'. Deminutio genus modo de-
tegit, ut, ne ab eodem exemplo recedam, 'funem' masculinum esse 'funiculus' ostendit.
7   Eadem in verbis quoque ratio comparationis, ut, si quis
antiquos secutus 'fervere' brevi media syllaba dicat, deprendatur vitiose loqui, quod omnia quae E et O litteris fatendi modo terminantur, eadem, si in infinitis E litteram
media syllaba acceperunt, utique productam habent:
'prandeo' 'pendeo' 'spondeo', 'prandere' 'pendere' 'spon-

² *del. H. Meyer*

---

³ Compare Horace, *Ars poetica* 59, Fortunatianus 3.3 Halm
(*RLM* 122.9).

⁴ See *OCD*³, s.v. Analogy and Anomaly: Varro, *De lingua
Latina* 8–10 is the main source for this dispute.

⁵ *Anus* ("old woman") and *manus* ("hand") make -*u* in the ablative and -*uum* in the genitive plural, and so support *domu* and

162

Finally, Usage is the surest teacher of speaking, and we should treat language like money marked with the public stamp.[3]

Reason: (1) Analogy

But all these criteria need keen judgement, especially Analogy, a term which those who translate from the Greek most closely have rendered as *proportio*.[4] The essence of Analogy is that it refers any doubtful matter to something similar about which there is no question, and tests the uncertain by the certain. This is done in two ways: by comparing similar words, especially with regard to their final syllables (hence monosyllables are said not to be subject to this principle); and by the study of diminutives. In nouns, the comparison reveals either the gender or the declension. (1) Gender: if (for instance) the question is whether *funis* ("rope") is masculine or feminine, *panis* ("bread") is a parallel. (2) Declension: if the question is whether we should say *hac domu* or *hac domo, domuum* or *domorum,* then *anus* and *manus* would be parallels.[5] Diminutives only reveal gender: for instance (to keep to the same example) *funiculus* proves that *funis* is masculine.

The same principle of comparison applies also to verbs. If, following the ancients, someone pronounces *fervere* with a short middle syllable, he can be shown to be wrong, because all verbs which end in *-eo* in the indicative, if they have *e* in the middle syllable of the infinitive, always make it long (*prandeo, pendeo, spondeo, prandēre,*

domuum against the second-declension forms prevalent in older Latin.

8 dere'. At quae O solam habent, dummodo per eandem litteram in infinito exeant, brevia fiunt: 'lego' 'dico' 'curro',
'legere' 'dicere' 'currere': etiamsi est apud Lucilium:

> fervit aqua et fervet: fervit nunc, fervet ad annum.

9 Sed pace dicere hominis eruditissimi liceat: si 'fervit' putat
illi simile 'currit' et 'legit', 'fervo' dicet ut 'lego' et 'curro',
quod nobis inauditum est. Sed non est haec vera comparatio: nam 'fervit' est illi simile 'servit'. Quam proportionem
sequenti dicere necesse est 'fervire' ut 'servire'.

10   Prima quoque aliquando positio ex obliquis invenitur,
ut memoria repeto convictos a me qui reprenderant quod
hoc verbo usus essem: 'pepigi'; nam id quidem dixisse
summos auctores confitebantur, rationem tamen negabant
permittere, quia prima positio 'paciscor', cum haberet naturam patiendi, faceret tempore praeterito 'pactus sum'.

11 Nos praeter auctoritatem oratorum atque historicorum
analogia quoque dictum tuebamur. Nam cum legeremus
in XII tabulis 'ni ita pagunt',[3] inveniebamus simile huic
'cadunt': inde prima positio, etiamsi vetustate exoleverat,
apparebat 'pago'[4] ut 'cado', unde non erat dubium sic 'pe-

12 pigi' nos dicere ut 'cecidi'. Sed meminerimus non per

---

[3] pacunt B   [4] paco B

---

[6] These are all "second-conjugation" verbs: *fervĕre* is "to boil";
prandere "to have lunch"; *pendere* "to hang"; *spondere* "to
pledge." Q.'s use of *fatendi modus* to mean "indicative" is unusual;
but see Charisius 1. 562 *GLK.*   [7] "Water boils now and will
boil next year": Lucilius 357 Marx = 374 Warmington (*ROL* 3.
116). *Fervĕre* (the earlier form) is still used by Vergil and other poets (see *OLD* s.v.). Compare also *fulgĕre/fulgēre* ("to shine").

pendēre, spondēre),[6] whereas those which have only *-o*, so long as they have *e* in the infinitive, make it short (*lego, dico, curro, legĕre, dicĕre, currĕre*). It is true that we find in Lucilius *fervit aqua et fervet: fervit nunc, fervet ad annum.*[7] But, with all respect to that learned man, if he thinks *fervit* is like *currit* and *legit,* he will have to say *fervo,* like *lego* and *curro;* but that is unheard of. "This however is not the true comparison: *fervit* is like *servit*": if you follow *this* analogy, you will have to say *fervire,* like *servire.*

The basic form[8] also can sometimes be discovered from the other tenses. I remember that I managed to refute people who had criticized me for using the form *pepigi;*[9] they admitted that good authorities had it, but they said that Reason rejected it, because the present indicative *paciscor,* being passive in form, made *pactus sum* in the past tense. Besides the authority of orators and historians, I defended the form by Analogy. Reading *ni ita pagunt* in the Twelve Tables,[10] I noted that it was like *cadunt;* so the first person, though now obsolete, seemed to be *pago,* like *cado;* whence there could be no doubt that we say *pepigi* like *cecidi.* But let us remember that the principle of Anal-

---

[8] I.e. the present indicative.

[9] Usually regarded as the perfect of *pango,* which, like the archaic *paco, pacĕre,* and its inceptive form *paciscor,* can mean "agree" or "covenant."

[10] If Q. gets his quotation (= 1.6 Warmington, *ROL* 3. 428) from *Ad Herennium* 2.20 ("When they have contract on the matter, let him plead; if they do not have contract (*ni pagunt*), let him state the case"), and if his text of *Ad Herennium,* like ours, had *pagunt,* it is right to follow A's reading here; but there seems little doubt that *paco* was the form used in the Law.

QUINTILIAN

omnia duci analogiae posse rationem, cum et sibi ipsa
plurimis in locis repugnet. Quaedam sine dubio conantur
eruditi defendere, ut, cum deprensum est 'lepus' et 'lupus'
similia positione quantum casibus numerisque dissentiant,
ita respondent non esse paria quia 'lepus' epicoenon sit,
'lupus' masculinum, quamquam Varro in eo libro quo initia
Romanae urbis enarrat lupum feminam dicit Ennium Pic-
toremque Fabium secutus. Illi autem idem, cum interro-
13 gantur cur 'aper' 'apri' et 'pater' 'patris' faciat, illud nomen
positum, hoc ad aliquid esse contendunt. Praeterea quoniam utrumque a Graeco ductum sit, ad eam rationem re-
14 currunt, ut πατρός 'patris', κάπρου 'apri' faciat. Illa tamen
quomodo effugient, ut [non],[5] quamvis feminina singulari
nominativo US litteris finita numquam genetivo casu RIS
syllaba terminentur, faciat tamen 'Venus' 'Veneris'? Item,
cum ES litteris finita per varios exeant genetivos, numquam tamen eadem RIS syllaba terminatos, 'Ceres' cogat
15 dici 'Cereris'? Quid vero quae tota positionis eiusdem in
diversos flexus eunt, cum 'Alba' faciat 'Albanos' et 'Alben-
sis', 'volo' 'volui' et 'volavi'? Nam praeterito quidem tempore varie formari verba prima persona O littera terminata
ipsa analogia confitetur, si quidem facit 'cado' 'cecidi',
'spondeo' 'spopondi', 'pingo' 'pinxi', 'lego' 'legi', 'pono'

5 *del. Halm*

11 *Lepus, leporis,* "hare"; *lupus, lupi,* "wolf."
12 Perhaps *De gente populi Romani.*
13 Ennius, *Annales* 68, 70 Vahlen = 71–74 Warmington = 65–
68 Skutsch; Fabius Pictor, fr. 2 Peter.

ogy cannot be applied universally, as it is often inconsistent
with itself. Scholars do indeed try to defend some inconsis-
tencies: for example, when it is observed how much *lepus*
and *lupus*,[11] though similar in the nominative singular,
differ in the other cases and numbers, they reply that the
reason they are not alike is that *lepus* is common, and *lupus*
masculine. Yet Varro, in the book in which he relates the
origins of Rome,[12] writes *lupus femina* ("female wolf"), following Ennius and Fabius Pictor.[13] But when they are
asked why *aper* ("boar") makes *apri* and *pater* ("father")
patris, they reply that *aper* is an "absolute" and *pater* a
"relative."[14] Again, since both words come from Greek,
they have recourse to the argument that *patris* comes from
patros and *apri* from *kaprou.* But how can they get over
the fact that, although feminines with a nominative singular in *-us* never have a genitive ending in *-ris*, *Venus* nevertheless makes *Veneris*; or that, although words ending in
-es have various forms in the genitive, but never end in *-ris*,
Ceres demands the form *Cereris*? Again, what of words
which, although identical in their primary form, have different inflexions? *Alba* has *Albani* and *Albenses*,[15] *volo* has
volui and *volavi.*[16] Analogy itself admits that verbs whose
present indicative ends in *-o* have a variety of forms in the
past tense: *cado cecidi, spondeo spopondi, pingo pinxi,*

---

[14] I.e. "father" implies "child," but "wild boar" has no corre-
lative. *Positum* here = *positivum*, Greek ὄνομα θεματικόν. *Ad
aliquid,* from Greek πρός τι, means "relative to something else."

[15] Compare Varro, *De lingua Latina* 8.35. *Albani* are from
Alba Longa, *Albenses* from Alba Fucens (see *Ad Herennium* 2.45;
a Latin colony of central Italy).

[16] *volo, volui,* "wish": *volo, volavi,* "fly."

16 'posui', 'frango' 'fregi', 'laudo' 'laudavi'. Non enim, cum primum fingerentur homines, Analogia demissa caelo formam loquendi dedit, sed inventa est postquam loquebantur, et notatum in sermone quo quidque[6] modo caderet. Itaque non ratione nititur sed exemplo, nec lex est loquendi sed observatio, ut ipsam analogian nulla res alia fecerit

17 quam consuetudo. Inhaerent tamen ei quidam molestissima diligentiae perversitate, ut 'audaciter' potius dicant quam 'audacter', licet omnes oratores aliud sequantur, et 'emicavit', non 'emicuit', et 'conire', non 'coire'. His permittamus et 'audivisse' et 'scivisse' et 'tribunale' et 'faciliter' dicere ; 'frugalis' quoque sit apud illos, non 'frugi':

18 nam quo alio modo fiet 'frugalitas'? Idem 'centum milia nummum' et 'fidem deum' ostendant duplices quoque soloecismos esse, quando et casum mutant et numerum: nesciebamus enim ac non consuetudini et decori serviebamus, sicut in plurimis quae M. Tullius in Oratore divine ut

19 omnia exequitur. Sed Augustus quoque in epistulis ad C. Caesarem scriptis emendat quod is 'calidam'[7] dicere quam 'caldam'[8] malit, non quia id non sit Latinum, sed quia sit odiosum[9] et, ut ipse Graeco verbo significavit, περίεργον.

---

6 *Spalding*: quid quoque *B*: quid quo *A*   7 *Keil*:   calidum *AB*   8 *Keil*: caldum *AB*   9 otiosum *Burman*

---

17 "Fall," "pledge," "paint," "read," "place," "break," "praise," in present and perfect tenses.
18 Q. implies that normal usage is *audisse, scisse, tribunal, facile.* (Compare 9.4.59 for the infinitive forms.)   19 See below, 1.6.29; and Cicero, *Tusculanae Disputationes* 3.18.
20 Cicero, *Orator* 155. *Nummum* and *deum* are genitive plurals, though they look like accusative singulars.

lego legi, pono posui, frango fregi, laudo laudavi.[17] Analogy was not sent down from heaven to frame the rules of language when men were first created, but was discovered only when they were already using language and note was taken of the way in which particular words ended in speech. It rests therefore not upon Reason but upon Precedent; it is not a law of speech, but an observed practice, Analogy itself being merely the product of Usage. Some scholars however cling to it with such perverse and irritating pedantry that they say *audaciter* rather than *audacter* (contrary to the usage of all the orators), *emicavit* for *emicuit* and *conire* for *coire.* Let us let them have *audivisse* and *scivisse* and *tribunale* and *faciliter,*[18] and even *frugalis* instead of *frugi*: for how else can we get *frugalitas*?[19] Let them point out the double Solecisms in *centum milia nummum* ("100,000 *nummi*") and *fidem deum* ("faith of the gods"),[20] when case and number are both changed; of course this was our ignorance, and we were not simply obeying the demands of Usage and Elegance, as in the many instances which Cicero discusses, with his unfailing mastery, in the *Orator.* Augustus also, in his letter to Gaius Caesar,[21] corrects him for saying *calidam* rather than *caldam,* not on the ground that it is not Latin, but as being repulsive, and, in his own Greek word, *periergon.* Yet some

---

[21] *Epist.* fr. XXIII Malcovati. The emperor reproves his grandson for being too pedantic. Keil's probable *calidam . . . caldam* makes the assumption that they are talking about hot water (*aquam*): in this usage, the shortened form *calda* is normal. Burman's *otiosum,* "otiose," may be closer to περίεργον; but see 8.3.30.

20 Atqui hanc quidam ὀρθοέπειαν solam putant, quam ego
minime excludo. Quid enim tam necessarium quam recta
locutio? Immo inhaerendum ei iudico, quoad licet, diu
etiam mutantibus repugnandum: sed abolita atque abro-
gata retinere insolentiae cuiusdam est et frivolae in parvis
21 iactantiae. Multum enim litteratus qui sine adspiratione et
producta secunda syllaba salutarit ('avete'[10] est enim), et
'calefacere' dixerit potius quam quod dicimus et 'conservavisse', his adiciat 'face' et 'dice' et similia. Recta est haec
22 via: quis negat? Sed adiacet et mollior et magis trita.

Ego tamen non alio magis angor quam quod obliquis
casibus ducti etiam primas sibi positiones non invenire sed
mutare permittunt, ut cum 'ebur' et 'robur', ita dicta ac
scripta summis auctoribus, in O litteram secundae syllabae
transferunt, quia sit 'roboris' et 'eboris', 'sulpur' autem
et 'guttur' U litteram in genetivo servent: ideoque 'iecur'
23 etiam et 'femur' controversiam fecerunt. Quod non minus
est licentiosum quam si 'sulpuri' et 'gutturi' subicerent in
genetivo litteram O mediam quia esset 'eboris' et 'roboris':
sicut Antonius Gnipho, qui 'robur' quidem et 'ebur' atque
etiam 'marmur' fatetur esse, verum fieri vult ex his 'ebura'

10 R: avere AB

---

22 Ăvē would be pedantic, hăvĕ the normal "iambic shortening" (Sihler 1995, 79): that the plural is avete, not avite, shows that
the strictly correct form is avē, the verb being of the second conju-
gation. Calfacere ("make warm") is usual, as are conservasse ("to
have preserved") and the imperatives fac ("do") and dic ("say").

23 Iecur, "liver," has genitive iecinoris or iecoris; femur, "thigh,"
has feminis or femoris. For the origin of these forms, see Sihler
(1995) 298–299.

think this is only verbal correctness ("orthoepy"); and I am certainly not against this! For what is so necessary as correct speech? Indeed, my rule is that one should stick to this principle as far as possible, and keep up resistance against innovators even for a long time; but to maintain obsolete and extinct forms is a sign of a certain presumption and petty ostentation in matters of small importance. The man of learning who says the usual word of greeting *without* an aspirate and *with* a long second syllable (it is long in *avēte*), and says *calefacere* instead of what we all say, and likewise *conservavisse,* might as well add *face* and *dice* and the like.[22] His road is the right one, of course; but there is an easier and more frequented one at hand.

There is, however, nothing which annoys me more in these people than their allowing themselves not only to discover but actually to change nominative forms on the basis of the other cases: thus in *ebur* ("ivory") and *robur* ("strength"), which the highest authorities pronounce and write like that, they change the vowel of the second syllable to *o,* on the ground that we have *roboris* and *eboris,* while *sulpur* and *guttur* keep *u* in the genitive. *Iecur* and *femur* therefore also have given rise to controversy.[23] This is no less arbitrary than if they were to foist an *o* on *sulpur* ("sulphur") and *guttur* ("throat") in the genitive, because there is one in *eboris* and *roboris.* Thus Antonius Gnipho,[24] who allows *robur* and *ebur* and even *marmur* ("marble") to be correct, wants the plurals to be *ebura, robura,*

---

[24] See Suetonius, *De grammaticis* 7. Tutor to Caesar, he is said to have written a commentary on Ennius.

24 'robura' 'marmura'. Quodsi animadverterent litterarum adfinitatem, scirent sic ab eo quod est 'robur' 'roboris' fieri quo modo ab eo quod est 'miles limes' 'militis limitis', 'iu-
25 dex vindex' 'iudicis vindicis', et quae supra iam attigi. Quid vero quod, ut dicebam, similes positiones in longe diversas figuras per obliquos casus exeunt, ut 'virgo Iuno,' 'fusus lusus', 'cuspis puppis' et mille alia: cum illud etiam accidat, ut quaedam pluraliter non dicantur, quaedam contra singulari numero, quaedam casibus careant, quaedam a primis statim positionibus tota mutentur, ut 'Iuppiter'?
26 Quod verbis etiam accidit, ut illi 'fero', cuius praeteritum perfectum et ulterius non invenitur. Nec plurimum refert nulla haec an praedura sint. Nam quid 'progenies' genetivo singulari, quid plurali 'spes' faciet? Quo modo autem 'quire' et 'urgere'[11] vel in praeterita patiendi modo vel in
27 participia transibunt? Quid de aliis dicam, cum 'senatus' [senatui][12] 'senati' an 'senatus' faciat incertum sit? Quare mihi non invenuste dici videtur aliud esse Latine, aliud grammatice loqui. Ac de analogia nimium.

[11] ruere B: luere *Colson*
[12] *del. Spalding*

---

25 See 1.4.12, 1.5.49. The examples illustrate assimilation and analogy: Sihler (1995) 67.

26 *Virgo, virginis*; *Iuno, Iunonis*; *fusus, fusi*; *lusus, lusūs*; *cuspis, cuspidis*; *puppis, puppis* ("virgin," "Juno," "spindle," "game," "spear," "(stern of a) ship").

27 *Iovem, Iovis, Iovi, Iove*: see Lindsay, *Latin Language* 377.

28 *Tuli* serves as the perfect of *fero* ("carry"), *tuleram* as pluperfect, *tulerim* as perfect subjunctive.

marmura. If they attended to the affinities[25] between letters, they would realize that *roboris* comes from *robur* in the same way as *militis limitis iudicis* and *vindicis* come from *miles* ("soldier") *limes* ("frontier") *iudex* ("judge") and *vindex* ("avenger"), or the other examples which I touched on above. And what about the similar nominatives which, as I said, develop very different forms in the oblique cases, like *virgo* and *Iuno, fusus* and *lusus, cuspis* and *puppis,* and a thousand others?[26] It also happens that some nouns have no plural, some no singular, some lack cases, and some (like *Iuppiter*)[27] are totally changed from their nominative forms. The same occurs in verbs, as in *fero,* of which no perfect or further inflexion is found.[28] It does not much matter whether these forms are non-existent or just very harsh. What will be the genitive singular of *progenies* ("offspring") or the genitive plural of *spes* ("hope")?[29] How can *quire* and *urgere*[30] form passive perfect tenses or participles? And why should I give more examples, when we are uncertain whether *senatus* makes *senati* or *senatūs*?[31] It seems to me that it was quite a neat remark to say that speaking Latin is one thing, and speaking grammatically quite another. This is more than enough about Analogy.

[29] *Progeniei* and *sperum* are both unattested.

[30] "To be able," "to press." But Terence, *Hecyra* 572 has *quita. Urgeo* is one of many verbs "lacking a supine."

[31] *Senatus* normally has genitive *senatūs,* but *senati* is quite well attested, and there is evidence in grammarians for *senatuis* (Aulus Gellius 4.16; Sisenna fr. 136 Peter), not for *senatui.* So *either* delete *senatui* (as I have done) *or* read *senatuis.*

28   Etymologia, quae verborum originem inquirit, a Cicerone dicta est notatio, quia nomen eius apud Aristotelen
invenitur σύμβολον, quod est 'nota'. Nam verbum ex verbo ductum, id est veriloquium, ipse Cicero qui finxit refor-
midat. Sunt qui vim potius intuiti originationem vocent.

29   Haec habet aliquando usum necessarium, quotiens inter-
pretatione res de qua quaeritur eget, ut cum M. Caelius se
esse hominem frugi vult probare, non quia abstinens sit
(nam id ne mentiri quidem poterat) sed quia utilis multis,
id est fructuosus, unde sit ducta frugalitas. Ideoque in

30 definitionibus adsignatur etymologiae locus. Nonnumquam etiam barbara ab emendatis conatur discernere, ut
.cum 'Triquetram' dici Siciliam an 'Triquedram', 'meridiem' an 'medidiem' oporteat quaeritur: aliquando con-

31 suetudini servit. Continet autem in se multam erudicio-
nem, sive ex Graecis orta tractemus, quae sunt plurima
praecipueque Aeolica ratione, cui est sermo noster simillimus, declinata, sive ex historiarum veterum notitia nomina
hominum locorum gentium urbium requiramus: unde
Bruti, Publicolae, Pythici? cur Latium, Italia, Beneventum? quae Capitolium et collem Quirinalem et Argiletum

---

32 *Topica* 35, "we use *notatio* because words are *notae* ("signs")
of things": compare Aristotle, *On interpretation* 16a3, 16a27—
though these passages are not particularly close.

33 "True speech"; *etymon = verum, -loquium* corresponds to
-logia.

34 *ORF* p. 486. The indeclinable adjective *frugi* is the dative of
frux, "fruit."

35 "Three-cornered," equivalent to Greek *Trinakria* (so
Isidore, *Etymologiae* 14.6.32).

BOOK 1.6

Reason: (2) Etymology

Etymology, which inquires into the origin of words, was called *notatio* by Cicero,[32] because we find in Aristotle the term *symbolon,* which means *nota.* Cicero, who himself devised the literal rendering of "etymology," *veriloquium,*[33] is afraid to use it. Some, with an eye rather to the essential meaning, call it "origination." It is sometimes necessary, when the subject in question needs interpretation, as when Marcus Caelius[34] seeks to prove that he is *homo frugi* ("an honest man"), not because he is abstemious (he could not even pretend to be that), but because he is useful to many, that is "fruitful," and from this is derived *frugalitas.* Etymology therefore has a place in definitions. Sometimes, again, it tries to distinguish barbarous from correct forms: for instance, when we ask if Sicily should be called *Triquetra* or *Triquedra,*[35] and whether *meridiem* or *medidiem*[36] is correct for "midday." Sometimes too it is the servant of Usage. It involves much erudition, whether we have to deal with words coming from the Greek, which are very numerous and are chiefly derived from Aeolic (this is the dialect which our language most closely resembles),[37] or to investigate the names of persons, places, nations or cities from our knowledge of old histories: why were *Brutus, Publicola,* or *Pythicus* so called? Why do we say *Latium, Italia, Beneventum*? What is the reason for the

---

[36] Varro (*De lingua Latina* 6.4) reports *medidie* inscribed on a sundial at Praeneste. *Meridies* is a result of dissimilation (Palmer, *Latin Language* 231; Sihler (1995) 151).

[37] See on 1.5.58.

175

appellandi ratio ?

32   Iam illa minora in quibus maxime studiosi eius rei fatigantur, qui verba paulum declinata varie et multipliciter ad
veritatem reducunt aut correptis aut porrectis aut adiectis
aut detractis aut permutatis litteris syllabisve. Inde pravis
ingeniis ad foedissima usque ludibria labuntur. Sit enim
'consul' a consulendo vel a iudicando: nam et hoc 'consulere' veteres vocaverunt, unde adhuc remanet illud 'rogat

33   boni consulas', id est 'bonum iudices': senatui dederit nomen aetas, nam idem patres sunt: sit[13] rex rector, et alia
plurima indubitata: nec abnuerim tegulae regulaeque et
similium his rationem; iam sit et classis a calando et lepus

34   'levipes' et vulpes 'volipes': etiamne a contrariis aliqua si-
nemus trahi, ut 'lucus' quia umbra opacus parum luceat, et
'ludus' quia sit longissime a lusu, et 'Ditis' quia minime
dives? Etiamne 'hominem' appellari quia sit humo natus

---

13 *H. Meyer*: et *AB*

---

38 According to these popular etymologies, *Brutus* means
"stupid"; *Publicola* "cultivator of the people"; *Pythicus* comes
from the snake Python whom Apollo killed; *Latium* from *latēre*,
"lie hidden" (because Saturn "lay hidden" there: Vergil, *Aeneid*
8.323); *Italia* from *vitulus*, "calf"; *Beneventum*, "good wind," is a
euphemism for an unhealthy place; *Capitolium* means "head of
Olus"; the hill *Quirinalis* is named from *Quirinus*, i.e. Romulus;
and *Argiletum* means "death of Argus."

39 Presumably from *tego*, "cover," and *rego*, "rule."

40 An old word meaning "to summon."

41 The hare is "light of foot" (compare Cicero, *Aratea* 121), the
fox "flying foot." Both these etymologies come from Aelius Stilo
(see Varro, *De re rustica* 3.126, *De lingua Latina* 5.101).

42 A common device of popular etymology: for *lucus* com-

names *Capitolium, Quirinalis, Argiletum*?[38]

And so we come to the minor points on which students of etymology spend so much energy, restoring words which have become slightly altered to their true form by many varied devices—shortening, lengthening, adding, taking away, or interchanging letters or syllables. Their perverse ingenuity causes them to fall into hideous absurdities. Let us grant that *consul* comes from "consulting" or "judging" (for the ancients used *consulere* in this sense too, and the phrase *rogat boni consulas*—that is "asks you to judge it good"—still survives); that the senate owes its name to the seniority of the members (they are also called "fathers"); that *rex* ("king") is a *rector* (ruler); and many other unquestionable facts of this kind. Nor would I reject the explanation given of *tegula, regula*[39] and the like. Let *classis* ("class") come from *calare*,[40] *lepus* from *levipes,* and *vulpes* from *volipes.*[41] But shall we also allow that some names come from opposites[42]—*lucus,* because a grove is dark and shady and does not "shine"; *ludus* ("school") because it is very far from being *lusus* ("play"); and *Dis,* because he is anything but *dives,* "rich"? Or that man is called *homo* because he is born of the earth, *humus,*[43] as though

pare, for example, Servius on Vergil, *Aeneid* 1.443, Isidore, *Etymologiae* 14.8.30. Of Q.'s examples, *ludus* represents Greek σχολή—"leisure" and also "school"—and Dis represents Πλού-των, Pluto, the underworld god seen as a source of wealth (Plato, *Cratylus* 403A, Cicero, *De natura deorum* 2.66); Q.'s explanation of this name as an "opposite" seems to be unique.

[43] Not an absurd etymology, according to Ernout–Meillet, *Dictionnaire étymologique du latin,* s.v. *homo;* found also in Hyginus (*Fabulae* 220), and exploited in Christian tradition (e.g. Tertullian, *Apologeticus* 18).

(quasi vero non omnibus animalibus eadem origo, aut illi
primi mortales ante nomen imposuerint terrae quam sibi),
35 et 'verba' ab aëre verberato? Pergamus: sic perveniemus
eo usque ut 'stella' luminis stilla credatur, cuius etymologiae auctorem clarum sane in litteris nominari in ea
36 parte qua a me reprenditur inhumanum est. Qui vero talia
libris complexi sunt, nomina sua ipsi inscripserunt, inge-
nioseque visus est Gavius 'caelibes' dicere veluti 'caelites',
quod onere gravissimo vacent, idque Graeco argumento
iuvit: ἠϊθέους enim eadem de causa dici adfirmat. Nec ei
cedit Modestus inventione: nam, quia Caelo Saturnus ge-
nitalia absciderit, hoc nomine appellatos qui uxore careant
ait; Aelius 'pituitam' quia petat vitam. Sed cui non post
37 Varronem sit venia? Qui 'agrum' quia in eo agatur aliquid,
et 'gragulos' quia gregatim volent dictos voluit persuadere
Ciceroni (ad eum enim scribit), cum alterum ex Graeco sit
38 manifestum duci, alterum ex vocibus avium. Sed huic¹⁴

14 *edd.*: hoc *AB*

44 This (quite common) etymology (see especially Augustine,
De dialectica 6.9) would suit the philosophical definition of sound
as "air struck" or "beaten": compare the Stoic definitions (H.
Diels, *Doxographi Graeci* 409a; *SVF* 1. 21, 30; 2. 33, 43, etc.) according to which sound is produced by the air being "struck" or
"beaten."

45 An etymology not attested elsewhere; the scholar responsible is unknown: Maltby (1990) 582.

46 Perhaps Gavius Bassus, cited by Gellius (3.19.3) for etymologies.

47 Ēitheoi ("young unmarried men") seems to contain *theoi*,
"gods," as *caelibes* suggests *caelites*, "gods in heaven."

all living things did not have that same origin, or the first
mortals gave a name to the earth before they gave one to
themselves? Can *verbum* ("word") come from the "rever-
beration" of the air?[44] Let us go a little further: we shall
thus come to believe that *stella* means a drop (*stilla*) of
light;[45] it would be cruel of me to name the famous scholar
who produced this etymology solely because of something
for which I have to criticize him. But those who have made
such things the subject of books have happily put their
names to them. Gavius[46] has been thought very clever for
identifying *caelibes* and *caelites,* because both bachelors
and gods are free of the heaviest burdens; he even supported this by a Greek argument, saying that *ēïtheoi* were
so called for the same reason.[47] Modestus[48] was no less ingenious; he says that bachelors are called *caelibes* because
Saturn cut off Caelus' genitals. And Aelius[49] derives *pituita*
("catarrh") from *petere vitam,* "to threaten life." But we
can pardon anyone after Varro,[50] who tried to persuade
Cicero (to whom he addressed his book) that *ager* comes
from *agere,* because things are *done* in a field, and *gragulus*
from *gregatim,* because jackdaws are *gregarious* in flight,
though the first word is obviously derived from the
Greek[51] and the second from the cry of the bird. But

[48] Presumably taken from the miscellany known to Gellius
(3.9.1). Caelus (Ouranos) was, in the myth, castrated by his son
Saturn (Kronos).

[49] L. Aelius Stilo, a learned scholar to whom both Cicero (see
Brutus 205–207) and Varro were indebted. Kaster (1995) 68–70.

[50] *De lingua Latina* 5.34 and 76.

[51] ἀγρός.

tanti fuit vertere, ut 'merula', quia sola volat, quasi mera volans nominaretur.

Quidam non dubitarunt etymologiae subicere omnem nominis causam, ut ex habitu, quem ad modum dixi, 'Longos' et 'Rufos', ex sono 'stertere' 'murmurare', etiam derivata, ut a 'veloci'[15] dicitur 'velocitas,'[16] et composita pleraque his similia, quae sine dubio alicunde[17] originem ducunt, sed arte non egent, cuius in hoc opere non est usus nisi in dubiis.

39   Verba a vetustate repetita non solum magnos adsertores habent, sed etiam adferunt orationi maiestatem aliquam non sine delectatione: nam et auctoritatem antiquitatis habent et, quia intermissa sunt, gratiam novitati
40   similem parant. Sed opus est modo, ut neque crebra sint haec nec manifesta, quia nihil est odiosius adfectatione, nec utique ab ultimis et iam oblitteratis repetita temporibus, qualia sunt 'topper' et 'antegerio' et 'exanclare' et 'prosapia' et Saliorum carmina vix sacerdotibus suis satis

---

[15] *Gertz*: velocitate *AB*
[16] *Gertz*: velox *AB*
[17] *Mueller*: aliunde *AB*

---

[52] Ibid. 5.76. Isidore (*Etymologiae* 12.7.45) agrees with Q.: see Maltby (1990) 262.

[53] 1.4.25.

[54] So Varro, *De lingua Latina* 6.67.

[55] Gertz' conjecture gives an example of *derivatio* where etymology is not needed, and it seems more natural to "derive" the noun from the adjective than *vice versa*. Later grammarians, how-

Varro[52] thought this sort of interpretation so important that he says that the word *merula* ("blackbird"), because it flies by itself, was named as *mera volans*.

Some scholars have not hesitated to make every explanation of a name a matter of etymology; for them, Longus and Rufus come from personal appearance (as I have said),[53] *stertere* ("snore") and *murmurare*[54] from the sound; they etymologize even derivatives, as *velocitas* from *velox*,[55] and compounds, and many other words like these, which no doubt do have an origin somewhere, but do not need this science, which has no use in the business except in doubtful cases.

Antiquity

Words taken from past ages not only have great men to urge their claims but also give the style a certain grandeur, not unmixed with charm; they have both the authority of age and, because they have fallen into disuse, an attraction like that of novelty. But moderation is essential; they must not be frequent or obvious (nothing is more tiresome than affectation), and certainly not taken from remote and now forgotten ages, like *topper, antegerio, exanclare, prosapia*,[56] and the hymns of the Salii that their own

---

ever, derive *velocitas* from *velo cita* (Charisius 393.20 Barwick), and *velox* from *velum* (Priscian 2.140 *GLK*).

[56] These words mean respectively "quickly," "very," "exhaust," "family." *Exanclare* and *prosapia* were used occasionally by Cicero; the other archaisms were not revived till after Q.'s time. See also 8.3.25–26.

41 intellecta. Sed illa mutari vetat religio et consecratis utendum est: oratio vero, cuius summa virtus est perspicuitas,
quam sit vitiosa si egeat interprete! Ergo ut novorum optima erunt maxime vetera, ita veterum maxime nova.

42 Similis circa auctoritatem ratio. Nam etiamsi potest
videri nihil peccare qui utitur iis verbis quae summi auctores tradiderunt, multum tamen refert non solum quid
dixerint, sed etiam quid persuaserint. Neque enim 'tubur-
chinabundum' et 'lurchinabundum' iam in nobis quisquam ferat, licet Cato sit auctor, nec 'hos lodices', quamquam id Pollioni placet, nec 'gladiola', atqui Messala dixit,
nec 'parricidatum', quod in Caelio vix tolerabile videtur,
nec 'collos' mihi Calvus persuaserit: quae nec ipsi iam
dicerent.

43 Superest igitur consuetudo: nam fuerit paene ridiculum malle sermonem quo locuti sint homines quam quo
loquantur. Et sane quid est aliud vetus sermo quam vetus
loquendi consuetudo? Sed huic ipsi necessarium est iudicium constituendumque in primis id ipsum quid sit quod
44 consuetudinem vocemus. Quae si ex eo quod plures fa-

---

57 Grammarians (including Varro) quote some passages of
these poems, which puzzled everyone (Horace, *Epistulae* 2.1.80)
and on which Aelius Stilo wrote a commentary. Text in Morel, *PLF*
1–5. The Salii, "dancers," were companions of priests who performed certain rites in honour of Mars and Quirinus. See also
1.10.20. See L. A. Holford-Strevens in *OCD*3, s.v. Carmen Saliare.

58 *ORF* p. 96. Both words mean "greedy, guzzling."

59 *ORF* p. 536: "these blankets." Q. takes the word to be
normally feminine.   60 *ORF* p. 534: "small swords." Neuter
plural instead of masculine *gladiolos*.

61 *ORF* p. 489: "parricide."

priests now hardly understand.[57] These indeed religion
forbids us to change; what is sacred must be kept in use.
But how faulty oratory (whose basic virtue is clarity) would
be if it needed an interpreter! So, as the best new words
will be the oldest, so the best old words will be the newest.

Authority

A similar principle applies to Authority. For though
anyone who uses the words recommended by the best
authors is sure not to go astray, it matters a great deal not
only what they said but what they made acceptable. No
one nowadays would put up with *tuburchinabundus* and
lurchinabundus, though Cato[58] is the authority for these
words, or with *hos lodices* (though Pollio approves)[59] or
gladiola (though Messala used it)[60] or *parricidatus*, which
is barely to be borne in Caelius.[61] Nor will Calvus persuade
me to say *collos*.[62] They would not use these words nowadays themselves.

Usage

So Usage remains: it would be almost laughable to use
the language people used to speak rather than that which
they speak today. Indeed, what is ancient speech except
the ancient Usage of speech? But here too we need judgement; we must first decide what we mean by Usage. If it
simply means "what most people do," it will give a very

---

[62] *ORF* p. 500: "neck" or "necks." Neuter was normal in imperial times, masculine in early Latin.

ciunt nomen accipiat, periculosissimum dabit praeceptum
non orationi modo sed, quod maius est, vitae: unde enim
tantum boni ut pluribus quae recta sunt placeant? Igitur ut
velli et comam in gradus frangere et in balneis perpotare,
quamlibet haec invaserint civitatem, non erit consuetudo,
quia nihil horum caret reprensione (at lavamur et tonde-
mur et convivimus ex consuetudine), sic in loquendo non
si quid vitiose multis insederit pro regula sermonis acci-
45 piendum erit. Nam ut transeam quem ad modum vulgo
imperiti loquantur, tota saepe theatra et omnem circi
turbam exclamasse barbare scimus. Ergo consuetudinem
sermonis vocabo consensum eruditorum, sicut vivendi
consensum bonorum.

7

1 Nunc, quoniam diximus quae sit loquendi regula, dicendum quae scribentibus custodienda, quod Graeci ortho-
graphian vocant, nos recte scribendi scientiam nomine-
mus. Cuius ars non in hoc posita est ut noverimus quibus
quaeque syllaba litteris constet (nam id quidem infra
grammatici officium est), sed totam, ut mea fert opinio,
2 subtilitatem in dubiis habet: ut longis syllabis omnibus
adponere apicem ineptissimum est, quia plurimae natura
ipsa verbi quod scribitur patent, sed interim necessarium,

63 See on 12.10.47. Similar analogies in Cicero, *Orator* 78,
Brutus 262.
1 See on 1.5.23.

dangerous rule, not only for oratory but (much more important) for life. For where can we be lucky enough to find a situation in which the majority like what is right? Plucking the hairs of the legs or armpits, arranging one's coiffure in tiers,[63] getting dead drunk at the baths—however universal these things have become in our society, they cannot be Usage, because they are all open to censure; yet we do of course wash and go to the barber's and have dinner parties, and all this *is* in accordance with Usage. So too in speech; we must not accept as a rule of language any bad habits which have become ingrained in many people. To say nothing of the language of the uneducated, we know that whole theatres and the entire circus crowd often commit Barbarisms in the shouting they make. I shall therefore define Usage in speech as the consensus of the educated, just as Usage in life is the consensus of the good.

CHAPTER 7

Correct writing: orthography

Having stated the rules of speaking, we must now give those which are to be observed in writing: the Greeks call this *orthographia;* let us call it the science of correct writing. This art does not consist simply in knowing the letters composing each syllable (for this is beneath the dignity of the *grammaticus*) but, as I see it, employs all its subtlety in doubtful cases. For example: it would be very silly to put an apex[1] over all long syllables, because the length of most of them is obvious from the nature of the word which is written, but it is *sometimes* necessary, namely when the same

185

cum eadem littera alium atque alium intellectum, prout
3 correpta vel producta est, facit: ut 'malus' arborem signi-
ficet an hominem non bonum apice distinguitur, 'palus'
aliud priore syllaba longa. aliud sequenti significat, et cum
eadem littera nominativo casu brevis, ablativo longa est,
utrum sequamur plerumque hac nota monendi sumus.
4 Similiter putaverunt illa quoque servanda discrimina, ut
'ex' praepositionem si verbum sequeretur 'specto', adiecta
secundae syllabae s littera, si 'pecto', remota scriberemus.
5 Illa quoque servata est a multis differentia, ut 'ad', cum
esset praepositio, D litteram, cum autem coniunctio, T ac-
ciperet, itemque 'cum', si tempus significaret, per 'quom,'
6 si comitem, per C ac duas sequentis scriberetur. Frigidiora
his alia, ut 'quidquid' C quartam haberet ne interrogare bis
videremur, et 'quotidie' non 'cotidie', ut sit quot diebus:
verum haec iam etiam inter ipsas ineptias evanuerunt.

7   Quaeri solet, in scribendo praepositiones sonum quem
iunctae efficiunt an quem separatae observare conveniat,
ut cum dico 'optinuit' (secundam enim B litteram ratio
8 poscit, aures magis audiunt P) et 'immunis' (illud enim

---

² *Pălūs* "marsh"; *pālŭs* "wooden stake."

³ *Exspecto* "expect"; *expecto* "comb out."

⁴ I.e. the preposition and the conjunction should be distinguished: on both Q.'s instances, see Marius Victorinus 4.30–33,
with I. Mariotti, *Marii Victorini Ars Grammatica* (Florence,
1967) 188–189.

⁵ "What? what?" This passage is evidence that Q. himself
wrote *quidquid*: Winterbottom (1970) 42.

⁶ "Every day." Velius Longus (7.79.17 *GLK*) declares *quotidie*
mistaken, because the word comes *non a quoto die sed a con-*

letter produces different senses if it is long and if it is short. Thus, in *malus,* an apex indicates that it means "apple tree" and not "bad man"; *palus* also means one thing if the first syllable is long and another if the second is long;[2] and when the same letter is found as short in the nominative and as long in the ablative, we commonly need to be reminded which interpretation to choose. Scholars have held on similar grounds that we should observe such distinctions as adding *s* to the second syllable when the preposition *ex* is compounded with the verb *specto,* but not if it is compounded with *pecto.*[3] Other distinctions observed by many scholars have included: *ad* as a preposition with a *d,* as a conjunction with a *t; cum* ("when") indicating time as *quom,* indicating accompaniment ("with") as *cum.*[4] Other recommendations were more unattractive: *c* as the fourth letter of *quidquid,* so as not to seem to be asking a question twice;[5] *quotidie* for *cotidie,* to show that it means *quot diebus.*[6] But these refinements have disappeared, even as specimens of folly.

The question is often asked whether, in writing prepositions, we should be guided by the sound they make in compounds or when separate: for example, when I say *optinuit* (Reason requires *b* as the second letter, but our ears hear *p*)[7] or *immunis*[8] (the *nm,* which the true sense

tinenti die. Victorinus (see Mariotti, op. cit. 191) also prefers *cotidie,* but keeps the derivation from *quoto die.*

[7] The etymological spelling (the one "Reason" demands) has affected derivatives (English *obtain*), but Q. must be right about the Latin pronunciation: Sihler (1995) 200.

[8] "Exempt": the negative prefix *in* + *munis: n* is always assimilated to following *m.* I hesitantly accept Colson's conjecture.

187

NM[1] quod veritas exigit, sequentis syllabae sono victum, M gemina commutatur).

9   Est et in dividendis verbis observatio, mediam litteram consonantem priori an sequenti syllabae adiungas. 'Haruspex' enim, quia pars eius posterior a spectando est, s litteram tertiae dabit, 'abstemius', quia ex abstinentia temeti composita vox est, primae relinquet.

10   Nam K quidem in nullis verbis utendum puto nisi quae significat etiam si[2] sola ponatur. Hoc eo non omisi quod quidam eam quotiens A sequatur necessariam credunt, cum sit C littera, quae ad omnis vocalis vim suam perferat.

11   Verum orthographia quoque consuetudini servit ideoque saepe mutata est. Nam illa vetustissima transeo tempora, quibus et pauciores litterae nec similes his nostris earum formae fuerunt et vis quoque diversa, sicut apud Graecos O litterae, quae interim longa ac brevis, ut apud nos, interim pro syllaba quam nomine suo exprimit posita

12   est: ut a Latinis veteribus D plurimis in verbis ultimam adiectam esse[3] manifestum est etiam ex columna rostrata, quae est Duilio in foro posita, interim G quoque, ut in pul-

---

[1] illud enim ‹NM› *Colson*: illud enim *K*: illud N *AB*
[2] *D.A.R.*: ut *AB*: ubi *Keil*: cum *Watt* 1988
[3] *D.A.R.*: quod *AB*

---

[9] *Tēmētum* is an old word for "wine" (see Aulus Gellius, 10.23.1). *Haruspex* probably does mean "an inspector of the intestines" of the sacrificial animals.

[10] E.g. *Kalendae, Kaeso.* See 1.4.9.

[11] The classical name of the letter o (omicron) was ου (Plato, *Cratylus* 414C), and it originally stood for the various sounds later expressed by o, ω, and ου.

demands, gives way to the sound of the second syllable, and is changed into a double *m*).

In dividing words also, one has to consider whether a middle consonant belongs to the preceding syllable or the following one: in *haruspex*, the second part of which comes from *specto*, the *s* belongs to the third syllable; whereas in *abstemius*, which is a compound meaning *abstinentia temeti*,[9] the *s* stays with the first syllable.

As for *k*, my view is that it should not be used in any words except those which it stands for even if it is put by itself.[10] I mention this because some hold that it is obligatory when *a* follows, although we possess *c*, which is capable of passing its force on to any vowel.

But orthography too is the servant of Usage, and has therefore often undergone change. I pass over the earliest period, when there were fewer letters and the shapes were different from ours, and also the value. Thus in Greek the letter *o* was sometimes long and short (as with us) and sometimes stood for the syllable which its name expresses;[11] just as the fact that in old Latin writings *d* was added at the end of many words[12] is established by the column with the beaks of ships erected in honour of Duilius in the Forum;[13] so sometimes also is *g*, as in *vesperug* on the

[12] Many forms in -*ē* had -*ēd* in older Latin (*mēd*, *tēd*) and there were ablatives in -*ōd*, -*ād*, and -*īd*. This old Indo-European feature was preserved in Italic dialects. Sihler (1995) 228.

[13] C. Duilius (Duellius, Cicero, *Orator* 153) defeated the Carthaginian fleet at Mylae in 260 BC. His victory was commemorated by a column decorated with the beaks of captured ships: for the inscription (*CIL* 1. 2, a copy made in imperial times), see Warmington, *ROL* 4. 128: note *pucnandod*, *marid*, *in altod*, to prove Q.'s point.

189

vinari Solis, qui colitur iuxta aedem Quirini, 'vesperug',
13 quod 'vesperuginem' accipimus. De mutatione etiam litterarum, de qua supra dixi, nihil repetere hic necesse est:
fortasse enim sicut scribebant, etiam loquebantur.
14 Semivocalis geminare diu non fuit usitatissimi moris,
atque e contrario usque ad Accium et ultra porrectas sylla-
15 bas geminis, ut dixi, vocalibus scripserunt. Diutius duravit
ut E et I iungendis eadem ratione qua Graeci [ei][4] uteren-
tur: ea casibus numerisque discretio[5] est, ut Lucilius praecipit:

> iam 'puerei venere': E postremum facito atque I
> ut pueri plures fiant

ac deinceps idem:

> mendaci furique addes E, cum dare furi[6]
> iusseris.

16 Quod quidem cum supervacuum est quia I tam longae
quam brevis naturam habet, tum incommodum aliquando;
nam in iis quae proximam ab ultima litteram E habebunt et
I longa terminabuntur, illam rationem sequentes utemur

---

[4] *del. Colson*
[5] *Watt* 1988: discreta *AB*
[6] furei *Lachmann*

---

[14] "Evening star." *Vesperug* cannot possibly be an archaic
form, and must be from a damaged or wrongly carved inscription.
A *pulvinar* is a couch on which images of the gods were laid in
certain ceremonials *(lectisternia),* but here it is a substantial and
permanent object: note that the Greek version of *Monumentum
Ancyranum* (19) renders *pulvinar ναόν,* "temple"; and Servius
(on Vergil, *Georgics* 3.532) speaks of using the word catachres-

pulvinar of the Sun near the temple of Quirinus: we understand this as *vesperugo*.[14] Of the interchange of letters I
have already spoken,[15] and need not repeat anything here;
maybe they actually spoke in those days as they wrote.

The doubling of semivowels was for a long time not the
most common usage, while on the contrary long syllables
were written (as I have said)[16] with double vowels down
to the time of Accius and beyond. The practice of joining *e*
and *i* on the same principle as the Greeks lasted longer;
it marks a distinction in cases and numbers, as Lucilius
tells us:[17]

> *iam puerei venere:* E *postremum facito atque* I,
> *ut pueri plures fiant;*

and later on:

> *mendaci furique addes* E, *cum dare furi*
> *iusseris.*

This is both unnecessary, because *i* can be either long or
short, and at times inconvenient, because if we follow this
principle, we shall have to use two *e*'s in words which have
e as the penultimate and a long *i* as the final letter, such as

---

tically for "temple." The reference here is to the cult of Sol Indiges
on the Quirinal, with a festival on 9 August.

[15] See 1.4.13.

[16] 1.4.10.

[17] Frs. 364–365 Marx = 377–378 Warmington, *ROL* 3. 116:
"Now the boys have come—make the ending *ei* to make sure the
boys are plural"; fr. 367 Marx = 380 Warmington (q.v. for discussion): "Add *e* to 'liar' and 'thief' when you tell someone to give to
the thief." (It is possible that we should read *furei* in Q.)

E gemina, qualia sunt haec 'aurei' 'argentei' et his similia:
17 idque iis praecipue qui ad lectionem instituentur etiam
impedimento erit, sicut in Graecis accidit adiectione ι
litterae, quam non solum dativis casibus in parte ultima
adscribunt, sed quibusdam etiam interponunt, ut in
ΛΗΙΣΤΗΙ, quia etymologia ex divisione in tris syllabas facta
desideret eam litteram.
18 AE syllabam, cuius secundam nunc E litteram ponimus,
varie per A et I efferebant, quidam semper ut Graeci,
quidam singulariter tantum, cum in dativum vel geneti-
vum casum incidissent, unde 'pictai vestis' et 'aquai' Vergi-
19 lius amantissimus vetustatis carminibus inseruit. In isdem
plurali numero E utebantur: 'hi Sullae, Galbae'. Est in hac
quoque parte Lucili praeceptum, quod quia pluribus
explicatur versibus, si quis parum credet apud ipsum in
nono requirat.
20 Quid quod Ciceronis temporibus paulumque infra,
fere quotiens S littera media vocalium longarum vel subiecta longis esset, geminabatur, ut 'caussae' 'cassus' 'divissiones'? Quo modo et ipsum et Vergilium quoque scrip-
21 sisse manus eorum docent. Atqui paulum superiores etiam
illud quod nos gemina dicimus 'iussi' una dixerunt.

---

18 "Golden" and "silver," nominative plural or genitive singular of the adjectives *aureus, argenteus*. Q. argues that the theory
he is attacking would require *aureei, argenteei*.
19 "Robber." This noun (from verb $\lambda\eta\ifmmode\zeta\else ί\fi\zeta\omega$) is in fact disyllabic
($\lambda\eta\sigma\tau\acute{\eta}\varsigma$) in Attic, but has three syllables in Ionic and in poetic
texts.
20 *Aeneid* 9.26, 7.464. *-āī* was thought a particularly characteristic feature of old poetry: see above on 1.5.17, and note Q.'s con-

aurei, argentei,[18] and the like, and this will actually be a hindrance, especially to those who are learning to read. We may compare the situation which arises in Greek from the addition of the letter iota, which they write not only in the ending of datives, but sometimes inside words, as in ΛΗΙΣΤΗΙ (*lēistēi*),[19] since etymology demands this letter because of the division of the word into three syllables.

The syllable *ae,* which now has *e* as second letter, was formerly expressed by *a* and *i,* by some writers in all circumstances (as in Greek), and by others only in the singular, when they came to the dative or genitive; hence that great lover of antiquity, Vergil, put *pictai vestis* and *aquai* in his verse.[20] In the same words, *e* was usual in the plural: *hi Sullae, Galbae.* Lucilius has advice to give about this too; but it occupies several lines, and I must ask the sceptical reader to consult the poet himself, in Book Nine.[21]

Again, in Cicero's days and somewhat later, it was the general practice to write *s* double when it occurred between two long vowels or after a long vowel, as in *caussae, cassus, divissiones.* That Cicero himself and Vergil both used this spelling is shown by their autographs.[22] And yet somewhat earlier writers spelt *iussi,* in which we have the double *s,* with one *s.*[23]

---

temporary Martial (11.90), who, in a short poem, ridicules both *Luceilei* and *terrai frugiferai.*

[21] See fr. 388 Warmington (we do not have the context).

[22] Simplification of -*ss*- to -*s*- after long vowels or diphthongs is quite late (*caussa* still in *Monumentum Ancyranum*): Allen (1965) 36, Sihler (1995) 222.

[23] This suggests that the *u* of *iussi* was short (Lindsay, *Latin Language* 111).

Iam 'optimus' 'maximus' ut mediam I litteram, quae veteribus U fuerat, acciperent C. primum Caesaris inscriptione traditur factum.

22   'Here' nunc E littera terminamus: at veterum comicorum adhuc libris invenio 'heri ad me venit': quod idem in epistulis Augusti, quas sua manu scripsit aut emendavit,

23   deprenditur. Quid? non Cato Censorius 'dicam' et 'faciam' 'dicae' et 'faciae' scripsit, eundemque in ceteris quae similiter cadunt modum tenuit? Quod et ex veteribus eius libris manifestum est et a Messala in libro de S littera posi-

24   tum. 'Sibe' et 'quase' scriptum in multorum libris est, sed an hoc voluerint auctores nescio: T. Livium ita his usum ex Pediano comperi, qui et ipse eum sequebatur. Haec nos I

25   littera finimus. Quid dicam 'vortices' et 'vorsus' ceteraque ad eundem modum, quae primus Scipio Africanus in E

26   litteram secundam vertisse dicitur? Nostri praeceptores 'servum' 'cervum'que U et O litteris scripserunt, quia subiecta sibi vocalis in unum sonum coalescere et confundi nequiret; nunc U gemina scribuntur ea ratione quam red-

---

24 Almost certainly the dictator, not Caligula as some have thought.

25 See 1.4.8.

26 "He came to me yesterday": Terence, *Phormio* 38. See 1.4.8.

27 We have *heri* in Suetonius, *Augustus* 71 and *Caligula* 8 (= *Fr. epist.* VII, XXV Malcovati). See also *Augustus* 87 for his use of colloquialisms, and ibid. 71.2 for reference to an autograph letter. Gellius 10.24.1 attests Augustus' great care for language.

28 Compare 9.4.39, where Q. speaks of Cato's "softening" the final *m* into *e;* but the statement remains puzzling.

29 Compare 9.4.38. Why should Messala's book on *s* contain this information? Perhaps he defended his views on suppressed

Again, an inscription of Gaius Caesar[24] is said to be the first authority for writing *optimus maximus* with *i* in the middle syllables, instead of *u*, as in older texts.[25]

We now write *here* with final *e*, but I still find in texts of the old comic writers *heri ad me venit*,[26] and this is also found in the letters of Augustus, which he either wrote or at least corrected himself.[27] And did not Cato the Censor write *dicam* and *faciam* as *dicae* and *faciae*,[28] and follow the same pattern in words of similar endings? We see this in old texts of his works and from what Messala says in his book on the letter *s*.[29] *Sibe* and *quase*[30] are found in texts of many writers, but whether the authors intended them or not, I do not know; I learn the fact that Livy used these forms from Pedianus,[31] who himself followed the example. We spell these words with a final *i*. And what about *vortices* and *vorsos* and the like, which Scipio Africanus is said to have been the first to spell with an *e* as second letter?[32] My teachers wrote *servos* ("slave") and *cervos* ("stag") with *vo*, on the ground that a vowel following itself could not coalesce or be blended to form a single sound. Today we

final *s* by citing the analogy of suppressed final *m*. Niedermann would read DICAΣ, FACIAΣ, assuming that Cato used *M* on its side for the final letter: this would look like *sigma*, and might be mentioned in Messala's book on *s*. The puzzle remains.

[30] For *sibi* ("for himself") and *quasi* ("as if").

[31] Asconius Pedianus is best known for his extant Cicero commentaries; Q.'s form of expression suggests that he knew him personally.

[32] Inscriptions confirm that *vert-* became dominant in the course of the second century BC; *vort-* is regular in early texts (e.g. Plautus) and was favoured by Sallust and later archaists like Apuleius.

didi: neutro sane modo vox quam sentimus efficitur, nec
inutiliter Claudius Aeolicam illam ad hos usus litteram
27 adiecerat. Illud nunc melius, quod 'cui' tribus quas prae-
posui litteris enotamus, in quo pueris nobis ad pinguem
sane sonum QU et OI utebantur, tantum ut ab illo 'qui'
distingueretur.

28   Quid quae scribuntur aliter quam enuntiantur? Nam et
'Gaius' C littera significatur, quae inversa mulierem decla-
rat, quia tam Gaias esse vocitatas quam Gaios etiam ex
29 nuptialibus sacris apparet: nec 'Gnaeus' eam litteram in
praenominis nota accipit qua sonat, et 'columnam' et
'consules' exempta N littera legimus, et 'Subura', cum tribus litteris notatur, C tertiam ostendit. Multa sunt generis
huius, sed haec quoque vereor ne modum tam parvae
quaestionis excesserint.

30   Iudicium autem suum grammaticus interponat his omnibus: nam hoc valere plurimum debet. Ego, nisi quod
consuetudo optinuerit, sic scribendum quidque iudico
31 quomodo sonat. Hic enim est usus litterarum ut custodiant
voces et velut depositum reddant legentibus. Itaque id exprimere debent quod dicturi sumus.

---

33 See 1.4.10–11.

34 See 1.4.8. Claudius' three new letters were to represent the
consonantal *u*, the sound in the second syllable of *optumus,* and
the sound of Greek *psi.* See Suetonius, *Claudius* 41 and the note
ad loc. in the LCL Suetonius, vol. II.

35 See *OLD* s.v. *qui* for these archaic forms.

36 For the formula "ubi tu Gaius, ibi ego Gaia" see Plutarch,
Quaestiones Romanae 30, Treggiari (1991) 26–27. Q.'s phraseol-
ogy is close to Cicero, *Pro Murena* 27.

37 Gnaeus is abbreviated Cn.

spell with two *u*'s, for the reason I gave.[33] Neither spelling really expresses the sound we hear. Claudius did a useful thing in adding the Aeolic letter for this purpose.[34] It is a modern improvement that we spell *cui* ("to whom") with these three letters; when I was a boy people used *quoi,* giving a very full sound, only to distinguish it from *qui.*[35]

And what about words written otherwise than they are pronounced? *C,* for instance, is used as an abbreviation for Gaius, and when inverted stands for a woman; for we see even in the marriage ceremony that Gaia as well as Gaius was a familiar name.[36] With Gnaeus, the abbreviation of the praenomen does not represent the pronunciation;[37] we read *columna*[38] and *consules*[39] without an *n*; and when *Subura* is represented by a three-letter abbreviation, the third letter is *c.*[40] There are many things of this kind; but I fear that these examples are already too many for such a trivial subject.

In all this, the *grammaticus* must apply his own judgement; this is what should have most weight. For my own part, I hold that (except where usage prevails) we should write everything just as it sounds. The use of letters is to keep safe sounds entrusted to them, as it were, and to restore them faithfully to readers. They ought therefore to represent what we are going to say.

[38] "Column." Compare the diminutive *columella.*

[39] "Consuls." The abbreviation is cos., coss.; *cosol* is a spelling found on an early inscription.

[40] Compare Varro, *De lingua Latina* 5.48: "I think it is rather called *Succusa* from the *pagus Succusanus* . . . it is now abbreviated SUC."

32   Hae fere sunt emendate loquendi scribendique partes: duas reliquas significanter ornateque dicendi non equidem grammaticis aufero, sed, cum mihi officia rhetoris supersint, maiori operi reservo.

33   Redit autem illa cogitatio, quosdam fore qui haec quae diximus parva nimium et impedimento[7] quoque maius aliquid agentibus putent: nec ipse ad extremam usque anxietatem et ineptas cavillationes descendendum atque his

34   ingenia concidi et comminui credo. Sed nihil ex grammatice nocuerit nisi quod supervacuum est. An ideo minor est M. Tullius orator quod idem artis huius diligentissimus fuit et in filio, ut epistulis apparet, recte loquendi asper quoque exactor? Aut vim C. Caesaris fregerunt editi de

35   analogia libri? Aut ideo minus Messala nitidus quia quosdam totos libellos non verbis modo singulis sed etiam litteris dedit? Non obstant hae disciplinae per illas euntibus, sed circa illas haerentibus.

8

1   Superest lectio: in qua puer ut sciat ubi suspendere spiritum debeat, quo loco versum distinguere, ubi cludatur sensus, unde incipiat, quando attollenda vel summittenda sit vox, quo quidque[1] flexu, quid lentius celerius concita-

---

[7] *Winterbottom*: impedimenta *AB*
[1] *Spalding*: quid quoque *AB*

---

[41] *Fr. epist.* VIII.5 Watt, Servius on Vergil, *Aeneid* 8.168: Cicero complains of his son's using *litteras duas* for "two epistles," since the plural *litterae* means "one epistle."
[42] See 1.5.63.   [43] See 1.5.15, 1.6.42, 1.7.23.

These are, in general, the topics concerned with correctness in speaking and writing; the two remaining topics, namely speaking with significance and elegance, I do not, of course, take away from the *grammaticus,* but, as I have yet to deal with the rhetor's duties, I reserve them for that more important work.

I am however still troubled by the thought that some readers will think what I have said very trivial and even an obstacle to those who have more important things to do. Nor do I myself think that one should descend into extreme meticulousness and foolish quibbling: natural talents, I think, are damaged and destroyed by this. But there is not much harm in *grammaticē,* except in its superfluous parts. Is Cicero less great as an orator for having been a close student of this science or for being (as his letters show) so stern in insisting on correct speech from his son?[41] Was Gaius Caesar's vigour impaired by his publishing books on Analogy?[42] Is Messala any less elegant because he devoted whole books not only to words but to letters?[43] These studies are no obstacle if they are taken as a stage to pass through, but only if you get stuck in them.

CHAPTER 8

Reading for boys

Reading remains to be discussed. In this, it is impossible, except by actual practice, to make it clear how a boy is to learn when to take a fresh breath, where to make a pause in a verse, where the sense ends or begins, when the voice is to be raised or lowered, what inflection should be given to

199

tius lenius dicendum, demonstrari nisi in opere ipso non
2 potest. Unum est igitur quod in hac parte praecipiam, ut
omnia ista facere possit: intellegat. Sit autem in primis lectio virilis et cum sanctitate[2] quadam gravis, et non quidem
prorsae similis, quia et carmen est et se poetae canere testantur, non tamen in canticum dissoluta nec plasmate, ut
nunc a plerisque fit, effeminata: de quo genere optime C.
Caesarem praetextatum adhuc accepimus dixisse: 'si can-
3 tas, male cantas: si legis, cantas'. Nec prosopopoeias, ut
quibusdam placet, ad comicum morem pronuntiari velim,
esse tamen flexum quendam quo distinguantur ab iis in
quibus poeta persona sua utetur.
4   Cetera admonitione magna egent, in primis ut tenerae
mentes tracturaeque altius quidquid rudibus et omnium
ignaris insederit non modo quae diserta sed vel magis quae
5 honesta sunt discant. Ideoque optime institutum est ut ab
Homero atque Vergilio lectio inciperet, quamquam ad in-
tellegendas eorum virtutes firmiore iudicio opus est: sed
huic rei superest tempus, neque enim semel legentur.
Interim et sublimitate heroi carminis animus adsurgat et
ex magnitudine rerum spiritum ducat et optimis inbuatur.
6 Utiles tragoediae: alunt et lyrici, si tamen in iis non auctores modo sed etiam partes operis elegeris: nam et Graeci
licenter multa et Horatium nolim in quibusdam interpretari. Elegia vero, utique quae[3] amat, et hendecasyllabi, qui

---

[2] suavitate B   [3] t: qua AB (qua amatur Colson)

---

[1] An otherwise unknown story, which may be about the young
Caligula rather than Julius Caesar; but see Suetonius, *Divus Iulius*
56.7 for a collection of Julius' juvenile sayings, suppressed by Augustus.   [2] Compare 11.3.91.

each phrase, and what should be spoken slowly or quickly, excitedly or calmly. So the only advice I can give on this subject, to enable him to do all these things, is: let him understand his text. The first point is that his reading should be manly and dignified, and display a certain solemnity, not like prose (because this is poetry and the poets claim to "sing") but not degenerating into sing-song or the effeminate artificiality that is now so popular. There is an excellent remark about this attributed to Gaius Caesar as a boy: "If you are singing, you are singing badly; if you are reading, you are singing."[1] Nor do I think that Prosopopoeiae, as some advise, should be pronounced in the manner of the comic stage, though there should be some inflection of the voice to distinguish them from passages in which the poet speaks in his own person.[2]

The other aspects of reading require important cautions: above all, these tender minds, which will be deeply affected by whatever is impressed upon them in their untrained ignorance, should learn not only eloquent passages but, even more, passages which are morally improving. The practice of making reading start with Homer and Vergil is therefore excellent. Of course it needs a more developed judgement to appreciate their virtues; but there is time enough for this, for they will be read more than once. Meanwhile, let the mind be uplifted by the sublimity of the heroic poems, and inspired and filled with the highest principles by the greatness of their theme. Tragedy is useful; and even lyric poets are educative, so long as you select not only the authors but the parts of their works to be read, because the Greeks have a good deal that is licentious, and there are some things in Horace that I should not care to explain in class. Elegy (especially when it is about love) and

sunt commata sotadeorum (nam de sotadeis ne praecipiendum quidem est), amoveantur si fieri potest, si minus,
7   certe ad firmius aetatis robur reserventur. Comoediae,
quae plurimum conferre ad eloquentiam potest, cum per
omnis et personas et adfectus eat, quem usum in pueris
putem paulo post suo loco dicam: nam cum mores in tuto
8   fuerint, inter praecipua legenda erit. De Menandro loquor, nec tamen excluserim alios, nam Latini quoque auctores adferent utilitatis aliquid; sed pueris quae maxime
ingenium alant atque animum augeant praelegenda: ceteris, quae ad eruditionem modo pertinent, longa aetas spatium dabit. Multum autem veteres etiam Latini conferunt,
quamquam plerique plus ingenio quam arte valuerunt, in
primis copiam verborum: quorum in tragoediis gravitas, in
comoediis elegantia et quidam velut atticismos inveniri
9   potest. Oeconomia quoque in iis diligentior quam in plerisque novorum erit, qui omnium operum solam virtutem
sententias putaverunt. Sanctitas certe et, ut sic dicam, viri-
litas ab iis petenda est, quando nos in omnia deliciarum vi-
10 tia dicendi quoque ratione defluximus. Denique credamus
summis oratoribus, qui veterum poemata vel ad fidem cau-
11 sarum vel ad ornamentum eloquentiae adsumunt. Nam
praecipue quidem apud Ciceronem, frequenter tamen

---

3 Hendecasyllables (---∪∪-∪-∪--) and Sotadeans (see
9.4.6, 9.4.90) are light-verse metres. Marius Victorinus (6.153
GLK) illustrates Q.'s point by showing that the hendecasyllable
carmen Pierides dabunt sorores can be turned into a Sotadean by
adding one word: *carmen lepidae Pierides dabunt sorores.*

4 See 10.1.69–72.   5 See 1.11. on the value of training in
acting techniques.   6 So Ovid (*Tristia* 2.424) of Ennius:
ingenio maximus, arte rudis.

hendecasyllables, which are portions of sotadeans³ (no advice is needed about sotadeans themselves!), should be banned if possible, or, if not, at least reserved for more mature years. As to comedy,⁴ whose contribution to eloquence can be very great, since it involves every kind of character and emotion, I shall point out soon, in its proper place, what use I think it is to boys.⁵ Of course, once the moral character is secure, it will be among the principal things to be read—Menander, I mean—though I should not rule out others either, for even the Latin authors will be of some service. But with boys, the texts to be read should be those which will best nourish the mind and develop the character. Life will give time enough for the rest, which are important only for academic scholarship. The old Latin poets also, though most of them were stronger in natural talent than in art,⁶ can make an important contribution, especially in richness of vocabulary; in their tragedies one can find dignity, in their comedies elegance and a kind of Attic quality. They are also more careful about organization than most of the moderns, who have come to think that clever phrases *(sententiae)* are the only virtue in any work. Certainly a high moral tone, and, if I may say so, manliness, has to be sought from them, now that we have degenerated into all the vices of voluptuousness even in our style of speaking. Finally, let us trust the great orators, who use the works of the early poets either to support their cases or to adorn their eloquence. Particularly in Cicero,⁷

---

⁷ Quotations from comedy are numerous in *Pro Caelio*; but Cicero uses poetical passages much more freely in his philosophical works than in his speeches.

apud Asinium etiam et ceteros qui sunt proximi, videmus
Enni Acci Pacuvi Lucili Terenti Caecili et aliorum inseri
versus, summa[4] non eruditionis modo gratia sed etiam
iucunditatis, cum poeticis voluptatibus aures a forensi
12 asperitate respirant. Quibus accedit non mediocris utilitas,
cum sententiis eorum velut quibusdam testimoniis quae
proposuere confirment.

Verum priora illa ad pueros magis, haec sequentia ad
robustiores pertinebunt, cum grammatices amor et usus
lectionis non scholarum temporibus sed vitae spatio terminentur.

13 In praelegendo grammaticus et illa quidem minora
praestare debebit, ut partes orationis reddi sibi soluto ver-
su desideret et pedum proprietates, quae adeo[5] debent
esse notae in carminibus ut etiam in oratoria compositione
14 desiderentur. Deprendat quae barbara, quae inpropria,
quae contra legem loquendi sint posita, non ut ex his
utique improbentur poetae (quibus, quia plerumque servire metro coguntur, adeo ignoscitur ut vitia ipsa aliis in
carmine appellationibus nominentur: metaplasmus enim
et schematismus seu[6] schemata, ut dixi, vocamus et laudem virtutis necessitati damus), sed ut commoneat arti-

[4] summae *Buchheit*   [5] ideo *Colson*
[6] *Spalding*: et *AB*

[8] See 10.1.113; Tacitus, *Dialogus* 21.7 reports Pollio's liking
for early tragedy; for his own tragedies (no fragment extant) see
Horace, *Carmina* 2.1.9, *Sermones* 1.10.42, Vergil, *Eclogues* 8.10.

[9] Some translators prefer "nearest to *our* times."

[10] *Priora* means the advice to read poems, *sequentia* the remarks on the use of quotations (§§10–12).

but often also in Asinius[8] and others nearest to their
times,[9] we find inserted lines from Ennius, Accius,
Pacuvius, Lucilius, Terence, Caecilius and others, producing great charm not only from the learning shown but from
the pleasure given by allowing the audience to relax from
the asperities of the courtroom in the delights of poetry.
There is considerable practical advantage in this also, because orators adduce the sentiments of the poets as a kind
of evidence to support their own positions.

Reading for older students

What I said first applies more to small boys; what came
next will be found relevant to older students;[10] the love
of *grammaticē* and the habit of reading do not end with
schooldays, but only with life.

In expounding his text, the *grammaticus* must also deal
with more elementary matters. He must ask the pupils to
break up the verse and give the parts of speech and the
qualities of the metrical feet, which need to become so
familiar in poetry that the need for them is felt also in rhetorical Composition. He must point out Barbarisms, improper usages, and anything contrary to the laws of speech,
not by way of censuring the poets for these (for poets are
often forced to be the slaves of metre, and are so far for-
given that the faults themselves have other names when
they occur in poetry; we call them, as I said,[11] Metaplasms
and Schematisms or Schemata, and make a virtue of necessity), but to remind the pupil of technical rules and activate

[11] 1.5.52–53.

ficialium et memoriam agitet.

15   Id quoque inter prima rudimenta non inutile demonstrare, quot quaeque verba modis intellegenda sint. Circa
glossemata etiam, id est voces minus usitatas, non ultima
16 eius professionis diligentia est. Enimvero iam maiore cura
doceat tropos omnes, quibus praecipue non poema modo
sed etiam oratio ornatur, schemata utraque, id est figuras,
quaeque lexeos quaeque dianoeas vocantur: quorum ego
sicut troporum tractatum in eum locum differo quo mihi
17 de ornatu orationis dicendum erit. Praecipue vero illa
infigat animis, quae in oeconomia virtus, quae in decore
rerum, quid personae cuique convenerit, quid in sensibus
laudandum, quid in verbis, ubi copia probabilis, ubi
modus.

18   His accedet enarratio historiarum, diligens quidem illa,
non tamen usque ad supervacuum laborem occupata: nam
receptas aut certe claris auctoribus memoratas exposuisse
satis est. Persequi quidem quid quis umquam vel con-
temptissimorum hominum dixerit aut nimiae miseriae aut
inanis iactantiae est, et detinet atque obruit ingenia melius
19 aliis vacatura. Nam qui omnis etiam indignas lectione sci-
das excutit, anilibus quoque fabulis accommodare operam
potest: atqui pleni sunt eius modi impedimentis grammati-
corum commentarii, vix ipsis qui composuerunt satis noti.
20 Nam Didymo, quo nemo plura scripsit, accidisse comper-

---

12 See 1.1.35.

13 I.e. in Books Eight and Nine.

14 See on 1.4.4.

15 Said to have written up to 4000 books (Seneca, *Epistulae*
88.37) and nicknamed "brazenguts" *(chalcenteros)* for his indefat-

his memory of them.

At this elementary stage, it is also useful to show in how many ways particular words may be understood. "Glosses"[12] also, that is to say words not in common use, are not the least important area of grammatical scholarship. The *grammatici,* however, should take greater care in teaching all the Tropes, which are the main ornaments not only of poetry but also of oratory, and both kinds of Schemata—that is to say, Figures of Speech *(lexis)* and of Thought *(dianoia)* as they are called; these, like the Tropes, I postpone till I come to deal with the ornaments of style.[13] Above all, he should impress upon their minds what is meant by excellence in organization, and in propriety of subject matter; what is appropriate to particular characters; what is praiseworthy in thought or word; and when abundance is acceptable, and when restraint.

A further task will be the explanation of historical allusions;[14] this must be scholarly, but not overloaded with superfluous labour. It is quite enough to expound versions which are traditional or at any rate rest on good authority. To hunt down everything ever said even by the most despised writer means either wretched pedantry or ostentatious vanity. It suppresses and smothers talents which would be better kept free for other matters. For anyone who goes carefully through every page, whether worth reading or not, may just as well deploy his energies on old wives' tales. Commentaries by *grammatici* are full of this sort of lumber, and are scarcely known to their authors themselves. There is a well-known story of Didymus[15]

igable energy. Part of a commentary on Demosthenes' *Philippics* is extant, ed. L. Pearson and S. Stephens (1983).

tum est ut, cum historiae cuidam tamquam vanae repug-
21 naret, ipsius proferretur liber qui eam continebat. Quod
evenit praecipue in fabulosis usque ad deridicula quaedam, quaedam etiam pudenda, unde improbissimo cuique
pleraque fingendi licentia est, adeo ut de libris totis et auctoribus, ut succurrit, mentiantur tuto, quia inveniri qui
numquam fuere non possunt: nam in notioribus frequentissime deprenduntur a curiosis. Ex quo mihi inter virtutes
grammatici habebitur aliqua nescire.

9

1 Et finitae quidem sunt partes duae quas haec professio
pollicetur, id est ratio loquendi et enarratio auctorum,
quarum illam methodicen, hanc historicen vocant. Adicia-
mus tamen eorum curae quaedam dicendi primordia
quibus aetatis nondum rhetorem capientis instituant.

2 Igitur Aesopi fabellas, quae fabulis nutricularum
proxime succedunt, narrare sermone puro et nihil se supra
modum extollente, deinde eandem gracilitatem stilo exigere condiscant. Versus primo solvere, mox mutatis verbis

---

The *Parallela Minora* ascribed to Plutarch (*Moralia* 305A–316B) contains references to authorities which seem to be inventions of this sort: see in general W. Speyer, *Die literarische Falschung in Altertum* (1971) 75–78.

1 See 1.4.2 above. This division resembles that given by Diomedes (1.426 *GLK*) into "exegetic" and "horistic," the latter being concerned with normative rules, parts of speech, and so on. *Grammaticē* was divided in various ways: Blank (1998) 146–148.

2 See 2.1.7.

(and no one ever wrote more than he did), that when he was arguing against some historical account as being absurd, one of his own books was produced which contained the story in question. This happens especially in mythology, and sometimes reaches ludicrous or even scandalous extremes, so that the most unscrupulous writer has plenty of scope for invention, and can even lie in any way that occurs to him about whole books or authorities—all quite safely, because those which never existed cannot be found.[16] When they venture on more familiar ground, such people are often caught out by the curious. That is why I shall reckon it among the virtues of the *grammaticus* not to know some things.

CHAPTER 9

Progymnasmata taught by the grammaticus

This concludes the two subjects which this profession claims to undertake, namely the principles of speech and the exegesis of the authors; the first of these is called "methodical" and the second "historical" *grammaticē*.[1] Let us add to these duties, however, some elements of oratory in which they are to instruct pupils still too young for the rhetor.[2]

Let them learn then to tell Aesop's fables, which follow on directly from their nurses' stories,[3] in pure and unpretentious language; then let them achieve the same slender elegance in a written version. Verse they should first break

---

[3] *Mūthos*, "fable," generally comes first in the curriculum of progymnasmata, though Theon (72 Spengel) treats *chria* first.

interpretari, tum paraphrasi audacius vertere, qua et
breviare quaedam et exornare salvo modo poetae sensu
3 permittitur. Quod opus, etiam consummatis professoribus
difficile, qui commode tractaverit cuicumque discendo
sufficiet.

Sententiae quoque et chriae et ethologiae[1] subiectis
dictorum rationibus apud grammaticos scribantur, quia
initium ex lectione ducunt: quorum omnium similis est
ratio, forma diversa, quia sententia universalis est vox,
4 ethologia[2] personis continetur. Chriarum plura genera traduntur: unum simile sententiae, quod est positum in voce
simplici: 'dixit ille' aut 'dicere solebat'; alterum quod est
in respondendo: 'interrogatus ille', vel 'cum hoc ei dictum
esset, respondit'; tertium huic non dissimile: 'cum quis
5 dixisset aliquid' vel 'fecisset'. Etiam in ipsorum factis esse

---

[1] *Regius*: aet(h)iologiae *AB*

[2] *Regius*: aet(h)iologia *AB* (aetiologia ‹rebus, chria› personis
Winterbottom)

---

[4] "Aphorism," Greek *gnōmē*, consists of paraphrasing and il-
lustrating a common saying (e.g. "Welcome the coming, speed the
parting guest"); *chria* (χρεία) is a saying or anecdote of a notable
person, and includes remarks on the person concerned (e.g.
"Isocrates said that the root of education is bitter, but its fruit
is sweet"). For the third progymnasma, the manuscripts give
aethiologia or *aetiologia*. This could mean (1) explanation of
causes (see 2.4.26, where exercises developing the *aition* of some
practice or symbol are regarded as a type of *chria*), or (2) a brief
argument making a doubtful proposition seem convincing
(Rutilius Lupus 2.19). Neither seems very appropriate; neither
"depends on persons." *Ethologia,* read by most editors down to
Radermacher, and meaning "description of character" or "speech

up, then interpret in different words, then make a bolder paraphrase, in which they are allowed to abbreviate and embellish some parts, so long as the poet's meaning is preserved. This task is difficult even for fully trained teachers; any pupil who handles it well will be capable of learning anything.

Aphorisms, Chriae, and Ethologiae[4] may also be written under the *grammatici*, so long as the arguments are supplied, because the themes can come out of reading.[5] The principle of all these exercises is similar, but their forms are very different: an Aphorism is a universal statement, Ethologia depends on persons. As to Chriae,[6] there are several sorts of these: one is akin to Aphorism and rests on a simple statement ("he said" or "he used to say"); another includes an answer ("being asked" or "when this was said to him, he answered"). There is a third type, much the same: "when someone said"—or "did"—"something." A Chria may also, it is thought, consist only of the subject's

---

in character" (like *ēthopoiia*) seems on balance to be preferred. But see Winterbottom (1970) 67–68, Morgan (1998) 192 n. 9 for the contrary view. See 2.4 for these exercises as taught by the rhetor.

[5] Q. means that, with all these exercises, the pupils' reading provides the quotations or anecdotes which are the material; at this stage, the pupils will not be able to develop the arguments for themselves.

[6] On types of *chria*, see Theon 98–106 Spengel. Recent literature on the subject is listed in *CRHP* pp. 764, 767: note especially R. F. Hock and E. N. O'Neil, *The Chreia in Ancient Rhetoric, I, The Progymnasmata* (Atlanta, 1986). There is a good brief sketch of the early history in A. S. F. Gow, *Machon* (Cambridge, 1965) 12–15.

QUINTILIAN

chrian putant, ut: 'Crates, cum indoctum puerum vidisset,
paedagogum eius percussit', et aliud paene par ei, quod
tamen eodem nomine appellare non audent, sed dicunt
χρειῶδες, ut: 'Milo, quem vitulum adsueverat ferre, tau-
rum ferebat'. In his omnibus et declinatio per eosdem
ducitur casus et tam factorum quam dictorum ratio est.

6   Narratiunculas a poetis celebratas notitiae causa, non
eloquentiae tractandas puto. Cetera maioris operis ac spiritus Latini rhetores relinquendo necessaria grammaticis
fecerunt: Graeci magis operum suorum et onera et modum norunt.

10

1   Haec de grammatice, quam brevissime potui, non ut omnia dicerem sectatus, quod infinitum erat, sed ut maxime
necessaria. Nunc de ceteris artibus quibus instituendos
priusquam rhetori tradantur pueros existimo strictim
subiungam, ut efficiatur orbis ille doctrinae quem Graeci
encyclion paedian vocant.

7 Also told of Diogenes ([Hermogenes] p. 6 Rabe, Aphthonius, *Progymnasmata* p. 4 Rabe).   8 This is a Chria "without
words," like "Diogenes lit a lamp in broad daylight and started
looking for a human being" (Diomedes 1. 310 *GL*).

9 The "declension" of Chriae was an exercise in grammar, in
which all the cases and numbers were used: "the philosopher Pythagoras advised his pupils . . . " is turned, e.g., into "it is said that
the two philosophers Pythagoras advised . . . " (E. Ziebarth (1913)
16; Morgan (1998) 156–157). See also Theon 101–102 Spengel.

10 Perhaps "confirmation," "refutation," "introduction of a
law," "thesis."

1 This phrase is the origin of "encyclopaedia." It is used by

action: "When Crates[7] saw an ill-educated boy, he beat his *paedagogus.*" A very similar example—which they do not venture to call a Chria but say it is "of the Chria type"—is "Milo[8] carried a grown bull which he had been used to carry as a calf." All these can be declined through the same range of cases,[9] and the principle applies to Chriae based on actions as well as those based on words.

Short narratives found in the poets should, in my view, be taught for general knowledge, not for developing eloquence. Larger and more ambitious exercises[10] have been forced on the *grammatici* by Latin rhetors who have abandoned them; the Greeks know the burdens and the limits of their work better.

CHAPTER 10

What other arts should the orator learn?

I have been as concise as possible in this discussion of *grammaticē,* making no attempt to mention everything (that would have been an endless task) but selecting the most essential points. I shall now briefly add something about the other arts in which I think boys should be trained before they are passed on to the rhetor, so as to complete the course of learning which the Greeks call *enkyklios paideia.*[1]

Hellenistic and Roman writers to cover a range of studies, both literary and mathematical, not always the same, but conceived as forming a whole (Vitruvius 1.1.12: *encyclios enim disciplina uti corpus unum ex his membris est composita* "the cycle of learning is formed as a single body out of these limbs, as it were"). This educational ideal developed later into the medieval *trivium* and *quadrivium.* See Hadot (1984) chs. 1–2; Morgan (1998) 33–38.

2   Nam isdem fere annis aliarum quoque disciplinarum studia ingredienda sunt: quae quia et ipsae artes sunt et esse perfectae sine orandi scientia possunt nec rursus ad efficiendum oratorem satis valent solae, an sint huic operi

3 necessariae quaeritur. Nam quid, inquiunt, ad agendam causam dicendamve sententiam pertinet scire quem ad modum in data linea constitui triangula aequis lateribus possint? Aut quo melius vel defendet reum vel reget consilia qui citharae sonos nominibus et spatiis distinxerit?

4 Enumerent etiam fortasse multos quamlibet utiles foro qui neque geometren audierint nec musicos nisi hac communi voluptate aurium intellegant.

   Quibus ego primum hoc respondeo, quod M. Cicero scripto ad Brutum libro frequentius testatur: non eum a nobis institui oratorem qui sit aut fuerit, sed imaginem quandam concepisse nos animo perfecti illius et nulla

5 parte cessantis. Nam et sapientem formantes eum qui sit futurus consummatus undique et, ut dicunt, mortalis quidam deus, non modo cognitione caelestium et[1] mortalium putant instruendum, sed per quaedam parva sane, si ipsa demum aestimes, ducunt, sicut exquisitas interim ambiguitates: non quia κερατίναι aut κροκοδίλιναι possint facere sapientem, sed quia illum ne in minimis quidem

---

[1] *Andresen*: vel *AB*

---

[2] *Orator* 3–6, 7–10, 100–101.

[3] "If you have not lost something, you have it; but you have not lost horns; therefore you have horns" (Diogenes Laertius 7.186 = *SVF* 2. 279: compare Seneca, *Epistulae* 49.8).

[4] "If the crocodile catches your slave and then promises to give

It is during these same years that the study of other subjects too must generally begin. Now, as they are arts in their own right and can be perfected without any knowledge of oratory, and on the other hand are not sufficient on their own to produce an orator, the question arises whether they are necessary to our work. What relevance (say some) to pleading a Cause or stating your opinion has the knowledge of how to construct an equilateral triangle on a given line? Will it make a man better at defending a client or guiding policy if he knows the different names and intervals of the notes of a lyre? Perhaps they will even give a long list of people, very serviceable in the courts, who never heard a mathematician lecture and know nothing of the musicians except from the pleasure of listening which we all share.

My answer to these critics is, in the first place, what Marcus Cicero[2] frequently says in the book he addressed to Brutus: I am not educating an orator who really exists or has existed, but I have in my mind an image of the ideal orator who has no imperfections at all. Even those who seek to form the Wise Man who is to be perfect in all respects, and, as they say, a sort of mortal god, not only require him to be instructed in the knowledge of things divine and human, but train him in some matters which, if you look at them in themselves, are quite trivial—subtle ambiguities for example—not of course because the fallacies of the "horn"[3] and the "crocodile"[4] can make a man wise, but because he ought not to make mistakes even in little things.

him back if you say correctly what he has decided to do about returning him, what will you say he has decided?" (Lucian, *Sale of Lives* 22 = SVF 2. 287).

6   oporteat falli. Similiter oratorem, qui debet esse sapiens, non geometres faciet aut musicus quaeque his alia subiungam, sed hae quoque artes ut sit consummatus iuvabunt: nisi forte antidotus quidem atque alia quae oculis aut vulneribus medentur ex multis atque interim contrariis quoque inter se effectibus componi videmus, quorum ex diversis fit una illa mixtura quae nulli eorum[2] similis est ex

7   quibus constat, sed proprias vires ex omnibus sumit, et muta animalia mellis illum inimitabilem humanae rationi saporem vario florum ac sucorum genere perficiunt: nos mirabimur si oratio, qua nihil praestantius homini dedit providentia, pluribus artibus egeat, quae, etiam cum se non ostendunt in dicendo nec proferunt, vim tamen occul-

8   tam suggerunt et tacitae quoque sentiuntur. 'Fuit aliquis sine iis disertus'. Sed ego oratorem volo. 'Non multum adiciunt'. Sed aeque non erit totum cui vel parva deerunt. Et optimum quidem hoc esse conveniet: cuius etiamsi in arduo spes est, nos tamen praecipiamus omnia, ut saltem plura fiant. Sed cur deficiat animus? Natura enim perfectum oratorem esse non prohibet, turpiterque desperatur quidquid fieri potest.

9   Atque ego vel iudicio veterum poteram esse contentus. Nam quis ignorat musicen, ut de hac primum loquar, tantum iam illis antiquis temporibus non studii modo verum etiam venerationis habuisse ut idem musici et vates et sapientes iudicarentur (mittam alios) Orpheus et Linus: quorum utrumque dis genitum, alterum vero, quia rudes

---

    [2] *Spalding*: earum *AB*

---

    [5] Compare 12.11.25–30.

Similarly, the orator, who ought to be a wise man, will not be produced by the mathematician or the musician or any of the other subjects I shall mention, but these arts will help him to attain perfection. We see that antidotes and other remedies for eyes or wounds are composed of many ingredients which sometimes have effects which counteract one another, and from this diversity is formed a single mixture which is unlike any of the ingredients but acquires its own qualities from them all; likewise, dumb creatures turn various kinds of flowers and juices into that flavour of honey which no human skill can imitate: are we then to be surprised if oratory, the highest gift of providence to man, stands in need of a number of arts which, even if they do not display or intrude themselves in speaking, nevertheless supply some secret force and make their silent presence felt? "But people have been fluent speakers without these." Yes: but I am asking for the real orator. "They add little." Yes, but if even small parts are missing, the whole is just as incomplete. It will be acknowledged that this is the ideal; if hopes of it are difficult to fulfil, let us none the less give advice on everything, so that at any rate more of it can be achieved. But why should our courage fail? Nature does not forbid the appearance of the perfect orator, and it is disgraceful to despair of anything that is possible.[5]

Music

Personally, I should be happy simply to accept the view of antiquity. Everyone knows that music (to speak of this first) was not only so much studied in ancient times but also so much venerated that Orpheus and Linus (to mention no others) were regarded both as musicians and as

quoque atque agrestes animos admiratione mulceret, non
feras modo sed saxa etiam silvasque duxisse posteritatis
10 memoriae traditum est. Itaque et Timagenes auctor est
omnium in litteris studiorum antiquissimam musicen extitisse, et testimonio sunt clarissimi poetae, apud quos inter
regalia convivia laudes heroum ac deorum ad citharam
canebantur. Iopas vero ille Vergili nonne

canit errantem lunam solisque labores

et cetera? Quibus certe palam confirmat auctor eminentis-
simus musicen cum divinarum etiam rerum cognitione
11 esse coniunctam. Quod si datur, erit etiam oratori necessaria, si quidem, ut diximus, haec quoque pars, quae ab oratoribus relicta a philosophis est occupata, nostri operis fuit
ac sine omnium talium scientia non potest esse perfecta
12 eloquentia. Atqui claros nomine sapientiae viros nemo dubitaverit studiosos musices fuisse, cum Pythagoras atque
eum secuti acceptam sine dubio antiquitus opinionem vul-
gaverint mundum ipsum ratione esse compositum, quam
postea sit lyra imitata, nec illa modo contenti dissimilium
concordia, quam vocant harmonian, sonum quoque his
13 motibus dederint. Nam Plato cum in aliis quibusdam tum

---

6 Orpheus was the son of the Muse Calliope, Linus of Apollo.

7 So (e.g.) Euripides, *Iphigenia at Aulis* 1211; Horace, *Carmina* 1.12.6, 3.11.12.

8 *F Gr Hist* 88 A 10; G. Bowersock, *Augustus and the Greek World* (Oxford, 1965) 124–126; see 10.1.75.

prophets and wise men. Both, we are told, were of divine birth,[6] while the former, because admiration of him calmed even rude and savage minds, has been believed by later ages to have drawn not only the animals but the rocks and stones after him.[7] So too Timagenes[8] asserts that music is the oldest of all literary arts, and this is confirmed by the evidence of the greatest poets, in whom the praises of heroes and gods were sung to the accompaniment of the lyre at royal banquets.[9] And does not Vergil's Iopas[10] "sing of the wandering moon and the sun's labours" and so on? This is open confirmation by a very great writer that music is connected also with the knowledge of things divine. If this is granted, it will be essential also to the orator, because (as we said) this area too, though abandoned by orators and taken over by philosophers, once belonged to our work, and eloquence cannot be perfect without the knowledge of all such things. In any case, no one can doubt that some men famous for wisdom have been students of music; Pythagoras and his followers, after all, popularized the belief, which no doubt they inherited from antiquity, that the world itself was constructed on the principle which the lyre later imitated; furthermore, not content with the "concord of unlikes" which they call "harmony," they attributed a sound also to these motions.[11] Various passages in Plato,

[9] Q. is thinking of scenes like the performance of Demodocus at the court of Alcinous in Homer, *Odyssey* 8.

[10] *Aeneid* 1.740–746.

[11] The "music of the spheres" was familiar from, e.g., Plato, *Republic* 10. 617B, Cicero, *Somnium Scipionis* 18–19 (where Q.'s idea that human music *imitates* heavenly is also found), *De natura deorum* 3.27 (see A. S. Pease ad loc.).

praecipue in Timaeo ne intellegi quidem nisi ab iis qui
hanc quoque partem disciplinae diligenter perceperint
potest. Quid[3] de philosophis loquar,[4] quorum fons ipse
14   Socrates iam senex institui lyra non erubescebat? Duces
maximos et fidibus et tibiis cecinisse traditum, exercitus
Lacedaemoniorum musicis accensos modis. Quid autem
aliud in nostris legionibus cornua ac tubae faciunt? Quorum concentus quanto est vehementior, tantum Romana
15   in bellis gloria ceteris praestat. Non igitur frustra Plato
civili viro, quem πολιτικόν vocat, necessariam musicen
credidit, et eius sectae, quae aliis severissima aliis asperri-
ma videtur, principes in hac fuere sententia, ut existima-
rent sapientium aliquos nonnullam operam his studiis
accommodaturos, et Lycurgus, durissimarum Lacedae-
16   moniis legum auctor, musices disciplinam probavit. Atque
eam natura ipsa videtur ad tolerandos facilius labores velut
muneri nobis dedisse, siquidem et remigem cantus horta-
tur; nec solum in iis operibus in quibus plurium conatus
praeeunte aliqua iucunda voce conspirat, sed etiam singu-
lorum fatigatio quamlibet se rudi modulatione solatur.
17   Laudem adhuc dicere artis pulcherrimae videor, nondum eam tamen oratori coniungere. Transeamus igitur id
quoque, quod grammatice quondam ac musice iunctae

---

[3] *om. B*
[4] loquor *B*

---

[12] Especially 34B–36D, the so-called psychogonia, the mathematical account of the construction of the soul.

[13] Plato, *Euthydemus* 272C; Cicero, *De senectute* 26.

[14] Thucydides 5.70, Xenophon, *Constitution of the Lacedae-
monians* 13.8.

and particularly in the *Timaeus*,[12] cannot even be understood by anyone who has not thoroughly grasped this branch of study. But why speak only of philosophers, whose fountainhead, Socrates, was not ashamed to learn to play the lyre in his old age?[13] We are told that the greatest generals played on the lyre and the pipe, and that Spartan armies were inspired by the strains of music.[14] And what else is the function of the horns and trumpets in our legions? The more assertive their sound, the more does Roman military glory dominate the world. It was therefore not without reason that Plato believed music to be essential for his statesman, or the *politikos* as he calls him, and that the leaders of the sect which some regard as the strictest, and others as the harshest, of all,[15] held the view that some of their Wise Men might give some attention to this subject. Lycurgus too, the originator of the severest laws of Sparta, approved of training in music.[16] Indeed, Nature herself seems to have given this to us as a gift to lighten our labours, for song heartens even the rower at his oar.[17] Nor is this effect confined to work in which the efforts of many are coordinated by a pleasant voice that sets the time; the weariness of the solitary worker also finds comfort in a tune, however crude it may be.

Thus far, I seem to have been giving an encomium of this noble art, but not yet associating it with the orator. So let us pass over the fact that *grammaticē* and music were

[15] I.e. the Stoics: see *SVF* 3. 221 (Diogenes of Babylon).

[16] Plutarch, *Lycurgus* 21, Athenaeus 14. 632F–633A.

[17] Compare Aristides Quintilianus 2.4 (57.27–29 Winnington-Ingram).

fuerunt: siquidem Archytas atque Euenus[5] etiam subiec-
tam grammaticen musicae putaverunt, et eosdem utriusque rei praeceptores fuisse cum Sophron ostendit, mimo-
rum quidem scriptor sed quem Plato adeo probavit ut
suppositos capiti libros eius cum moreretur habuisse cre-
18   datur, tum Eupolis, apud quem Prodamus et musicen et
litteras docet et Maricas, qui est Hyperbolus, nihil se ex
musice scire nisi litteras confitetur. Aristophanes quoque
non uno libro sic institui pueros antiquitus solitos esse
demonstrat, et apud Menandrum in Hypobolimaeo senex,
qui reposcenti filium patri velut rationem inpendiorum
quae in educationem contulerit exponens psaltis se et
19   geometris multa dicit dedisse. Unde etiam ille mos ut in
conviviis post cenam circumferretur lyra, cuius cum se im-
peritum Themistocles confessus esset, ut verbis Ciceronis
20   utar, 'est habitus indoctior'. Sed veterum quoque Romanorum epulis fides ac tibias adhibere moris fuit: versus
quoque Saliorum habent carmen. Quae cum omnia sint a
Numa rege instituta, faciunt manifestum ne illis quidem

---

[5] *B: Aristoxenus A after correction, edd.*

---

[18] If this reading is right, the person meant is presumably
Euenos of Paros, sophist and poet, mentioned by Plato (*Apology*
20B, *Phaedrus* 267A). See *AS* 127–128. But many accept that
Aristoxenus is meant (fr. 72 Wehrli): see note on §22 below.

[19] This anecdote (Riginos (1976) 174) is known from various
sources, but Q. is the earliest. However, Duris of Samos (*F Gr Hist*
76 F 72) knew about Plato's admiration for the Syracusan mime-
writer Sophron, and Aristotle (*Poetics* 1447b10–11) associated
Sophron's work with the Socratic dialogue.

once united, if it is true that Archytas and Euenus[18] regarded *grammaticē* as subordinate to music, and that the identity of the teachers of the two arts is shown both by Sophron, a writer of mimes whom nevertheless Plato approved so warmly that he is believed to have died with Sophron's books under his pillow,[19] and by Eupolis,[20] in whose play Prodamus teaches both music and letters and Maricas (that is to say, Hyperbolus) confesses to knowing nothing of music except his letters. Aristophanes also, in more than one work, shows that boys were brought up in music in the old times;[21] and the old man in Menander's *Hypobolimaeus,*[22] who, in giving an account to the boy's real father (who is claiming him back) of the expenses he has incurred on his education, says that he has paid large sums to "teachers of the lyre, and teachers of geometry." Hence also the practice of taking a lyre round the company after dinner; when Themistocles admitted he could not play, he was (to use Cicero's words) "regarded as rather uneducated."[23] It was the practice also to have lyres and pipes at banquets among the ancient Romans. Even the hymns of the Salii have a tune. And as all this was introduced by King Numa,[24] it is obvious that even our rude and warlike

[20] Fr. 17 Kock = 17 Kassel–Austin. Aristophanes (*Knights* 188) also makes his sausage-seller hero say that he knows nothing of *mousikē* "except the letters": here *mousikē* covers all literary and musical education.

[21] See *Clouds* 966ff., *Frogs* 729.

[22] "The Foundling" (fr. 430a Koerte): the play is also called *Agroikos,* "The Countryman." For the situation see 7.1.4, 9.2.89.

[23] Cicero, *Tusculanae Disputationes* 1.4, Plutarch, *Themistocles* 2.4.   [24] Livy 1.20.

qui rudes ac bellicosi videntur curam musices, quantam
21 illa recipiebat aetas, defuisse. Denique in proverbium usque Graecorum celebratum est indoctos a Musis atque a
Gratiis abesse.

22   Verum quid ex ea proprie petat futurus orator dissera-
mus.

      Numeros musice duplices habet, in vocibus et in cor-
pore: utriusque enim rei aptus quidam modus desideratur.
Vocis rationem Aristoxenus musicus dividit in ῥυθμόν et
μέλος, quorum alterum modulatione, alterum canore ac
sonis constat. Num igitur non haec omnia oratori necessaria? Quorum unum ad gestum, alterum ad conlocationem
verborum, tertium ad flexus vocis, qui sunt in agendo quo-
23 que plurimi, pertinet: nisi forte in carminibus tantum et in
canticis exigitur structura quaedam et inoffensa copulatio
vocum, in agendo supervacua est, aut non compositio et
sonus in oratione quoque varie pro rerum modo adhibetur
24 sicut in musice. Namque et voce et modulatione grandia
elate, iucunda dulciter, moderata leniter canit totaque arte
25 consentit cum eorum quae dicuntur adfectibus. Atqui in
orando quoque intentio vocis, remissio, flexus pertinet ad
movendos audientium adfectus, aliaque et conlocationis et
vocis, ut eodem utar verbo, modulatione concitationem iu-

---

25 Compare Aelian, *On the Characteristics of Animals* 12.6,
12.19: "those who (so they say) are far from the Muses and the
Graces care nothing for dolphins."
26 Testimonium 39, da Rios (1954). Q.'s analogy is somewhat
obscure: presumably gesture in oratory is analogous to rhythmi-
cal movement "in the body," word arrangement to rhythm "in
sounds," and the inflection of the voice to *melos*.
27 But *cantica* may mean "songs" in general (as in 1.2.8) or be

ancestors did not neglect music, in so far as that age allowed. Finally, there is a well-known Greek proverb that says that "the uneducated are far away from the Muses and the Graces."[25]

But let us discuss the advantages which the future orator in particular may derive from music.

Music has patterns of two kinds, in sounds and in the movement of the body, for both need proper control of some kind. The musical theorist Aristoxenus[26] divides what concerns sound into rhythm *(rhythmos)* and melody *(melos),* the former comprising the "modulation," and the latter the tone and the quality of the sound. Now are not *all* these essential to the orator? One point is relevant to gesture, the second to word arrangement, and the third to the inflexions of the voice, many of which are also involved in making a speech. Or do you imagine that some kind of structure and euphonious combination of sounds is necessary only for poetry or the sung parts of plays,[27] and not essential in pleading? Or that oratory does not employ various kinds of Composition and sounds according to the needs of the subject just as music does? Music indeed employs sound and modulation, to express sublime thoughts loftily, pleasing thoughts with sweetness, and ordinary thoughts with easy grace; it uses all its skill to accord with the emotions required by the words it accompanies. Yet in oratory too, raising, lowering, or inflecting the voice is a means of affecting the hearers' feelings; we use one "modulation" (if I may use the same term) of phrasing and of voice to arouse the judge's indignation and a different

contrasted with *carmina* as a lower, less respectable genre (so Colson).

dicis, alia misericordiam petimus, cum etiam organis, quibus sermo exprimi non potest, adfici animos in diversum
26 habitum sentiamus. Corporis quoque aptus et decens motus, qui dicitur εὐρυθμία, et est necessarius nec aliunde peti potest: in quo pars actionis non minima consistit, qua de re sepositus nobis est locus.

27 Age, non habebit in primis curam vocis orator? Quid tam musices proprium? Sed ne haec quidem praesumenda pars est: uno interim contenti simus exemplo C. Gracchi, praecipui suorum temporum oratoris, cui contionanti consistens post eum musicus fistula, quam tonarion vocant,
28 modos quibus deberet intendi ministrabat; haec ei cura inter turbidissimas actiones vel terrenti optimates vel iam timenti fuit.

Libet propter quosdam imperitiores et[6] 'crassiore', ut vocant, 'Musa', dubitationem huius utilitatis eximere.
29 Nam poetas certe legendos oratori futuro concesserint: num igitur hi sine musice? Ac si quis tam caecus animi est ut de aliis dubitet, illos certe qui carmina ad lyram composuerunt. Haec diutius forent dicenda si hoc studium velut
30 novum praeciperem. Cum vero antiquitus usque a Chirone atque Achille ad nostra tempora apud omnis, qui

---

6 *recc.*: etiam *AB*: ⟨vel⟩ etiam *Watt* 1988

---

28 11.3 (which includes a study of the voice).

29 See Cicero, *De oratore* 3.225; a slightly different account is given in Plutarch, *Tiberius Gracchus* 2.4, and Valerius Maximus 8.10.1.

30 Compare Horace's *crassa Minerva* (*Sermones* 2.2.3).

31 [Plutarch], *On music* 40: "We learn that Heracles made use of music, and Achilles, and many others, whose teacher is said to

one for arousing pity; why, we even feel that mental attitudes are affected in various ways by instruments which
are incapable of articulate speech. Moreover, an apt and
becoming movement of the body—what the Greeks call
eurhythmia—is essential, and cannot be obtained from
any other source. A large part of the subject of Delivery
depends on this; we have a place reserved for it.[28]

Again, will not the orator, as a priority, take trouble
about his voice? What is so specially the concern of music
as this? Here too I must not anticipate; let us be content for
the moment with the example of Gaius Gracchus, the leading orator of his age, who, when he was addressing the assembly, used to have a musician standing behind him with
a pipe (in Greek, it is called a *tonarion*) with which the man
indicated the tones in which he was to pitch his voice.[29] He
took this trouble in his most turbulent speeches, when he
was either terrifying the aristocrats, or beginning to be
afraid of them.

I should like, for the sake of some persons who are less
well instructed and have a "coarser Muse"[30] (as the saying
is), to remove all doubts about the usefulness of this art.
They are bound to admit that the reading of the poets is of
use to the future orator; but do poets exist without music?
If anyone should be blind enough to be doubtful about
the others, this must at least be true of those who wrote
songs for the lyre. The point would need arguing at greater
length if I were recommending some novel discipline; but
music has in fact lasted from the old days of Chiron and
Achilles[31] down to our own time among everyone who has

have been the wise Chiron, instructor in music and righteousness
and medicine."

modo legitimam disciplinam non sint perosi, duraverit,
non est committendum ut illa dubia faciam defensionis

31 sollicitudine. Quamvis autem satis iam ex ipsis quibus sum
modo usus exemplis credam esse manifestum quae mihi
et quatenus musice placeat, apertius tamen profitendum
puto non hanc a me praecipi quae nunc in scaenis effeminata et inpudicis modis fracta non ex parte minima si quid
in nobis virilis roboris manebat excidit, sed qua laudes for-
tium canebantur quaque ipsi fortes canebant: nec psalteria
et spadicas, etiam virginibus probis recusanda, sed cogni-
tionem rationis, quae ad movendos leniendosque adfectus

32 plurimum valet. Nam et Pythagoran accepimus concitatos
ad vim pudicae domui adferendam iuvenes iussa mutare
in spondium modos tibicina composuisse, et Chrysippus
etiam nutricum illi quae adhibetur infantibus adlectationi

33 suum quoddam carmen adsignat. Est etiam non inerudite
ad declamandum ficta materia, in qua ponitur tibicen qui
sacrificanti Phrygium cecinerat, acto illo in insaniam et per
praecipitia delato, accusari quod causa mortis extiterit:
quae si dici debet ab oratore nec dici citra scientiam musices potest, quomodo non hanc quoque artem necessariam
esse operi nostro vel iniqui consentient?

34   In geometria partem fatentur esse utilem teneris aeta-

---

32 A small lyre (Pollux 4.59).   33 See Iamblichus, *Life of Pythagoras* 25; Hermogenes 383 Rabe.

34 *SVF* 3. 735. Presumably what is meant is a lullaby.

35 This declamation theme is not attested elsewhere. Q. follows the Aristotelian view of the Phrygian mode as orgiastic and
ecstatic (*Politics* 1342b3); contrast Plato, *Republic* 399A.

36 *Geometria* (see §35) here embraces arithmetic and mathematics generally.

228

not conceived a dislike for regular study, and so I must not make the mistake of casting doubt on my case by too anxious a defence. It will, I believe, be already clear from the examples I have adduced what music I approve of, and to what extent. Nevertheless, I think I ought to state more plainly that I do *not* recommend the effeminate music of the modern stage, emasculated by indecent rhythms, which has done so much to destroy any manly strength we still had left, but rather the music to which the praises of brave men were sung, and which brave men themselves used to sing. Nor do I advise the psaltery and the spadix,[32] instruments which not even respectable girls should handle, but rather a knowledge of the principles that possess such power to arouse or sedate the emotions. We are told that Pythagoras, when some young men were roused to commit an outrage on a respectable family, calmed them by ordering the piper to change her tune to a spondaic one.[33] Chrysippus[34] also suggests a special tune for nurses' attempts to coax babies. And there is a fictitious declamation theme which shows considerable learning, in which a piper who had played a Phrygian air to a man making a sacrifice is accused of causing his death, because the man was driven mad and threw himself over a precipice.[35] If this speech has to be made by an orator, and it cannot be made without knowledge of music, how can the most prejudiced critics fail to agree that music is necessary for our enterprise?

Geometry[36]

As for geometry, it is admitted that some parts of it are useful for young children, because it exercises the mind,

tibus: agitari namque animos et acui ingenia et celeritatem percipiendi venire inde concedunt, sed prodesse eam non, ut ceteras artis, cum perceptae sint sed cum discatur existi-
35 mant. Id vulgaris opinio est: nec sine causa summi viri etiam inpensam huic scientiae operam dederunt.

Nam cum sit geometria divisa in numeros atque formas, numerorum quidem notitia non oratori modo sed cuicumque primis saltem litteris erudito necessaria est. In causis vero vel frequentissime versari solet: in quibus actor, non dico si circa summas trepidat, sed si digitorum saltem incerto aut indecoro gestu a computatione dissentit,
36 iudicatur indoctus. Illa vero linearis ratio et ipsa quidem cadit frequenter in causas (nam de terminis mensurisque sunt lites), sed habet maiorem quandam aliam cum arte
37 oratoria cognationem. Iam primum ordo est geometriae necessarius; nonne et eloquentiae? Ex prioribus geometria probat insequentia et certis incerta: nonne id in dicendo facimus? Quid? illa propositarum quaestionum conclusio non fere tota constat syllogismis? Propter quod pluris invenias qui dialecticae similem quam qui rhetoricae fateantur hanc artem. Verum et orator, etiamsi raro,
38 non tamen numquam probabit dialectice. Nam et syllogismis si res poscet utetur, et certe enthymemate, qui rhetoricus est syllogismus. Denique probationum quae

---

37 This refers to the conventional system of indicating numbers and doing calculations by various positions and movements of the fingers: see 11.3.117, Juvenal 10.249, Apuleius, *Apology* 89, and LCL *Greek Mathematical Works,* ed. I. Thomas, 1. 31. Units and tens were expressed by the left hand, hundreds and thousands by the right; higher numbers involved moving one hand or the other about. Nestor (Juvenal, loc. cit.), who has lived three gener-

sharpens the wits, and generates quickness of perception. But it is thought that the advantages come not (as with other arts) when it has been learned, but only during the learning process. This is an uneducated view. It is not without good reason that some great men have expended enormous effort on this science.

Geometry is divided into two parts, one dealing with Number, the other with Form. Knowledge of numbers is essential not only to the orator, but to anyone who has had even a basic education. It is indeed very frequently involved in actual cases. There the speaker is thought an ignoramus, I will not say if he hesitates in adding up, but if he contradicts his calculations by shaky and inappropriate movements with his fingers.[37] The theory of lines also frequently comes into actual cases (there are disputes about boundaries and measurements) but it has a more important relation to oratory than this. In the first place, order is a necessary element in geometry: is it not also in eloquence? Geometry proves subsequent propositions from preceding ones, the uncertain from the certain: do we not do the same in speaking? Again: does not the solution of the problems rest almost wholly on Syllogisms? This is why you find the majority of people thinking that it is closer to dialectic than to rhetoric. But even the orator will sometimes, if rarely, prove his point by dialectic, seeing that, if the subject demands it, he will use Syllogisms, and certainly the Enthymeme, which is a rhetorical Syllogism.[38]

ations, "is beginning to count his years on the right hand." The rules were complex and confusion easy: see Butler and Owen on Apuleius, loc. cit.

[38] See 5.10, 5.14.

sunt potentissimae grammicae apodixis vulgo dicuntur:
39 quid autem magis oratio quam probationem petit? Falsa
quoque veris similia geometria ratione deprendit. Fit hoc
et in numeris per quasdam quas pseudographias vocant,
quibus pueri ludere solebamus. Sed alia maiora sunt. Nam
quis non ita proponenti credat: 'quorum locorum extremae lineae eandem mensuram colligunt, eorum spatium
40 quoque quod iis lineis continetur par sit necesse est ?' At id
falsum est: nam plurimum refert cuius sit formae ille
circumitus, reprehensique a geometris sunt historici qui
magnitudinem insularum satis significari navigationis ambitu crediderunt. Nam ut quaeque forma perfectissima,
41 ita capacissima est. Ideoque illa circumcurrens linea, si
efficiet orbem, quae forma est in planis maxime perfecta,
amplius spatium complectetur quam si quadratum paribus
oris efficiat, rursus quadrata triangulis, triangula ipsa plus
aequis lateribus quam inaequalibus.
42   Sed alia[7] forsitan obscuriora: nos facillimum etiam im-
peritis sequamur experimentum. Iugeri mensuram ducen-
tos et quadraginta longitudinis pedes esse dimidioque in
latitudinem patere non fere quisquam est qui ignoret, et
qui sit circumitus et quantum campi cludat colligere expe-
43 ditum. At centeni et octogeni in quamque partem pedes
idem spatium extremitatis sed multo amplius clusae quat-

[7] talia *Halm*

39 Compare 1.10.49. For the rigour of plane geometry, Colson
compares Galen's statement (*De libris suis* 11 = xix.41 Kuhn)
recommending the study of these "linear" proofs as a preliminary
to his own logic.   40 Obscure; presumably "trick diagrams"
which lead to impossible conclusions. But the term may cover

Finally, the most powerful proofs are commonly called "linear demonstrations."[39] And what is the aim of oratory if not proof? Geometry also uses reasoning to detect falsehoods which appear like truths. This also happens with numbers, by means of the so-called "pseudographs"[40] which we used to amuse ourselves with as boys. There are other more important points. Who would not believe the following proposition? "When the lines bounding two figures are equal in length, the areas contained by these lines must also be equal." But it is false, for everything depends on the shape of the figure, and historians have been taken to task by geometers for thinking that the size of islands is given by the length of the circumnavigation.[41] In fact, the more perfect the shape, the greater the area it contains. So, if the boundary line is a circle, which is the most perfect plane figure, it will enclose a larger area than a square, and a square will enclose more than a triangle, and an equilateral triangle more than one with unequal sides.

Other aspects of this may be rather obscure, but let me take an example which is easy even for the inexpert. Almost everyone knows than a *iugerum* is 240 feet long and 120 feet broad,[42] and its perimeter and the area of ground enclosed are easily calculated. But a square of 180 feet gives the same perimeter, but a much larger area enclosed

arithmetical fallacies also: see "Archytas" *On Principles* in Stobaeus 1.41, p. 283 Wachsmuth (= H. Thesleff, *The Pythagorean Texts of the Hellenistic Period* (Åbo, 1965) p. 36, 25).

41 Colson cites Thucydides 6.1 (on Sicily) and Polybius 9.21 (on the relative size of Sparta and Megalopolis).

42 I.e. a *iugerum* is two *actus quadrati,* each being a square of 120 feet.

233

tuor lineis areae faciunt. Id si computare quem piget, bre-
vioribus numeris idem discat. Nam deni in quadram pedes
quadraginta per oram, intra centum erunt. At si quini deni
per latera, quini in fronte sint, ex illo quod amplectuntur
44 quartam deducent eodem circumductu. Si vero porrecti
utrimque undeviceni singulis distent, non plures intus
quadratos habebunt quam per quot longitudo ducetur:
quae circumibit autem linea eiusdem spatii erit cuius ea
quae centum continet. Ita quidquid formae quadrati de-
45 traxeris, amplitudini quoque peribit. Ergo etiam id fieri
potest, ut maiore circumitu minor loci amplitudo cludatur.
Haec in planis; nam in collibus vallibusque etiam imperito
patet plus soli esse quam caeli.

46   Quid quod se eadem geometria tollit ad rationem
usque mundi? In qua, cum siderum certos constitutosque
cursus numeris docet, discimus nihil esse inordinatum
atque fortuitum: quod ipsum nonnumquam pertinere ad
47 oratorem potest. An vero, cum Pericles Athenienses solis
obscuratione territos redditis eius rei causis metu libera-
vit, aut cum Sulpicius ille Gallus in exercitu L. Pauli de
lunae defectione disseruit, ne velut prodigio divinitus facto militum animi terrerentur, non videtur esse usus orato-
48 ris officio? Quod si Nicias in Sicilia scisset, non eodem
confusus metu pulcherrimum Atheniensium exercitum
perdidisset: sicut Dion, cum ad destruendam Dionysi
tyrannidem venit, non est tali casu deterritus.

---

43 Plutarch, *Pericles* 35.

44 Livy 44.37 (168 BC).

45 Thucydides 7.50–51; Plutarch, *Nicias* 22.

46 Plutarch, *Dion* 24. This was in 357 BC; Dion and his friends
were not perturbed, but his troops were, and the seer Miltas had

by its four sides. If the calculation is too much for you, you can learn the same fact from smaller numbers. A 10-foot square has a perimeter of 40 feet and encloses an area of 100 feet. But if it is 15 feet by 5, the area enclosed is a quarter less, the perimeter being the same. And if we have a parallelogram measuring 19 feet by one, the number of square feet will be no more than the linear feet of one of the longer sides, though the perimeter will be the same as that of the 100-foot area. So the size of the enclosed area will diminish the more you depart from the square shape. Hence it is even possible that a larger perimeter may enclose a smaller area. This applies to level areas. In hills and valleys, even the inexpert can see that the ground area is greater than the sky that covers it.

But geometry also soars higher, to the very system of the universe. Here, when it teaches by its calculations the fixed and ordained courses of the stars, we learn that nothing is without order or fortuitous. This itself is sometimes relevant for the orator. When Pericles[43] freed the Athenians from the terror caused by the darkening of the sun by explaining the cause, or when Sulpicius Gallus[44] spoke about the lunar eclipse to Lucius Paullus' army, to prevent the soldiers from being terrified by what seemed a portent from heaven, does he not seem to have been performing an orator's function? If Nicias in Sicily had known this,[45] he would not have been confused by that same terror, and so ruined that splendid Athenian army. Dion, when he arrived to put down the tyranny of Dionysius, was not deterred by a similar occurrence.[46]

to tell them that the eclipse signified the eclipse of Dionysius' tyranny.

235

Sint extra licet usus bellici transeamusque quod Archi-
49 medes unus obsidionem Syracusarum in longius traxit; illud utique iam proprium ad efficiendum quod intendimus,
plurimas quaestiones, quibus difficilior alia ratione expli-
catio est, ut de ratione dividendi,[8] de sectione in infinitum,
de celeritate augendi,[9] linearibus illis probationibus solvi
solere: ut, si est oratori, quod proximus demonstrabit liber,
de omnibus rebus dicendum, nullo modo sine geometria
esse possit orator.

11

1 Dandum aliquid comoedo quoque, dum eatenus qua pro-
nuntiandi scientiam futurus orator desiderat. Non enim
puerum quem in hoc instituimus aut femineae vocis exili-
2 tate frangi volo aut seniliter tremere. Nec vitia ebrietatis
effingat nec servili vernilitate inbuatur nec amoris ava-
ritiae metus discat adfectum: quae neque oratori sunt
necessaria et mentem praecipue in aetate prima teneram
adhuc et rudem inficiunt; nam frequens imitatio transit
3 in mores. Ne gestus quidem omnis ac motus a comoedis
petendus est. Quamquam enim utrumque eorum ad quendam modum praestare debet orator, plurimum tamen aberit a scaenico, nec vultu nec manu nec excursionibus

---

8 *recc.*: vivendi *A*: videndi *B*   9 augenda *B*

---

47 By his ingenuity in inventing catapults etc.: Livy 24.34, Plutarch, *Marcellus* 14.
48 These examples are obscure: "division" may be any one of a
number of mathematical procedures; "speed of increase" seems
to allude to the study of geometrical and arithmetical progression.

But let us take uses in war to be none of our business, and pass over the fact that Archimedes,[47] on his own, prolonged the siege of Syracuse. What is important for our purpose is that many problems, which are difficult to solve in other ways, are often solved by these "linear proofs," such as the method of division, infinite section, and speed of increase.[48] So, if (as the next book will prove)[49] an orator has to speak on all subjects, he cannot be an orator without geometry.

CHAPTER 11

Acting techniques: Delivery and gesture

The comic actor too should be given some part, but only in so far as the future orator needs a knowledge of Delivery. I do not want the boy we are educating for this purpose to have a weak and womanish voice or to quaver like an old man. Nor ought he to mimic the failings of drunkenness, be taught the cringing manners of a slave, or learn the emotions of love, greed, or fear. These things are not necessary for an orator, and they infect the mind, especially in the early years when it is malleable and unformed. Frequent imitation develops into habit. Nor should all kinds of gesture and movement be sought from the comic actors. Though the orator must indeed master both to a certain extent, he will keep well clear of staginess and of anything excessive in facial expression, or in the way he uses his

Colson's defence of *videndi ratio* as meaning "optics" is unconvincing.
    49 2.20.

nimius. Nam si qua in his ars est dicentium, ea prima est
ne ars esse videatur.

4   Quod est igitur huius doctoris officium? In primis vitia
si qua sunt oris emendet, ut expressa sint verba, ut suis
quaeque litterae sonis enuntientur. Quarundam enim
vel exilitate vel pinguitudine nimia laboramus, quasdam
velut acriores parum efficimus et aliis non dissimilibus sed
5   quasi hebetioribus permutamus. Quippe et rho litterae,
qua Demosthenes quoque laboravit, labda succedit, quarum vis est apud nos quoque, et cum C ac similiter G[1] non
6   evaluerunt, in T[2] ac D molliuntur. Ne illas quidem circa s
litteram delicias hic magister feret, nec verba in faucibus
patietur audiri nec oris inanitate resonare nec, quod minime sermoni puro conveniat, simplicem vocis naturam
pleniore quodam sono circumliniri, quod Graeci cata-
7   peplasmenon dicunt (sic appellatur cantus tibiarum quae,
praeclusis quibus clarescunt foraminibus, recto modo
8   exitu graviorem spiritum reddunt). Curabit etiam ne
extremae syllabae intercidant, ut par sibi sermo sit, ut quotiens exclamandum erit lateris conatus sit ille, non capitis,
ut gestus ad vocem, vultus ad gestum accommodetur.

[1] T *Philander*
[2] G *Philander*

---

[1] See the detailed advice given in 11.3.72–136.
[2] See *Ad Herennium* 4.10 with Caplan's note.
[3] Cicero, *De oratore* 1.260: Demosthenes was unable to pronounce the first letter of the art he practised, i.e. *rh*etoric.
[4] If this reading is right (Philander's emendations make the
error consist in pronouncing *c* and *t* as voiced), the phenomenon
described is perhaps just a childish fault.

hands or moves around.[1] If speakers do possess an art of these things, its first rule is not to seem to be art.[2]

So what is this instructor's duty? In the first place he must correct any faults of enunciation, so that words are clearly pronounced and the proper sound is given to each letter. There are some letters which we have a bad tendency to make too thin or too full; others we stifle as too harsh, and replace by similar but duller-sounding ones. For instance, *lambda* is substituted for *rho*, with which even Demosthenes had difficulty.[3] (We have the equivalents of these letters in our own language.) Again, when *c* and *g* are not given full value, they are softened into *t* and *d*.[4] The teacher is also not to tolerate that affected pronunciation of *s*,[5] or to let words come from the throat or resonate in the cavity of the mouth, or allow the natural quality of the voice be overlaid with a fuller sound, a fault very damaging to pure speech (the Greeks call this *katapeplasmenon*, a term applied to the sound of a pipe, when the stops which produce the higher notes are closed and a lower note is produced through the main aperture only). He will also make sure that final syllables are not lost, that the speech maintains an even level, that when the voice has to be raised the effort comes from the lungs and not from the head, and that the gesture is appropriate to the voice and the facial expression to the gesture. He should

[5] Butler suggests that this is the tendency to insert *i* before initial *st, sp, sc* (so also Corsi: for this feature of late Latin see Lindsay (1894) 105); it might also be the tendency to slur over final -*s*, as in archaic usage but also in current speech (so Colson: see also W. D. Elcock, *The Romance Languages* (London, 1960) 51); or just an exaggerated hissing; or almost anything. We do not know.

9   Observandum erit etiam ut recta sit facies dicentis, ne labra detorqueantur, ne inmodicus hiatus rictum distendat, ne supinus vultus, ne deiecti in terram oculi, ne inclinata
10   utrolibet cervix. Nam frons pluribus generibus peccat. Vidi multos quorum supercilia ad singulos vocis conatus adlevarentur, aliorum constricta, aliorum etiam dissidentia, cum alterum in verticem tenderet[3] altero paene oculus
11   ipse premeretur. Infinitum autem, ut mox dicemus, in his quoque rebus momentum est, et nihil potest placere quod non decet.
12   Debet etiam docere comoedus quomodo narrandum, qua sit auctoritate suadendum, qua concitatione consurgat ira, qui flexus deceat miserationem: quod ita optime faciet si certos ex comoediis elegerit locos et ad hoc maxime ido-
13   neos, id est actionibus similes. Idem autem non ad pronuntiandum modo utilissimi, verum ad augendam quoque
14   eloquentiam maxime accommodati erunt. Et haec dum infirma aetas maiora non capiet: ceterum cum legere orationes oportebit, cum virtutes earum iam sentiet, tum mihi diligens aliquis ac peritus adsistat, neque solum lectionem formet, verum ediscere etiam electa ex iis cogat et ea dicere stantem clare et quem ad modum agere oportebit, ut protinus pronuntiationem vocem memoriam exerceat.

[3] tenderent *B*

also take care that the speaker faces his audience, that his lips are not distorted, nor his mouth split open in a wide grin, that his face is not turned upwards, his eyes fixed on the ground, or his neck turned to one side. The forehead can go wrong in many ways: I have seen many who raised their eyebrows at every effort of their voice, others whose brows were always bent, others again who could not keep them level, one making its way towards the top of the head, and the other almost covering the eye itself. As we shall observe later,[6] even these little things are matters of infinite moment; and nothing can give pleasure which is not becoming.

Our actor will also have to teach how to deliver a narrative, how to lend authority to advice, what stimulus to use in order to produce a surge of anger, what change of tone is appropriate to an appeal to pity. The best way he can do this is by choosing particular passages from comedy which are most suitable for the purpose, that is, most resembling actual pleadings.[7] These are not only very useful for training in Delivery, but will prove admirably adapted to develop a speaker's eloquence. All this should be done while the child is not yet strong enough to undertake more serious exercises; but when he has to read speeches, and begins to appreciate their merits, he should then have available to him some careful and experienced teacher, not only to train his reading, but to force him to learn select passages by heart and repeat them standing, clearly and in the way he will one day have to plead; this will train Delivery, voice, and Memory at a single stroke.

[6] See 9.3.101, 11.3.72–81.
[7] See 10.1.70 for (Greek) examples.

15   Ne illos quidem reprehendendos puto qui paulum
etiam palaestricis vacaverunt. Non de iis loquor quibus
pars vitae in oleo pars in vino consumitur, qui corporum
cura mentem obruerunt; hos enim abesse ab eo quem in-
16   stituimus quam longissime velim: sed nomen est idem iis a
quibus gestus motusque formantur, ut recta sint bracchia,
ne indoctae rusticae‹ve›[4] manus, ne status indecorus, ne
qua in proferendis pedibus inscitia, ne caput oculique ab
17   alia corporis inclinatione dissideant. Nam neque haec esse
in parte pronuntiationis negaverit quisquam neque ipsam
pronuntiationem ab oratore secernet: et certe quod facere
oporteat non indignandum est discere, cum praesertim
haec chironomia, quae est (ut nomine ipso declaratur) lex
gestus, et ab illis temporibus heroicis orta sit et a summis
Graeciae viris atque ipso etiam Socrate probata, a Platone
quoque in parte civilium posita virtutum, et a Chrysippo
in praeceptis de liberorum educatione compositis non
18   omissa. Nam Lacedaemonios quidem etiam saltationem
quandam tamquam ad bella quoque utilem habuisse inter
exercitationes accepimus. Neque id veteribus Romanis
dedecori fuit: argumentum est sacerdotum nomine[5] ac re-

---

[4] *add. edd.*
[5] ‹cum› nomine *Watt* 1988

---

[8] Xenophon, *Symposium* 2.15–20. "Chironomy"—i.e. gesticu-
lation: Q.'s explanation is hardly right—is part of dancing.

[9] *Laws* 7. 795D–796E. Plato approves both of imitative dancing (so long as dignity is preserved) and of dancing as exercise.

[10] *SVF* 3. 737.

[11] And not only the Spartans: the "Pyrrhic" dance, imitating
the movements of armed combat, was not exclusively Spartan. For

Gymnastics

I do not think there is any cause to blame those who have found a little time also for the teachers of gymnastics. I do not mean the people who spend half their lives rubbing themselves with oil and the other half drinking, and who smother the mind by their care for the body. I should indeed like to keep these folk as far away from my pupil as possible. But the same name applies to those who train gesture and movement to ensure that the arms are held straight, the hands show no lack of education and no country-bred manners, the stance is proper, there is no clumsiness in moving the feet, and the head and eyes do not move independently of the general inclination of the body. No one will deny that these matters come under Delivery, or attempt to separate Delivery from the person of the orator. Nor of course should anyone disdain to learn what he ought to do, especially as "chironomy"—which, as its name tells us, is the "law of gesture"—originated in heroic times and was approved by the greatest of the Greeks, including Socrates himself,[8] while it was given a place by Plato[9] among the accomplishments of the citizen, and included by Chrysippus[10] in his advice on the education of children. We are told that the Spartans even counted a certain kind of dancing among their military exercises, as being useful even in war.[11] Nor did the Romans of old think it disgraceful; this is clear from the fact that dance has survived to the present day in the name of a priesthood[12] and in ritual, and

a dance that mimics warlike action, see that performed by the Thracians in Xenophon's presence (*Anabasis* 6.1).

[12] The Salii, see on 1.6.40, 1.10.20.

ligione durans ad hoc tempus saltatio et illa in tertio Ciceronis de Oratore libro verba Crassi, quibus praecipit ut
orator utatur 'laterum inclinatione forti ac virili, non a
scaena et histrionibus, sed ab armis aut etiam a palaestra'.
Cuius disciplinae usus in nostram usque aetatem sine re-
19 prehensione descendit. A me tamen nec ultra puerilis annos retinebitur nec in his ipsis diu. Neque enim gestum
oratoris componi ad similitudinem saltationis volo, sed sub-
esse aliquid ex hac exercitatione puerili, unde nos non id
agentis furtim decor ille discentibus traditus prosequatur.

12

1 Quaeri solet an, etiamsi discenda sint haec, eodem tempore tamen tradi omnia et percipi possint. Negant enim
quidam, quia confundatur animus ac fatigetur tot disciplinis in diversum tendentibus, ad quas nec mens nec corpus
nec dies ipse sufficiat, et, si maxime patiatur hoc aetas ro-
2 bustior, pueriles annos onerari non oporteat. Sed non satis
perspiciunt quantum natura humani ingenii valeat, quae
ita est agilis ac velox, sic in omnem partem, ut ita dixerim,
spectat, ut ne possit quidem aliquid agere tantum unum, in
plura vero non eodem die modo sed eodem temporis mo-
3 mento vim suam intendat. An vero citharoedi non simul et
memoriae et sono vocis et plurimis flexibus serviunt, cum

---

13 3.220.

from the words of Crassus in the third book of Cicero's *De oratore*,[13] in which he lays it down that the orator should have "bold and manly movement of the body, derived not from the stage and the acting profession, but from weapon training or even from the gymnasium." And the use of this sort of training has persisted uncensured down to our own time. In my practice, however, it will not be kept up beyond the years of boyhood, and even so not for very long. I do not want the orator's gestures to be modelled on the dance; but I do want something of these boyhood exercises to underpin them, so that the grace acquired in learning them stays with us, though unobserved, when our minds are on other things.

CHAPTER 12

Should several subjects be taught at once?

The question is often asked whether, even if these things have to be learned, they can all be taught and absorbed at the same time. Some say no, on the ground that the mind is confused and wearied by so many studies that lead in different directions, for which neither mind nor body nor indeed time can suffice; even though the older boys can stand it, it is wrong (they say) for children's minds to be so burdened. These critics do not fully appreciate the power of the human mind; it is so nimble and quick, so ready (if I may put it like this) to look in all directions, that it cannot even concentrate exclusively on one thing at a time, but applies its powers to many objects, not only on the same day but at the same moment. Singers to the lyre simultaneously attend to their memory and to the sound and vari-

interim alios nervos dextra percurrunt, alios laeva trahunt
continent praebent, ne pes quidem otiosus certam legem
4 temporum servat—et haec pariter omnia? Quid? nos
agendi subita necessitate deprensi nonne alia dicimus alia
providemus, cum pariter inventio rerum, electio verborum, compositio gestus pronuntiatio vultus motus desiderentur? Quae si velut sub uno conatu tam diversa parent
simul, cur non pluribus curis horas partiamur—cum praesertim reficiat animos ac reparet varietas ipsa, contraque
sit aliquanto difficilius in labore uno perseverare? Ideo et
stilus lectione requiescit et ipsius lectionis taedium vicibus
5 levatur; quamlibet multa egerimus, quodam tamen modo
recentes sumus ad id quod incipimus. Quis non optundi
possit si per totum diem cuiuscumque artis unum magistrum ferat? Mutatione recreabitur sicut in cibis, quorum
diversitate reficitur stomachus et pluribus minore fastidio
6 alitur. Aut dicant isti mihi quae sit alia ratio discendi.
Grammatico soli deserviamus, deinde geometrae tantum,
omittamus interim quod didicimus? mox transeamus ad
musicum, excidant priora? Et cum Latinis studebimus litteris, non respiciamus ad Graecas? [et]¹ Ut semel finiam,
7 nihil faciamus nisi novissimum? Cur non idem suademus
agricolis, ne arva simul et vineta et oleas et arbustum
colant, ne pratis et pecoribus et hortis et alvearibus avi-

---

¹ del. Radermacher

---

¹ Greek was begun before Latin (1.1.12, 1.4.1); *litteris* covers
both linguistic and literary study, i.e. both parts of *grammaticē*.

ous inflexions of the voice, meanwhile running over certain
strings with the right hand, and plucking, stopping, or re-
leasing others with the left; even the foot is kept occupied
in beating time; and all this goes on simultaneously. And
do we not ourselves, when called upon to plead in a sudden
emergency, speak and plan ahead at the same time, because Invention, Choice of Words, Composition, Gesture,
Delivery, expression, and movement are all called for at
once? If all these different things obey our orders in the
course of a single effort, why should we not divide our
hours among a number of concerns, especially as variety
refreshes and restores the mind, while on the other hand it
is a good deal harder to stick continuously to one job? The
pen takes a rest during reading, and the monotony of reading itself is relieved by a change of subject. No matter how
many things we have done, in a sense we come fresh to any
new activity. Who could fail to have his mind blunted, if
he had to listen to a single teacher all day long, whatever
the subject? The learner will be refreshed by change, just
as the stomach is refreshed by variety of sustenance and
nourished more appetizingly by a number of different
foods. If my critics disagree, let them tell me what other
method of learning there is. Are we to be subject to the
grammaticus alone, and then to the mathematician alone,
and forget meanwhile what we learned before? Are we
then to move on to the music teacher, and let our earlier
studies slip out of mind? When we study Latin, are we not
to look back at Greek?[1] To cut a long story short, are we to
do nothing except the last thing to come our way? By the
same token, why not recommend farmers not to cultivate
arable, vineyards, olives, and fruit trees at the same time,
and not to divide their attentions between meadowland,

247

busque accommodent curam? Cur ipsi aliquid forensibus
negotiis, aliquid desideriis amicorum, aliquid rationibus
domesticis, aliquid curae corporis, nonnihil voluptatibus
cotidie damus? Quarum nos una res quaelibet nihil inter-
mittentis fatigaret: adeo facilius est multa facere quam diu.

8   Illud quidem minime verendum est, ne laborem studiorum pueri difficilius tolerent; neque enim ulla aetas
minus fatigatur. Mirum sit forsitan sed experimentis de-
9   prehendas. Nam et dociliora sunt ingenia priusquam
obduruerunt. Id vel hoc argumento patet, quod intra biennium quam verba recte formare potuerunt quamvis nullo
instante omnia fere locuntur: at noviciis nostris per quot
annos sermo Latinus repugnat! Magis scias si quem iam
robustum instituere litteris coeperis non sine causa dici
παιδομαθεῖς eos qui in sua quidque arte optime faciant.
10   Et patientior est laboris natura pueris quam iuvenibus.
Videlicet ut corpora infantium nec casus quo in terram
totiens deferuntur tam graviter adfligit nec illa per manus
et genua reptatio nec post breve tempus continui lusus et
totius diei discursus, quia pondus illis abest nec se ipsi
gravant: sic animi quoque, credo quia minore conatu mo-
ventur nec suo nisu studiis insistunt sed formandos se tan-
11   tummodo praestant, non similiter fatigantur. Praeterea
secundum aliam aetatis illius facilitatem velut simplicius
docentis secuntur nec quae iam egerint metiuntur: abest
illis adhuc etiam laboris iudicium. Porro, ut frequenter ex-

---

2 Conversely, "late learners," ὀψιμαθεῖς, are thought not to
know their subject properly.

cattle, gardens, beehives, and poultry? Why do we ourselves daily give some attention to court business, some to our friends' needs, some to our domestic accounts, some to the care of the body, and a little to pleasures? Any one of these activities, if we never broke off from it, would wear us out. So true it is that it is easier to do many things than to do one thing for long!

At least we do not have to fear that young boys will find the labour of study too exhausting. No age gets tired less easily. This may seem surprising; but you will find it true by experience. For one thing, the mind absorbs teaching better before it is set hard. This is shown simply by the fact that, within two years of their being able to form words properly, they can say practically anything, without pressure from anyone. Yet think how many years Latin remains an obstacle to our newly-imported slaves! Try to teach an adult to read, and you will understand better that it was with good reason that anyone who does everything really well in his own art is said to have "learned as a child."[2] Secondly, children bear hard work better than young men. Just as infants come to less harm from their frequent falls on the ground, or from their crawling on hands and knees, or (a little later) from their endless games and rushing around all day, because they have no great weight and are no burden to themselves, so their minds too are less likely to get tired, because, presumably, their movements need less exertion, and they do not need an effort of their own to apply themselves to study, but merely present themselves to be formed and moulded. Moreover, thanks to the general malleability of children, they follow their teachers more naively, as it were, and do not measure what they have done. They have as yet no sense of work. Moreover, as

249

QUINTILIAN

perti sumus, minus adficit sensus fatigatio quam cogitatio.

12 Sed ne temporis quidem umquam plus erit, quia his aetatibus omnis in audiendo profectus est. Cum ad stilum secedet, cum generabit ipse aliquid atque componet, tum

13 inchoare haec studia vel non vacabit vel non libebit. Ergo cum grammaticus totum diem occupare non possit, nec debeat ne discentis animum taedio avertat, quibus potius

14 studiis haec temporum velut subsiciva donabimus? Nam nec ego consumi studentem in his artibus volo: nec moduletur aut musicis notis cantica excipiat nec utique ad minutissima usque geometriae opera descendat; non comoedum in pronuntiando nec saltatorem in gestu facio. Quae si omnia exigerem, suppeditabat tamen tempus; longa est enim quae discit aetas et ego non de tardis ingeniis loquor.

15 Denique cur in his omnibus quae discenda oratori futuro puto eminuit Plato? Qui non contentus disciplinis quas praestare poterant Athenae, non Pythagoreorum, ad quos in Italiam navigaverat, Aegypti quoque sacerdotes adiit atque eorum arcana perdidicit.

16 Difficultatis patrocinia praeteximus segnitiae; neque enim nobis operis amor est, nec quia sit honesta ac rerum pulcherrima eloquentia petitur ipsa, sed ad vilem usum et

17 sordidum lucrum accingimur. Dicant sine his in foro multi et adquirant, dum sit locupletior aliquis sordidae mercis

---

3 Plato's travels are reported in Diogenes Laertius 3.6–7. He goes to Italy to study with Pythagoreans (Archytas, Philolaus, Eurytus) and to Egypt for the priests (Cicero, *De finibus* 5.87, *De republica* 1.16; Diodorus 1.96.2). Details in Riginos (1976) ch. 6.

I have often found, fatigue has less effect on the mind than the thought of it.

Again, there will never be more time than now, for at this age all progress comes from listening. When the boy goes off by himself to write, when he is producing and composing something of his own, he will either have no time or no inclination to begin these other studies. So, as the *grammaticus* neither can nor ought to fill the whole day, for fear of putting his pupil off the subject by boring him, to what studies, rather than these, are we to devote the balance of the time? I have no wish for the student to wear himself out with these subjects; he has no need to compose tunes, or to take down songs in musical notation, and certainly not to descend into the smallest minutiae of geometry; I am not training an actor in delivery or a dancer in gesture. But if I did make all these demands, there would yet be time enough. The learning period is long, and I am not speaking of slow minds. And finally, why did Plato excel in all the things which I believe a future orator should learn? Because he was not content with the teaching which Athens could provide, or with that of the Pythagoreans, whom he had travelled to Italy to see, but also visited the priests of Egypt and learned their secrets.[3]

The excuse of "difficulty" is a cloak for our idleness. We do not love the work, nor is eloquence sought for its own sake because it is honourable and the fairest thing in the world; we gird up our loins for mercenary ends and filthy lucre. Let many speak in the courts and make money without these arts, so long as traders in any vile commodity are

negotiator et plus voci suae debeat praeco. Ne velim quidem lectorem dari mihi quid studia referant computaturum. Qui vero imaginem ipsam eloquentiae divina quadam[2] mente conceperit, quique illam, ut ait non ignobilis tragicus, 'reginam rerum orationem' ponet ante oculos, fructumque non ex stipe advocationum sed ex animo suo et contemplatione ac scientia petet perpetuum illum nec fortunae subiectum, facile persuadebit sibi ut tempora, quae spectaculis campo tesseris, otiosis denique sermonibus, ne dicam somno et conviviorum mora conteruntur, geometrae potius ac musico inpendat, quanto plus delectationis habiturus quam ex illis ineruditis voluptatibus. Dedit enim hoc providentia hominibus munus, ut honesta magis iuvarent.

19   Sed nos haec ipsa dulcedo longius duxit. Hactenus ergo de studiis quibus antequam maiora capiat puer instituendus est: proximus liber velut novum sumet exordium et ad rhetoris officia transibit.

---

[2] divinam quandam *Stroux*

richer, and the public crier[4] earns more by *his* voice! I do not want to have a reader even who will calculate the return on his studies. But the man who, by some divine instinct, has formed a real concept of eloquence, who sets before his eyes that "speech, queen of the world," of which the famous tragic poet[5] speaks, and who seeks that enduring reward which does not depend on fortune, not in the fees of advocacy but in his own heart and contemplation and knowledge—*he* will easily persuade himself to spend the time which is wasted in the theatre or the Campus, in gaming or idle talk—not to say sleep and long-drawn-out dinners—in listening to the geometrician and the teacher of music. How much greater will be the delight he gets from these than from those uneducated pleasures! It was a gift of Providence to mankind, that the truly good should give us the greater pleasure.

But the charm of all this has made me go on too long. So much, then, for the studies in which the boy is to be trained before he is capable of greater things. The next book will make a new beginning, as it were, and pass on to the duties of the rhetor.

[4] The *praeco* (auctioneer, public crier) has a despised trade. Martial (5.56) advises a friend to make his son a *praeco* or an architect if he proves stupid.

[5] Pacuvius, *Hermiona* fr. 187 Warmington (*ROL* 2. 232), from Cicero, *De oratore* 2.187: *O flexanima atque omnium regina rerum oratio,* "mind-bender speech, queen of the world." The line is based on Euripides, *Hecuba* 816.

BOOK TWO

INTRODUCTION

Book Two (detailed commentary by M. Winterbottom, Oxford D.Phil. thesis, 1962, unpublished) falls into two parts: (a) chapters 1–13 extend to the rhetor's department the practical educational perspectives of Book One; (b) chapters 14–21 deal with traditional general questions about the nature of rhetoric which had been debated at least from the time of Plato and still form the staple of the many Byzantine "prolegomena" to rhetoric (texts in H. Rabe, *Prolegomenon Sylloge*, 1931).

(a) 2.1 discusses the point at which the pupil should be transferred from *grammaticus* to rhetor—the answer is "when he is fit" (2.1.7). This depends however on the division of the progymnasmata between the two teachers. Quintilian would like the rhetor to take them all over except the simplest. Before coming to details, he insists (2.2) on the need to inquire into the teacher's good character. There are many risks, especially if older and younger boys are taught together. (Quintilian clearly hints at sexual abuse.) Moreover (2.3), it is wrong to fob off beginners with a less than expert teacher; quality counts at this stage, and ensures that the pupil will not have things to unlearn later.

We now come to the progymnasmata: first Narrative (2.4.1–17, including a digression on correcting students' work), then Refutation and Confirmation (2.4.18–19), Encomia and Invective (2.4.20–21), Commonplaces (2.4.22–23), Theses (2.4.24–32), and Discussion of Laws (2.4.33–40). We have ample comparative material in the Greek progymnasmata of Theon (Quintilian's near contemporary), "Hermogenes" (with Priscian's Latin adaptation, *RLM* 551–560), Libanius, Aphthonius, and Nicolaus. Lausberg §§ 1104–1139 summarizes the material; D. L. Clark, *Rhetoric in Greco-Roman Education* (1957) 176–212, gives a good brief account. The curriculum varied somewhat (Quintilian's order is not exactly that of other rhetors) but progress from simple narrative through isolated argument to something like a whole speech (e.g. "a proposal for a law") is universal. Familiarity with these exercises is to be assumed in all rhetorically trained writers of the Roman period; they are building-bricks in all sorts of work, poetry as well as prose.

In 2.5, Quintilian recommends reading orators and historians with guidance from the rhetor. He regards this as somewhat controversial, because it takes time away from practice in declamation, which is what parents want. In discussing what beginners should read (2.5.18–24), Quintilian stresses Livy and Cicero, and the avoidance of the archaic or the decadent. A classical taste for lucidity and amplitude is to be formed. Fuller advice comes much later, in 10.1. Theon 13 (pp. 102–105 Patillon–Bolognesi: a chapter known only from the Armenian version) also advises on reading.

2.6–9 offer commonsense tips to the teacher: advice on correcting declamations (how much help to give, when to produce a "fair copy"), a warning against allowing pupils to memorize too much of their own work (though this is something parents like), and a repeated insistence on adapting teaching to individual needs. Pupils too have their obligations. Finally (2.10), Quintilian takes a position on declamation: it should be as realistic as possible, so as to give the pupil an idea of what he will encounter in real life. The structure of 2.1–10 is analysed in detail by R. Granatelli, *Rhetorica* 13 (1995) 137–160.

(b) Quintilian begins the second part of the book (2.11–12) by defending "Art" against those who think Nature can do everything. Though this is a commonplace prefatory topic (e.g. "Longinus" 2.1), he sounds as if he has a particular target in mind, persons who win cheap success by an intemperate and violent manner. It is not that Art can do everything (2.13); the circumstances of Causes demand a great variety of approaches, to be judged not by textbook rules but by the two general criteria of "the expedient" and "the becoming" (2.13.8).

After briefly discussing (2.14) the name "rhetoric" and possible Latin equivalents, and its division into "art, artist, work"—a division which he makes use of in the general scheme of his own work (12.10; Lausberg §§ 42–45; General Introduction)—Quintilian moves on (2.15) to a doxographical account of definitions of rhetoric. He comes down firmly on the side of those which include a moral element, and do not speak simply of an "art of persuasion." He goes back to Plato (2.14.24–30), whom he defends against what he regards as inadequate interpretations. While Quintilian's "doxography" is the fullest we have, it should be read in the light of Cicero, *De oratore* 1.45–73 (with Leeman–Pinkster ad loc.) and Sextus Empiricus, *Adversus mathematicos* 2 (*Adversus rhetoras:* LCL 4.188–243);

some later texts, especially Doxapatres' commentary on Aphthonius' *Progymnasmata* (= *Prolegomenon Sylloge* 103–124 Rabe), also provide useful parallels and information. See in general Martin (1974) 2–6, Kennedy (1980) 3–7.

The next question (2.16) is whether rhetoric is useful: of course it is, if the orator is to be a "good man." More difficult (2.17) is the question whether it is an Art (*technē*). This was an issue for philosophers, and we have many texts about it: Sextus Empiricus, op. cit.; Philodemus, *Rhetorica* 1 and 2; Cicero, *De oratore* 1.102–112; Olympiodorus' commentary on Plato's *Gorgias,* 69ff. Westerink. For a discussion of these, see especially J. Barnes, *Discourse Analysis Research Group Newsletter* 2.2 (Calgary, 1986) 2–22. The debate arose in Hellenistic times; and the denial of the status of *technē* to rhetoric seems to have been part of the anti-Stoic polemic of the Peripatetic Critolaus (frs. 25–39 Wehrli). The whole subject—the "quarrel" of philosophy and rhetoric—has often been discussed; but H. von Arnim, *Dio von Prusa* (1898) 4–114 remains fundamental.

For Quintilian, of course, rhetoric *is* a *technē*: but what sort (2.18)? Using the Aristotelian distinction between "theoretical," "practical (active)," and "poetic (productive)" forms of knowledge, he concludes that it is essentially "active," but has features in common with the other two kinds. He next (2.19) raises the familiar question whether Art or Nature contributes more to it; he does not (as many do) distinguish Art from "practice," but simply sees Nature as giving the raw material and Art the form.

That rhetoric may be a "virtue" (2.20) is also a philosopher's question. The Stoics held that it was, and that only the Wise Man can be the true "orator" (*SVF* 3. 654–656).

(On the nature of Stoic rhetoric and Quintilian's reaction to it, see C. Atherton, *Classical Quarterly* 38 (1988) 392–427.) Quintilian offers a worldly version of this. Acknowledging that rhetoric may be a "non-art" or a "bad" or "pointless" art, he would claim that the ideal rhetoric towards which his education is intended to lead is indeed a "virtue." (For his general view of the relation between oratory and morality, see M. Winterbottom in *Journal of Roman Studies* 54 (1964) 90–97 and the same writer's "Quintilian the Moralist" in *QHAR* 1. 317–336.)

Finally (2.21) Quintilian deals with another topic of the Hellenistic debate, and opposes the view that rhetoric cannot be an art because it has no special subject matter.

LIBER SECUNDUS

1

1   Tenuit consuetudo, quae cotidie magis invalescit, ut prae-
    ceptoribus eloquentiae, Latinis quidem semper, sed etiam
    Graecis interim, discipuli serius quam ratio postulat trade-
    rentur. Eius rei duplex causa est, quod et rhetores utique
    nostri suas partis omiserunt et grammatici alienas occupa-
2   verunt. Nam et illi declamare modo et scientiam decla-
    mandi ac facultatem tradere officii sui ducunt idque intra
    deliberativas iudicialisque materias (nam cetera ut pro-
    fessione sua minora despiciunt), et hi non satis credunt
    excepisse quae relicta erant (quo nomine gratia quoque iis
    habenda est), sed ad prosopopoeias usque ⟨et⟩[1] ad suaso-
    rias, in quibus onus dicendi vel maximum est, inrumpunt.
3   Hinc ergo accidit ut quae alterius artis prima erant opera
    facta sint alterius novissima, et aetas altioribus iam disci-
    plinis debita in schola minore subsidat ac rhetoricen apud

----

[1] add. recc. (ad suasorias del. Winterbottom, ad prosopopoeias
del. Granatelli, Rhetorica 13.144)

----

[1] In 1.9, Q. allowed *grammatici* to teach fable, *gnōmē*, chria,
and (?) speeches in character; here he complains that they have
gone too far. If the reading *suasoriae* ("deliberative exercises") is

BOOK TWO

CHAPTER 1

When should the study of rhetoric be begun?

The custom has come to prevail, and grows stronger every day, of sending pupils to the teachers of rhetoric later than reason demands—invariably as regards Latin rhetors, but sometimes also as regards Greek. There are two reasons for this: the rhetors, and certainly our own, have abandoned their own sphere, and the *grammatici* have taken over what belongs to others. The rhetors think that their only function is to declaim and teach the theory and practice of declamation, restricted moreover to deliberative and judicial themes (because they regard everything else as beneath the dignity of their profession). The *grammatici* do not think it is enough to pick up what was left for them (and we should indeed be grateful to them for this), but make inroads as far as *prosopopoeiae* and *suasoriae,* in which the burden of speaking is very great.[1] Hence subjects which once formed the first stages of one discipline have come to form the final stages of another, and an age-group which ought to go on to higher studies is kept back in

right (see text notes), the reference is to advanced exercises like "proposal for a law" (νόμου εἰσφορά). See 2.1.8, 2.4.22.

grammaticos exerceat. Ita, quod est maxime ridiculum, non ante ad declamandi magistrum mittendus videtur puer quam declamare sciat.

4 Nos suum cuique professioni modum demus: et grammatice, quam in Latinum transferentes litteraturam vocaverunt, fines suos norit, praesertim tantum ab hac appellationis suae paupertate, intra quam primi illi constitere, provecta; nam tenuis a fonte adsumptis [historicorum criticorumque]² viribus pleno iam satis alveo fluit, cum praeter rationem recte loquendi non parum alioqui copiosam prope omnium maximarum artium scientiam amplexa sit:

5 et rhetorice, cui nomen vis eloquendi dedit, officia sua non detrectet nec occupari gaudeat pertinentem ad se laborem: quae, dum opere cedit, iam paene possessione depul-

6 sa est. Neque infitiabor aliquem ex his qui grammaticen profiteantur eo usque scientiae progredi posse ut ad haec quoque tradenda sufficiat. Sed cum id aget, rhetoris officio fungetur, non suo.

7 Nos porro quaerimus quando iis quae rhetorice praecipit percipiendis puer maturus esse videatur: in quo quidem non id est aestimandum, cuius quisque sit aetatis, sed quantum in studiis iam effecerit. Et ne diutius disseram quando sit rhetori tradendus, sic optime finiri credo: cum poterit.

---

² *del. Winterbottom*: poetarum historicorumque *B*: historicorum oratorumque *t*

---

² Compare Cicero, *Orator* 61. *Rhētor* literally means "speaker."

a lower school, and practises rhetoric under the *grammatici*. So (ridiculous as it is) a boy is not thought fit to go to the declamation master until he knows how to declaim.

Grammaticus and rhetor: the place of progymnasmata in the curriculum

We must however give the two professions their proper spheres. *Grammaticē* (it has been translated *litteratura* in Latin) must learn to know its own limits, especially as it has advanced so far beyond the modest bounds which its name implies, within which its earlier professors confined themselves. At its source a tiny trickle, it has gathered strength [from historians and critics] and now flows in full flood, having come to comprise not only the principles of correct speech (in itself no inconsiderable matter) but the knowledge of almost all the major arts. Rhetoric for its part, named as it is from the power of speaking,[2] must not shirk its proper duties or rejoice to see burdens which belong to it taken up by others; indeed, by surrendering some of the work, it has almost been driven out of its rightful possessions. I shall not deny, of course, that some individual among those who profess *grammaticē* may progress to a stage of knowledge which makes him fully capable of teaching these things too; but when he does so, he will be performing the rhetor's function, not his own.

We next ask when a boy may be thought mature enough to grasp the precepts of rhetoric. For this purpose, we must think not of the actual age of the person, but of what progress he has already made in his studies. To save longer discussion of the question "When should he be sent on to the rhetor?" the best answer, I think, is "When he is fit."

8   Sed hoc ipsum ex superiore pendet quaestione. Nam si grammatices munus usque ad suasorias prorogatur, tardius rhetore opus est: at[3] si rhetor prima officia operis sui non recusat, a narrationibus statim et laudandi vituperandique

9   opusculis cura eius desideratur. An ignoramus antiquis hoc fuisse ad augendam eloquentiam genus exercitationis, ut thesis dicerent et communes locos et cetera citra complexum rerum personarumque quibus verae fictaeque controversiae continentur? Ex quo palam est quam turpiter deserat eam partem rhetorices institutio quam et pri-

10   mam habuit et diu solam.[4] Quid autem est ex his de quibus supra dixi quod non cum in alia quae sunt rhetorum propria, tum certe in illud iudiciale causae genus incidat? An non in foro narrandum est? Qua in parte nescio an sit vel

11   plurimum. Non laus ac vituperatio certaminibus illis frequenter inseritur? Non communes loci, sive qui sunt in vitia derecti, quales legimus a Cicerone compositos, seu quibus quaestiones generaliter tractantur, quales sunt editi a Quinto quoque Hortensio, ut 'sitne parvis argumentis credendum' et 'pro testibus' et 'in testes', in mediis litium

12   medullis versantur? Arma sunt haec quodam modo prae-

---

[3] om. B   [4] prima . . . sola *Güngerich* 1973 (*"of which it was the first and for a long time the sole possessor"*)

---

[3] See 3.5.11. A "thesis" is a general statement or question, not attached to any particular circumstances: "Should one marry?" as opposed to "Should Cato marry?" Lausberg §§ 1134–1138.

[4] Another type of general discussion, e.g. "against tyranny," "on luxury," "on the value of witnesses." Lausberg §§ 407–409; J. de Decker, *Iuvenalis Declamans* (Ghent, 1913) 19–70.

[5] No other references are known to collections of common-

But this itself depends on the previous question. For if the duties of the *grammaticus* are extended to include *suasoriae,* the rhetor will not be needed till later. But if the rhetor does not shirk the first duties of his task, he is needed as soon as the pupil gets to Narratives and short Encomia and Vituperations. Have we forgotten that the ancients developed their eloquence by the exercises of Thesis[3] and Commonplace,[4] and others which do not have a particular context of circumstances and persons, such as form the substance of real and imaginary *controversiae*? It is surely plain now that it is a scandal that rhetorical teaching has abandoned its original, and for a long time its only, sphere. And what is there in the exercises of which I have just spoken which does not fall within the general functions of the rhetor, and indeed also within the forensic genre? Do we not have to give Narratives in court? I suspect it may be the most important thing we do there. Are not Encomium and Vituperation frequently introduced in our contests? Do not Commonplaces belong at the very heart of lawsuits, whether they are like those which we read that Cicero composed, against vices, or are general discussions of questions, like those published also by Quintus Hortensius—"should small arguments carry weight?" "for witnesses," and "against witnesses?"[5] These are, in a sense, weapons always to be kept ready,[6] to be

places by Cicero or Hortensius. Q. implies that he does not know the Cicero collection at first hand. Examples in the speeches are numerous: see e.g. *In Verrem* 2.4.60, *Philippics* 2.97.

[6] Compare 7.10.14, and Pope's praise of Q. (*Essay on Criticism* 671–672): "Thus useful Arms in Magazines we place, All rang'd in Order and dispos'd with Grace."

paranda semper, ut iis cum res poscet utaris. Quae qui pertinere ad orationem non putabit, is ne statuam quidem
inchoari credet cum eius membra fundentur.

13   Neque hanc, ut aliqui putabunt, festinationem meam
sic quisquam calumnietur tamquam eum qui sit rhetori
traditus abducendum protinus a grammaticis putem. Dabuntur illis tum quoque tempora sua, neque erit verendum ne binis praeceptoribus oneretur puer. Non enim
crescet, sed dividetur qui sub uno miscebatur labor, et erit
sui quisque operis magister utilior: quod adhuc optinent
Graeci, a Latinis omissum est, et fieri videtur excusate,
quia sunt qui labori isti successerint.

2

1   Ergo cum ad eas in studiis vires pervenerit puer ut quae
prima esse praecepta rhetorum diximus mente consequi
possit, tradendus eius artis magistris erit.

2   Quorum in primis inspici mores oportebit: quod ego
non idcirco potissimum in hac parte tractare sum adgres-
sus quia non in ceteris quoque doctoribus idem hoc exami-
nandum quam diligentissime putem, sicut testatus sum
libro priore, sed quod magis necessariam eius rei mentio-

used as the occasion demands. Anyone who denies that these things are not relevant to oratory might as well believe that a statue is not begun when the limbs are being cast!

No one should criticize this haste of mine (as some will think it) as though I were recommending that the pupil who has been handed over to the rhetor should forthwith be taken away from the *grammatici*. They will have their place in the timetable at this stage also, and there is no reason to fear that a boy will be overloaded by having two masters, for the work that was formerly all done under one will not increase, but simply be divided, and each teacher will be more serviceable in his own department. The Greeks still maintain this system, the Latins have given it up—excusably, we may think, because others have taken over this work from the *grammatici*.

CHAPTER 2

The duties and personal qualifications of the rhetor

So as soon as the boy has progressed in his studies to the point when he can follow what I have called the first stage of instruction in rhetoric, he should be handed over to the teachers of that art.

The first necessity will be to inquire into their good character. The reason which leads me to tackle this issue particularly in the present context is not that I do not think that the most careful inquiries possible are necessary in regard to other teachers also (as I showed in the previous book) but because the age of the pupils makes it more es-

3   nem facit aetas ipsa discentium. Nam et adulti fere pueri
ad hos praeceptores transferuntur et apud eos iuvenes
etiam facti perseverant, ideoque maior adhibenda tum
cura est ut et teneriores annos ab iniuria sanctitas docentis
4   custodiat et ferociores a licentia gravitas deterreat. Neque
vero sat est summam praestare abstinentiam, nisi disciplinae severitate convenientium quoque ad se mores ad-
strinxerit.

    Sumat igitur ante omnia parentis erga discipulos suos
animum, ac succedere se in eorum locum a quibus sibi
5   liberi tradantur existimet. Ipse nec habeat vitia nec ferat.
Non austeritas eius tristis, non dissoluta sit comitas, ne
inde odium, hinc contemptus oriatur. Plurimus ei de
honesto ac bono sermo sit: nam quo saepius monuerit, hoc
rarius castigabit; minime iracundus, nec tamen eorum
quae emendanda erunt dissimulator, simplex in docendo,
6   patiens laboris, adsiduus potius quam inmodicus. Inter-
rogantibus libenter respondeat, non interrogantes per-
contetur ultro. In laudandis discipulorum dictionibus nec
malignus nec effusus, quia res altera taedium laboris, alte-
7   ra securitatem parit. In emendando quae corrigenda erunt
non acerbus minimeque contumeliosus; nam id quidem
multos a proposito studendi fugat, quod quidam sic obiur-
8   gant quasi oderint. Ipse aliquid, immo multa cotidie dicat
quae secum auditores referant. Licet enim satis exem-
plorum ad imitandum ex lectione suppeditet, tamen viva

---

[1] They are with the rhetor from, say, 13 to 18 or 19.

sential to discuss it now. Boys are approaching adulthood when they are passed on to the rhetor, and they remain with him even as young men;[1] that is why we must take particular care at this stage that the impeccable character of the teacher should preserve the younger pupils from injury, and his authority deter the more aggressive from licentious behaviour. It is not sufficient that he should himself set an example of perfect self-control unless he also restrains the behaviour of those who attend his classes by the severity of his discipline.

First of all, then, let him adopt a paternal attitude towards his pupils, and regard himself as taking the place of those whose children are entrusted to him. Let him be free of vice himself and intolerant of it in others. Let him be strict but not grim, and friendly but not too relaxed, so as to incur neither hatred nor contempt. He should talk a great deal about what is good and honourable; the more often he has admonished his pupils, the more rarely will he need to punish them. He must not be given to anger, but he must not turn a blind eye to things that need correction; he must be straightforward in his teaching, willing to work, persistent but not obsessive. He must answer questions readily, and put questions himself to those who do not ask any. In praising his pupils' performances he must be neither grudging nor fulsome: the one produces dislike of the work, the other complacency. In correcting faults, he must not be biting, and certainly not abusive. Many have been driven away from learning because some teachers rebuke pupils as though they hate them. He should himself deliver at least one speech, preferably several, a day, for his class to take away with them. For even if he provides them with plenty of examples for imitation from their reading, better

illa, ut dicitur, vox alit plenius, praecipueque praeceptoris
quem discipuli, si modo recte sunt instituti, et amant et ve-
rentur. Vix autem dici potest quanto libentius imitemur
eos quibus favemus.

9   Minime vero permittenda pueris, ut fit apud plerosque,
adsurgendi exultandique in laudando licentia: quin etiam
iuvenum modicum esse, cum audient, testimonium debet.
Ita fiet ut ex iudicio praeceptoris discipulus pendeat, atque

10   id se dixisse recte quod ab eo probabitur credat. Illa vero
vitiosissima, quae iam humanitas vocatur, invicem qualia-
cumque laudandi cum est indecora et theatralis et severe
institutis scholis aliena, tum studiorum perniciosissima
hostis: supervacua enim videntur cura ac labor parata

11   quidquid effuderint laude. Vultum igitur praeceptoris intueri tam qui audiunt debent quam ipse qui dicit: ita enim
probanda atque improbanda discernent; sic stilo facultas

12   continget, auditione iudicium. At nunc proni atque suc-
cincti ad omnem clausulam non exsurgunt modo verum
etiam excurrunt et cum indecora exultatione conclamant.
Id mutuum est et ibi declamationis fortuna. Hinc tumor et
vana de se persuasio usque adeo ut illo condiscipulorum
tumultu inflati, si parum a praeceptore laudentur, ipsi de
illo male sentiant.

13   Sed se quoque praeceptores intente ac modeste audiri
velint: non enim iudicio discipulorum dicere debet magis-

nourishment comes, as they say, from the "living voice," and especially from a teacher whom, if they are properly taught, the pupils love and respect. It is difficult to over-estimate how much readier we are to imitate those whom we like.

We should definitely not allow boys (as happens in many teachers' classrooms) to stand up or jump out of their seats to applaud. Even young adults, when they are listen-ing to a speech, should be restrained in their approval. In this way, the pupil will come to depend on the teacher's judgement, and think that he has spoken well when *he* ap-proves. The extremely undesirable "humanity," as it is now called, which consists of mutual praise without any regard to quality, is unseemly, reeks of the theatre, and is quite alien to properly disciplined schools; it is also a very dan-gerous enemy of study, because, if there is praise on hand for every effusion, care and effort appear superfluous. The audience, therefore, as well as the pupil who is speaking, should keep their eyes on the teacher's face; they will thereby learn to distinguish what deserves approval from what does not, and will thus acquire judgement by listen-ing as well as facility by writing. Nowadays however, lean-ing forward, all ready to go, they not only stand up at the end of every sentence, but rush forward with shouts of un-seemly enthusiasm. It is a mutual service; this is what makes the declamation a success. The result is a swollen head and a very false idea of themselves, carried to the point where, intoxicated by their fellow-students' uproar, they come to have bad feelings about their teacher if he fails to praise them warmly enough.

But teachers too should expect to be heard attentively and quietly. The master does not have to speak to suit the

ter, sed discipulus magistri. Quin, si fieri potest, intenden-
dus animus in hoc quoque, ut perspiciat quae quisque et
quo modo laudet, et placere quae bene dicet non suo magis quam eorum nomine delectetur qui recte iudicabunt.

14   Pueros adulescentibus permixtos sedere non placet
mihi. Nam etiamsi vir talis qualem esse oportet studiis
moribusque praepositum modestam habere potest etiam
iuventutem, tamen vel infirmitas a robustioribus separan-
da est, et carendum non solum crimine turpitudinis verum
15   etiam suspicione. Haec notanda breviter existimavi. Nam
ut absit ab ultimis vitiis ipse ac schola ne praecipiendum
quidem credo. Ac si quis est qui flagitia manifesta in eli-
gendo filii praeceptore non vitet, iam hinc sciat cetera
quoque quae ad utilitatem iuventutis componere conamur
esse sibi hac parte omissa supervacua.

3

1   Ne illorum quidem persuasio silentio transeunda est, qui,
etiam cum idoneos rhetori pueros putaverunt, non tamen
continuo tradendos eminentissimo credunt, sed apud minores aliquamdiu detinent, tamquam instituendis artibus
magis sit apta mediocritas praeceptoris cum ad intellectum atque imitationem facilior, tum ad suscipiendas ele-
2   mentorum molestias minus superba. Qua in re mihi non
arbitror diu laborandum ut ostendam quanto sit melius op-

pupils' judgement, the pupil has to speak to suit his. If possible, too, he should watch to see what each boy praises and how, and should be pleased if the good things in his speech are appreciated, not so much for his own sake as for that of the pupils who judge it correctly.

I do not approve of boys and young men sitting all together. Even if a teacher who is the right type to be in charge of studies and morals may be able to keep the young men also under control, the weaker should all the same be kept apart from the stronger, and one must avoid not only charges of immorality but the bare suspicion. I thought a brief note was needed on this; there is surely no need even to specify that both teacher and school must be free from the grosser vices. And should there be any father who fails to avoid obvious vices in choosing his son's teacher, let him have no doubt that, if this is neglected, everything else that we are trying to put together for the use of young people is pointless.

CHAPTER 3

Should the best teacher be employed
from the start?

I must not pass over in silence the view of those who, even when they have judged boys fit for the rhetor, still do not think they ought to be put straight into the charge of the most eminent teacher, but keep them for a time with lesser men, as though a mediocre teacher were better suited to the early stages of the art, both because he is easier to understand and to imitate and because he will not be too proud to take on the troublesome business of elementary teaching. On this, I do not think there is any need to em-

timis inbui, quanta in eluendis quae semel insederint vitiis
difficultas consequatur, cum geminatum onus succedentis
premat, et quidem dedocendi gravius ac prius quam do-
3 cendi: propter quod Timotheum clarum in arte tibiarum
ferunt duplices ab iis quos alius instituisset solitum exigere
mercedes quam si rudes traderentur.

Error tamen est in re duplex: unus, quod interim sufficere illos minores existimant et bono sane stomacho
4 contenti sunt: quae quamquam est ipsa reprensione digna
securitas, tamen esset utcumque tolerabilis si eius modi
praeceptores minus docerent, non peius; alter ille etiam
frequentior, quod eos qui ampliorem dicendi facultatem
sint consecuti non putant ad minora descendere, idque
interim fieri quia fastidiant praestare hanc inferioribus cu-
5 ram, interim quia omnino non possint. Ego porro eum qui
nolit in numero praecipientium non habeo, posse autem
maxime, si velit, optimum quemque contendo: primum
quod eum qui eloquentia ceteris praestet illa quoque per
quae ad eloquentiam pervenitur diligentissime percepisse
6 credibile est, deinde quia plurimum in praecipiendo valet
ratio, quae doctissimo cuique plenissima est, postremo
quia nemo sic in maioribus eminet ut eum minora de-
ficiant: nisi forte Iovem quidem Phidias optime fecit, illa

---

1 The story is not told elsewhere, but Lucian's *Harmonides*
features Timotheus as a teacher of the *aulos*.

2 At Olympia. This vast seated figure, ivory and gold over a
hardwood core, was decorated with many smaller representations
of mythical subjects and all sorts of other ornament. Coins and the
description by Pausanias (5.11) give an idea of it; it was the theme
of the Olympic Oration (12) of Q.'s younger contemporary Dio of
Prusa.

phasize how much better it is to absorb the best models, and how hard it is at a later stage to eradicate faults which have once become ingrained, because this puts a double burden on the teachers who take over, namely that of un-teaching, which is a heavier task than teaching, and has to be given priority. It is for this reason that the famous piper Timotheus[1] is said to have charged those who had had another teacher double the fee he asked of complete be-ginners.

The mistake here, however, is twofold. (1) For the time being, they think the lesser men perfectly adequate, and are indeed comfortable and content with them. This com-placency is certainly in itself blameworthy, but it would still be tolerable, if it was only the quantity, and not the quality, of such persons' teaching that was inferior. (2) Sec-ondly—an even commoner error—they think that those who have acquired superior gifts of eloquence will not condescend to lesser matters, and that the reason for this is sometimes that they disdain to take trouble over what is beneath them, and sometimes that they just cannot do it. Personally, I do not count anyone who is unwilling to do this as a teacher at all; and, as for capacity, my view is that the best man, if he chooses, will do it best, because (1) it is reasonable to believe that a man who surpasses others in eloquence has thoroughly understood the steps by which eloquence is attained; (2) the reasoning faculty, which is most highly developed in the most learned, is of crucial im-portance in teaching; and (3) no one excels in big things who fails in small things. Or are we to think that, though Phidias' Zeus[2] is a masterpiece, the decorative additions to

autem quae in ornamentum operis eius accedunt alius
melius elaborasset, aut orator loqui nesciet aut leviores
morbos curare non poterit praestantissimus medicus.

7   Quid ergo? non est quaedam eloquentia maior quam ut
eam intellectu consequi puerilis infirmitas possit? Ego
vero confiteor: sed hunc disertum praeceptorem pruden-
tem quoque et non ignarum docendi esse oportebit, sum-
mittentem se ad mensuram discentis, ut velocissimus
quoque, si forte iter cum parvolo faciat, det manum et gra-
dum suum minuat nec procedat ultra quam comes possit.

8   Quid si plerumque accidit ut faciliora sint ad intellegendum et lucidiora multo quae a doctissimo quoque dicuntur? Nam et prima est eloquentiae virtus perspicuitas, et,
quo quis ingenio minus valet, hoc se magis attollere et dila-
tare conatur, ut statura breves in digitos eriguntur et plura

9   infirmi minantur. Nam tumidos et corruptos et tinnulos et
quocumque alio cacozeliae genere peccantes certum habeo non virium sed infirmitatis vitio laborare, ut corpora
non robore sed valetudine inflantur, et recto itinere lassi
plerumque devertunt. Erit ergo etiam obscurior quo
quisque deterior.

10   Non excidit mihi scripsisse me in libro priore, cum
potiorem in scholis eruditionem esse quam domi dicerem,
libentius se prima studia tenerosque profectus ad imitationem condiscipulorum, quae facilior esset, erigere: quod a
quibusdam sic accipi potest tamquam haec quam nunc

11   tueor sententia priori diversa sit. Id a me procul aberit;
namque ea causa vel maxima est cur optimo cuique prae-
ceptori sit tradendus puer, quod apud eum discipuli quo-

---

3 Compare 9.4.66.   4 See 8.3.56.
5 Compare "Longinus" 3.4.   6 1.2.26.

that work would have been better done by someone else? Or that an orator will not know how to conduct an ordinary conversation? Or that a great doctor will not be able to treat minor illnesses?

What then? Is there not a type of eloquence too great to be understood by immature boys? I admit that there is. But our eloquent teacher will also need to be sensible and knowledgeable about teaching, and prepared to come down to his pupil's level, just as a very fast walker, if he were walking with a child, would give him his hand, shorten his own stride, and never go beyond what his companion could manage. Again, it commonly happens that what the most learned teachers say is also easier to understand and much clearer. For clarity is the first virtue of eloquence, and the less talented a speaker is, the harder he will strive after elevation and expansion, just as little men walk on tiptoe and weak men use more threats. As for the turgid, the perverse, the jingling,[3] and any who suffer from any other species of affectation,[4] I am persuaded that they do so not out of strength but out of weakness, just as bodies swell not with strength but with illness,[5] and people who are tired of the direct road often turn aside from it. So the worse a teacher is, the more obscure he will be also.

I have not forgotten that I said in the previous book,[6] when I was arguing that school education was preferable to home education, that the beginnings and the early progress of the young are stimulated more by imitating fellow pupils, because this is easier. Some may interpret this as implying that the position I am now defending is contrary to my earlier one. But that is far from my intention; perhaps the strongest reason why the boy should be entrusted to the best possible teacher is that the pupils are better

que melius instituti aut dicent quod inutile non sit imitari,
aut, si quid erraverint, statim corrigentur: at indoctus ille
etiam probabit fortasse vitiosa et placere audientibus iudicio suo coget.

12   Sit ergo tam eloquentia quam moribus praestantissimus qui ad Phoenicis Homerici exemplum dicere ac
facere doceat.

4

1   Hinc iam quas primas in docendo partis rhetorum putem
tradere incipiam, dilata parumper illa quae sola vulgo
vocatur arte rhetorica: ac mihi oportunus maxime videtur
ingressus ab eo cuius aliquid simile apud grammaticos
puer didicerit.

2   Et quia narrationum, excepta qua in causis utimur, tris
accepimus species, fabulam, quae versatur in tragoediis
atque carminibus non a veritate modo sed etiam a forma
veritatis remota, argumentum, quod falsum sed vero simile comoediae fingunt, historiam, in qua est gestae rei
expositio, grammaticis autem poeticas dedimus: apud rhetorem initium sit historica, tanto robustior quanto verior.

3   Sed narrandi quidem quae nobis optima ratio videtur

---

7 *Iliad* 9.443, "to be a speaker of words and a doer of deeds."

1 For this important classification, see *Ad Herennium* 1.12–13
(with Caplan's note), Sextus Empiricus, *Adversus grammaticos*
252–253 and 263 (with D. Blank's commentary, 1998); Cicero, *De
inventione* 1.27; R. Meijering, *Literary and Rhetorical Theories in
Greek Scholia* (Groningen, 1987) 76ff.; W. Trimpi (1983) 291–
295.   2 1.9.6.

taught in his school and will themselves either speak in a way worth imitating or be corrected at once if they make mistakes, whereas the unlearned teacher may well approve faulty work and force his pupils to like it because of his own judgement.

So the teacher who (like Phoenix in Homer)[7] teaches his pupils "to speak and to do" must be as distinguished for his eloquence as for his character.

CHAPTER 4

Preliminary exercises (Progymnasmata)

I shall now proceed to indicate what I take to be the first areas to be covered by the rhetor, postponing for the moment what is commonly regarded as the sole field of the "art of rhetoric." The handiest approach seems to me to be by way of something which is closely related to what the child has learned with the *grammatici*.

Narrative

We are told that there are three species of Narrative,[1] apart from the one used in actual Causes. One is Fable, found in tragedies and poems, and remote not only from truth but from the appearance of truth. The second is Plot, which is the false but probable fiction of comedy. The third is History, which contains the narration of actual events. We have given poetical Narratives to the *grammatici*;[2] the rhetor should begin with historical ones, which are more grown-up because they are more real.

I shall discuss what I think to be the best principles of

tum demonstrabimus cum de iudiciali parte dicemus: interim admonere illud sat est, ut sit ea neque arida prorsus
atque ieiuna (nam quid opus erat tantum studiis laboris
inpendere si res nudas atque inornatas indicare satis videretur?), neque rursus sinuosa et arcessitis descriptionibus,
in quas plerique imitatione poeticae licentiae ducuntur,
4 lasciva.[1] Vitium utrumque, peius tamen illud quod ex ino-
pia quam quod ex copia venit. Nam in pueris oratio perfecta nec exigi nec sperari potest: melior autem indoles laeta
generosique conatus et vel plura iusto concipiens interim
5 spiritus. Nec umquam me in his discentis annis offendat si
quid superfuerit. Quin ipsis doctoribus hoc esse curae velim, ut teneras adhuc mentes more nutricum mollius alant,
et satiari velut quodam iucundioris disciplinae lacte pa-
tiantur. Erit illud plenius interim corpus quod mox adulta
6 aetas adstringat. Hinc spes roboris: maciem namque et
infirmitatem in posterum minari solet protinus omnibus
membris expressus infans. Audeat haec aetas plura et
inveniat et inventis gaudeat, sint licet illa non satis sicca
interim ac severa. Facile remedium est ubertatis, sterilia
7 nullo labore vincuntur. Illa mihi in pueris natura minimum
spei dederit in qua ingenium iudicio praesumitur. Materiam esse primum volo vel abundantiorem atque ultra
quam oporteat fusam. Multum inde decoquent anni, multum ratio limabit, aliquid velut usu ipso deteretur, sit modo
unde excidi possit et quod exculpi; erit autem, si non ab

---

[1] *edd.*: lasciviat *AB*

---

[3] 4.2.

Narrative later, when I come to speak of forensic oratory.[3] Meanwhile, it is sufficient to note that it should be neither quite dry and jejune (for why spend so much labour on our studies if it was thought satisfactory to set things out baldly and without embellishment?) nor, on the other hand, tortuous and revelling in those irrelevant Descriptions to which many are tempted by their wish to imitate the licence of poets. Both are faults, but the one which comes from deficiency is worse than the one which comes from abundance. In boys, a perfect style is neither to be demanded nor expected; but there is a better prospect in a fertile mind, ambitious effort, and a spirit that sometimes has too many bold ideas. I should never feel troubled by a certain amount of excess in a pupil of this age. Indeed, I should like the teachers themselves to take trouble to nourish the tender minds gently, like nurses, and let them have their fill of the milk, as it were, of pleasanter learning. That will put flesh on them for a time, but growing up will in due course slim them down. This is where one sees hope of future strength. The baby whose limbs are all distinctly visible from the start threatens to be skinny and weak later on. The young should be more daring and inventive, and take pleasure in their inventions, even if for the time being these are not sober and correct enough. Exuberance is easily remedied; no effort can overcome barrenness. The quality in a boy which, to my mind, gives least promise is the premature growth of judgement at the expense of creative talent. I like the raw material at the start to be over-abundant, poured out more generously even than it ought to be. The passing years will reduce it greatly, method will file it down, use will rub some of it away, so long as there is something there to be cut out and chiselled; and that will

283

initio tenuem nimium laminam duxerimus et quam caela-
8 tura altior rumpat. Quod me de his aetatibus sentire minus
mirabitur qui apud Ciceronem legerit: 'volo enim se effe-
rat in adulescente fecunditas'.

Quapropter in primis evitandus, et in pueris praecipue,
magister aridus, non minus quam teneris adhuc plantis sic-
9 cum et sine umore ullo solum. Inde fiunt humiles statim et
velut terram spectantes, qui nihil supra cotidianum sermonem attollere audeant. Macies illis pro sanitate et iudicii
loco infirmitas est, et, dum satis putant vitio carere, in id
ipsum incidunt vitium, quod virtutibus carent. Quare mihi
ne maturitas quidem ipsa festinet nec musta in lacu statim
austera sint: sic et annos ferent et vetustate proficient.
10 Ne illud quidem quod admoneamus indignum est, ingenia puerorum nimia interim emendationis severitate
deficere; nam et desperant et dolent et novissime oderunt
et, quod maxime nocet, dum omnia timent nihil conantur.
11 Quod etiam rusticis notum est, qui frondibus teneris non
putant adhibendam esse falcem, quia reformidare ferrum
12 videntur et nondum cicatricem pati posse. Iucundus ergo
tum maxime debet esse praeceptor, ut remedia, quae
alioqui natura sunt aspera, molli manu lenientur: laudare
aliqua, ferre quaedam, mutare etiam reddita cur id fiat ratione, inluminare interponendo aliquid sui. Nonnumquam
hoc quoque erit utile, totas ipsum dictare materias, quas et
13 imitetur puer et interim tamquam suas amet: at si tam

---

4 *De oratore* 2.88.   5 The must (see Cicero, *Brutus* 288 for
the metaphor) should be too sweet (i.e. the boy's talent too rich) to
begin with, so that a due balance is obtained in maturity, when the
wine begins to be more acid (and the mind to lose vigour).

6 Compare Vergil, *Georgics* 2.369.

be so, if we do not draw the plate too thin to begin with, so that it breaks if the engraving goes too deep. That I think in this way about the young will be less surprising to anyone who has read Cicero's words: "I like fecundity to run riot in a young man."[4]

It is therefore especially important, particularly with little boys, to avoid a dry teacher, just as we avoid a dry soil without moisture for young plants. For with this sort of teaching, they instantly become stunted, and look down at the ground, as it were, because they dare not rise above the level of daily speech. They think leanness means health and weakness good judgement, and while they think it is enough to be without fault they fall into the fault of being without virtues. I would not want even maturity to come too soon, or the must to become tart straight away in the vat; in this way it will bear its years better and improve with age.[5]

It is worth noting too that boys' minds sometimes cannot stand up to undue severity in correction. They despair, they feel hurt, they come ultimately to hate the work, and (most damaging of all) they make no effort because they are frightened of everything. Farmers know this: they do not believe in applying the pruning hook to the tender leaves, because these seem to be afraid of the knife[6] and not yet able to bear a scar. So at this stage the teacher should be particularly kind, so that the remedies, which are otherwise harsh by nature, can be made easier by a gentle touch. He must praise some things, tolerate others, suggest changes (always also giving reasons for them), and brighten up passages by putting in something of his own. He will sometimes also find it useful to dictate whole themes himself for the boy to imitate and sometimes love

285

neglegens ei stilus fuerit ut emendationem non recipiat,
expertus sum prodesse quotiens eandem materiam rursus
a me retractatam scribere de integro iuberem: posse enim
eum adhuc melius: quatenus nullo magis studia quam spe
14 gaudent. Aliter autem alia aetas emendanda est, et pro
modo virium et exigendum et corrigendum opus. Solebam
ego dicere pueris aliquid ausis licentius aut laetius laudare
illud me adhuc, venturum tempus quo idem non permitte-
rem: ita et ingenio gaudebant et iudicio non fallebantur.
15 Sed ut eo revertar unde sum egressus: narrationes stilo
componi quanta maxima possit adhibita diligentia volo.
Nam ut primo, cum sermo instituitur, dicere quae audierint utile est pueris ad loquendi facultatem, ideoque et retro agere expositionem et a media in utramque partem
discurrere sane merito cogantur, sed ad gremium praeceptoris et dum ‹maiora›[2] non possunt et dum res ac verba
conectere incipiunt, ut protinus memoriam firment: ita
cum iam formam rectae atque emendatae orationis acci-
pient, extemporalis garrulitas nec expectata cogitatio et
16 vix surgendi mora circulatoriae vere iactationis est. Hinc
parentium imperitorum inane gaudium, ipsis vero contemptus operis et inverecunda frons et consuetudo pes-
sime dicendi et malorum exercitatio et, quae magnos
quoque profectus frequenter perdidit, adrogans de se
17 persuasio innascitur. Erit suum parandae facilitati tempus,

[2] *add. Winterbottom*

as if they were his own. If, however, the written work is so careless that it cannot be corrected, I have found that it helped if I treated the same theme again myself and made my pupil write it out afresh, telling him he could do even better; for nothing makes for happy work as much as hope. But different ages need different methods of correction, and the original assignment and the correction have both to be proportionate to the pupil's strength. I used to say to boys who ventured on some rather free or exuberant expression that I approved of it now, but the time would come when I should not let it pass. So they were happy with their creativity, and not deceived in their judgement.

But to return to the point from which I digressed. I want written Narratives to be as carefully composed as possible. When children are first being taught to talk, it is useful for them to repeat what they have heard, so as to improve their facility of speech, and they may quite properly be made to tell the story orally in reverse, and to start in the middle and go either backwards or forwards, but only privately with the teacher, and only so long as they cannot do more, but are merely beginning to put things and words together; this helps to strengthen the memory from the start. Similarly, when they are beginning to understand the nature of correct and accurate speech, extempore chatter, not waiting to think and hardly hesitating before getting up, suggests simply the self-advertisement of a street-seller's patter. Ignorant parents get a foolish pleasure from this, but the boys themselves come to despise their work, lose all shame, acquire very bad habits of speaking, practise their faults, and develop an arrogant conceit of themselves—a development which has often put a stop to impressive progress. There will be a proper

QUINTILIAN

nec a nobis neglegenter locus iste transibitur. Interim satis
est si puer omni cura et summo, quantum illa aetas capit,
labore aliquid probabile scripserit: in hoc adsuescat, huius
sibi rei naturam faciat. Ille demum in id quod quaerimus
aut ei proximum poterit evadere qui ante discet recte
dicere quam cito.

18   Narrationibus non inutiliter subiungitur opus restruen-
di[3] confirmandique eas, quod ἀνασκευή et κατασκευή vocatur. Id porro non tantum in fabulosis et carmine traditis
fieri potest, verum etiam in ipsis annalium monumentis:
ut, si quaeratur 'an sit credibile super caput Valeri pugnan-
tis sedisse corvum, qui os oculosque hostis Galli rostro
atque alis everberaret', sit in utramque partem ingens ad
19   dicendum materia: aut de serpente, quo Scipio traditur
genitus, et lupa Romuli et Egeria Numae; nam Graecis
historiis plerumque poeticae similis licentia est. Saepe
etiam quaeri solet de tempore, de loco, quo gesta res dicitur, nonnumquam de persona quoque, sicut Livius frequentissime dubitat et alii ab aliis historici dissentiunt.
20   Inde paulatim ad maiora tendere incipiet, laudare claros viros et vituperare improbos: quod non simplicis utili-

3 destruendi A (cf 2.17.30, 10.5.12, Stat. Theb. 10.879)

7 See 10.1.   8 See especially Theon (76 and 93 Spengel);
in general Lausberg §§ 1122–1125.
9 All these examples (Valerius: Livy 7.26; Scipio: Livy 26.19.7;
she-wolf: Livy 1.4; Egeria: Livy 1.19, 1.21) are historical, not
mythical in the way that, e.g., the story of Apollo and Daphne (the
example in Aphthonius' *Progymnasmata* 10–16 Rabe = 28–32
Spengel) is. Q. wishes to maintain a Roman, and not too unrealistic, tone even in this exercise.

time for acquiring facility, and I shall not neglect that topic.[7] Meanwhile, it is enough if a boy, by taking pains and working as hard as his age permits, writes something that one can approve. Let him get used to this, and make it second nature. It is only the pupil who learns to speak correctly before he learns to speak quickly who will be able to achieve our ideal, or the nearest thing to it.

Refutation and Confirmation

To Narrative is usefully added the exercise of refuting and confirming, which is called *anaskeuē* and *kataskeuē*.[8] This too can be applied not only to mythical and poetic traditions, but also to the records of history. For example, there is a great deal to be said on both sides if we ask whether it is credible that a raven should have settled on Valerius' head as he was fighting, and struck the face and eyes of his Gallic opponent with its beak and wings; or we can take the serpent by which Scipio is supposed to have been begotten, or Romulus' she-wolf, or Numa's Egeria.[9] (Greek historical narratives often display an almost poetic licence.) The time and place of a supposed occurrence, and sometimes also the person involved, is often questioned. Thus Livy very frequently expresses doubt, and historians very frequently disagree with one another.

Encomia and Invectives

The pupil will then gradually begin to attempt more ambitious themes: Encomia of famous men and Invective

tatis opus est. Namque et ingenium exercetur multiplici
variaque materia et animus contemplatione recti pravique
formatur, et multa inde cognitio rerum venit exemplisque,
quae sunt in omni genere causarum potentissima, iam tum
21 instruit, cum res poscet usurum. Hinc illa quoque exercitatio subit comparationis, uter melior uterve deterior:
quae quamquam versatur in ratione simili, tamen et dupli-
cat materiam et virtutum vitiorumque non tantum naturam sed etiam modum tractat. Verum de ordine laudis
contraque, quoniam tertia haec rhetorices pars est, prae-
cipiemus suo tempore.
22 Communes loci (de iis loquor quibus citra personas in
ipsa vitia moris est perorare, ut in adulterum, aleatorem,
petulantem) ex mediis sunt iudiciis et, si reum adicias, ac-
cusationes: quamquam hi quoque ab illo generali tractatu
ad quasdam deduci species solent, ut si ponatur adulter
caecus, aleator pauper, petulans senex. Habent autem
23 nonnumquam etiam defensionem; nam et pro luxuria et
pro amore dicimus, et leno interim parasitusque defenditur sic ut non homini patrocinemur sed crimini.
24 Theses autem quae sumuntur ex rerum comparatione

---

10 See Theon, 109–112 Spengel. Q. deals with this type of
speech in more detail in 3.7.   11 See Theon 112 Spengel;
Lausberg § 1130. F. Focke (*Hermes* 58 (1923) 327–368) gives still
the best general study of "comparison" (*synkrisis*). The "Comparisons" in Plutarch's *Lives* are an ingenious historical elaboration of
this exercise.   12 3.7.

13 See on 2.1.8.

14 Hermogenes (25.17 Rabe) treats these as "double theses."
For a rhetorical "town and country" comparison, see Libanius,
Progymnasmata 10.5 (8.353–360 Foerster); the theme is trans-
muted into high poetry by Vergil, *Georgics* 2.458–474.

against the wicked.[10] This is useful in more ways than one: the mind is exercised by the variety and multiplicity of the material; the character is moulded by the contemplation of right and wrong; a wide knowledge of facts is acquired, and this provides the speaker with a ready-made store of examples—a very powerful resource in all sorts of cases—which he will use when occasion demands. From this follows the exercise of Comparison:[11] which of the two men is the better and which is the worse? This rests on a similar principle, but doubles the material and handles not only the nature of virtues and vices but their degree. The method of Encomium and its opposite (which form the third part of rhetoric) I shall prescribe when its time comes.[12]

Commonplaces

Commonplaces[13] (I mean those in which we orate against vices in themselves—the adulterer, the gambler, the profligate—without naming individuals) are at the heart of judicial cases: if you add the defendant's name, they become accusations. But the usual treatment of Commonplaces is to modify the generality by bringing it down to some more specific case: a *blind* adulterer, a *poor* gambler, an *old* profligate. They sometimes contribute to a defence, for we speak "in defence of luxury" or "in defence of love," and a pimp or a parasite may occasionally be defended, so as to plead the cause not of the individual but of the crime itself.

Theses

Theses which are taken from comparisons of things[14]—

(ut 'rusticane vita an urbana potior', 'iuris periti an milita-
ris viri laus maior') mire sunt ad exercitationem dicendi
speciosae atque uberes, quae vel ad suadendi officium vel
etiam ad iudiciorum disceptationem iuvant plurimum:
nam posterior ex praedictis locus in causa Murenae copio-
25   sissime a Cicerone tractatur. Sunt et illae paene totae ad
deliberativum pertinentes genus: 'ducendane uxor', 'pe-
tendine sint magistratus'; namque et hae personis modo
adiectis suasoriae erunt.

26   Solebant praeceptores mei neque inutili et nobis etiam
iucundo genere exercitationis praeparare nos coniecturali-
bus causis cum quaerere atque exequi iuberent 'cur arma-
ta apud Lacedaemonios Venus' et 'quid ita crederetur
Cupido puer atque volucer et sagittis ac face armatus' et
similia, in quibus scrutabamur voluntatem, cuius in controversiis frequens quaestio est: quod genus chriae videri
potest.

27   Nam locos quidem, quales sunt de testibus 'semperne
his credendum' et de argumentis 'an habenda etiam parvis fides', adeo manifestum est ad forensis actiones pertinere ut quidam neque ignobiles in officiis civilibus scriptos eos memoriaeque diligentissime mandatos in promptu
habuerint, ut, quotiens esset occasio, extemporales eorum
28   dictiones his velut emblematis exornarentur: quo quidem

---

15 22ff.

16 See Pausanias 3.15.10.

17 A common theme: *Anthologia Palatina* 5.177, Horace,
Carmina 3.27.67–68, Tibullus 2.1.81, Propertius 2.12, Isidore,
Etymologiae 8.11.80 ("He is painted as winged, because nothing is
more fickle and changeable than lovers; as a boy, because love is
foolish and irrational. He is imagined as carrying an arrow and a

for example "Is country life or town life to be preferred?" "Does the lawyer or the soldier deserve the greater praise?"—are remarkably attractive and rewarding ways of exercising the skill of speaking; they are extremely helpful both for deliberative and also for forensic duties, for the second of the two themes I have suggested is handled very fully by Cicero in *Pro Murena*.[15] Other theses are relevant almost entirely to the deliberative genre: "Should a man marry?" "Should one compete for office?" Simply add specific persons, and these too become *suasoriae*.

My own teachers used to prepare us for Conjectural Causes by means of a useful exercise, which we also found amusing: they told us to inquire into and develop such questions as "Why is Venus portrayed as armed at Sparta?"[16] or "Why was Love believed to be a winged boy armed with arrows and a torch?"[17] In this, we investigated Intention, which is a frequent topic in *controversiae*. This exercise may be thought of as a kind of Chria.[18]

General topics, such as on witnesses ("should we always believe them?"), or on rational arguments ("should we rely on them, however trivial?"), so obviously relate to forensic pleadings that some people, by no means undistinguished in public life, have been known to write these topics out,[19] carefully commit them to memory, and have them ready at hand so as to embellish their extempore speeches with these insertions when necessary. I used to think—I cannot

torch; an arrow because love wounds the heart; a torch, because it sets it on fire").

[18] Because it involves discussing and justifying an authoritative opinion. Lausberg §§ 1117–1120.

[19] Compare 2.1.11.

QUINTILIAN

(neque enim eius rei iudicium differre sustineo) summam
videbantur mihi infirmitatem de se confiteri. Nam quid hi
possint in causis, quarum varia et nova semper est facies,
proprium invenire, quo modo propositis ex parte adversa
respondere, altercationibus velociter occurrere, testem
rogare, qui etiam in iis quae sunt communia et in plurimis
causis tractantur vulgatissimos sensus verbis nisi tanto ante
29 praeparatis prosequi nequeant? Necesse[4] vero his, cum
eadem iudiciis pluribus dicunt, aut fastidium moveant velut frigidi et repositi cibi, aut pudorem deprensa totiens
audientium memoria infelix supellex, quae sicut apud pau-
peres ambitiosos pluribus et diversis officiis conteratur:
30 cum eo quidem, quod vix ullus est tam communis locus qui
possit cohaerere cum causa nisi aliquo propriae quaestionis vinculo copulatus; appareatque eum non tam insertum
31 quam adplicitum, vel quod dissimilis est ceteris, vel quod
plerumque adsumi etiam parum apte solet, non quia desideratur, sed quia paratus est, ut quidam sententiarum gratia verbosissimos locos arcessunt, cum ex locis debeat nasci
32 sententia: ita sunt autem speciosa haec et utilia si oriuntur
ex causa; ceterum quamlibet pulchra elocutio, nisi ad victoriam tendit, utique supervacua, sed interim etiam contraria est. Verum hactenus evagari satis fuerit.

[4] *Zumpt*: nec *AB*

---

[20] I.e. postpone the subject to the discussion of Improvisation,
10.7.   [21] The imagery suggests a situation like that of the
people of Egesta (Thucydides 6.46) who borrowed gold and silver
plate from one another to entertain the Athenian envoys and
create the impression that they were all rich.   [22] Compare
Horace, *Ars poetica* 15, on the "purple patch sewn on."

bear to hold my opinion back[20]—that this amounted to an admission of great weakness. For what specific arguments can these people find in the course of cases which continually present new features of various kinds? How can they answer points raised by the other side, make a quick response in debate, or interrogate a witness, if they cannot so much as express the most banal sentiments over common matters which occur in great numbers of Causes without having prepared their words so long before? Inevitably, when they say the same things in several cases, they will either produce the disgust we feel for cold, twice-served-up food, or else will be disgraced by the detection of their wretched stock-in-trade, so familiar to the audience's memory, and worn to shreds, as it were, by doing numerous different services for poor men who want to put on a show.[21] What is more, there is scarcely any topic so general that it can fit any real case, unless it is connected with it by some link arising out of the particular question—and even so it would be obvious that it was not so much an insertion as a patch stuck on,[22] either because it is different from its surroundings, or because it is commonly added even irrelevantly, not because it is needed, but because it is ready to hand. (Similarly, some speakers drag in very diffuse general "topics" for the sake of their *sententiae,* when the *sententia* ought rather to grow out of the topic.) These things are attractive and useful if, and only if, they arise naturally out of the Cause; but the most beautiful verbal expression, unless it helps us to win, is always unnecessary, and sometimes actually damaging. But I have wandered far enough from the point.

33   Legum laus ac vituperatio iam maiores ac prope summis operibus suffecturas vires desiderant: quae quidem
suasoriis an controversiis magis accommodata sit exercitatio consuetudine et iure civitatium differt. Apud Graecos
enim lator earum ad iudicem vocabatur, Romanis pro
contione suadere ac dissuadere moris fuit; utroque autem
modo pauca de his et fere certa dicuntur: nam et genera
34   sunt tria sacri, publici, privati iuris. Quae divisio ad laudem
magis spectat, si quis eam per gradus augeat, quod lex,
quod publica, quod ad religionem deum comparata sit. Ea
35   quidem de quibus quaeri solet communia omnibus. Aut
enim de iure dubitari potest eius qui rogat, ut de P. Clodi,
qui non rite creatus tribunus arguebatur: aut de ipsius ro-
gationis, quod est varium, sive non trino forte nundino
promulgata sive non idoneo die sive contra intercessionem
vel auspicia aliudve quid quod legitimis obstet dicitur lata
36   esse vel ferri, sive alicui manentium legum repugnare. Sed
haec ad illas primas exercitationes non pertinent: nam sunt
eae citra complexum personarum temporum causarum.

   Reliqua eadem fere vero fictoque certamine huius

---

23 Theon 128 Spengel. "Proposal of law" is a commoner exercise; either form could easily be developed into a complete
speech. Lausberg § 1139.
   24 A proposed law could be challenged at Athens (by a *graphē
paranomōn*) as unconstitutional. A number of Demosthenes'
speeches are concerned with such cases: see especially *Orations*
22, 23 (*Against Androtion, Against Timocrates*).
   25 See Cicero, *De domo* 32–33.
   26 Ibid. 34. Clodius was not eligible to be a tribune because (as
Cicero claimed) he was a patrician, his adoption into a plebeian
family not being valid.

Criticism of laws

Praise and denunciation of laws[23] need greater powers, such as are almost equal to the highest tasks of the orator. Whether this exercise is more like a deliberative or a forensic declamation depends on the custom and law of the states concerned. Among the Greeks, the proposer of a law was called before a judge;[24] in Rome, the practice was to speak for and against the proposal in an assembly of the people. In both cases, the points made are few and pretty well defined. For there are in fact just three kinds of law: sacred, public, and private. This division is more relevant when a law is being commended, because then one can advance step by step: it is (1) a law, (2) a public law, (3) a law designed to safeguard religion.[25] The Questions which usually arise are common to all three types. Doubts may be raised either (1) about the legal status of the proposer (as with Publius Clodius, who was shown not to have been properly elected tribune),[26] or (2) about the legality of the proposal itself; this opens up various possibilities: it may be said not to have been promulgated for the statutory three market days,[27] or to have been, or now to be, carried on an improper day, or contrary to a tribune's intercession or to the auspices, or to be subject to some other objection as to its legitimacy; or again, it may be said to be inconsistent with some existing law. But these matters are not relevant to the elementary exercises, which do not involve specific persons, times, or cases.

The other points handled are more or less the same in

[27] I.e. for seventeen days, since the bill could not be debated till the third *nundinae* from its promulgation.

37 modi tractantur: nam vitium aut in verbis aut in rebus est.
In verbis quaeritur satis significent an sit in iis aliquid
ambiguum: in rebus, an lex sibi ipsa consentiat, an in praeteritum ferri debeat, an in singulos homines. Maxime vero
38 commune est quaerere an sit honesta, an utilis. Nec ignoro
plures fieri a plerisque partes, sed nos iustum pium religio-
sum ceteraque his similia honesto complectimur.

Iusti tamen species non simpliciter excuti solet. Aut
enim de re ipsa quaeritur, ut dignane poena vel praemio
sit, aut de modo praemii poenaeve, qui tam maior quam
39 minor culpari potest. Utilitas quoque interim natura dis-
cernitur, interim tempore. Quaedam an optineri possint
ambigi solet. Ne illud quidem ignorare oportet, leges aliquando totas, aliquando ex parte reprendi solere, cum
exemplum rei utriusque nobis claris orationibus praebe-
40 atur. Nec me fallit eas quoque leges esse quae non in perpetuum rogentur, sed de honoribus aut imperiis, qualis
Manilia fuit, de qua Ciceronis oratio est. Sed de his nihil
hoc loco praecipi potest: constant enim propria rerum de
quibus agitur, non communi, qualitate.
41 His fere veteres facultatem dicendi exercuerunt, ad-

---

28 Cicero, *De domo* 43; Cicero there invokes the Laws of the
Twelve Tables to denounce *privilegium,* the enactment of a law
which specially targeted an individual citizen.

29 For *iustum* as a subdivision of *honestum,* see Cicero, *De
officiis* 1.20, where it is the second main *locus* of *honestum,* viz.
civil society.

30 No classical speeches can be found to illustrate this: Cousin
and Corsi cite various episodes in Livy (4.2, 6.40, 10.7–8, 34.5),
but it is not clear what Q. has in mind.

31 Cicero, as praetor in 66 BC, supported the proposal of the

all cases of this kind, whether real or imaginary. Any defect must be either in the words or in the substance. As regards the words, the Question is whether they are clear enough or in some respect ambiguous. As regards the substance, it is whether the law is consistent with itself, whether it should be retrospective, and whether it should apply to individuals.[28] The most generally applicable Questions are whether it is right and whether it is expedient. I know many people make more subdivisions; but I include justice, piety, religion and the like under "right."

Justice[29] however usually receives quite a complex treatment. Questions are raised either about the action itself with which the law is concerned—for example, does it deserve punishment or reward?—or about the level of reward or punishment, which can be criticized as either too high or too low. Expediency too is sometimes determined by the nature of the matter, sometimes by the occasion. With some laws, the common doubt is whether they can be enforced. And it must be borne in mind also that laws are sometimes criticized in their entirety and sometimes in part, for we have examples of both in famous speeches.[30] I have not forgotten that there are also laws which are not meant to be permanent, but which concern honours or appointments to commands, like the Lex Manilia[31] which is the subject of Cicero's speech. But no advice on these is in place here; they are based on the special Quality of the matters they address, not on a common Quality.

Such, in general, were the ways in which the ancients exercised their powers of speaking, though they took over

tribune C. Manilius to give Pompey supreme command in the war against Mithridates.

sumpta tamen a dialecticis argumentandi ratione. Nam
fictas ad imitationem fori consiliorumque materias apud
Graecos dicere circa Demetrium Phalerea institutum fere
42   constat. An ab ipso id genus exercitationis sit inventum, ut
alio quoque libro sum confessus, parum comperi: sed ne ii
quidem qui hoc fortissime adfirmant ullo satis idoneo auc-
tore nituntur. Latinos vero dicendi praeceptores extremis
L. Crassi temporibus coepisse Cicero auctor est: quorum
insignis maxime Plotius fuit.

5

1   Sed de ratione declamandi post paulo: interim, quia prima
rhetorices rudimenta tractamus, non omittendum videtur
id quoque, ut moneam quantum sit conlaturus ad profec-
tum discentium rhetor si, quem ad modum a grammaticis
exigitur poetarum enarratio, ita ipse quoque historiae atque etiam magis orationum lectione susceptos a se discipulos instruxerit. Quod nos in paucis, quorum id aetas
2   exigebat et parentes utile esse crediderant, servavimus: ceterum sentientibus iam tum optima duae res impedimento
fuerunt, quod et longa consuetudo aliter docendi fecerat
legem, et robusti fere iuvenes nec hunc laborem desi-

---

32 For Demetrius' supposed role as the initiator of a decadent
phase of eloquence, see 10.1.80, and Cicero, *Orator* 92, 96, *Bru-*
tus 37ff. Q. is rightly sceptical about his importance in the history
of declamation: see *GD* 18–19, and, for full discussion, Heldemann (1982) 99–122.   33 Presumably *De causis corruptae*
eloquentiae.   34 *De oratore* 3.93, but with no specific reference to declamation.   35 L. Plotius Gallus (see Suetonius, *De*
rhetoribus 26, citing a letter of Cicero: Kaster (1995) 291–297)

the method of argument from the dialecticians. Speaking on imaginary themes, constructed to imitate judicial or deliberative cases, is said to have begun with the Greeks around the time of Demetrius of Phalerum.[32] Whether he himself invented this type of exercise, I have been unable to discover, as I have admitted in another work.[33] Even those who affirm it most strongly have no sufficient authority to rely upon. As for Latin teachers of oratory, Cicero[34] assures us that they began in the last days of Lucius Crassus. The most famous of these teachers was Plotius.[35]

CHAPTER 5

The rhetor should read oratory and history with his pupils

I shall be speaking of the method of declamation a little later.[1] Meanwhile, as we are dealing with the first rudiments of rhetoric, I think I should not fail to point out what a contribution the rhetor will make to his pupils' progress if—as a parallel to the interpretation of the poets we demand from the *grammatici*—he too instructs the pupils he takes over in reading history and, even more, oratory. I myself observed this practice in a few cases, where the children's age made it necessary and the parents thought it useful. But, though my views were then clearly right, there were two obstacles in the way: long custom had established another way of teaching, and the mature young men (as

seems to have taught in Rome before 92 BC, when Crassus, as censor, banned Latin teaching of rhetoric. Q. knows his work on gesture: 11.3.143.   [1] 2.10.

3 derantes exemplum nostrum[1] sequebantur. Nec tamen,
etiam si quid novi vel sero invenissem, praecipere in posterum puderet: nunc vero scio id fieri apud Graecos, sed
magis per adiutores, quia non videntur tempora suffectura
4 si legentibus singulis praeire semper ipsi velint. Et hercule
praelectio quae in hoc adhibetur, ut facile atque distincte
pueri scripta oculis sequantur, etiam illa quae vim cuiusque verbi, si quod minus usitatum incidat, docet, multum
5 infra rhetoris officium existimanda est. At demonstrare
virtutes vel, si quando ita incidat, vitia, id professionis eius
atque promissi quo se magistrum eloquentiae pollicetur
maxime proprium est, eo quidem validius quod non utique
hunc laborem docentium postulo, ut ad gremium revocatis
6 cuius quisque eorum velit libri lectione deserviant. Nam
mihi cum facilius tum etiam multo videtur magis utile facto silentio unum aliquem (quod ipsum imperari per vices
optimum est) constituere lectorem, ut protinus pronun-
7 tiationi quoque adsuescant: tum exposita causa in quam
scripta legetur oratio (nam sic clarius quae dicentur intellegi poterunt), nihil otiosum pati quodque in inventione
quodque in elocutione adnotandum erit: quae in prohoe-
mio conciliandi iudicis ratio, quae narrandi lux brevitas
fides, quod aliquando consilium et quam occulta calliditas
8 (namque ea sola in hoc ars est, quae intellegi nisi ab artifice
non possit): quanta deinceps in dividendo prudentia,

[1] *del. Shackleton Bailey*

[2] I.e. Q.'s model declamations. So Spalding, following Regius;
an alternative (but less likely) interpretation is that the older boys,
instead of doing more advanced exercises, chose to do the reading, which was a waste of their time.   [3] Compare 1.11.3. Q.

they mostly were) who did not need this work were following my models.[2] However, even if I had made a new discovery too late for myself, I should have no qualms about passing it on to future generations. In fact, I know that it is
practised in the Greek schools, but more by means of assis-
tants, because time is seen to be too short for the masters
themselves always to supervise pupils' reading individually. Indeed, reading the text out to ensure that the boys
follow the written word easily and clearly, and even the sort
of reading which is meant to explain the force of any unfa-
miliar word, are both to be judged far beneath the rhetor's
proper office. On the other hand, it certainly is part of his
profession and claim as teacher of eloquence to point out
merits and, where necessary, faults—all the more so because I am not of course imposing on teachers the task of
calling the pupil up to stand at their side, and helping him
in reading any book he may choose! It seems to me both
easier and much more profitable to call for silence and ap-
point one boy as reader (it is best to do this by giving each a
turn), so that they accustom themselves also to speaking in
public. Then the Cause for which the speech to be read
was written should be explained, because that will enable
the spoken words to be better understood. Nothing must
pass unnoticed: every noteworthy point of Invention or
Elocution is to be observed—the way in which the judge is
conciliated in the Prooemium; the clarity, brevity, and
credibility of the Narrative; the speaker's plan and hidden
artifice (in this business the only art is that which can only
be seen by an artist!);[3] the wisdom shown in dividing the

runs through the various parts of the speech, enumerating the various qualities which the teacher is to point out.

quam subtilis et crebra argumentatio, quibus viribus in-
spiret, qua iucunditate permulceat, quanta in maledictis
asperitas, in iocis urbanitas, ut denique dominetur in adfectibus atque in pectora inrumpat animumque iudicum
9   similem iis quae dicit efficiat; tum, in ratione eloquendi,
quod verbum proprium ornatum sublime, ubi amplificatio
laudanda, quae virtus ei contraria, quid speciose tralatum,
quae figura verborum, quae levis et quadrata, virilis tamen
compositio.

10   Ne id quidem inutile, etiam corruptas aliquando et vi-
tiosas orationes, quas tamen plerique iudiciorum pravitate
mirentur, legi palam, ostendique in his quam multa inpropria obscura tumida humilia sordida lasciva effeminata
sint: quae non laudantur modo a plerisque, sed, quod est
11   peius, propter hoc ipsum quod sunt prava laudantur. Nam
sermo rectus et secundum naturam enuntiatus nihil habere ex ingenio videtur; illa vero quae utcumque deflexa
sunt tamquam exquisitiora miramur non aliter quam dis-
tortis et quocumque modo prodigiosis corporibus apud
quosdam maius est pretium quam iis quae nihil ex commu-
12   nis habitus bonis perdiderunt, atque etiam qui specie ca-
piuntur vulsis levatisque et inustas comas acu comentibus
et non suo colore nitidis plus esse formae putant quam
possit tribuere incorrupta natura, ut pulchritudo corporis

---

4 Compare [Quintilian], *Declamationes minores* 298f.: "one
pleases by weakness, another by the wretched condition of a crippled body." Plutarch (*Moralia* 520c) tells us of a market at Rome in
abnormal or monstrously deformed slaves.

materials; the delicate and dense argument; the vigour that stirs and the charm that delights; the sharpness of the invective, the wit of the jokes; and how finally the orator reigns over the jury's emotions, forces his way into their hearts, and makes their feelings reflect his words. As for Elocution, he will point out the exact use, elegance, or sublimity of each word; where Amplification is to be praised, and where the opposite quality is to be seen; the brilliance of the metaphors, the Figures of Speech, and how the Composition is smooth and well-formed while remaining masculine.

It can also be useful sometimes to read aloud bad or faulty speeches, but of the kind that many admire out of bad taste, and to point out what a lot of expressions in these are inexact, obscure, turgid, low, mean, extravagant, or effeminate. These expressions are not only praised by many people but, what is worse, praised just for their badness. For straightforward, natural speech is judged to owe nothing to talent; we admire things which are in some way distorted as being more sophisticated—just as some people set a higher value on human bodies which are crippled or somehow deformed than on those which have lost none of the blessings of normality,[4] while others again, who are captivated by appearances, fancy that there is more beauty in those who have had their hairs plucked and skin smoothed, who singe their hair and keep it in order with pins, and whose complexion is anything but their own, than in anything that uncorrupted nature can confer:

venire videatur ex malis morum.

13   Neque solum haec ipse debebit docere praeceptor, sed frequenter interrogare et iudicium discipulorum experiri. Sic audientibus securitas aberit nec quae dicentur superfluent aures: simul ad id perducentur quod ex hoc quaeritur, ut inveniant ipsi et intellegant. Nam quid aliud agimus docendo eos quam ne semper docendi sint?

14   Hoc diligentiae genus ausim dicere plus conlaturum discentibus quam omnes omnium artes, quae iuvant sine dubio multum, sed latiore quadam comprensione per omnes quidem species rerum cotidie paene nascentium

15   ire qui possunt? Sicut de re militari quamquam sunt tradita quaedam praecepta communia, magis tamen proderit scire qua ducum quisque ratione in quali re tempore loco sit sapienter usus aut contra: nam in omnibus fere minus

16   valent praecepta quam experimenta. An vero declamabit quidem praeceptor ut sit exemplo suis auditoribus: non plus contulerint lecti Cicero aut Demosthenes? Corrigetur palam si quid in declamando discipulus erraverit: non potentius erit emendare orationem, quin immo etiam iucundius? Aliena enim vitia reprendi quisque mavult quam sua.

17   Nec deerant plura quae dicerem: sed neminem haec utilitas fugit, atque utinam tam non pigeat facere istud quam non displicebit.

---

[5] This second error is to take artificial elegance (of complexion or hair) for real beauty. Translated into literary terms, this means that some (§ 11) like the deliberately uncouth, others (§ 12) excessive polish. A similar argument is found in Seneca, *Epistulae* 114.

thus beauty of body seems to come from depravity of character.[5]

The teacher will not only be required to give instruction on these things himself, but to ask frequent questions and test his pupils' judgement. This will get rid of inattentiveness while they are listening, and ensure that what is said does not go in at one ear and out at the other; at the same time they will be led to form their own ideas and to understand, which is the object of the exercise. After all, what else do we aim at by teaching them except to ensure that they do not always need to be taught?

I would venture to say that this kind of effort will contribute more to learners than all the textbooks of all the writers on rhetoric; these are no doubt a great help, but how can they possibly so extend their range as to go through all the specific cases that arise almost every day? War is like this. Although some general principles are traditionally taught, it will be more useful to know the methods employed, whether wisely or not, by particular generals in various circumstances, times, and places. Precept is less important than experience in almost every field. If the teacher declaims to provide his pupils with models, would not reading Cicero and Demosthenes make a bigger contribution? If the pupil is corrected in public when he makes a mistake in declaiming, would it not be more effective, and indeed pleasanter, to correct an existing speech? Everyone prefers to hear the faults of others criticized rather than his own.

There is more that I could say. But the practical value of this method escapes no one. I only wish the reluctance that is felt about it was not as great as the satisfaction it is sure to give!

QUINTILIAN

18   Quod si potuerit optineri, non ita difficilis supererit
quaestio, qui legendi sint incipientibus. Nam quidam illos
minores, quia facilior eorum intellectus videbatur, pro-
baverunt, alii floridius genus, ut ad alenda primarum aeta-
19   tium ingenia magis accommodatum. Ego optimos quidem
et statim et semper, sed tamen eorum candidissimum
quemque et maxime expositum velim, ut Livium a pueris
magis quam Sallustium (etsi hic[2] historiae maior est auctor, ad quem tamen intellegendum iam profectu opus sit).
20   Cicero, ut mihi quidem videtur, et iucundus incipientibus
quoque et apertus est satis, nec prodesse tantum sed etiam
amari potest: tum, quem ad modum Livius praecipit, ut
quisque erit Ciceroni simillimus.
21   Duo autem genera maxime cavenda pueris puto:
unum, ne quis eos antiquitatis nimius admirator in Gracchorum Catonisque et aliorum similium lectione dures-
cere velit; fient enim horridi atque ieiuni: nam neque vim
eorum adhuc intellectu consequentur et elocutione, quae
tum sine dubio erat optima, sed nostris temporibus aliena
est, contenti, quod est pessimum, similes sibi magnis viris
22   videbuntur. Alterum, quod huic diversum est, ne recentis
huius lasciviae flosculis capti voluptate prava deleniantur,

2 etsi hic *Halm, after Spalding*: et hic A: et B

---

6 Compare 10.1.101.

7 In a letter to his son; see 10.1.39.

8 Cicero (*Brutus* 126) recommended C. Gracchus, but Q. includes no pre-Ciceronian orators in his recommendations for
reading in 10.1. His reserved approval in § 23 is presumably
meant to encourage the appreciation of progress. The old-fash-
ioned Messala in Tacitus, *Dialogus* 26 "prefers the vigour of C.

Choice of reading

If this point is won, what remains will be the comparatively easy question of what authors should be read by beginners. Some have recommended the less pretentious authors, because they seemed easier to understand; others,
the more florid school, as being better suited to nourish
the talents of the very young. I think the best should come
both first and always, but among the best the most straightforward and accessible: for example, Livy for boys rather
than Sallust.[6] (Sallust indeed is the greater historian, but
one needs further progress to understand him.) Cicero, in
my view at least, is both pleasant reading for beginners,
and perfectly accessible; he can not only be useful but can
be a favourite. Next (to follow Livy's advice)[7] should come
whoever is most like Cicero.

There are two types of writing against which I think
boys should be particularly protected. First, let no fanatic
devotee of the archaic hope to make them grow stiff
by reading the Gracchi,[8] Cato, and the like; this will only
make them uncouth and jejune, for they will not yet
be able to grasp the force of these writers with their
understanding, and if they content themselves with the
style—doubtless excellent in its day but quite alien to our
times—they will think themselves on a par with these great
men, and nothing could be worse than that. The second
thing to be avoided is the opposite: they must not fall for
the prettiness of modern self-indulgence, and grow soft
with its depraved pleasures, so as to fall in love with that

Gracchus or the ripe eloquence of L. Crassus" to the affectations
of Maecenas and Gallio.

ut praedulce illud genus et puerilibus ingeniis hoc gratius
quo propius est adament.

23   Firmis autem iudiciis iamque extra periculum positis
suaserim et antiquos legere (ex quibus si adsumatur solida
ac virilis ingenii vis deterso rudis saeculi squalore, tum
noster hic cultus clarius enitescet) et novos, quibus et

24 ipsis multa virtus adest: neque enim nos tarditatis natura
damnavit, sed dicendi mutavimus genus et ultra nobis
quam oportebat indulsimus: ita non tam ingenio illi nos
superarunt quam proposito. Multa ergo licebit eligere, sed
curandum erit ne iis quibus permixta sunt inquinentur.

25 Quosdam vero etiam quos totos imitari oporteat et fuisse
nuper et nunc esse quidni libenter non concesserim modo

26 verum etiam contenderim? Sed hi qui sint non cuiuscumque est pronuntiare. Tutius circa priores vel erratur,
ideoque hanc novorum distuli lectionem, ne imitatio iudicium antecederet.

6

1 Fuit etiam in hoc diversum praecipientium propositum,
quod eorum quidam materias quas discipulis ad dicendum
dabant, non contenti divisione derigere, latius dicendo

---

1 I.e. the plan or organization to be followed (to be dealt with
in Book Seven), the "sinews" of the cases ([Quintilian], *Declamationes minores* 270). Sopater's collection (see Innes and Winterbottom, 1988) gives the clearest view of what is meant.

luscious sweetness which is all the more attractive to boys because it is closer to their natural instincts.

Once tastes have been formed and are secure from danger, I should recommend reading both the older orators (because, if the solid, masculine force of their genius can be acquired, but without the layer of uncouthness incident to that primitive age, our own more polished product will shine with extra brilliance) and the moderns, who also have many good qualities. Nature has not condemned us to be slow-witted; but we have changed our style and indulged ourselves more than we ought. It is not in natural talent that the ancients are better than we are, but in their aims. There are thus many texts which can well be chosen, but we shall have to take care that they are not contaminated by the contexts in which they are embedded. I am of course happy to admit—indeed, I should positively contend—that there have been in recent times, and still are, orators who ought to be imitated in all their features. But who they are, it is not in everyone's power to decide. It is safer to stick with the earlier writers, even at the price of error, and I have therefore set the reading of the moderns for a later stage, lest imitation should run ahead of judgement.

CHAPTER 6

*How should the teacher set
and correct declamations?*

There is another way in which teachers' practice has varied. Some, not content with suggesting the Division[1] of the themes which they set for their pupils, worked them out at

prosequebantur, nec solum probationibus implebant sed
2 etiam adfectibus: alii, cum primas modo lineas duxissent,
post declamationes quid omisisset quisque tractabant,
quosdam vero locos non minore cura quam cum ad dicendum ipsi surgerent excolebant. Utile utrumque, et ideo
neutrum ab altero separo; sed si facere tantum alterum necesse sit, plus proderit demonstrasse rectam protinus viam
3 quam revocare ab errore iam lapsos: primum quia emendationem auribus modo accipiunt, divisionem vero ad cogitationem etiam et stilum perferunt; deinde quod libentius praecipientem audiunt quam reprehendentem. Si qui
vero paulo sunt vivaciores, in his praesertim moribus,
4 etiam irascuntur admonitioni et taciti repugnant. Neque
ideo tamen minus vitia aperte coarguenda sunt: habenda
enim ratio ceterorum, qui recta esse quae praeceptor non
emendaverit credent.

Utraque autem ratio miscenda est et ita tractanda ut
5 ipsae res postulabunt. Namque incipientibus danda erit
velut praeformata materia secundum cuiusque vires. At
cum satis composuisse se ad exemplum videbuntur, brevia
quaedam demonstranda[1] vestigia, quae persecuti iam suis
6 viribus sine adminiculo progredi possint. Nonnumquam
credi sibi ipsos oportebit, ne mala consuetudine semper
alienum laborem sequendi nihil per se conari et quaerere
sciant. Quodsi satis prudenter dicenda viderint, iam prope
consummata fuerit praecipientis opera: si quid erraverint

---

[1] demonstranda <velut> *Watt* 1993

some length themselves, and supplied not only proofs but also emotional appeals. Others, having given only the basic outline, used to handle points which each pupil had omitted after the declamation had been given, and spent as much trouble on some set pieces as if they were standing up to speak themselves. Both methods have their uses, and I do not want to choose between them. However, if we can have only one, it will be found more helpful to have pointed out the right course at the start than to rescue a pupil from errors into which he has already fallen; first, because they only *hear* the correction, whereas they take the Division to heart in their preparation and in their writing; and secondly because they are more willing to listen to advice than to criticism. Indeed, our livelier pupils, especially in the present moral climate, are actually angered by admonition, and silently resist it. But it does not follow that faults should not be openly reproved. We have, after all, to think of the others, who will believe that anything the teacher has not criticized must be right.

The two methods should in fact be combined, and used as circumstances require. Beginners should be given the material predigested, as it were, according to their individual powers; when they seem to have formed their style sufficiently on their model, brief hints only should be given them—a sort of track which they can follow and then proceed along under their own power without help. Sometimes they should be left entirely to their own devices, for fear that the bad habit of always following someone else's work should prevent them from learning how to make an effort or seek out material on their own. Once they come to have a satisfactory view of what needs to be said, the teacher's work is almost done; if they still make mistakes,

313

7   adhuc, erunt ad ducem reducendi. Cui rei simile quiddam
facientes aves cernimus, quae teneris infirmisque fetibus
cibos ore suo conlatos partiuntur: at cum visi sunt adulti,
paulum egredi nidis et circumvolare sedem illam prae-
cedentes ipsae docent: tum expertos[2] vires libero caelo
suaeque ipsorum fiduciae permittunt.

7

1   Illud ex consuetudine mutandum prorsus existimo in iis de
quibus nunc disserimus aetatibus, ne omnia quae scripserint ediscant et certa, ut moris est, die dicant: quod
quidem maxime patres exigunt, atque ita demum studere
liberos suos si quam frequentissime declamaverint cre-
2   dunt, cum profectus praecipue diligentia constet. Nam
ut scribere pueros plurimumque esse in hoc opere plane
velim, sic ediscere electos ex orationibus vel historiis aliove
quo genere dignorum ea cura voluminum locos multo
3   magis suadeam. Nam et exercebitur acrius memoria aliena
complectendo quam sua, et qui erunt in difficiliore huius
laboris genere versati sine molestia quae ipsi composuerint[1] iam familiaria animo suo adfigent, et adsuescent
optimis, semperque habebunt intra se quod imitentur, et
iam non sentientes formam orationis illam quam mente

[2] *recc.*: expertas *AB*
[1] composuerunt *B*

---

[1] Compare 10.5.21 and Persius 3.45–47.

they must be brought back under his guidance. We can observe birds doing something like this: when their young are tender and feeble, they collect food in their own mouths and divide it among them; but when the young seem fully grown, they teach them to go a little way from the nest and circle round it, leading the way themselves, until they have proved their strength and are allowed the freedom of the sky and left to rely on their own self-confidence.

CHAPTER 7

Learning by heart

There is one current practice in teaching boys of the age we are discussing which I think ought to be radically altered. They should not learn by heart everything they write and recite it, as is the custom, on a fixed day. This is particularly expected by fathers,[1] and they are not convinced that their children are learning unless they declaim as often as possible. Yet the truth is that progress depends mainly on patient application. For while I certainly believe in boys writing and being mainly occupied with this, I should much prefer them to learn by heart selected passages of speeches or histories or some other type of book that is worth treating in this way. For (1) it is a better exercise for the memory to take in other people's words than one's own; (2) those who are trained in this more difficult task will easily fix their own compositions in their mind, because these are already familiar; (3) they will get used to the best models and always have objects of imitation in their minds; (4) they will now unconsciously reproduce the style of the speech which they have so thoroughly ab-

4   penitus acceperint expriment. Abundabunt autem copia
verborum optimorum et compositione ac figuris iam non
quaesitis sed sponte et ex reposito velut thesauro se offe-
rentibus. Accedit his et iucunda in sermone bene a quoque
dictorum relatio et in causis utilis. Nam et plus auctoritatis
adferunt ea quae non praesentis gratia litis sunt comparata, et laudem saepe maiorem quam si nostra sint conci-
liant.

5   Aliquando tamen permittendum quae ipsi scripserint
dicere, ut laboris sui fructum etiam ex illa quae maxime
petitur laude plurium capiant. Verum id quoque tum fieri
oportebit cum aliquid commodius elimaverint, ut eo velut
praemio studii sui donentur ac se meruisse ut dicerent
gaudeant.

8

1   Virtus praeceptoris haberi solet, nec inmerito, diligenter
in iis quos erudiendos susceperit notare discrimina ingeniorum, et quo quemque natura maxime ferat scire. Nam
est in hoc incredibilis quaedam varietas, nec pauciores ani-
2   morum paene quam corporum formae. Quod intellegi
etiam ex ipsis oratoribus potest, qui tantum inter se distant
genere dicendi ut nemo sit alteri similis, quamvis plurimi
se ad eorum quos probabant imitationem composuerint.

sorbed. They will also acquire a plentiful and choice vocabulary, and a command of Composition and Figures, not now artificially sought but spontaneously appearing, as it were, out of their hoarded treasure. A further benefit is a capacity to recall the good remarks of the various authors, which is both a source of pleasure in conversation and a useful resource in court, because things which have not been contrived for the sake of the Cause in hand have more authority, and often win more praise, than if they were our own.

Sometimes, however, pupils *should* be allowed to deliver what they have written themselves, so as to reap the reward of their labours in the coveted form of the praises of a large audience. But even this ought not to happen until they have produced a decently finished piece of work, so that they are given the privilege as a sort of prize for their efforts and can feel pleased that they have deserved the right to speak.

CHAPTER 8

On suiting the teaching to the individual

It is generally and deservedly regarded as a virtue in a teacher that he should carefully observe the differences in the abilities of the pupils whose education he has undertaken, and understand the direction to which their various talents incline. There is incredible variety in this; there are almost as many different kinds of mind as of body. This can be seen even in the orators themselves; they differ in style so much that no one is like another, though most of them trained themselves to imitate the models they admired.

3 Utile deinde plerisque visum est ita quemque instituere ut
propria naturae bona doctrina foverent, et in id potissimum ingenia quo tenderent adiuvarent:[1] ut si quis pa-
laestrae peritus, cum in aliquod plenum pueris gymnasium
venerit, expertus eorum omni modo corpus animumque

4 discernat cui quisque certamini praeparandus sit, ita praeceptorem eloquentiae, cum sagaciter fuerit intuitus cuius
ingenium presso limatoque genere dicendi, cuius acri gravi dulci aspero nitido urbano maxime gaudeat, ita se com-
modaturum singulis ut in eo quo quisque eminet proveha-

5 tur, quod et adiuta cura natura magis evalescat et qui in
diversa ducatur neque in iis quibus minus aptus est satis
possit efficere et ea in quae natus videtur deserendo faciat
infirmiora.

6 Quod mihi (libera enim vel contra receptas persua-
siones rationem sequenti sententia est) in parte verum
videtur: nam proprietates ingeniorum dispicere prorsus

7 necessarium est. In his quoque certum studiorum facere
dilectum nemo dissuaserit. Namque erit alius historiae
magis idoneus, alius compositus ad carmen, alius utilis studio iuris, [ut][2] nonnulli rus fortasse mittendi: sic discernet
haec dicendi magister quomodo palaestricus ille cursorem
faciet aut pugilem aut luctatorem aliudve quid ex iis quae

8 sunt sacrorum certaminum. Verum ei qui foro destinabitur
non in unam partem aliquam sed in omnia quae sunt eius

[1] *Meister*: adiuvarentur *AB*
[2] *del. H. Meyer*

[1] Perhaps with special reference to the Ludi Capitolini, insti-
tuted by Nero and important under Domitian; but the phrase

318

Many teachers have consequently thought it useful to train each individual so as to nurture his natural gifts by instruction, and to direct his talents especially towards the goal to which they were tending. Just as an expert trainer, coming into a gymnasium full of boys, tests them, body and mind, in all ways, and decides for what event each should be prepared, so also (it has been thought) the teacher of eloquence, having shrewdly perceived whose talents were happiest with a concise and terse style, and whose with one that is energetic, dignified, pleasing, rough, elegant, or witty, will adapt himself to each in such a way as to bring out his special qualities; nature (it is argued) gains in strength by cultivation, and the pupil who is led in the opposite direction cannot achieve much in areas in which he has no aptitude, while he weakens the talents he seems born to exploit by abandoning them.

Now I have to say—for one is surely free to dissent even from received wisdom if one follows reason—that this view is true only in part. It is certainly necessary to distinguish special types of talent; no one can persuade me not to make these part of the basis for the choice of study. One person will be better suited for history, another for poetry, another for law, and some perhaps will have to be sent home to the farm. The teacher of rhetoric will mark these down, just as the trainer will produce a runner or a boxer or a wrestler, or a contestant in one of the other events that make up the Sacred Games.[1] On the other hand, a pupil who is destined for the courts must make great efforts not only in one department but in everything

covers all festival games (Pythian at Delphi, Olympian at Olympia, etc.).

operis, etiam si qua difficiliora discenti videbuntur, elabo-
randum est; nam et omnino supervacua erat doctrina si na-

9 tura sufficeret. An si quis ingenio corruptus ac tumidus, ut
plerique sunt, inciderit, in hoc eum ire patiemur? Aridum
atque ieiunum non alemus et quasi vestiemus? Nam si
quaedam detrahere necessarium est, cur non sit adicere

10 concessum? Neque ego contra naturam pugno: non enim
deserendum id bonum, si quod ingenitum est, existimo,

11 sed augendum, addendumque quod cessat. An vero claris-
simus ille praeceptor Isocrates, quem non magis libri bene
dixisse quam discipuli bene docuisse testantur, cum de
Ephoro atque Theopompo sic iudicaret ut alteri frenis,
alteri calcaribus opus esse diceret, aut in illo lentiore tarditatem aut in illo paene praecipiti concitationem adiu-
vandam docendo existimavit, cum alterum alterius natura
miscendum arbitraretur ?

12 Inbecillis tamen ingeniis sane sic obsequendum sit ut
tantum in id quo vocat natura ducantur; ita enim quod solum possunt melius efficient. Si vero liberalior materia
contigerit et in qua merito ad spem oratoris simus adgressi,

13 nulla dicendi virtus omittenda est. Nam licet sit aliquam in
partem pronior, ut necesse est, ceteris tamen non repugna-
bit, atque ea cura paria faciet iis in quibus eminebat, sicut
ille, ne ab eodem exemplo recedamus, exercendi corpora
peritus non, si docendum pancratiasten susceperit, pugno
ferire vel calce tantum aut nexus modo atque in iis certos

---

2 Compare 10.1.74; Cicero, *Brutus* 204, *De oratore* 3.36.
Ephorus and Theopompus both won fame as historians rather
than as orators.

3 The *pankration* was a form of all-in fighting, involving both
boxing and wrestling techniques.

that belongs to his profession, even the things which seem particularly difficult to the learner. If nature were sufficient on her own, learning would be altogether unnecessary! If we come across a mind naturally decadent and inflated, as many are, shall we let him go on in this direction? As for the dry and jejune, shall we not nourish and clothe them, as it were? If it is necessary to take some things away, why should it not be permissible to add some others? I am not fighting nature, of course. I do not believe that innate good qualities should be abandoned, but that they should be developed, and deficiencies made good. When the famous educator Isocrates, whose pupils testify to his excellence as a teacher as much as his books do to his own eloquence, judged of Ephorus and Theopompus that the one needed the spur and the other the curb,[2] did he believe that the tardiness of the slower one and the hastiness of his daring fellow pupil should be mitigated by teaching, when he really thought that each needed a dose of the qualities of the other?

With weaker talents, on the other hand, one must indeed follow their bent by guiding them exclusively towards the goal that their nature suggests. They will then do better the only thing they can do. But if we encounter richer material, where we have justifiably come to hope for a real orator, no virtue of speaking should be forgotten. For though such a pupil will inevitably have a bias towards some qualities, he will not be resistant to others, but will apply himself to developing them to the same level as those in which he already excels—just as the trainer (let us keep to the same example) who knows about exercising the body, if he has a pancratiast[3] to train, will not only teach him to punch and kick and to master the holds—and cer-

321

aliquos docebit, sed omnia quae sunt eius certaminis. Erit
qui ex iis aliqua non possit: in id maxime quod poterit
14 incumbet. Nam sunt haec duo vitanda prorsus: unum, ne
temptes quod effici non possit, alterum, ne ab eo quod quis
optime facit in aliud cui minus est idoneus transferas. At
si fuerit qui docebitur ille, quem adulescentes senem vidi-
mus, Nicostratus, omnibus in eo docendi partibus similiter
utetur, efficietque illum, qualis hic fuit, luctando pug-
nandoque, quorum utroque certamine isdem diebus coro-
15 nabatur, invictum. Et quanto id magis oratoris futuri
magistro providendum erit! Non enim satis est dicere
presse tantum aut subtiliter aut aspere, non magis quam
phonasco acutis tantum aut mediis aut gravibus sonis aut
horum etiam particulis excellere. Nam sicut cithara, ita
oratio perfecta non est nisi ab imo ad summum omnibus
intenta nervis consentiat.

9

1 Plura de officiis docentium locutus discipulos id unum interim moneo, ut praeceptores suos non minus quam ipsa
studia ament et parentes esse non quidem corporum, sed
2 mentium credant. Multum haec pietas conferet studio;
nam ita et libenter audient et dictis credent et esse similes
concupiscent, in ipsos denique coetus scholarum laeti

---

4 Victor in wrestling and pankration at the 204th Olympiad
(AD 37); said to have been an ugly man (Lucian, *On writing history* 9); see also Tacitus, *Dialogus* 10.5. He could have been
known by Q. in the fifties or sixties.

tain particular holds at that—but everything that is relevant to the competition. Some will be incapable of some things; they must concentrate on what they can do. The two things most to be avoided are (1) trying to do the impossible, and (2) diverting the pupil from what he can do best to something for which he is less well suited. But if the potential pupil is like the famous Nicostratus[4] (who was already old when I saw him in my young days), the trainer will give him lessons in all departments, and will make him also (as *he* was) invincible in wrestling and boxing, for both of which Nicostratus won crowns on the same occasion. How much more must the teacher of the future orator foster this versatility! It is not enough just to speak concisely, elegantly, or vehemently, any more than it would be for a professional singer to excel exclusively in the higher, lower, or middle register, or in some part of one of these. Oratory is like the lyre; unless all its strings, from bottom to top, are in tune, it cannot be perfect.

CHAPTER 9

Pupils' responsibilities

Having said a good deal about teachers' duties, I have, for the time being, only one piece of advice for pupils: that they should love their teachers as they do their studies, and think of them as the parents not of their bodies but of their minds. This feeling of affection will do much for their studies. They will be ready to listen, have confidence in what is said, and want to be like the teacher; they will go to classes

alacresque[1] convenient, emendati non irascentur, laudati
3 gaudebunt, ut sint carissimi studio merebuntur. Nam ut
illorum officium est docere, sic horum praebere se dociles:
alioqui neutrum sine altero sufficit; et sicut hominis ortus
ex utroque gignentium confertur, et frustra sparseris
semina nisi illa praemollitus foverit sulcus, ita eloquentia
coalescere nequit nisi sociata tradentis accipientisque concordia.

10

1 In his primis operibus, quae non ipsa parva sunt sed maio-
rum quasi membra atque partes, bene instituto ac satis
exercitato iam fere tempus adpetet adgrediendi suasorias
iudicialesque materias: quarum antequam viam ingredior,
pauca mihi de ipsa declamandi ratione dicenda sunt, quae
quidem ut ex omnibus novissime inventa, ita multo est uti-
2 lissima. Nam et cuncta illa de quibus diximus in se fere
continet et veritati proximam imaginem reddit, ideoque
ita est celebrata ut plerisque videretur ad formandam eloquentiam vel sola sufficere. Neque enim virtus ulla perpetuae dumtaxat orationis reperiri potest quae non sit cum
3 hac dicendi meditatione communis. Eo quidem res ista
culpa docentium reccidit ut inter praecipuas quae corrum-
perent eloquentiam causas licentia atque inscitia decla-
mantium fuerit.

[1] alacres *B*

---

[1] See 2.4.41; *GD* 18.
[2] Compare the attack on declamation in Petronius 1–2. For
Q.'s own attitude, see General Introduction.

cheerfully and eagerly, they will not be angry when corrected, they will be pleased when they are praised, they will try to earn affection by their application. As the teachers' business is to teach, so theirs is to make themselves teachable. Neither is sufficient without the other. And just as it takes two parents to produce a human being, and seed is scattered in vain if the ground has not been softened in advance to nurture it, so eloquence cannot develop unless teacher and learner work in harmony together.

CHAPTER 10

Uses and methods of Declamation

Once the pupil has been well instructed and sufficiently exercised in these first tasks (which are indeed not trivial, but are parts or members of the greater whole), the time will be approaching for him to attempt deliberative and forensic themes. But before I embark on this, I must say a little about the general principles of Declamation, the last to be invented of all the exercises[1] but by far the most useful, because it both embraces in itself all the things of which we have been speaking, and provides the closest image of reality. Consequently it has become so popular that many think that it is sufficient by itself for the formation of an orator. No excellence—or at least no excellence of continuous speech—can be found which is not also to be found in this type of practice oration. Yet the thing has degenerated to such an extent (and this is the fault of the teachers) that the licence and ignorance of declaimers has become one of the prime causes of the decadence of eloquence.[2]

4   Sed eo quod natura bonum est bene uti licet. Sint ergo
et ipsae materiae quae fingentur quam simillimae veritati,
et declamatio, in quantum maxime potest, imitetur eas ac-
5   tiones in quarum exercitationem reperta est. Nam magos
et pestilentiam et responsa et saeviores tragicis novercas
aliaque magis adhuc fabulosa frustra inter sponsiones et
interdicta quaeremus. Quid ergo? numquam haec supra
fidem et poetica, ut vere dixerim, themata iuvenibus tractare permittamus, ut expatientur et gaudeant materia et
6   quasi in corpus eant? Erat optimum, sed certe sint grandia
et tumida, non stulta etiam et acrioribus oculis intuenti
ridicula, ut, si iam cedendum est, impleat se declamator
aliquando, dum sciat, ut quadrupedes, cum viridi pabulo
distentae sunt, sanguinis detractione curantur et sic ad cibos viribus conservandis idoneos redeunt, ita sibi quoque
tenuandas adipes, et quidquid umoris corrupti contraxerit
7   emittendum si esse sanus ac robustus volet. Alioqui tumor
ille inanis primo cuiuscumque veri operis conatu depre-
hendetur.

Totum autem declamandi opus qui diversum omni
modo a forensibus causis existimant, hi profecto ne rationem quidem qua ista exercitatio inventa sit pervident;
8   nam si foro non praeparat, aut scaenicae ostentationi aut
furiosae vociferationi simillimum est. Quid enim attinet
iudicem praeparare qui nullus est, narrare quod omnes
sciant falsum, probationes adhibere causae de qua nemo

---

³ *Sponsio* involves a litigant undertaking to pay his adversary a
determined sum in the event of his losing his case. *Interdictum* is
an injunction or provisional order made by a praetor. The terms
exemplify humdrum litigation.

However, what is by nature good is capable of good use. So let the fictitious themes themselves be as close to real life as they can be, and the declamation itself, so far as possible, reproduce the pleadings for which it was devised as a training. We shall look in vain, among the forfeits and the interdicts,[3] for the magicians, the plagues, the oracles, the stepmothers more cruel than any in tragedy, and the other still more fabulous elements. What then? Are we never to let young men handle these unrealistic or, to put it more accurately, poetical themes, so as to give them their head and let them enjoy the subject and, as it were, put on more flesh? In an ideal world, yes; but at least let the themes be grand, even exaggerated; let them not also be silly or laughable to a critical eye. Thus, if we do now have to make concessions, let the declaimer satisfy his longings occasionally—so long as he realizes that he will one day have to get rid of the fat and discharge the corrupt humours if he wants to be healthy and strong—just as cattle, bloated with green fodder, are cured by blood-letting[4] and then get back to food suitable for maintaining their strength. If this is not done, the empty swelling will be detected at the first attempt at real work.

Those who think that Declamation in general is in every way distinct from forensic cases completely fail to see the reason why this exercise was invented. If it is not a preparation for the courts, it is like nothing so much as a stage performance or the cries of a lunatic. What is the point of conciliating a non-existent judge, narrating what everyone knows to be false, or producing proofs to support

4 See Palladius, *De veterinaria medicina* 6.6, 12.1, 12.4, 14.5.

sit pronuntiaturus? Et haec quidem otiosa tantum: adfici
vero et ira vel luctu permoveri cuius est ludibrii nisi quibusdam pugnae simulacris ad verum discrimen aciemque
iustam consuescimus!

9   Nihil ergo inter forense genus dicendi atque hoc de-
clamatorium intererit? Si profectus gratia dicimus, nihil.
Utinamque adici ad consuetudinem posset ut nominibus
uteremur et perplexae magis et longioris aliquando actus
controversiae fingerentur et verba in usu cotidiano posita
minus timeremus et iocos inserere moris esset: quae nos,
quamlibet per alia in scholis exercitati simus, tirones in
foro inveniunt.

10   Si vero in ostentationem comparetur declamatio, sane
paulum aliquid inclinare ad voluptatem audientium de-
11   bemus. Nam et iis actionibus quae in aliqua sine dubio
veritate versantur, sed sunt ad popularem aptatae delectationem, quales legimus panegyricos totumque hoc de-
monstrativum genus, permittitur adhibere plus cultus,
omnemque artem, quae latere plerumque in iudiciis debet, non confiteri modo sed ostentare etiam hominibus in
12   hoc advocatis. Quare declamatio, quoniam est iudiciorum
consiliorumque imago, similis esse debet veritati, quoniam autem aliquid in se habet epidicticon, nonnihil sibi
nitoris adsumere.

13   Quod faciunt actores comici, qui neque ita prorsus ut
nos vulgo loquimur pronuntiant, quod esset sine arte,

---

5 Q.'s view is clearly sensible, but Menander Rhetor (331.16
Spengel) is more precise: "The *epideixeis* of public speeches composed by the people known as sophists [i.e. high-class professional
declaimers] I regard as practice for real cases (μελέτην ἀγώνων),
not as *epideixis.*"

a case on which no decision will be given? This indeed is no worse than a waste of time; but think of the absurdity of working ourselves into a passion or getting stirred up by sorrow, unless we are seeking to prepare ourselves by a sort of mock battle for genuine perils and a real engagement!

Is there to be no difference then between the forensic genre and the declamatory? If the point of practice speaking is to make progress, none. I wish indeed that we could add to present practice the use of actual names and sometimes the invention of more complex cases which require longer pleadings; and also that we were less frightened of words that are in daily use, and thought it quite normal to insert some jokes. However well we have been trained in school in other respects, these things find us novices in court.

But if Declamation is really for show, then we ought indeed to bend over somewhat to give the audience pleasure. For even in speeches which, though undoubtedly concerned with real events, are designed to entertain the people (such as the Panegyrics which we read, and the epideictic genre as a whole), it is permissible to introduce more ornament, and not only confess but actually display, before an audience assembled for this purpose, the art which in forensic oratory must generally be concealed. Thus Declamation, inasmuch as it is the image of forensic and deliberative eloquence, must bear a resemblance to real life; but inasmuch as it has an epideictic element, it must assume a degree of elegance.[5]

Comic actors in fact do this: they neither deliver their speeches exactly as we talk in ordinary life, because that

neque procul tamen a natura recedunt, quo vitio periret imitatio, sed morem communis huius sermonis decore quodam scaenico exornant.

14   Sic quoque aliqua nos incommoda ex iis quas finxerimus materiis consequentur, in eo praecipue quod multa in iis relincuntur incerta, quae sumimus ut videtur, aetates facultates liberi parentes, urbium ipsarum vires iura mo-
15   res, alia his similia: quin aliquando etiam argumenta ex ipsis positionum vitiis ducimus.

Sed haec suo quoque loco. Quamvis enim omne propositum operis a nobis destinati eo spectet ut orator instituatur, tamen, ne quid studiosi requirant, etiam si quid erit quod ad scholas proprie pertineat in transitu non omittemus.

11

1   Iam hinc ergo nobis inchoanda est ea pars artis ex qua capere initium solent qui priora omiserunt: quamquam video quosdam in ipso statim limine obstaturos mihi, qui nihil egere eius modi praeceptis eloquentiam putent, sed natura sua et vulgari modo scholarum exercitatione contenti rideant etiam diligentiam nostram exemplo magni quoque nominis professorum, quorum aliquis, ut opinor, interrogatus quid esset schema et noema, nescire se quidem, sed si ad rem pertineret esse in sua declamatione
2   respondit. Alius percontanti Theodoreus an Apollodoreus

---

6 I.e. the declaimer supplies details as he wants to fill gaps in the theme as set.   7 7.2.54.   1 *Schēma* is the normal Greek word for Figure; *noēma* (not a common term: Lausberg § 690) is said in 8.5.12 to be a modern expression to indicate an idea which is understood but not made explicit.

would be inartistic, nor on the other hand do they depart much from nature, which would destroy the mimicry; instead, they enhance the manner of our ordinary speech with some of the graces of the stage.

Even so, some problems will arise from the themes we invent, especially because many details in them are left vague, and we assume these at will: ages, resources, children, parents, the strength, laws, and customs of the cities themselves, and so on. Indeed we sometimes draw arguments from defects in the setting of the themes.[6]

But more of this in its due place.[7] For, although the whole purpose of this work as I intend it is to educate an orator, I do not want students to feel anything is lacking, and shall therefore touch in passing even on topics which strictly belong only to school practice.

CHAPTER 11

The need for training; weaknesses and strengths of those who rely on natural talent

At this point, I must make a start on that part of the art of rhetoric with which writers who have omitted the earlier stages normally begin. I can see, however, that some are going to block my path right at the outset, because they believe that eloquence needs no rules at all of this sort; content with their own abilities and the mere common exercises of the schools, they even laugh at the trouble I take. In this, they are following the example of some professors of high repute, one of whom, as I understand, when asked what was meant by Figure and Thought,[1] said that he didn't know, but, if it was relevant, it was in his declamation! Another, when asked whether he was a Theodorean

esset, 'egone?'[1] inquit 'parmularius'. Nec sane potuit urbanius ex confessione inscitiae suae elabi. Porro hi, quia et beneficio ingenii praestantes sunt habiti et multa etiam memoria digna exclamaverunt, plurimos habent similes
3 neglegentiae suae, paucissimos naturae. Igitur impetu dicere se et viribus uti gloriantur: neque enim opus esse probatione aut dispositione in rebus fictis, sed, cuius rei gratia plenum sit auditorium, sententiis grandibus, quarum opti-
4 ma quaeque a periculo petatur. Quin etiam in cogitando nulla ratione adhibita aut tectum intuentes magnum aliquid quod ultro se offerat pluribus saepe diebus expectant, aut murmure incerto velut classico instincti concitatissimum corporis motum non enuntiandis sed quaerendis
5 verbis accommodant. Nonnulli certa sibi initia priusquam sensum invenerint destinant, quibus aliquid diserti subiungendum sit: eaque diu secum ipsi clareque meditati desperata conectendi facultate deserunt et ad alia deinceps atque inde alia non minus communia ac nota devertunt.
6 tunt. Qui plurimum videntur habere rationis non in causas tamen laborem suum sed in locos intendunt, atque in iis

---

[1] *D.A.R.*: ego *AB*

---

[2] See 3.1.17–18. Theodorus and Apollodorus headed opposing schools, Apollodorus laying more emphasis on rigorous order and observance of rules. Bulk of the evidence in Anonymus Seguierianus (ed. Dilts–Kennedy, 1997); fragments collected by R. Granatelli (Rome, 1991). General account in Kennedy, *ARRW* 337–342.

[3] A *parmularius* was a fan of the "Thracian" gladiators, who were armed with a sword and small shield *(parmula),* as opposed

or an Apollodorean,[2] replied "Me? I'm a Parmularian!"[3] To be sure, he could have found no neater way of sliding out of a confession of ignorance. Moreover, because these people are regarded as having exceptional natural gifts and have made many memorable remarks, they have found many to match them in negligence, but very few to match them in natural ability. So they take pride in speaking by inspiration[4] and innate strength; there is no need (they say) for proofs and organization in a fictitious theme, but only for what fills the lecture room, namely impressive *sententiae*, the best of which come from taking risks. Neither have they any settled procedure for thinking out what they intend to say. They either stare at the ceiling[5] and wait, often for several days, for some great thought to present itself, or else work themselves up by an inarticulate mumbling, which serves as a trumpet call, and gesture violently, not to help them speak, but to help them search for words! Some fix on particular set openings before they have thought out their idea, with a view to hanging some clever remark on them, and then, having rehearsed them both to themselves and aloud for a long time, despair of finding the connecting link and accordingly abandon them, and proceed to turn to one cliché after another, each equally hackneyed and banal. Those who appear to be the most methodical of them nevertheless put their work not into the Causes as a whole but into set commonplaces, and even in these they do

to the *murmillones*, who wore Gallic armour and a helmet with an image of a fish on top.

[4] On such people and Q.'s attitude, see M. Winterbottom in *Ethics and Rhetoric* (ed. Innes, Hine, Pelling (Oxford, 1995)) 313–322.　　[5] Compare 10.3.15.

non corpori prospiciunt, sed abrupta quaedam, ut forte ad
7 manum venere, iaculantur. Unde fit ut dissoluta et ex diversis congesta oratio cohaerere non possit, similisque sit
commentariis puerorum in quos ea quae aliis declamanti-
bus laudata sunt regerunt. Magnas tamen sententias et res
bonas (ita enim gloriari solent) elidunt: nam et barbari et
servi, et, si hoc sat est, nulla est ratio dicendi.

12

1 Ne hoc quidem negaverim, sequi plerosque[1] hanc opinionem, ut fortius dicere videantur indocti, primum vitio
male iudicantium, qui maiorem habere vim credunt ea
quae non habent artem, ut effringere quam aperire, rum-
pere quam solvere, trahere quam ducere putant robustius.
2 Nam et gladiator qui armorum inscius in rixam ruit et
luctator qui totius corporis nisu in id quod semel invasit
incumbit fortior ab his vocatur, cum interim et hic frequenter suis viribus ipse prosternitur et illum vehementis
3 impetus excipit adversarii mollis articulus. Sed sunt in hac
parte quae imperitos etiam naturaliter fallant; nam et
divisio, cum plurimum valeat in causis, speciem virium
minuit, ut[2] rudia politis maiora et sparsa compositis nume-
4 rosiora creduntur. Est praeterea quaedam virtutum vitiorumque vicinia, qua maledicus pro libero, temerarius pro

---

[1] E: plerumque AB   [2] Winterbottom: et AB

---

[1] The notion that vices are "near neighbours" to corresponding virtues is common to ethics and stylistics: Aristotle, *Nico-
machean Ethics* 1125a17–34, Demetrius 114, Juvenal 14.109,
Horace, *Ars poetica* 25–31.

not look to the whole context, but simply fire off brusque phrases as they happen to come to hand. Consequently, the fragmented speech, made up of such diverse elements, cannot hold together; it becomes like a boy's notebook in which he records admired passages in other people's declamations. Nevertheless, they do manage to force out some grand *sententiae* and, as they boast, "good things." So do barbarians and slaves. If this is all that is needed, there is no rational method in oratory at all.

CHAPTER 12

I would not wish to deny either that most people follow this view, with the result that the untrained are thought to speak with more vigour. This is partly the fault of bad critics, who think that where there is no art there is more force—just as they think it shows more strength to burst something open than to unlock it, to break something than to unfasten it, to drag than to lead. These people also call a gladiator "braver" if he rushes into the fight however unskilled in arms he is, and a wrestler "braver" if he puts the whole weight of his body behind the first hold, even though that wrestler is often brought down by his own strength, and the gladiator who rushes in is met by his adversary's supple parry. However, in our field, there are matters which in the very nature of things deceive the inexperienced critic. Thus even Division, though very important in Causes, reduces the appearance of strength, on the principle that the unpolished seems more impressive than the polished, and things scattered around seem more numerous than things well arranged. Moreover, there is a close connection between virtues and vices,[1] which en-

forti, effusus pro copioso accipitur. Maledicit autem ineru-
ditus apertius et saepius vel cum periculo suscepti litigato-
5 ris, frequenter etiam suo. Adfert et ista res opinionem,
quia libentissime homines audiunt ea quae dicere ipsi no-
luissent. Illud quoque alterum quod est in elocutione ipsa
periculum minus vitat, conaturque perdite, unde evenit
nonnumquam ut aliquid grande inveniat qui semper quaerit quod nimium est: verum id et raro provenit et cetera
vitia non pensat.
6   Propter hoc quoque interdum videntur indocti copiam
habere maiorem, quod dicunt omnia, doctis est et electio
et modus. His accedit quod a cura docendi quod intende-
rint recedunt: itaque illud quaestionum et argumentorum
apud corrupta iudicia frigus evitant, nihilque aliud quam
quod[3] vel pravis voluptatibus aures adsistentium permul-
7 ceat[4] quaerunt. Sententiae quoque ipsae, quas solas pe-
tunt, magis eminent cum omnia circa illas sordida et abiec-
ta sunt, ut lumina non inter umbras, quem ad modum
Cicero dicit, sed plane in tenebris clariora sunt. Itaque in-
geniosi vocentur, ut libet, dum tamen constet contume-
8 liose sic laudari disertum. Nihilo minus confitendum est
etiam detrahere doctrinam aliquid, ut limam rudibus et
cotes hebetibus et vino vetustatem, sed vitia detrahit,
atque eo solo minus est quod litterae perpolierunt quo
melius.

[3] quo *B*
[4] permulceant *B*

---

[2] *De oratore* 3.101.
[3] Compare 10.1.40.

ables rudeness to pass for frankness, rashness for courage, and extravagance for abundance. Now the unskilled speaker is more openly and more frequently rude, even endangering his clients, and often also himself. But this itself earns good opinions, because people are only too pleased to listen to what they would not have been prepared to say themselves. The unskilled speaker is also less able to avoid the other danger, which is actually a matter of style: he makes desperate efforts, and hence, just because he is always looking for too much, sometimes succeeds in finding something impressive. But this is a rare piece of luck, and it does not compensate for his other faults.

Another reason why the untrained sometimes seem to have greater resources of language is that they say everything, whereas the trained speaker shows selection and restraint. The untrained also exempt themselves from the trouble of explaining their position. They thus avoid the chilly reception that our decadent courts give to Questions and Proofs, and seek only for effects which charm the ears of the audience, even if the pleasure is a perverse one. The very *sententiae*, the sole object of their efforts, become more conspicuous when all around is squalid and dreary— just as lights shine brighter not so much "in the shade" (as Cicero puts it)[2] but in total darkness! So let them be called "talented," if they like, as long as it is understood that it is an insult to a man of eloquence to be praised in these terms.[3] All the same, it has to be admitted that learning does take something away—as a file takes something from a rough surface, or a whetstone from a blunt edge, or age from wine—but it takes away faults, and the work that has been polished by literary skills is diminished only in so far as it is improved.

9   Verum hi pronuntiatione quoque famam dicendi fortius quaerunt; nam et clamant ubique et omnia levata, ut
ipsi vocant, manu emugiunt, multo discursu, anhelitu, iac-
10   tatione gestus, motu capitis furentes. Iam collidere manus,
terrae pedem incutere, femur pectus frontem caedere,
mire ad pullatum circulum facit: cum ille eruditus, ut in
oratione multa summittere variare disponere, ita etiam in
pronuntiando suum cuique eorum quae dicet colori accommodare actum sciat, et, si quid sit perpetua observa-
11   tione dignum, modestus et esse et videri malit. At illi hanc
vim appellant quae est potius violentia: cum interim non
actores modo aliquos invenias sed, quod est turpius, praeceptores etiam qui, brevem dicendi exercitationem consecuti, omissa ratione ut tulit impetus passim tumultuentur,
eosque qui plus honoris litteris tribuerunt ineptos et ieiu-
nos et tepidos et infirmos, ut quodque verbum contume-
liosissimum occurrit, appellent.
12   Verum illis quidem gratulemur sine labore, sine ratione, sine disciplina disertis: nos, quando et praecipiendi
munus iam pridem deprecati sumus et in foro quoque
dicendi, quia honestissimum finem putabamus desinere
dum desideraremur, inquirendo scribendoque talia conso-
lemur otium nostrum quae futura usui bonae mentis iuvenibus arbitramur, nobis certe sunt voluptati.

---

4 See 11.3.119.

5 These are the bystanders, not wearing the toga, and despised
by correctly dressed advocates and others in court. See Suetonius,
Augustus 40, Pliny, *Epistulae* 7.17.9.

6 See 12.11 (on the right time for retirement).

These people, however, also claim a reputation for "strong" speaking by their delivery. They shout at every point, and bellow everything out, with "uplifted hand" (as they say),[4] with much running up and down, panting, gesticulating violently, and tossing their heads like madmen. Clapping your hands, stamping on the floor, striking your thigh and chest and forehead, are all wonderfully effective with the dingier part of the audience.[5] But the educated speaker, just as he knows how to lower the tension often in his speech and constantly vary his style and arrange his material, also knows, in his delivery, how to suit his action to the tone of each part of his speech; if there is any rule which deserves to be always observed, it is to keep, and be seen to keep, within the bounds of decency. My opponents however use the word "force" for what is better described as violence. At the same time, you can find not only some pleaders, but (what is worse) some teachers too, who, having had a little training in speaking, forget method altogether and riot all over the place, as the impulse takes them, calling anyone who has paid more respect to literature a foolish, empty, dithering weakling, or whatever particularly insulting name comes into their mind.

But let us congratulate these people for becoming so competent without effort, method, or training. For myself, having now long since given up both my teaching duties and also my work in the courts, because I thought the most honourable end of my career would be to stop while I was still in demand,[6] me console my leisure hours by research and writing such as this, which I believe will be of use to right-minded young men and is certainly a pleasure to myself.

13

1 Nemo autem a me exigat id praeceptorum genus quod est
a plerisque scriptoribus artium traditum, ut quasi quasdam leges inmutabili necessitate constrictas studiosis dicendi feram: utique prohoemium et id quale, proxima huic
narratio, quae lex deinde narrandi, propositio post hanc
vel, ut quibusdam placuit, excursio, tum certus ordo
quaestionum, ceteraque quae, velut si aliter facere fas non
2 sit, quidam tamquam iussi secuntur. Erat enim rhetorice
res prorsus facilis ac parva si uno et brevi praescripto
contineretur: sed mutantur pleraque causis temporibus
occasione necessitate. Atque ideo res in oratore praecipua
consilium est, quia varie et ad rerum momenta convertitur.
3 Quid si enim praecipias imperatori, quotiens aciem
instruet derigat frontem, cornua utrimque promoveat,
equites pro cornibus locet? Erit haec quidem rectissima
fortasse ratio quotiens licebit, sed mutabit[1] natura loci, si
mons occurret, si flumen obstabit, < si >[2] collibus silvis aspe-
4 ritate alia prohibebitur; mutabit hostium genus, mutabit
praesentis condicio discriminis: nunc acie derecta, nunc
cuneis, nunc auxiliis, nunc legione pugnabitur, nonnum-
5 quam terga etiam dedisse simulata fuga proderit. Ita prohoemium necessarium an supervacuum, breve an longius,

1 *Francius*: mutabitur *AB*
2 *add. edd.*

---

1 To be discussed in 6.5.

CHAPTER 13

Rhetoric cannot be bound by hard and fast laws

No one however should expect from me the sort of rules that most writers of textbooks have handed down, or ask me to lay down for students a set of laws, as it were, bound by immutable necessity: a Prooemium in every case, and of a certain kind; next, Narrative, and the rules of Narrative; then the Proposition, or, as some prefer, Digression; then a fixed order of Questions, and all the other things which some follow as commands, as if to do otherwise was a sin. Rhetoric would be a very easy and trivial affair if it could be comprised in a single short set of precepts. In fact, almost everything depends on Causes, times, opportunity, and necessity. Hence a specially important feature in an orator is prudent planning,[1] because this adjusts itself in various ways to the trend of events. Suppose you were to advise a general, every time he draws up his troops for battle, to keep the line straight, advance the two wings, and position the cavalry on the flanks. This may indeed be the best plan, when it is feasible; but the nature of the terrain will force a change, if there is a mountain ahead or a river in the way, or if he is held up by hills or woods or other unfavourable features. The character of the enemy will also force a change, so will the nature of the immediate danger. The battle will sometimes be fought in line, sometimes in column, with the auxiliaries or with the legions; it will even be a good plan sometimes to feign flight and turn your back on the enemy. Similarly, it is the Cause that will dictate whether a Prooemium is obligatory or superfluous, short

341

ad iudicem omni sermone derecto an aliquando averso per aliquam figuram dicendum sit, constricta an latius fusa narratio, continua an divisa, recta an ordine permutato,

6 causae docebunt, itemque de quaestionum ordine, cum in eadem controversia aliud alii parti prius quaeri frequenter expediat. Neque enim rogationibus plebisve scitis sancta sunt ista praecepta, sed hoc quidquid est utilitas excogita-

7 vit. Non negabo autem sic utile esse plerumque, alioqui nec scriberem. Verum si eadem illa nobis aliud suadebit utilitas, hanc relictis magistrorum auctoritatibus seque-mur.

8 Equidem id maxime praecipiam ac 'repetens iterum-que iterumque monebo': res duas in omni actu spectet ora-tor, quid deceat, quid expediat. Expedit autem saepe mu-tare ex illo constituto traditoque ordine aliqua, et interim decet, ut in statuis atque picturis videmus variari habitus

9 vultus status; nam recti quidem corporis vel minima gratia est: nempe enim adversa fit[3] facies et demissa bracchia et iuncti pedes et a summis ad ima rigens opus. Flexus ille et, ut sic dixerim, motus dat actum quendam et adfectum: ideo nec ad unum modum formatae manus et in vultu

10 mille species; cursum habent quaedam et impetum, se-dent alia vel incumbunt, nuda haec, illa velata sunt, quae-dam mixta ex utroque. Quid tam distortum et elaboratum

---

[3] *Gibson*: sit *AB*

---

[2] I.e. by the Figure of Apostrophe (*aversio*).

or long, whether the whole of it should be addressed to the judge or some parts, by means of a Figure, to another person;[2] whether the Narrative should be brief or full, continuous or split up, straightforward or in reverse order. And the same holds for the order of the Questions, since it often happens that in the same case one party may find it expedient to put one Question first, and the other another. These rules are not authorized by bills or plebiscites; such as they are, they are the product of expediency. I do not deny that there is generally some practical use in them; otherwise, I should not be writing this book. But if expediency persuades us of something else, we shall disregard the authority of the professors, and go along with her.

My personal advice, which I shall enjoin, "repeat, and urge again, again,"[3] is that in all his activities the orator should keep two things in mind: what is becoming and what is expedient.[4] And it is often expedient, and sometimes becoming, to make changes in the set traditional order, just as we see dress, expression, and stance varied in statues and pictures. The upright body has very little grace: the face looks straight at you, the arms hang down, the feet are joined together, and the work is entirely stiff from top to bottom. That flexibility—I might almost say "movement"—produces a sort of action and emotion. For the same reason, the hands are not always positioned in the same way, and there are a thousand kinds of facial expression. Some figures are shown running or dashing forward, others sit or lie; some are naked, some clothed, some half and half. What is so contorted and elaborately wrought

[3] *Aeneid* 3.436 (inexact quotation).
[4] So 11.1.8.

quam est ille discobolos Myronis? Si quis tamen ut parum
rectum improbet opus, nonne ab intellectu artis afuerit, in
qua vel praecipue laudabilis est ipsa illa novitas ac difficultas ?

11   Quam quidem gratiam et delectationem adferunt figurae, quaeque in sensibus quaeque in verbis sunt. Mutant
enim aliquid a recto, atque hanc prae se virtutem ferunt,
12 quod a consuetudine vulgari recesserunt. Habet in pictura speciem tota facies: Apelles tamen imaginem Antigo-
ni latere tantum altero ostendit, ut amissi oculi deformitas
lateret. Quid? non in oratione operienda sunt quaedam,
sive ostendi non debent sive exprimi pro dignitate non pos-
13 sunt? Ut fecit Timanthes, opinor, Cythnius in ea tabula qua
Coloten Teium vicit. Nam cum in Iphigeniae immolatione
pinxisset tristem Calchantem, tristiorem Ulixem, addidis-
set Menelao quem summum poterat ars efficere mae-
rorem: consumptis adfectibus non reperiens quo digne
modo patris vultum posset exprimere, velavit eius caput et
14 suo cuique animo dedit aestimandum. Nonne huic simile
est illud Sallustianum: 'nam de Carthagine tacere satius
puto quam parum dicere' ?

        Propter quae mihi semper moris fuit quam minime alli-
gare me ad praecepta quae καθολικά vocitant, id est, ut

---

5 Copies of this famous bronze statue of a discus-thrower
crouched for action (described by Lucian, *Philopseudes* 18) are
well known: critique and illustration, for example, in *Oxford History of Classical Art,* ed. J. Boardman (Oxford, 1993) 94–95. See
also 12.10.7.

6 So Pliny, *Nat. Hist.* 35.90.

7 Cicero, *Orator* 74 tells the story, but without names: more
detail in Pliny, *Nat. Hist.* 35.73.

as Myron's famous Discobolus?[5] But would not any critic
who disapproved of it because it was not upright show how
far he was from understanding its art, in which the very
novelty and difficulty of the pose are what most deserve
praise?

The same grace and charm are produced by Figures,
whether of Thought or of Speech. They represent a deviation from the norm, and make a virtue of their distance
from common or vulgar usage. In a picture, the full face
displays the beauty; yet Apelles painted Antigonus in pro-
file, so as to conceal the blemish of his lost eye.[6] Are not
certain things likewise to be covered up in a speech, either
because they ought not to be disclosed or because they
cannot be expressed adequately? This is what Timanthes
of Cythnus (I think it was he) did in the picture with which
he won the prize over Colotes of Teos.[7] Having depicted,
in his Sacrifice of Iphigenia, Calchas sad, Ulysses even sad-
der, and given Menelaus the most complete expression of
grief that his art could produce, he found he had used up
all his means of representing emotion and could discover
no way of adequately portraying her father's face; so he
covered his head in a veil, and left it to the imagination of
the spectators. There is a parallel to this, surely, in Sallust's
words: "As to Carthage, I think it better to say nothing than
to say too little."[8]

Because of this, it has always been my custom to tie
myself down as little as possible to what the Greeks call
"catholic"[9] rules—that is (to translate as well as we can)

8 *Jugurtha* 19 (not an exact quotation).
9 Compare Cicero, *Ad Atticum* 14.20.3 καθολικὸν θεώρημα.

dicamus quo modo possumus, universalia vel perpetualia;
raro enim reperitur hoc genus, ut non labefactari parte aliqua et subrui possit.

15   Sed de his plenius suo quidque loco tractabimus: interim nolo se iuvenes satis instructos si quem ex his qui breves plerumque circumferuntur artis libellum edidicerint
et velut decretis technicorum tutos putent. Multo labore,
adsiduo studio, varia exercitatione, plurimis experimentis,
altissima prudentia, praesentissimo consilio constat ars
16 dicendi. Sed adiuvatur his quoque, si tamen rectam viam,
non unam orbitam monstrent: qua declinare qui crediderit
nefas, patiatur necesse est illam per funes ingredientium
tarditatem. Itaque et stratum militari labore iter saepe de-
serimus compendio ducti, et si rectum limitem rupti tor-
rentibus pontes inciderint circumire cogemur, et si ianua
17 tenebitur incendio per parietem exibimus. Late fusum
opus est et multiplex et prope cotidie novum et de quo
numquam dicta erunt omnia. Quae sint tamen tradita,
quid ex his optimum, et si qua mutari adici detrahi melius
videbitur, dicere experiar.

14

1 Rhetoricen in Latinum transferentes tum oratoriam, tum
oratricem nominaverunt. Quos equidem non fraudaverim
debita laude quod copiam Romani sermonis augere temp-
tarint: sed non omnia nos ducentes ex Graeco secuntur,

---

[10] This is a general reference to the many places in which Q.,
discussing some rule (e.g. relating to the Parts of a Speech, Disposition, Composition, or Gesture), will show that experience must
often temper the rigidity of theory.

"universal" or "perpetual" rules. Rules are rare indeed that cannot be weakened or subverted in some respect.

But I will say more about these things in their proper places.[10] For the time being, I do not want young men to think their education complete if they have learned by heart one of the little textbooks which are in general circulation, or to believe that the decrees of the technical writers will ensure their salvation. The art of speaking depends on much effort, continual study, varied kinds of exercise, long experience, profound wisdom, and unfailing strategic sense. But rules too are an aid to it, if they indicate the main road, and not just some one narrow track such that anyone who thinks it a sin to stray will need to walk as slowly as a tightrope walker. We often leave the paved military road for the attraction of a short cut; if a flood has brought down the bridges and made the direct road impassable, we shall be forced to make a detour; if a door is blocked by fire, we shall escape through the wall. Our work is extensive, varied, and new almost every day; never will everything have been said about it. What I shall try to do is to set out the traditional doctrines, what is best in them, and whatever changes, additions, or omissions seem desirable.

CHAPTER 14

The name "rhetoric" and its first main division

Rhētorikē has been translated into Latin as *oratoria* or *oratrix*. I have no intention of depriving the translators of the praise they deserve for trying to enrich the Latin language. But our words do not always perform well when we base

sicut ne illos quidem quotiens utique suis verbis signare
2 nostra voluerunt. Et haec interpretatio non minus dura
est quam illa Plauti 'essentia' et 'queentia', sed ne propria
quidem; nam oratoria sic effertur ut elocutoria, oratrix ut
elocutrix, illa autem de qua loquimur rhetorice talis est qualis eloquentia. Nec dubie apud Graecos quoque duplicem
3 intellectum habet; namque uno modo fit adpositum—ars
rhetorica, ut navis piratica—altero nomen rei, qualis est
philosophia, amicitia. Nos ipsam nunc volumus significare
substantiam, ut grammatice litteratura est, non litteratrix
quem ad modum oratrix, nec litteratoria quem ad modum
4 oratoria: verum id in rhetorice non fit. Ne pugnemus igitur, cum praesertim plurimis alioqui Graecis sit utendum;
nam certe et philosophos et musicos et geometras dicam
nec vim adferam nominibus his indecora in Latinum sermonem mutatione: denique cum M. Tullius etiam ipsis
librorum quos hac de re primum scripserat titulis Graeco
nomine utatur, profecto non est verendum ne temere vi-
deamur oratori maximo de nomine artis suae credidisse.
5 Igitur rhetorice (iam enim sine metu cavillationis utemur hac appellatione) sic, ut opinor, optime dividetur ut
de arte, de artifice, de opere dicamus. Ars erit quae disci-

---

[1] Probably the Stoic Sergius Plautus (see also 3.6.23,
10.1.124). These innovations (see also 8.3.33) render Greek
οὐσία ("essence, being") and δύναμις ("potentiality").

[2] Q.'s argument is somewhat contorted. He explains that
rhētorikē in Greek is both a feminine adjective and used sub-
stantivally (with ellipse of *technē,* "art"). In this second use it corresponds to the abstract noun *eloquentia. Oratoria* and *oratrix* are
respectively an adjective and an agent noun, and so unsuitable to
translate the abstract substantive *rhētorikē.* In the parallel case of

them on the Greek, any more than theirs do, at any rate when they have chosen to express our concepts in their language. And this translation is no less awkward than Plautus'[1] *essentia* and *queentia,* and is not even exact. For *oratoria* is formed like *elocutoria* and *oratrix* like *elocutrix,* whereas *rhētorikē,* of which we are speaking, is the same sort of thing as *eloquentia.* The word undoubtedly has two senses in Greek too. In one, it is an adjective (*ars rhetorica,* like *navis piratica*), in the other a noun, like "philosophy" or "friendship." We need it here as a substantive, in the sense in which *grammatikē* is represented by *litteratura,* not by *litteratrix* on the analogy of *oratrix* or *litteratoria* on the analogy of *oratoria.* But this option is not available for *rhētorikē.*[2] So let us not put up any resistance; we have to use many Greek words anyway. I shall certainly use *philosophus, musicus* and *geometres,* and shall not do violence to these words by clumsy translation into Latin. And finally, since Cicero used a Greek word in the title of the first books he wrote on this subject,[3] we surely do not have to fear being thought rash in trusting to the greatest of orators in the matter of the name of his art.

"Rhetoric" then (I shall use this word from now on without fear of criticism) will be best, in my view, divided into (1) the art, (2) the artist, (3) the work. (1) The art is

grammatikē, Latin has the resource of the noun *litteratura* (see 2.1.4), but there is no similarly acceptable noun to correspond to *rhētorikē.* Latin *-icus* adjectives (Q.'s examples, *rhetoricus, piraticus,* are both, as it happens, borrowings from Greek) are indeed in use, but cannot be substantivized. It should be noted that Q. regularly gives Greek inflections to *grammaticē.*

[3] I.e. *De inventione,* normally referred to by Q. as *Rhetorica.*

plina percipi debet: ea est bene dicendi scientia. Artifex est
qui percepit hanc artem: id est orator, cuius est summa
bene dicere. Opus, quod efficitur ab artifice: id est bona
oratio. Haec omnia rursus diducuntur in species: sed illa
sequentia suo loco, nunc quae de prima parte tractanda
sunt ordiar.

15

1   Ante omnia, quid sit rhetorice. Quae finitur quidem varie,
    sed quaestionem habet duplicem: aut enim de qualitate ip-
    sius rei aut de comprensione verborum dissensio est. Pri-
    ma atque praecipua opinionum circa hoc differentia, quod
    alii malos quoque viros posse oratores dici putant, alii,
    quorum nos sententiae accedimus, nomen hoc artemque
2   de qua loquimur bonis demum tribui volunt. Eorum au-
    tem qui dicendi facultatem a maiore ac magis expetenda
    vitae laude secernunt, quidam rhetoricen vim tantum, qui-
    dam scientiam sed non virtutem, quidam usum, quidam
    artem quidem sed a scientia et virtute diiunctam, quidam
    etiam pravitatem quandam artis, id est κακοτεχνίαν, no-
3   minaverunt. Hi fere aut in persuadendo aut in dicendo
    apte ad persuadendum positum orandi munus sunt arbi-
    trati: id enim fieri potest ab eo quoque qui vir bonus non
    sit. Est igitur frequentissimus finis: 'rhetoricen esse vim
    persuadendi'. Quod ego vim appello, plerique potestatem,

    ⁴ In 12.1–9 and 12.10 respectively. On this division of the sub-
ject, see General Introduction.
    ¹ Epicurus (fr. 51 Usener) is said to have used this word of
forensic oratory: Sextus Empiricus (*Adversus mathematicos* 2.36,

what has to be acquired by study: it is the science of speaking well. (2) The artist is the man who has acquired the art, that is, the orator, whose goal is to speak well. (3) The work is what the orator produces, that is, a good speech. These are all subdivided into various parts. Of the two latter divisions I shall speak in due course;[4] I shall now begin the treatment of the first.

CHAPTER 15

The nature and purpose of rhetoric

First of all, what is rhetoric? It is defined in various ways, but there are really two areas of disagreement, one concerning the quality of the actual thing, and the other the way to define it in words. The first and main difference of opinion is that some think that bad men also can be orators, and others, with whose view I agree, confine this name, and the art of which we are speaking, to the good. Of those who divorce the faculty of speaking from any greater or more desirable achievement of life, some call rhetoric merely a power, some a science but not a virtue, some a practice, some an art, but not one linked with science and virtue, some again a perversion of art (*kakotechnia*).[1] They almost all believe that the function of oratory lies in persuading or in speaking in a way adapted to persuade. For this can be done even by one who is not a good man. So the commonest definition is that "rhetoric is the power of persuading." (What I call "power" many call "capacity," some

49, 68) naturally makes play with it in his demolition of the claims of rhetoric. See also 2.20.2.

nonnulli facultatem vocant: quae res ne quid adferat ambi-
4 guitatis, vim dico δύναμιν. Haec opinio originem ab Iso-
crate, si tamen re vera ars quae circumfertur eius est,
duxit. Qui cum longe sit a voluntate infamantium oratoris
officia, finem artis temere comprendit dicens esse rhetoricen persuadendi opificem, id est πειθοῦς δημιουργόν:
neque enim mihi permiserim eadem uti declinatione qua
5 Ennius M. Cethegum 'suadae medullam' vocat. Apud Platonem quoque Gorgias in libro qui nomine eius inscriptus
est idem fere dicit, sed hanc Plato illius opinionem vult accipi, non suam. Cicero pluribus locis scripsit officium ora-
6 toris esse dicere adposite ad persuadendum, in rhetoricis
etiam, quos sine dubio ipse non probat, finem facit persuadere. Verum et pecunia persuadet et gratia et auctoritas dicentis et dignitas, postremo aspectus etiam ipse sine voce,
quo vel recordatio meritorum cuiusque vel facies aliqua
7 miserabilis vel formae pulchritudo sententiam dictat. Nam
et Manium Aquilium defendens Antonius, cum scissa
veste cicatrices quas is pro patria pectore adverso suscepis-
set ostendit, non orationis habuit fiduciam, sed oculis populi Romani vim attulit: quem illo ipso aspectu maxime
8 motum in hoc, ut absolveret reum, creditum est. Servium

---

2 It is unlikely that Isocrates himself wrote a textbook, though
one (not now extant) passed under his name: Radermacher, *AS*
153–163. The "power of persuasion" definition was attributed to
Corax and Tisias; Plato's Socrates (*Gorgias* 453A) paraphrases
Gorgias' concept in the words *"dēmiourgos* ('craftsman') of persuasion." 3 Ennius, *Annales* 303 Vahlen = 305 Warmington =
304 Skutsch; Cicero, *Brutus* 59. 4 *De inventione* 1.6, *De
oratore* 1.138. In the earlier work, Cicero distinguishes the
officium of rhetoric, which is "to speak in a manner appropriate for

BOOK 2.15

"faculty." To avoid ambiguity, let me say that by "power" I mean *dynamis*.) This view originates with Isocrates[2] (if the "Art" passing under his name is really his). He, though far from sharing the aims of those who disparage the duties of an orator, defines the art somewhat carelessly, saying "rhetoric is the craftsman (*dēmiourgos*) of persuasion (*peithō*)." (I cannot bring myself to use the new coinage with which Ennius described Marcus Cethegus as *suadae medulla*, "marrow of persuasion.")[3] Gorgias, in the dialogue of Plato which takes its name from him, says much the same; but Plato wants it to be seen as Gorgias' view, not his own. Cicero writes in various places[4] that the duty of the orator is "to speak in a manner suited to persuade." In his *Rhetorica*, however (books which doubtless he does not himself approve), he says that the goal of rhetoric is "to persuade." But money also persuades, as do influence, the speaker's authority and dignity, and even the mere look of a man though he says nothing; for the memory of a person's services or a sad face or a beautiful body can determine a verdict. Antonius, defending Manius Aquilius,[5] tore open his client's clothes and disclosed the scars he bore in front, earned in his country's service, and thus, instead of relying on his own eloquence, delivered a shock to the eyes of the people of Rome, who, we are led to believe, were chiefly moved to acquit him by the mere sight. And a speech of

persuasion," from its *finis*, which is "to persuade by speech." Q. seems to treat these statements as contradictory, failing to draw Cicero's distinction, and using *finis* for both a descriptive definition (ὅρος) and a statement of aims (τέλος).

[5] Cicero, *De oratore* 2.124, 194; *In Verrem* 2.5.3. This celebrated defence (against a charge of extortion) was in 98 BC. *ORF* p. 227.

353

quidem Galbam miseratione sola, qua non suos modo liberos parvolos in contione produxerat, sed Galli etiam Sulpi-
ci filium suis ipse manibus circumtulerat, elapsum esse
cum aliorum monumentis, tum Catonis oratione testatum
9 est. Et Phrynen non Hyperidis actione quamquam admirabili, sed conspectu corporis, quod illa speciosissimum
alioqui diducta nudaverat tunica, putant periculo libera-
tam.

Quae si omnia persuadent, non est hic de quo locuti
10 sumus idoneus finis. Ideoque diligentiores sunt visi sibi
qui, cum de rhetorice idem sentirent, existimarunt eam
vim dicendo persuadendi. Quem finem Gorgias in eodem
de quo supra diximus libro velut coactus a Socrate facit; a
quo non dissentit Theodectes, sive ipsius id opus est quod
de rhetorice nomine eius inscribitur, sive, ut creditum est,
Aristotelis: in quo est finem esse rhetorices: 'ducere homines dicendo in id quod actor[1] velit'.
11 Sed ne hoc quidem satis est comprehensum: persuadent enim dicendo vel ducunt in id quod volunt alii
quoque, ut meretrices adulatores corruptores. At contra
non persuadet semper orator, ut interim non sit proprius
hic finis eius, interim sit communis cum iis qui ab oratore
12 procul absunt. Atqui non multum ab hoc fine abest Apollo-

[1] auctor *B*: *del. Winterbottom*

[6] Cato's speech against Galba (149 BC) was reported in his
Origines (Cicero, *Brutus* 89: frs. 106–110 Peter: see also *ORF*
pp. 79–80).   [7] See also 1.10.47. Presumably his son had been
left in Galba's guardianship.
[8] See also 10.5.2. This famous example is also used in Sextus
Empiricus, *Adversus mathematicos* 2.2.

Cato's,[6] as well as other records, is evidence that Servius Galba escaped condemnation solely through the pity he aroused by not only exhibiting his own little children before the assembly, but also carrying in his arms the child of Sulpicius Gallus.[7] So also, it is thought, Phryne was saved from danger not by Hyperides' pleading, admirable as it was, but by the sight of her lovely body, which she had further revealed by opening her dress.[8]

If all these things are persuasive, the definition of which we spoke is inadequate, and so those who, although holding the same general view of rhetoric, have judged it to be "the power of persuading by speaking," have claimed to be more accurate. This definition is given by Gorgias in the dialogue already mentioned, under compulsion apparently from Socrates.[9] Theodectes[10] does not dissent, whether the book on rhetoric attributed to him is his or, as has been believed, Aristotle's. It states that the end of rhetoric is "to lead men by speech to the conclusion desired by the speaker."

But even this does not say enough. Others besides orators persuade or induce compliance with their wishes by speech: for instance, courtesans, flatterers, corrupters. And on the other hand, the orator does not always succeed in persuading, so that sometimes this definition does not fit him, and sometimes it is common also to others who are far from being orators. Yet Apollodorus[11] does not move far

9 Plato, *Gorgias* 452E.

10 Poet and rhetorician; see Kennedy, *AP* 80–81, Radermacher, *AS* p. 202. See also 4.2.63, 11.2.51.

11 See on 2.11.2.

dorus dicens iudicialis orationis primum et super omnia
esse persuadere iudici et sententiam eius ducere in id
quod velit. Nam et ipse oratorem fortunae subicit, ut, si
non persuaserit, nomen suum retinere non possit.

13   Quidam recesserunt ab eventu, sicut Aristoteles dicit:
'rhetorice est vis inveniendi omnia in oratione persuasibilia'. Qui finis et illud vitium de quo supra diximus habet, et
insuper quod nihil nisi inventionem complectitur, quae
sine elocutione non est oratio.

14   Hermagorae, qui finem eius esse ait persuasibiliter dicere, et aliis qui eandem sententiam, non isdem tantum
verbis, explicant ac finem esse demonstrant dicere quae
oportet omnia ad persuadendum, satis responsum est
cum persuadere non tantum oratoris esse convicimus.

15   Addita sunt his alia varie. Quidam enim circa res
omnes, quidam circa civiles modo versari rhetoricen putaverunt: quorum verius utrum sit, in eo loco qui huius
16 quaestionis proprius est dicam. Omnia subiecisse oratori
videtur Aristoteles cum dixit vim esse videndi quid in quaque re possit esse persuasibile, et Iatrocles,[2] qui non
quidem adicit 'in quaque re', sed nihil excipiendo idem

---

[2] Patrocles A

---

[12] Compare Aristotle, *Rhetoric* 1. 1355b25 "capacity to per-
ceive what may possibly be convincing in any particular matter":
see Q.'s more accurate version below, §16.

[13] Fr. 2 Matthes: Kennedy, *AP* 303–321. Hermagoras' definition (fr. 3 Matthes) is said also to have included the qualification
that the orator's duty is to persuade "as far as the conditions of
circumstances and persons allow." Compare *Ad Herennium* 1.2,
Prolegomenon Sylloge 65 Rabe.

from this formulation when he says that the first and most important task of forensic oratory is "to persuade the judge and guide his decision towards that which the speaker desires." For Apollodorus too makes the orator subject to fortune by refusing to let him keep his title if he does not succeed in persuading.

Some are not concerned with results at all, like Aristotle, who says that "Rhetoric is the power of discovering all the persuasive elements in a speech."[12] This formulation has the fault already mentioned, and also covers only Invention, which does not constitute oratory without Elocution.

Hermagoras,[13] who says that the end is "to speak persuasively," and the others who express the same view in different words and say that it is "to say everything which ought to be said for the purposes of persuasion," were sufficiently answered when we proved that persuasion is not exclusively the domain of the orator.[14]

Various additions to these formulations have been suggested. Some think rhetoric has to do with "all things," others only with "public matters." I shall discuss which of these views is nearer the truth when I come to the proper context for this question.[15] Aristotle seems to have brought everything within the orator's field when he defined rhetoric as "the power of seeing what, in any matter, might be persuasive." Iatrocles,[16] without adding "in any matter," nevertheless excludes nothing and so shows that his view is

[14] Above, §11.

[15] 2.21.

[16] Here and at 3.6.44 the tradition is split between *Iatrocles* and *Patrocles*. Neither person is known.

ostendit: vim enim vocat inveniendi quod sit in oratione
persuasibile. Qui fines et ipsi solam complectuntur inventionem. Quod vitium fugiens Eudorus[3] vim putat
inveniendi et eloquendi cum ornatu credibilia in omni ora-
17 tione. Sed cum eodem modo credibilia quo persuasibilia
etiam non orator inveniat, adiciendo 'in omni oratione'
magis quam superiores concedit scelera quoque suadenti-
18 bus pulcherrimae rei nomen. Gorgias apud Platonem suadendi se artificem in iudiciis et aliis coetibus esse ait, de
iustis quoque et iniustis tractare: cui Socrates persuadendi, non docendi concedit facultatem.
19   Qui vero non omnia subiciebant oratori, sollicitius ac
verbosius, ut necesse erat, adhibuerunt discrimina, quorum fuit Ariston, Critolai Peripatetici discipulus, cuius hic
finis est: 'scientia videndi et agendi in quaestionibus civili-
20 bus per orationem popularis persuasionis'. Hic scientiam,
quia Peripateticus est, non ut Stoici virtutis loco ponit:
popularem autem comprendendo persuasionem etiam
contumeliosus est adversus artem orandi, quam nihil putat

---

[3] Theodorus *A*: Diodorus *Spengel*

---

[17] An almost identical definition ("rhetoric is the capacity to
discover and express with elegance all available credible argument in any speech") is attributed by Nicolaus (*Progymnasmata*
p. 2 Felten) and other late sources to a Diodorus. Hence Spengel
would read Diodorus here. Theodorus (the reading in A) is ruled
out, as he belongs to quite another group (§21). Eudorus might
be the well-known Alexandrian Platonist who flourished under
Augustus, though there is no evidence that he wrote on rhetoric.
If *superiores* means "predecessors" (as I translate it) and not just
"those mentioned above" (*OLD* s.v. 3), it is implied that the person meant is later than Apollodorus and Hermagoras.

the same. His definition is "the power of discovering what is persuasive in speech." These formulations also cover only Invention. To avoid this fault, Eudorus proposes "the power to discover and express with elegance whatever is credible in any speech."[17] But as even a non-orator may discover what is "credible" as well as "persuasive," Eudorus, even more than his predecessors, surrenders the name of our noble profession to inciters of crime by his addition of the phrase "in any speech." Gorgias in Plato[18] claims to be an expert in persuasion in the courts and other assemblies, and says that he treats justice and injustice as well; Socrates in reply allows him the faculty of persuading, but not of teaching.

Those who did not make everything a subject for the orator have necessarily introduced some rather forced and elaborate distinctions. They include Ariston,[19] the pupil of the Peripatetic Critolaus,[20] whose definition is: "the science of seeing and acting in public questions by means of speech of popular persuasiveness." Being a Peripatetic, he does not like the Stoics identify "science" and virtue; and by including in his definition "*popular*[21] persuasiveness" he actually insults the art of oratory, implying that it will

---

[18] *Gorgias* 454B–E.

[19] There seem to have been two Peripatetic philosophers called Ariston, this pupil of Critolaus being the younger. Sextus Empiricus, *Adversus mathematicos* 2.61 (= Wehrli, *Die Schule des Aristoteles, Ariston der jüngere*, fr. 2), gives his definition as "the aim (σκοπός) of rhetoric is persuasion and its end (τέλος) the achievement of persuasion."   [20] A strong opponent of the claims of rhetoric to be a branch of knowledge (below, §23).

[21] Was the Greek word δημοτικῆς or ὀχλικῆς? Q.'s criticism seems tendentious.

doctis persuasuram. Illud de omnibus qui circa civiles
demum quaestiones oratorem iudicant versari dictum sit,
excludi ab iis plurima oratoris officia, illam certe laudati-
vam totam, quae est rhetorices pars tertia.

21   Cautius Theodorus Gadareus, ut iam ad eos veniamus
qui artem quidem esse eam, sed non virtutem putaverunt.
Ita enim dicit, ut ipsis eorum verbis utar qui haec ex Graeco transtulerunt: 'ars inventrix et iudicatrix et enuntiatrix,
decente ornatu secundum mensionem, eius quod in quo-
22   que potest sumi persuasibile, in materia civili'. Itemque
Cornelius Celsus, qui finem rhetorices ait 'dicere persuasibiliter in dubia civili materia'. Quibus sunt non dissimiles
qui ab aliis traduntur, qualis est ille: 'vis videndi et eloquendi de rebus civilibus subiectis sibi cum quadam persuasione et quodam corporis habitu et eorum quae dicet
23   pronuntiatione'. Mille alia, sed aut eadem aut ex isdem
composita, quibus item cum de materia rhetorices dicendum erit respondebimus.

Quidam eam neque vim neque scientiam neque artem
putaverunt, sed Critolaus usum dicendi (nam hoc τριβή
24   significat), Athenaeus fallendi artem. Plerique autem,

---

22 Q. himself (3.4) recognizes the common ground between
Epideictic and the other two "genres" of Forensic and Deliberative: but πολιτικός (civilis) is often taken to exclude Epideictic
(e.g. Aristotle, *Rhetoric* 1391b16).   23 See on 2.11.2.

24 Translation uncertain: others take *secundum mensionem*
with what follows: "in accordance with the proportions of that
which can be taken." Q. is using someone else's translation, and
one can only guess at the underlying Greek: e.g. τέχνη εὑρετικὴ
καὶ κριτικὴ καὶ ἀπαγγελτικὴ μετὰ πρέποντος κόσμου κατὰ
μέτρον τοῦ ἐν ἑκάστῳ ἐνδεχομένου πιθανοῦ ἐν πράγματι
πολιτικῷ.   25 Fr. 1 Marx.   26 2.21.

not be persuasive to the educated. All those who confine
the field of the orator's activity to "public" questions may
be criticized as excluding most of the duties of an orator,
and certainly the whole encomiastic genre, which is one
third of rhetoric.[22]

Turning now to those who regard rhetoric as an art but
not a virtue, we find Theodorus[23] of Gadara taking a more
cautious line. He says (I quote the actual words of those
who have translated this from the Greek): "The art which
discovers and judges and expresses, with proper elegance
in accordance with due proportion, that which can be
taken as persuasive in each case, in subjects of public concern."[24] So also Cornelius Celsus,[25] who says that the aim
of rhetoric is "to speak persuasively on disputable public
matters." Similar definitions are given by others, for example: "the power of seeing and speaking on public matters
submitted to it, combined with a certain persuasiveness
and a certain physical presence and delivery of the words."
There are thousands of others, but they are all either the
same or made up out of the same elements. I shall respond
to these when I come to deal with the subject matter of
rhetoric.[26]

Some treat rhetoric neither as a power nor as a science
nor as an art. Critolaus[27] calls it "*knack* of speaking" (that is
what *tribē* means), Athenaeus "art of deceiving."[28] Many

[27] Fr. 26 Wehrli. But the use of $\tau\rho\iota\beta\dot{\eta}$ comes from Plato:
Gorgias 463B, *Phaedrus* 260E.   [28] Sextus Empiricus, *Adversus mathematicos* 2.62, attributes to this Athenaeus (of whom
nothing is known) a definition inconsistent with what Q. gives us
here: "rhetoric is a power of words which aims at the persuasion of
the hearers." See Kennedy, *AP* 320–321.

dum pauca ex Gorgia Platonis a prioribus imperite excerp-
ta legere contenti neque hoc totum neque alia eius volumi-
na evolvunt, in maximum errorem inciderunt, creduntque
eum in hac esse opinione, ut rhetoricen non artem sed
25 'peritiam quandam gratiae ac voluptatis' existimet, et alio
loco 'civilitatis particulae simulacrum et quartam partem
adulationis', quod duas partes civilitatis corpori adsignet,
medicinam et quam interpretantur exercitatricem, duas
animo, legalem atque iustitiam, adulationem autem medicinae vocet cocorum artificium, exercitatricis mangonum,
qui colorem fuco et verum robur inani sagina mentiantur,
26 legalis cavillatricem, iustitiae rhetoricen. Quae omnia sunt
quidem scripta in hoc libro dictaque a Socrate, cuius persona videtur Plato significare quid sentiat: sed alii sunt eius
sermones ad coarguendos qui contra disputant compositi,
quos ἐλεγκτικούς vocant, alii ad praecipiendum, qui δογ-
27 ματικοί appellantur. Socrates autem seu Plato eam quidem quae tum exercebatur rhetoricen talem putat (nam
et dicit his verbis τοῦτον τὸν τρόπον ὃν ὑμεῖς πολι-
τεύεσθε), veram autem et honestam intellegit; itaque dis-
putatio illa contra Gorgian ita cluditur: οὐκοῦν ἀνάγκη
τὸν ῥητορικὸν δίκαιον εἶναι, τὸν δὲ δίκαιον βούλεσθαι
28 δίκαια πράττειν. Ad quod ille quidem conticescit, sed ser-

---

[29] *Gorgias* 462C, 463D, 464B. *Gorgias* was the key text in the
debate between rhetoric and philosophy: Aelius Aristides' three
long speeches on the subject (*Orat.* 2, 3, 4) are largely directed
against it.   [30] These terms do not occur in this connection
elsewhere, but Q.'s division corresponds in effect to that between
"hyphegematic" ("expository") and "zetetic" ("investigative") dialogues made by Diogenes Laertius 3.49. *Gorgias* is there classed
as "anatreptic" ("subversive"), a subdivision of the "investigative."

writers, content to take excerpts from Plato's *Gorgias,* un-
wisely selected by their predecessors, and not reading the
whole dialogue or his other works, have fallen into the
great error of supposing that Plato believed that rhetoric
was not an art but "a certain expertise in charm and pleasure," and (from another passage) "the shadow of a part of
politics" and "the fourth type of flattery."[29] (Plato assigns
two parts of "politics" to the body, medicine and gymnastics (they translate this as *exercitatrix*), and two to the
mind, law and justice; he makes cookery a form of "flattery
of medicine," the expertise of the slave-dealers "flattery
of gymnastics," because they use paint to fake colour and
useless fat to fake real strength, and similarly sophistry
"flattery of law," and rhetoric "flattery of justice.") Now all
this is indeed written in this dialogue, and spoken by Socrates, in whose person Plato appears to represent his own
views. But some of his dialogues were composed to refute
opponents, and these are called "elenctic" dialogues, while
others are for teaching, and are called "dogmatic."[30] Now
Socrates (or Plato) applies this description to rhetoric as
practised in those days, for he speaks explicitly of "this way
in which you conduct public affairs,"[31] but he has an understanding of true and honourable rhetoric. The argument with Gorgias therefore ends with the words "And so
the rhetorical man must be just, and the just man must
wish to do just things."[32] This silences Gorgias, and the

For Q., however, it is "elenctic," and so contains arguments of various degrees of validity. For the history of this classification see O.
Nüsser, *Albins Prolog und die Dialogtheorie des Platonismus*
(1991) 101–168.

[31] *Gorgias* 500C.   [32] 460C.

monem suscipit Polus iuvenili calore inconsideratior, contra quem illa de simulacro et adulatione dicuntur. Tum Callicles adhuc concitatior, qui tamen ad hanc perducitur clausulam: τὸν μέλλοντα ὀρθῶς ῥητορικὸν ἔσεσθαι δίκαιον ἄρα δεῖ εἶναι καὶ ἐπιστήμονα τῶν δικαίων, ut appareat Platoni non rhetoricen videri malum, sed eam veram nisi iusto ac bono non contingere.

29   Adhuc autem in Phaedro manifestius facit hanc artem consummari citra iustitiae quoque scientiam non posse: cui opinioni nos quoque accedimus. An aliter defensionem Socratis et eorum qui pro patria ceciderant laudem scrip-

30   sisset? Quae certe sunt oratoris opera. Sed in illud hominum genus quod facilitate dicendi male utebatur invectus est. Nam et Socrates inhonestam sibi credidit orationem quam ei Lysias reo composuerat, et tum maxime scribere litigatoribus quae illi pro se ipsi dicerent erat moris, atque ita iuri quo non licebat pro altero agere fraus adhibebatur.

31   Doctores quoque eius artis parum idonei Platoni videbantur, qui rhetoricen a iustitia separarent et veris credibilia

32   praeferrent; nam id quoque dicit in Phaedro. Consensisse autem illis superioribus videri potest etiam Cornelius Celsus, cuius haec verba sunt: 'orator simile tantum veri petit',

---

33 508C.

34 260ff.

35 I.e. *Menexenus,* often taken in antiquity as a model of epideictic, without regard to its parodic quality.

36 For this supposed speech and Socrates' refusal, see below 11.1.11; Cicero, *De oratore* 1.231; [Plutarch], *Lives of the Ten Orators* 836B; Diogenes Laertius 2.40–41; Giannantoni 1 c 135. Q. is drawing attention in what follows to the difference between the Athenian practice of litigants pleading for themselves (though

conversation is taken up by Polus, whose youthful ardour makes him less circumspect, and it is against Polus that the passage about "shadow" and "flattery" is directed. Then comes Callicles, who is even more ardent, but who is nevertheless led to the conclusion that "the man who is going to be a rhetorician in the correct way must therefore be just and have knowledge of what is just."[33] It is obvious, then, that Plato does not think that rhetoric is a bad thing, but that real rhetoric can be attained only by the just and good man.

He makes it even clearer in the *Phaedrus*[34] that this art cannot be perfect without a knowledge of justice also. I agree with this. Otherwise, would Plato have written his Defence of Socrates and his encomium of the men who fell fighting for their country?[35] These are certainly orator's work. His attack was directed, however, against the class of men who made bad use of their facility in speaking. Socrates even thought the speech which Lysias composed for his defence dishonourable for him to use,[36] although it was the practice in those days to write speeches for litigants to deliver in court, thereby circumventing the law which forbade one man to speak on behalf of another. The teachers of rhetoric also seemed unsatisfactory to Plato, because they separated rhetoric from justice and preferred the credible to the true: he says this also in the *Phaedrus*.[37] Cornelius Celsus[38] seems to have been of the same opinion as these early rhetors, for he says "The orator seeks only

perhaps using a speech written by a professional) and the Roman relationship of advocate and client.

[37] 267A.

[38] Fr. 2 Marx.

deinde paulo post: 'non enim bona conscientia sed victoria litigantis est praemium': quae si vera essent, pessimorum hominum foret haec tam perniciosa nocentissimis moribus dare instrumenta et nequitiam praeceptis adiuvare.

33   Sed illi rationem opinionis suae viderint; nos autem ingressi formare perfectum oratorem, quem in primis esse virum bonum volumus, ad eos qui de hoc opere melius sentiunt revertamur.

Rhetoricen autem quidam eandem civilitatem esse iudicaverunt, Cicero scientiae civilis partem vocat (civilis autem scientia idem quod sapientia est), quidam eandem
34   philosophiam, quorum est Isocrates. Huic eius substantiae maxime conveniet finitio rhetoricen esse bene dicendi scientiam. Nam et orationis omnes virtutes semel complectitur et protinus etiam mores oratoris, cum bene di-
35   cere non possit nisi bonus. Idem valet Chrysippi finis ille ductus a Cleanthe, 'scientia recte dicendi'. Sunt plures eiusdem, sed ad alias quaestiones magis pertinent. Idem sentiret finis hoc modo comprensus: 'persuadere quod oporteat', nisi quod artem ad exitum alligat.
36   Bene Areus: 'dicere secundum virtutem orationis'.

---

39 *De inventione* 1.6.

40 Isocrates used φιλοσοφία regularly to describe his own brand of moral and rhetorical education.

41 Attributed to Xenocrates (fr. 13 Heinze = Sextus Empiricus, *Adversus mathematicos* 2.6) and then normal for Stoics (Cicero, *De oratore* 1.83). Sextus (loc. cit.) however points out that Xenocrates used "science" *(epistēmē)* as an equivalent of *technē*, whereas the Stoics meant it in their special sense of the possession of secure *katalēpseis*, only possible for the Wise Man, who is thus "the only orator."

the semblance of truth," and, a little later, "The reward is not a good conscience, but the victory of the litigant." If this were true, only a very bad man would give such dangerous weapons to criminals or help wickedness with his advice.

But it is up to these people to justify their own views. What I have undertaken is to fashion the perfect orator, and my first requirement is that he should be a good man. Let us therefore return to those who have sounder views on the subject.

Some think that rhetoric and politics are the same; Cicero[39] calls rhetoric a part of political science (and "political science" here means philosophy); and some think rhetoric and philosophy are the same (Isocrates was of this opinion).[40] The definition which will best suit this notion of its real nature is that "rhetoric is the science of speaking well."[41] This includes all the virtues of speech in one formula and at the same time also the character of the orator, because only a good man can speak "well." Chrysippus' definition, taken from Cleanthes, "the science of speaking rightly," comes to the same thing.[42] Chrysippus gives other definitions also, but they relate rather to other problems. The same view would be implied in the formulation "to persuade what it is right to do," except that this ties the art down to results.

Areus'[43] formula is a good one: "to speak according to the virtue of speech."

[42] *SVF* 1. 288–294, 491.
[43] See 3.1.16; probably to be distinguished (so H. Diels, *Doxographi Graeci* 86–87) from the philosopher Areios Didymos, a favourite companion of Augustus.

Excludunt a rhetorice malos et illi qui scientiam civilium officiorum eam putaverunt, si scientiam virtutem iudicant, sed anguste intra civiles quaestiones coercent.

Albucius non obscurus professor atque auctor scientiam bene dicendi esse consentit, sed exceptionibus peccat adiciendo 'circa civiles quaestiones et credibiliter': quarum iam utrique responsum est.

37   Probabilis et illi voluntatis qui recte sentire et dicere rhetorices putaverunt.

Hi sunt fere fines maxime inlustres et de quibus praecipue disputatur. Nam omnis quidem persequi neque attinet neque possum, cum pravum quoddam, ut arbitror, studium circa scriptores artium extiterit nihil isdem verbis quae prior aliquis occupasset finiendi: quae ambitio procul 38   aberit a me. Dicam enim non utique quae invenero, sed quae placebunt, sicut hoc: rhetoricen esse bene dicendi scientiam, cum, reperto quod est optimum, qui quaerit aliud peius velit.

His adprobatis simul manifestum est illud quoque, quem finem vel quid summum et ultimum habeat rhetorice, quod τέλος dicitur, ad quod omnis ars tendit: nam si est ipsa bene dicendi scientia, finis eius et summum est bene dicere.

Those who define rhetoric as "the science of public duties" also exclude bad men, if they regard "science" as virtue; but the restriction to public questions is too narrow.

Albucius,[44] a well-known teacher and writer, agrees that it is "the science of speaking well," but he goes wrong when he adds the restrictive phrases "in regard to public questions" and "credibly." I have already dealt with both these points.

The intention of those who have held that it is the business of rhetoric "to think and speak rightly" is also to be commended.

These, roughly, are the most famous and most seriously discussed definitions. It would be irrelevant and impossible for me to deal with all that have been proposed. It seems to me that there has grown up a perverse desire in writers of textbooks never to formulate anything in words which some predecessor has used. I shall have no such pretensions. What I say will not necessarily be what I have discovered, but what I think right. In this case, it is that rhetoric is "the science of speaking well." Once the best answer is found, to look for another is to seek something worse.

This granted, we also have a clear answer to the question of what the end, or highest aim or ultimate goal of rhetoric is—the *telos* as it is called, to which all arts tend. For if the art is "the science of speaking well," its end and highest aim is "to speak well."

[44] See Kaster (1995) 346–355.

QUINTILIAN

16

1 Sequitur quaestio an utilis rhetorice. Nam quidam vehementer in eam invehi solent, et, quod est[1] indignissimum,
2 in accusationem orationis utuntur orandi viribus: eloquentiam esse quae poenis eripiat scelestos, cuius fraude
damnentur interim boni, consilia ducantur in peius, nec
seditiones modo turbaeque populares sed bella etiam in-
expiabilia excitentur, cuius denique tum maximus sit usus
3 cum pro falsis contra veritatem valet. Nam et Socrati
obiciunt comici docere eum quo modo peiorem causam
meliorem faciat, et contra Tisian et Gorgian similia dicit
4 polliceri Plato. Et his adiciunt exempla Graecorum Roma-
norumque, et enumerant qui perniciosa non singulis tantum sed rebus etiam publicis usi eloquentia turbaverint
civitatium status vel everterint, eoque et Lacedaemoniorum civitate expulsam et Athenis quoque, ubi actor mo-
vere adfectus vetabatur, velut recisam orandi potestatem.
5 Quo quidem modo nec duces erunt utiles nec magistratus nec medicina nec denique ipsa sapientia: nam et dux

[1] *Halm*: sit *AB*

---

[1] Aristotle (*Rhetoric* 1. 1355a20–30) also treats this as a separate question, and argues (1) that we need rhetoric to avoid the re-
proach of letting a good cause fail; (2) that "scientific" proof does
not convince everybody; (3) that we need to know how to refute
opposing arguments, and only dialectic and rhetoric can help us
here; (4) that it is right to acquire skill to defend ourselves by
speech even more than by physical strength.

[2] E.g. Aristophanes, *Clouds* 97–98, 112–115, 882ff.

[3] *Phaedrus* 267A.   [4] Compare Cicero, *Brutus* 50, Tacitus,
Dialogus 40, but especially Chamaeleon fr. 35 Wehrli ("many cit-

CHAPTER 16

Is rhetoric useful?

The next question is whether rhetoric is useful.[1] Some are in the habit of making a violent attack upon it and (most disgracefully) using the power of oratory to denounce oratory. It is eloquence, they argue, that snatches criminals from punishment, conduces sometimes by its deception to the condemnation of the innocent, leads deliberations astray, and excites not only sedition and mob violence but wars that can never be expiated; in short (they say) its greatest use is to stand up for falsehood against truth. Thus the comic poets accuse Socrates of teaching how to make the worse cause seem the better,[2] and Plato,[3] on the other side, says that Tisias and Gorgias made similar promises. They add examples from Greece and from Rome and enumerate all those who have used an eloquence ruinous not only to individuals but to the common good in order to disturb or overthrow the institutions of states; this is why (they say) rhetoric was expelled from Sparta[4] and its powers curtailed at Athens, where speakers were forbidden to make emotional appeals.[5]

On this principle, neither generals nor magistrates nor medicine nor philosophy itself will be "useful." Flaminius

ies, and especially Sparta, do not accept philosophy or rhetoric because of your [sc. Athenian] rivalries and quarrels in words and untimely refutations").

[5] See also 6.1.7, 10.1.107. Aristotle (*Rhetoric* 1354a23) says that it was forbidden in the court of the Areopagus (not in the ordinary courts!) to speak "outside the subject," for fear of affecting the judges' emotions.

QUINTILIAN

Flaminius et Gracchi Saturnini Glauciae magistratus, et in
medicis venena, et in iis qui philosophorum nomine male
utuntur gravissima nonnumquam flagitia deprehensa sunt.
6   Cibos aspernemur: attulerunt saepe valetudinis causas.
Numquam tecta subeamus: super habitantes aliquando
procumbunt. Non fabricetur militi gladius: potest uti eodem ferro latro. Quis nescit ignes aquas, sine quibus nulla
sit vita, et, ne terrenis inmorer, solem lunamque praecipua
siderum aliquando et nocere ?
7   Num igitur negabitur deformem Pyrrhi pacem Caecus
ille Appius dicendi viribus diremisse? Aut non divina M.
Tulli eloquentia et contra leges agrarias popularis fuit et
Catilinae fregit audaciam et supplicationes, qui maximus
8   honor victoribus bello ducibus datur, in toga meruit? Non
perterritos militum animos frequenter a metu revocat oratio et tot pugnandi pericula ineuntibus laudem vita potiorem esse persuadet? Neque vero me Lacedaemonii atque
Athenienses magis moverint quam populus Romanus,
9   apud quem summa semper oratoribus dignitas fuit. Equidem nec urbium conditores reor aliter effecturos fuisse ut
vaga illa multitudo coiret in populos nisi docta voce com-
mota, nec legum repertores sine summa vi orandi conse-

---

6 Flaminius was the general defeated by Hannibal at Lake
Trasimene (217 BC); the Gracchi were demagogues; Saturninus
and Glaucia, tribune and praetor, controlled Rome in the revo-
lutionary years 102–100 BC. These *exempla* come mainly from
Cicero, *Brutus* 224.

7 Appius Claudius' speech (279 BC) against peace with Pyrrhus was known to Cicero (*De senectute* 16, *Brutus* 61); see also
Plutarch, *Pyrrhus* 19. Evidence collected in *ORF* 1–4.

8 The speeches *De lege agraria,* against the tribune Rullus,

372

was a general, the Gracchi, Saturninus and Glaucia were magistrates.[6] There are poisoners among doctors, and the most dreadful crimes are sometimes detected in those who discredit the name of philosopher. Let us have nothing to do with food: it often causes illness. Let us never go indoors: the roof sometimes falls on the people inside. Never let a sword be made for a soldier: a robber can use it. Who does not know that fire and water, without which life would not exist, and even—not to dwell on earthly things alone— the sun and the moon, the greatest of heavenly bodies, sometimes do harm as well as good?

Then will anyone deny that Appius the Blind destroyed the disgraceful peace with Pyrrhus by the power of his oratory?[7] Did not Cicero's divine eloquence earn popular support when he spoke against the agrarian laws?[8] Did it not crush Catiline's criminal audacity? Did it not win, in civilian life, the supplications which are the greatest honour given to victorious generals in war? Does not oratory often revive the courage of a frightened army and persuade the soldier, as he faces the many perils of battle, that glory is to be preferred to life? The examples of Sparta and Athens move me less than that of the Roman people, who have always held their orators in high regard. I cannot imagine how the founders of cities would have made a homeless multitude come together to form a people, had they not moved them by their skilful speech, or how legislators would have succeeded in restraining mankind in the servi-

date from Cicero's consulship (63 BC), as do the Catilinarian conspiracy and the honours granted for its suppression (3 December 63), which are mentioned next.

cutos ut se ipsi homines ad servitutem iuris adstringerent.
10 Quin ipsa vitae praecepta, etiam si natura sunt honesta,
plus tamen ad formandas mentes valent quotiens pulchri-
tudinem rerum claritas orationis inluminat. Quare, etiam
si in utramque partem valent arma facundiae, non est
tamen aecum id haberi malum quo bene uti licet.
11　Verum haec apud eos forsitan quaerantur qui summam
rhetorices ad persuadendi vim rettulerunt. Si vero est
bene dicendi scientia, quem nos finem sequimur, ut sit
orator in primis vir bonus, utilem certe esse eam confiten-
12 dum est. Et hercule deus ille princeps, parens rerum fabri-
catorque mundi, nullo magis hominem separavit a ceteris,
quae quidem mortalia essent, animalibus quam dicendi
13 facultate. Nam corpora quidem magnitudine viribus firmi-
tate patientia velocitate praestantiora in illis mutis videmus, eadem minus egere adquisitae extrinsecus opis; nam
et ingredi citius et pasci et tranare aquas citra docentem
14 natura ipsa sciunt, et pleraque contra frigus ex suo corpore
vestiuntur et arma iis ingenita quaedam et ex obvio fere
victus, circa quae omnia multus hominibus labor est. Rationem igitur nobis praecipuam dedit eiusque nos socios
15 esse cum dis inmortalibus voluit. Sed ipsa ratio neque tam
nos iuvaret neque tam esset in nobis manifesta nisi quae
concepissemus mente promere etiam loquendo possemus:
quod magis deesse ceteris animalibus quam intellectum et

9 Compare Isocrates, *Nicocles* 6, Cicero, *De oratore* 1.33, *De inventione* 1.2–5. Q. questions this view later (3.3.4) on the ground that nomadic and scattered peoples nevertheless pos-sessed orators.　10 I.e. the proponents of the definitions dis-cussed in 2.15.2–20.　11 For Q., *logos* (which also means "rea-son") is specifically speech; without this, even Reason would be

tude of the law, had they not had the highest gifts of oratory.[9] The very guiding principles of life, however intrinsically honourable they are, nevertheless possess more power to shape men's minds when the brilliance of eloquence illumines the beauty of the subject. And so, although the weapons of eloquence are powerful for good or ill, it is unfair to count as evil something which it is possible to use for good.

But these problems may perhaps be left to those who have reduced the end of rhetoric to "power of persuasion."[10] If however it is the science of speaking well (the definition I adopt), so that an orator is in the first place a good man, it must certainly be admitted that it is useful. And indeed, that first god, the father of all things and the maker of the universe, distinguished man from other living creatures that are subject to death by nothing so much as the faculty of speech.[11] We see in dumb animals bodies which surpass ours in size, strength, robustness, endurance, and speed, and we see that they need less external aids than we do. They know naturally, and without any teacher, how to run and feed and swim across water. Many are clothed against cold by the resources of their own bodies, have weapons born with them, and food almost always at hand; all these things give men much trouble. And so the creator gave us Reason as our special gift, and chose that we should share it with the immortal gods. Yet Reason itself would not help us so much, or be so evident in us, if we did not have the power to express the thoughts we have conceived in our minds; it is this, rather than some degree

little use (§15). *Irrationalia* (§16) translates ἄλογα, which means both "without reason" and "without speech."

16 cogitationem quandam videmus. Nam et mollire cubilia et
nidos texere et educare fetus et excludere, quin etiam re-
ponere in hiemem alimenta, opera quaedam nobis inimi-
tabilia, qualia sunt cerarum ac mellis, efficere nonnullius
fortasse rationis est; sed, quia carent sermone quae id fa-

17 ciunt, muta atque inrationalia vocantur. Denique homines
quibus negata vox est quantulum adiuvat animus ille caelestis!

Quare si nihil a dis oratione melius accepimus, quid
tam dignum cultu ac labore ducamus aut in quo malimus
praestare hominibus quam quo ipsi homines ceteris ani-

18 malibus praestant: eo quidem magis quod nulla in parte
plenius labor gratiam refert? Id adeo manifestum erit si
cogitaverimus unde et quo usque iam provecta sit orandi

19 facultas: et adhuc augeri potest. Nam ut omittam defendere amicos, regere consiliis senatum, populum exercitum
in quae velit ducere, quam sit utile conveniatque bono
viro: nonne pulchrum vel hoc ipsum est, ex communi intellectu verbisque quibus utuntur omnes tantum adsequi
laudis et gloriae ut non loqui et orare, sed, quod Pericli
contigit, fulgurare[2] ac tonare videaris ?

17

1 Finis non erit si expatiari parte in hac et indulgere voluptati velim. Transeamus igitur ad eam quaestionem quae se-

    [2] fulgere *B*

---

    [12] Aristophanes, *Acharnians* 530. See 12.2.22, 12.10.24;
Cicero, *Orator* 29; Pliny, *Epistulae* 1.20.19.

of understanding and thought, which we see to be lacking in other animals. Making soft beds, weaving nests, rearing and hatching the young, even storing up food against the winter, and other works which we cannot imitate (like making honey and wax)—all these are perhaps signs of a certain degree of Reason; but since the creatures which do these things lack speech, they are said to be dumb and irrational. Finally, how little does heaven's gift of mind help humans who have been denied a voice!

And so, if we have had no better gift from the gods than speech, what else should we think so deserving of careful cultivation? In what should we prefer to excel among men more than in that in which mankind excels other living creatures—especially as there is no activity in which labour brings its reward more generously? This will be obvious of course if we consider where oratory came from and how far it has now progressed; and it can still be developed further. To say nothing of how useful it is, and how right and proper for a good man, to defend friends, guide the senate by good counsel, and lead a people or an army in whatever direction he chooses, is there not a splendour in the very fact of using our common understanding and the words that all use to achieve such praise and glory that you seem not just to be speaking or pleading, but, like Pericles, to "lighten and thunder?"[12]

CHAPTER 17

Is rhetoric an art?

If I chose to expatiate on this subject and indulge my own pleasure, I should never reach the end. So let us pass to the

2   quitur, an rhetorice ars sit. Quod quidem adeo ex iis qui
praecepta dicendi tradiderunt nemo dubitavit ut etiam
ipsis librorum titulis testatum sit scriptos eos de arte rhetorica, Cicero vero eam[1] quae rhetorice vocetur esse arti-
ficiosam eloquentiam dicat. Quod non oratores tantum
vindicarunt, ut studiis aliquid suis praestitisse videantur,
sed cum iis philosophi et Stoici et Peripatetici plerique

3   consentiunt. Ac me dubitasse confiteor an hanc partem
quaestionis tractandam putarem; nam quis est adeo non ab
eruditione modo sed a sensu remotus hominis ut fabrican-
di quidem et texendi et luto vasa ducendi artem putet, rhetoricen autem maximum ac pulcherrimum, ut supra diximus, opus in tam sublime fastigium existimet sine arte

4   venisse? Equidem illos qui contra disputaverunt non tam
id sensisse quod dicerent quam exercere ingenia materiae
difficultate credo voluisse, sicut Polycraten, cum Busirim
laudaret et Clytaemestram: quamquam is, quod his dissimile non esset,[2] composuisse orationem quae est habita
contra Socraten dicitur.

5   Quidam naturalem esse rhetoricen volunt et tamen
adiuvari exercitatione non diffitentur, ut in libris Ciceronis

---

[1] *Halm*: etiam *B*: ea *A*
[2] est *A*

---

[1] *De inventione* 1.6.
[2] 1.12.16.
[3] The "Accusation of Socrates" by the sophist Polycrates was
well known in later antiquity (Radermacher, *AS* 128ff., Giannantoni (1990) 1 c 134–137) and was among the sources available
to Libanius for his "Apology" (Russell 1996, 18–20). It was generally known not to be contemporary with the trial (Favorinus F3

next question, which is whether rhetoric is an art. Nobody, of those who have laid down rules for oratory, has of course doubted this: the very titles of their books, "On the Art of Rhetoric," bear witness to it, and Cicero defines "what is called rhetoric" as "artistic eloquence."[1] But not only have orators made this claim, so as to give their studies some prestige, but both Stoic and Peripatetic philosophers for the most part agree with them. I must confess I had doubts about the need to deal with this part of the question: for who is there, I will not say so unlearned, but so lacking in ordinary human sense, as to imagine that there are arts of building and weaving and pottery, but that rhetoric—the greatest and most splendid of achievements, as we have said[2]—can have reached its lofty eminence without the aid of art? For my part, I think that those who have argued against this view did not mean what they said, but wanted rather to exercise their intellect on a difficult theme, like Polycrates praising Busiris and Clytemnestra—though he is said to have composed in a similar vein a speech which was delivered against Socrates.[3]

Some would have it that rhetoric is natural, but still admit that it is developed by practice. So Antonius, in

Mensching = Diogenes Laertius 2.39). Isocrates (*Busiris* 5) speaks of this and of an "Encomium of Busiris" (the monstrously cruel king of Egypt) and could be taken as implying the view reported by Q. (but not *asserted,* unless we read A's *est* for *esset*), that the "Accusation" too was not serious. No other explicit reference to a "Clytemnestra" is known; but Philodemus (*Rhetorica* 1. 217 Sudhaus) speaks of Penelope and Clytemnestra as themes of paradoxical speeches.

de Oratore dicit Antonius observationem quandam esse,
6 non artem. Quod non ideo ut pro vero accipiamus est positum, sed ut Antoni persona servetur, qui dissimulator artis
fuit: hanc autem opinionem habuisse Lysias videtur. Cuius
sententiae talis defensio est, quod indocti et barbari et servi, pro se cum locuntur, aliquid dicant simile principio,
narrent, probent, refutent et, quod vim habeat epilogi, de-
7 precentur. Deinde adiciunt illas verborum cavillationes,
nihil quod ex arte fiat ante artem fuisse: atqui dixisse homines pro se et in alios semper: doctores artis sero et circa
Tisian et Coraca primum repertos: orationem igitur ante
8 artem fuisse eoque artem non esse. Nos porro quando coeperit huius rei doctrina non laboramus, quamquam apud
Homerum et praeceptorem Phoenicem cum agendi tum
etiam loquendi, et oratores plures, et omne in tribus ducibus orationis genus, et certamina quoque proposita eloquentiae inter iuvenes invenimus, quin in caelatura clipei
Achillis et lites sunt et actores.
9   Illud enim admonere satis est, omnia quae ars consum-
maverit a natura initia duxisse: aut tollatur medicina, quae

---

4 2.232. Crassus summarizes Antonius' view as saying that
rhetoric is *observatio quaedam earum rerum quae in dicendo
valent*, "an observance of the things which are important in speaking."   5 Perhaps from Cicero, *Brutus* 48, where it is said on
the authority of Aristotle that Lysias at first believed in an *ars
dicendi* but then dispensed with it, because he saw that Theodorus' expertise in theory did not make him a successful speaker.

6 In 3.1.8, both are said to have written *artes,* though in fact
only Corax probably did. Radermacher, *AS* 28–35; the earliest evidence is Plato, *Phaedrus* 267A, 272C, 273A.

Cicero's *De oratore*,[4] calls it a kind of observation, not an art. This statement however is not put there for us to accept it as true, but to fit Antonius' character, because he was a man who concealed his art. Lysias,[5] however, seems to have been of the same opinion. The defence of it is that uneducated people, barbarians, and slaves, when they are speaking to defend themselves, produce something like a Prooemium, and then narrate, prove, refute, and finally beg for mercy in the equivalent of an Epilogue. Advocates of this view add some well-known sophistries: nothing based on art can have existed before the art; but men did speak to defend themselves or attack others, and the first teachers of the art came later, in the time of Tisias and Corax;[6] therefore oratory existed before the art, and cannot be an art. For my part, I am not concerned about when the teaching first began. However, in Homer we find Phoenix as a teacher of "doing and speaking," a number of other orators, examples of each type of style in the three leaders, and competition in eloquence among the young. Furthermore, law-suits and pleaders are to be seen in the engravings on Achilles' shield.[7]

It is sufficient to remind ourselves that everything which art makes perfect had its origin in nature. Otherwise, let us do away with medicine, which was discovered

---

[7] Q.'s arguments are: (1) Phoenix (*Iliad* 9.442) is shown as teaching speech as well as deeds; (2) Homer's descriptions of the oratory of Menelaus and Odysseus (*Iliad* 3.214, 221) and of Nestor (1.249) show that he knew the "three styles" (see 12.10.64); (3) in *Iliad* 15.283, Thoas is said to be excelled by few "whenever the young men contended in speech"; (4) Achilles' shield (*Iliad* 18.497ff.) represented a scene of litigation.

ex observatione salubrium atque his contrariorum reperta
est et, ut quibusdam placet, tota constat experimentis
(nam et vulnus deligavit aliquis antequam haec ars esset, et
febrem quiete et abstinentia, non quia rationem videbat,
10   sed quia id valetudo ipsa coegerat, mitigavit), nec fabrica
sit ars (casas enim primi illi sine arte fecerunt), nec musica
(cantatur ac saltatur per omnis gentes aliquo modo). Ita, si
rhetorice vocari debet sermo quicumque, fuisse eam ante-
11   quam esset ars confitebor: si vero non quisquis loquitur
orator est, et tum non tamquam oratores loquebantur,
necesse est oratorem factum arte nec ante artem fuisse
fateantur.

Quo illud quoque excluditur quod dicunt, non esse artis id quod faciat qui non didicerit: dicere autem homines
12   et qui non didicerint. Ad cuius rei confirmationem adferunt Demaden remigem et Aeschinen hypocriten oratores
fuisse. Falso: nam neque orator esse qui non didicit potest,
et hos sero potius quam numquam didicisse quis dixerit,
quamquam Aeschines ab initio sit versatus in litteris, quas
pater eius etiam docebat, Demaden neque non didicisse
certum sit et continua dicendi exercitatio potuerit tantum
quantuscumque postea fuit fecisse; nam id potentissimum

---

⁸ "Empiricists" formed a distinct school of ancient medicine,
beginning with Philinus of Cos and Serapion of Alexandria (third
century BC), and well known from treatises by Galen.

⁹ Supposed author of a speech "On the Twelve Years" (i.e.
338–326 BC): see LCL *Minor Attic Orators* 2. 334–359. Best
known however as an example of the self-taught orator who did
not publish:12.10.49, Cicero, *Brutus* 36.

¹⁰ Aeschines' acting career gave Demosthenes an opportunity
for insults (*De corona* 313); Q. counters (from *De corona* 258)

by the observation of things conducive to health and sickness and, according to some, is based entirely on experience:[8] somebody bandaged a wound before this art existed, and eased a fever by rest and starvation, not because he saw any reason for it, but because that is what the illness itself demanded. Let us not allow building to be an art either: primitive men constructed their huts without art. Music too: singing and dancing of some sort exist in all peoples. So if any speech whatever is to be called "rhetoric," then I must agree that rhetoric existed before there was an art; but if it is not true that everyone who speaks is an orator, and people did not speak like orators in those days, then they must admit that the orator is produced by art, and did not exist before art.

This also rules out their argument that anything done by a man who has not learned it cannot be an achievement of art, and yet there are men who can make speeches without having learned. In support of this view they adduce the fact that Demades[9] the rower and Aeschines[10] the actor were both orators. This is false reasoning: no man can be an orator who has not learned, and it is better to suppose that these men learned late than that they never learned, though in fact Aeschines was well versed in literature from his childhood, since his father was actually a teacher; as for Demades, it is not certain that he never learned, and continual practice could very well have made him what he came to be, for that is in fact the most effective way of

with the point that his father was a schoolmaster. Aeschines and Demades are cited together by Philodemus (*Rhetorica* 2. 97 Sudhaus); this argument is part of the Hellenistic controversy on "Is rhetoric an art?"

13 discendi genus est. Sed et praestantiorem si didicisset fu-
turum fuisse dicere licet: neque enim orationes scribere
est ausus, ut[3] eum multum valuisse in dicendo sciamus.

14 Aristoteles, ut solet, quaerendi gratia quaedam subtilitatis suae argumenta excogitavit in Grylo: sed idem et de
arte rhetorica tris libros scripsit, et in eorum primo non artem solum eam fatetur, sed ei particulam civilitatis sicut
15 dialectices adsignat. Multa Critolaus contra, multa Rhodius Athenodorus. Agnon quidem detraxit sibi inscriptione ipsa fidem, qua rhetorices accusationem professus
est. Nam de Epicuro, qui disciplinas omnes fugit, nihil
miror.

16 Hi complura dicunt, sed ex paucis locis ducta: itaque
potentissimis eorum breviter occurram, ne in infinitum
quaestio evadat.

17 Prima iis argumentatio ex materia est. Omnis enim artes aiunt habere materiam, quod est verum: rhetorices
nullam esse propriam, quod esse falsum in sequentibus
probabo.

18 Altera est calumnia nullam artem falsis adsentiri opi-
nionibus, quia constitui sine perceptione non possit, quae
semper vera sit: rhetoricen adsentiri falsis: non esse igitur

3 cum *Halm*

---

11 "Gryllus or On Rhetoric" (frs. 68–69 Rose, 1–3 Ross) was
Aristotle's tribute to Xenophon's son Gryllus (Γρῦλος seems the
more correct form), who was killed at Mantinea in 362 BC.

12 *Rhetoric* 1. 1356a30.

13 Fr. 25 Wehrli.

14 See also 12.2.24. Epicurus was famous for saying "take ship
and flee from all *paideia*" (Diogenes Laertius 10.6). Nothing is

learning. On the other hand, one can say that he would
have been more outstanding if he had learned; for he never
ventured to write down his speeches, though we know he
delivered them with great effect.

Aristotle, in his usual way, devised some arguments of
characteristic subtlety in his *Gryllus*,[11] for the sake of discussion; but he also wrote three books on the art of rhetoric and, in the first, not only admits it to be an art but says it
is a part both of "politics" and of "dialectic."[12] Critolaus[13]
and Athenodorus of Rhodes have argued at length on the
other side. Agnon diminished his own credibility by the title of his book, which he openly declared an "Accusation of
Rhetoric." As to Epicurus,[14] I feel no surprise; he rejected
all forms of education.

These writers have a great deal to say, but it is all based
on a few topics of argument. I shall deal briefly with the
most significant of these, so that the discussion does not go
on indefinitely.

(1) Their first argument is based on the subject matter.
All arts, they say, have a subject matter. This is true. Rhetoric, they say, has none of its own. In what follows I shall
show this to be false.[15]

(2) Their second slander is that no art assents to false
propositions, because it cannot exist without a cognitive
presentation which is invariably true,[16] whereas rhetoric
does assent to falsehoods, and therefore is not an art. I am

known of Athenodorus of Rhodes; Agnon (or Hagnon) is presumably the pupil of Carneades mentioned by Cicero and others.

[15] 2.21.

[16] This is said in Stoic terms (*perceptio* = κατάληψις or
καταληπτικὴ φαντασία, a perception which is bound to be true).

19 artem. Ego rhetoricen nonnumquam dicere falsa pro veris
confitebor, sed non ideo in falsa quoque esse opinione
concedam, quia longe diversum est ipsi quid videri et ut
alii videatur efficere. Nam et imperator falsis utitur saepe:
ut Hannibal, cum inclusus a Fabio, sarmentis circum cornua boum deligatis incensisque, per noctem in adversos
montes agens armenta speciem hosti abeuntis exercitus
dedit: sed illum fefellit, ipse quid verum esset non ignora-
20 vit. Nec vero Theopompus Lacedaemonius, cum permutato cum uxore habitu e custodia ut mulier evasit, falsam de
se opinionem habuit, sed custodibus praebuit. Item orator,
cum falso utitur pro vero, scit esse falsum eoque se pro
vero uti: non ergo falsam habet ipse opinionem, sed fallit
21 alium. Nec Cicero, cum se tenebras offudisse iudicibus in
causa Cluenti gloriatus est, nihil ipse vidit. Et pictor, cum
vi artis suae efficit ut quaedam eminere in opere, quaedam
recessisse credamus, ipse ea plana esse non nescit.

22 Aiunt etiam omnes artes habere finem aliquem propositum ad quem tendant: hunc modo nullum esse in
rhetorice, modo non praestari eum qui promittatur. Men-
tiuntur: nos enim esse finem iam ostendimus et quis esset
23 diximus; et praestabit hunc semper orator: semper enim
bene dicet. Firmum autem hoc quod opponitur adversus
eos fortasse sit qui persuadere finem putaverunt: noster
orator arsque a nobis finita non sunt posita in eventu; tendit quidem ad victoriam qui dicit, sed cum bene dixit,

---

17 Livy 22.16.   18 An episode of early Spartan history, also
told by Polyaenus 8.34, as an example of a "stratagem."

19 We do not know where; but Plutarch, *Cicero* 25 makes him
say much the same about his defence of Munatius Plancus Bursa,
some time before 52 BC.   20 2.15.38.

prepared to admit that rhetoric does sometimes say untrue things as if true, but I would not concede that it is therefore in a state of false opinion; there is a great difference between holding an opinion oneself and making someone else adopt it. Generals also often use falsehoods: Hannibal, when hemmed in by Fabius, gave the enemy the illusion that his army was in retreat by tying brushwood to the horns of oxen, setting fire to them, and driving the herd at night up into the mountains.[17] He deceived Fabius, but he knew the truth himself. Again, when the Spartan Theopompus[18] changed clothes with his wife and escaped from custody disguised as a woman, he had no false opinion about himself, but he gave his guards one. Similarly an orator, when he substitutes a falsehood for the truth, knows it is false and that he is substituting it for the truth; he does not therefore have a false opinion himself, but he deceives the other person. When Cicero boasted[19] that he had cast a cloud of darkness over the eyes of the jury, in the case of Cluentius, he saw clearly enough himself. And when a painter makes us believe, by his art, that some objects are in the foreground and others in the background, he himself knows they are all on the same plane.

(3) They also say that all arts have a definite end to which they are directed, but in rhetoric sometimes there is no such thing, and sometimes the promised end is not achieved. This is false. We have already shown that there is an end, and what it is.[20] Moreover, the real orator will always achieve it, because he will always speak well. However, this criticism may perhaps be valid against those who think that the "end" is to persuade. My orator, and the art that I have defined, do not depend on the outcome. The speaker certainly aims to win; but when he has spoken

24 etiam si non vincat, id quod arte continetur effecit. Nam et
gubernator vult salva nave in portum pervenire: si tamen
tempestate fuerit abreptus, non ideo minus erit guberna-
25 tor dicetque notum illud: 'dum clavum rectum teneam'; et
medicus sanitatem aegri petit: si tamen aut valetudinis vi
aut intemperantia aegri aliove quo casu summa non contigit,[4] dum ipse omnia secundum rationem fecerit, medicinae fine non excidet. Ita oratori bene dixisse finis est.
Nam est ars ea, ut post paulum clarius ostendemus, in actu
posita, non in effectu.
26 Ita falsum erit illud quoque quod dicitur, artes scire
quando sint finem consecutae, rhetoricen nescire: nam se
quisque bene dicere intelleget.
Uti etiam vitiis rhetoricen, quod ars nulla faciat, crimi-
27 nantur, quia et falsum dicat et adfectus moveat. Quorum
neutrum est turpe, cum ex bona ratione proficiscitur,
ideoque nec vitium; nam et mendacium dicere etiam sa-
pienti aliquando concessum est, et adfectus, si aliter ad ae-
quitatem perduci iudex non poterit, necessario movebit
28 orator: imperiti enim iudicant et qui frequenter in hoc ipsum fallendi sint, ne errent. Nam si mihi sapientes iudices
dentur, sapientium contiones atque omne consilium, nihil
invidia valeat, nihil gratia, nihil opinio praesumpta falsi-
que testes, perquam sit exiguus eloquentiae locus et prope
29 in sola delectatione ponatur. Sin et audientium mobiles

[4] contingit A

[21] Ennius, *Annales* 483 Vahlen = 538 Warmington = 508
Skutsch. Greek equivalent (ὀρθὰν τὰν ναῦν) in Cicero, *Ad
Quintum fratrem* 1.2.13 (where see Watt's note).
[22] See 12.1.38. Q. again speaks in Stoic terms.

well, even if he does not win, he has fulfilled the demands of his art. Thus a pilot wants to reach harbour with his ship safe; but if he is swept away by a storm, he is not thereby any less a pilot, and he can quote the well-known line, "So long as I hold the tiller straight";[21] likewise a doctor seeks his patient's health, but if the force of the disease or the foolish behaviour of the patient, or some other event, prevents this aim being achieved, he will not cease to be a doctor, so long as he does everything according to medical principles. Similarly, for the orator, to have spoken well is to have accomplished his end. For—as I shall show more clearly a little later—this art depends on the activity, not on the outcome.

(4) Hence there is no truth either in the argument that arts know when they have attained their end, but rhetoric does not. Everyone will realize when he is speaking well.

(5) They allege also that rhetoric makes use of vices, which no art does, in speaking falsehoods and exciting emotions. But neither of these is disgraceful when it is done for a good reason; therefore it is not a vice either. To tell a lie is something occasionally allowed even to the wise man;[22] and as for rousing emotions, the orator is bound to do this if the judge cannot be brought to give a fair judgement by other means. Judges can be inexperienced people who frequently need to be deceived, to save them from being wrong. If we had wise men as judges and assemblies and councils of all kinds were made up of the wise, if hatred, influence, prejudice, and false witness had no power, then the scope for eloquence would be very small, confined more or less to giving pleasure. But as the feelings of audiences are fickle and the truth is exposed to so many

QUINTILIAN

animi et tot malis obnoxia veritas, arte pugnandum est et
adhibenda quae prosunt: neque enim qui recta via depul-
sus est reduci ad eam nisi alio flexu potest.

30   Plurima vero ex hoc contra rhetoricen cavillatio est,
quod ex utraque causae parte dicatur. Inde haec: nullam
esse artem contrariam sibi, rhetoricen esse contrariam
sibi; nullam artem restruere[5] quod effecerit, accidere hoc
rhetorices operi. Item aut dicenda eam docere aut non dicenda: ita vel per hoc non esse artem, quod non dicenda
praecipiat, vel per hoc, quod, cum dicenda praeceperit,
31   etiam contraria his doceat. Quae omnia apparet de ea rhetorice dici quae sit a bono viro atque ab ipsa virtute seiunc-
ta: alioqui ubi iniusta causa est, ibi rhetorice non est, adeo
ut vix admirabili quodam casu possit accidere ut ex utraque
32   parte orator, id est vir bonus, dicat. Tamen quoniam hoc
quoque in rerum naturam cadit, ut duos sapientes aliquando iustae causae in diversum trahant, quando etiam pugna-
turos eos inter se, si ratio ita duxerit, credunt, respondebo
propositis, atque ita quidem ut appareat haec adversus eos
quoque frustra excogitata qui malis moribus nomen orato-
33   ris indulgent. Nam rhetorice non est contraria sibi: causa
enim cum causa, non illa secum ipsa componitur. Nec, si
pugnent inter se qui idem didicerunt, idcirco ars, quae
utrique tradita est, non erit: alioqui nec armorum, quia
saepe gladiatores sub eodem magistro eruditi inter se

---

[5] *D.A.R. (this may have been in A before correction into*
destruere): restituere *B*

---

[23] I.e. on Q.'s assumption that rhetoric has a moral basis.
[24] Stoicism recognized patriotic duties, and so it is conceivable
that two Wise Men might find themselves in opposing armies.

390

evils, we must fight with the weapons of art, and employ whatever means serve our purpose. A man who has been driven off the right road can only be brought back to it by changing course again.

Most of the captious objections to rhetoric, however, arise from the fact that speeches are made on both sides of any Cause. Hence the following arguments: (1) no art contradicts itself, but rhetoric does contradict itself; (2) no art tries to demolish its own work, but this does happen to the work of rhetoric; (3) it teaches either what ought to be said or what ought not to be said, and so it is not an art for one of two reasons: either because it teaches what ought not to be said, or because, having taught what ought to be said, it teaches also the opposite. All these points obviously apply to the rhetoric which is divorced from the good man and from virtue itself; on any other assumption,[23] where the Cause is unjust, there is no rhetoric, so that it can hardly happen, even in quite exceptional circumstances, that an orator, that is to say a good man, should speak on both sides. However, as it is possible in the nature of things that two wise men may sometimes be drawn by just causes to opposite sides (people believe that they would even fight each other if reason led them to this),[24] I shall answer these arguments, and in such a way as to make it clear that they have been contrived to no avail, even as regards those who allow the name of orator to persons of bad character. (1) Rhetoric does not contradict itself. Cause is pitted against Cause, not rhetoric against itself. And even if persons who have learned the same things fight one another, it does not follow that the art, which was imparted to both of them, is not an art. On any other view, there would be no art of arms, because gladiators trained under the same master

391

34 componuntur, nec gubernandi, quia navalibus proeliis gubernator est gubernatori adversus, nec imperatoria quia
imperator cum imperatore contendit. Item non evertit
opus rhetorice quod effecit:[6] neque enim positum a se
argumentum solvit orator; sed ne rhetorice quidem, quia
apud eos qui in persuadendo finem putant, aut si quis, ut
dixi, casus duos inter se bonos viros composuerit, veri similia quaerentur: non autem, si quid est altero credibilius, id
35 ei contrarium est quod fuit credibile. Nam ut candido can-
didius et dulci dulcius non est adversum, ita nec probabili
probabilius. Neque praecipit umquam non dicenda nec
dicendis contraria, sed quae in quaque causa dicenda sunt.
36 Non semper autem ei, etiamsi frequentissime, tuenda veritas erit, sed aliquando exigit communis utilitas ut etiam
falsa defendat.

Ponuntur hae quoque in secundo Ciceronis de Oratore
libro contradictiones: artem earum rerum esse quae scian-
tur: oratoris omnem actionem opinione, non scientia
contineri, quia et apud eos dicat qui nesciant, et ipse dicat
37 aliquando quod nesciat. Ex his alterum, id est an sciat iudex de quo dicatur, nihil ad oratoris artem; alteri respon-
dendum. 'Ars earum rerum est quae sciuntur.' Rhetorice
38 ars est bene dicendi, bene autem dicere scit orator. 'Sed
nescit an verum sit quod dicit.' Ne ii quidem qui ignem aut

6 *recc.*: efficit *AB*

25 2.30. What follows is put in indirect speech, and is not an
exact quotation.

are often matched against each other, or of piloting, because in naval battles one pilot is opposed to another, or of generalship, because general is pitted against general. (2) Rhetoric does *not* overthrow its own work. The orator does not refute the argument he has put up, nor does rhetoric either, because, if we take the view of those who regard persuasion as the end of rhetoric, or again if we consider two good men whom (as I suggested) chance may have pitted against each other, what will be sought will be probabilities; and, if one proposition is *more* credible than another, it is not contrary to that which is merely credible. Whiter is not contrary to white, nor sweeter to sweet; nor is the more probable contrary to the less probable. (3) Rhetoric never teaches what ought not to be said, or the contrary of what ought to be said, but what ought to be said in each individual Cause. However, although it most often has to defend truth, this is not always so: public interest sometimes requires it to defend what is false.

In the second book of Cicero's *De oratore*[25] the following objections also are put:

> Art deals with things which are known; an orator's entire pleading is based on opinions, not knowledge, because he is speaking before an audience who do not know, and he himself sometimes says what he does not know.

One of these points—namely whether the judge knows what is being spoken of—has nothing to do with the art of the orator. To the other, an answer must be given. "Art deals with things which are known." Yes: rhetoric is the art of speaking well, and the orator knows how to speak well. "But he does not know whether what he says is true." Well,

aquam aut quattuor elementa aut corpora insecabilia esse
ex quibus res omnes initium duxerint tradunt, nec qui
intervalla siderum et mensuras solis ac terrae colligunt:
disciplinam tamen suam artem vocant. Quodsi ratio efficit
ut haec non opinari sed propter vim probationum scire vi-
39   deantur, eadem ratio idem praestare oratori potest. 'Sed an
causa vera sit nescit.' Ne medicus quidem an dolorem capitis habeat qui hoc se pati dicet: curabit tamen tamquam
id verum sit, et erit ars medicina. Quid quod rhetorice non
utique propositum habet semper vera dicendi, sed semper
veri similia? Scit autem esse veri similia quae dicit.
40   Adiciunt his qui contra sentiunt quod saepe, quae in
aliis litibus inpugnarunt actores causarum, eadem in aliis
defendant. Quod non artis sed hominis est vitium.
Haec sunt praecipua quae contra rhetoricen dicantur,
alia et minora et tamen ex his fontibus derivata.
41   Confirmatur autem esse artem eam breviter. Nam sive,
ut Cleanthes voluit, ars est potestas via, id est ordine,
efficiens, esse certe viam atque ordinem in bene dicendo
nemo dubitaverit, sive ille ab omnibus fere probatus finis
observatur, artem constare ex perceptionibus consentien-
tibus et coexercitatis ad finem utilem vitae, iam ostendi-
42   mus nihil non horum in rhetorice inesse. Quid quod et inspectione et exercitatione, ut artes ceterae, constat? Nec

26 SVF 1. 490 (cf. also 1. 72): τέχνη ἐστὶν ἕξις ὁδῷ (= Q.'s via)
πάντα ἀνύουσα ("An art is a settled condition achieving everything methodically").
27 SVF 1. 73: τέχνη ἐστὶ σύστημα ἐκ καταλήψεων συγγε-
γυμνασμένων (Q.'s coexercitatis) πρός τι τέλος εὔχρηστον τῶν
ἐν τῷ βίῳ ("An art is a complex of cognitive perceptions exercised

neither do the people who tell us that the origin of all things lies in fire or water or the four elements or indivisible bodies (atoms), or indeed those who calculate the distances between the stars or the size of the sun and the earth; yet they all call their study an art. And if reason enables them to appear not just to have an opinion of these things but to know them, because of the cogency of their proofs, reason may very well do as much for the orator. "But he doesn't know whether his cause is true." Neither does the doctor know whether the man who says he has a headache really has one, but he will treat him just the same, on the assumption that it is true, and his medicine will be an art. Again, rhetoric does not necessarily have the intention of always speaking the truth, but only the probable, but the orator does know that what he says is probable.

A further objection made by our opponents is that advocates often defend in one case what they have attacked in another. This is a fault of the person, not of the art.

These are the main points made against rhetoric; others are less important but derived from the same sources.

The proof that it is an art can be brief. If, as Cleanthes suggested, art is "a capability which acts by method,"[26] that is to say in an orderly way, then no one can doubt that there is method and order in speaking well. If we maintain the almost universally approved definition that an art "consists of cognitions agreeing and trained to cooperate towards an end useful to life,"[27] we have already shown that none of these elements is lacking in rhetoric. Surely, like other arts, it is based on theory and on practice. And it must be an art,

in concert to achieve some useful good in life"). See also *Prolegomenon Sylloge* 45 Rabe.

potest ars non esse si est ars dialectice (quod fere constat),
cum ab ea specie magis quam genere differat. Sed nec illa
omittenda sunt: qua in re alius se inartificialiter, alius arti-
ficialiter gerat, in ea esse artem, et in eo quod qui didicerit
43 melius faciat quam qui non didicerit esse artem. Atqui non
solum doctus indoctum sed etiam doctior doctum in rhetorices opere superabit, neque essent eius aliter tam multa
praecepta tamque magni qui docerent. Idque cum omnibus confitendum est, tum nobis praecipue, qui rationem
dicendi a bono viro non separamus.

18

1 Cum sint autem artium aliae positae in inspectione, id est
cognitione et aestimatione rerum, qualis est astrologia nullum exigens actum, sed ipso rei cuius studium habet intellectu contenta, quae θεωρητική vocatur, aliae in agendo,
quarum in hoc finis est et ipso actu perficitur nihilque post
actum operis relinquit, quae πρακτική dicitur, qualis sal-
2 tatio est, aliae in effectu, quae operis quod oculis subicitur
consummatione finem accipiunt, quam ποιητικήν appella-
mus, qualis est pictura: fere iudicandum est rhetoricen in
3 actu consistere: hoc enim quod est officii sui perficit; atque
ita ab omnibus dictum est. Mihi autem videtur etiam ex
illis ceteris artibus multum adsumere. Nam et potest ali-

---

28 Both "deal with matters which are in a sense common for all
to know and not belonging to any definite branch of knowledge"
(Aristotle, *Rhetoric* 1. 1354a2).

1 The following tripartite division (Platonic, according to Diogenes Laertius 3.84) is familiar also from Aristotle: e.g. *Meta-
physics* 1025b25, 1064a17; *Topics* 145a15. See Lausberg §10.

if dialectic is, as is generally agreed, because it differs from dialectic in species only, not in genus.[28] Nor must we omit to point out that there is art implicit in anything which may be done either with art or without it, and also in anything which is better done by one who has learned it than by one who has not. In rhetoric, indeed, not only will the taught surpass the untaught, but the better taught will surpass the less well taught; otherwise there would not be so many rules and the teachers would not be such great men. This is something everyone must admit, but especially those of us who treat oratory as inseparable from the good man.

CHAPTER 18

The place of rhetoric among the arts

Some arts are based on theory,[1] that is, the knowledge and evaluation of things. An example is astronomy, which requires no action but is content with the simple understanding of its subject of study. This is called a "theoretical" art. Others consist of action; their end is in action, it is achieved by action and, once the act has been performed, nothing remains to do. Such an art is said to be "practical." Dancing is an example. Others again depend on a result, and achieve their end by the completion of a work which can be seen. We call these "poetic" arts. Painting is an example. We must, in general terms, conclude that rhetoric consists of action, for it is by this that it accomplishes what belongs to its duty. And this has indeed been the universal view. But I think rhetoric also takes much from those other arts.

quando ipsa per se inspectione esse contenta. Erit enim rhetorice in oratore etiam tacente, et si desierit agere vel proposito vel aliquo casu impeditus, non magis desinet
4 esse orator quam medicus qui curandi fecerit finem. Nam est aliquis ac nescio an maximus etiam ex secretis studiis fructus, ac tum pura voluptas litterarum cum ab actu, id est
5 opera, recesserunt et contemplatione sui fruuntur. Sed effectivae quoque aliquid simile scriptis orationibus vel historiis, quod ipsum opus in parte oratoria merito ponimus, consequetur. Si tamen una ex tribus artibus habenda sit, quia maximus eius usus actu continetur atque est in eo frequentissima, dicatur activa vel administrativa; nam et hoc eiusdem rei nomen est.

19

1 Scio quaeri etiam naturane plus ad eloquentiam conferat an doctrina. Quod ad propositum quidem operis nostri nihil pertinet (neque enim consummatus orator nisi ex utroque fieri potest), plurimum tamen referre arbitror
2 quam esse in hoc loco quaestionem velimus. Nam si parti utrilibet omnino alteram detrahas, natura etiam sine doctrina multum valebit, doctrina nulla esse sine natura poterit. Sin ex pari coeant, in mediocribus quidem utrisque

(1) It may sometimes be content with theory for its own sake. Rhetoric will be present in the orator even when he is silent; and if he ceases to practise, either by a conscious decision or through some chance, he will no more cease to be an orator than a doctor who has stopped treating patients ceases to be a doctor. For there is some reward—perhaps the greatest of all—in private study; the pleasure of literature is pure when it has withdrawn from activity, that is to say from hard work, and can enjoy contemplating itself. (2) But rhetoric will also acquire some features of an art which has an end product, by *writing* speeches or history, an activity which we rightly regard as itself coming within the sphere of oratory. Nevertheless, if it has to be regarded as belonging to one of the three classes, it must be called "active" or "administrative" (this is another name for the same thing) because its main concern and most frequent application are in action.

CHAPTER 19

Which matters more, nature or teaching?

I am aware that the question is also commonly raised, whether nature or teaching contributes more to eloquence. This is indeed irrelevant to my proposed work (because the perfect orator cannot come into existence except by a combination of the two), but I do think it very important to define what question it is that we want to ask in this context. For if you isolate one of the pair from the other altogether, nature will be able to do a lot without teaching, but without nature there can be no teaching. If they are equally matched, however, and both are unremarkable,

maius adhuc naturae credam esse momentum, consum-
matos autem plus doctrinae debere quam naturae putabo;
sicut terrae nullam fertilitatem habenti nihil optimus agri-
cola profuerit: e terra uberi utile aliquid etiam nullo co-
lente nascetur: at in solo fecundo plus cultor quam ipsa per
3   se bonitas soli efficiet. Et si Praxiteles signum aliquod ex
molari lapide conatus esset exculpere, Parium marmor
mallem rude: at si illud idem artifex expolisset, plus in manibus fuisset quam in marmore. Denique natura materia
doctrinae est: haec fingit, illa fingitur. Nihil ars sine materia, materiae etiam sine arte pretium est; ars summa materia optima melior.

20

1   Illa quaestio est maior, ex mediis artibus, quae neque laudari per se nec vituperari possunt, sed utiles aut secus secundum mores utentium fiunt, habenda sit rhetorice, an
sit, ut compluribus etiam philosophorum placet, virtus.
2   Equidem illud quod in studiis dicendi plerique exercuerunt et exercent aut nullam artem, quae ἀτεχνία nomina-
tur, puto (multos enim video sine ratione, sine litteris, qua
vel impudentia vel fames duxit ruentes), aut malam quasi
artem, quam κακοτεχνίαν dicimus: nam et fuisse multos
et esse nonnullos existimo qui facultatem dicendi ad homi-

---

1 μέσαι τέχναι (*SVF* 3. 505) are morally indifferent, and can
be used for good or bad purposes. The concept is a Stoic one, but
the Stoics (Cicero, *De oratore* 3.65) did in fact regard eloquence
both as "knowledge" and as "virtue," so that the Wise Man was the
only true orator (*SVF* 3. 654–656).
2 See 2.15.2.

nature, I think, will still have the greater influence, whereas perfect orators owe more to teaching than to nature. Similarly, an infertile soil will not be improved even by the best farmer, and good land will yield a useful crop even if no one tills it, but on any fertile ground the farmer will do more than the goodness of the soil can do by itself. If Praxiteles had tried to make a statue out of a millstone, I should have preferred an unworked block of Parian marble; but if he had worked the block of marble, the result would have owed more to his skill as a craftsman than to the stone. In a word: nature is the raw material of teaching; the one forms, the other is formed. Without material, art can do nothing; material has a value apart from art; the highest art is better than the best material.

CHAPTER 20

Is rhetoric a virtue?

A more important question is whether rhetoric is to be regarded as one of the "indifferent" arts,[1] which cannot be praised or blamed in themselves, but are useful or otherwise according to the character of the user, or, as many even among the philosophers maintain, as a virtue. For my part, I think that the practice of speaking which many have followed in the past, and still do today, is either a non-art, what is called an *atechnia* (for I see many people rushing in wherever impudence or fear of starvation has led them, without any method or literary training), or else a sort of bad art, what we call a *kakotechnia*.[2] For I believe that there have been many, and still are some, who have turned

3   num perniciem converterint. Ματαιοτεχνία quoque est
quaedam, id est supervacua artis imitatio, quae nihil sane
neque boni neque mali habeat, sed vanum laborem, qualis
illius fuit qui grana ciceris ex spatio distante missa in acum[1]
continuo et sine frustratione inserebat; quem cum spectas-
set Alexander, donasse dicitur eiusdem leguminis modio,
4   quod quidem praemium fuit illo opere dignissimum. His
ego comparandos existimo qui in declamationibus, quas
esse veritati dissimillimas volunt, aetatem multo studio ac
labore consumunt. Verum haec quam instituere conamur
et cuius imaginem animo concepimus, quae bono viro con-
5   venit quaeque est vere rhetorice, virtus erit. Quod philosophi quidem multis et acutis conclusionibus colligunt, mihi
vero etiam planiore hac proprieque nostra probatione
videtur esse perspicuum.

   Ab illis haec dicuntur. Si consonare sibi in faciendis ac
non faciendis virtus[2] est (quae pars eius prudentia voca-
6   tur), eadem in dicendis ac non dicendis erit. Et si virtutes
sunt ad quas nobis, etiam ante quam doceremur, initia
quaedam ac semina sunt concessa natura, ut ad iustitiam,
cuius rusticis quoque ac barbaris apparet aliqua imago, nos

---

[1] orcam *Badius*   [2] virtutis *B*

---

[3] A similar argument is found in *Prolegomenon Sylloge* 262
Rabe, where *kakotechniai* are those which actually do harm, like
the skills of sorcerers or thieves, and *mataiotechniai* are skills
which have no practical use, "as with this pea with holes in it" (ἐπὶ
τούτου τοῦ πολυτρήτου κέγχρου), which suggests a trick something like the one Q. goes on to mention, though apparently not
the same.

[4] Needles for sewing tents or sails or nets, for instance, would

their skill in speaking to the ruin of men. There is also something called *mataiotechnia*,[3] a pointless imitation of art, which has, to be sure, no good or bad in it, but just vain labour—like the man who threw chick peas from a distance through a needle,[4] and without ever missing; Alexander, having watched him, is said to have given him a bushel of the peas—a very appropriate reward for the work. Very comparable to these performers, I feel, are the people who spend their lives, with much study and effort, on declamations which they design to be as unreal as possible. The rhetoric which I am trying to establish, and of which I have formed an idea in my mind, the rhetoric which befits a good man and really *is* rhetoric, will be a virtue. Philosophers come to this conclusion by many ingenious arguments; to me it seems perfectly clear from the simpler and original proof which I give below.[5]

This is what the philosophers say. If consistency in what should and should not be done is a virtue (the part of virtue called prudence), the same virtue should appear in respect of what should and should not be said. Furthermore, if there are virtues of which nature has granted us some rudiments or seeds even before we are taught—justice for instance, some semblance of which is evident to countryfolk and barbarians—it is plain that we have been formed from

be large, and the eye (in netting needles) not necessarily closed. So, if the trick is to throw the pea through the needle's eye, it is not an impossibility. The story has had some popularity: Montaigne, Steele, Boswell, and Hegel all know it in some form. See M. S. Inwood, *Bulletin of the Hegel Society of Great Britain* 35 (1997) 92–93, arguing that Badius' *orcam* (a narrow-necked vessel) is an unnecessary emendation. [5] I.e. in §§8–10.

certe sic esse ab initio formatos ut possemus orare pro nobis, etiamsi non perfecte, tamen ut inessent quaedam, ut
7 dixi, semina eius facultatis, manifestum est. Non eadem
autem iis natura artibus est quae a virtute sunt remotae.
Itaque cum duo sint genera orationis, altera perpetua,
quae rhetorice dicitur, altera concisa, quae dialectice, quas
quidem Zenon adeo coniunxit ut hanc compressae in pug-
num manus, illam explicatae diceret similem, etiam dis-
putatrix virtus erit: adeo de hac, quae speciosior atque
apertior tanto est, nihil dubitabitur.
8   Sed plenius hoc idem atque apertius intueri ex ipsis
operibus volo. Nam quid orator in laudando faciet nisi ho-
nestorum et turpium peritus? aut in suadendo nisi utilitate
perspecta? aut in iudiciis si iustitiae sit ignarus? Quid? non
fortitudinem postulat res eadem, cum saepe contra turbu-
lentas populi minas, saepe cum periculosa potentium
offensa, nonnumquam, ut iudicio Miloniano, inter circum-
fusa militum arma dicendum sit: ut, si virtus non est, ne
perfecta quidem esse possit oratio ?
9   Quod si ea in quoque animalium est virtus qua praestat
cetera vel pleraque, ut in leone impetus, in equo velocitas,
hominem porro ratione atque oratione excellere ceteris
certum est: cur non tam in eloquentia quam in ratione virtutem eius esse credamus, recteque hoc apud Ciceronem
dixerit Crassus: 'est enim eloquentia una quaedam de
summis virtutibus', et ipse Cicero sua persona cum ad
Brutum in epistulis tum aliis etiam locis virtutem eam
appellet?

6 *SVF* 1. 75; Cicero, *Orator* 113.
7 *De oratore* 3.55, *Partitiones oratoriae* 78, *Academica* 1.5; fr.
epist. VII.14 Watt.

the beginning to be able to plead for ourselves, not perfectly of course, but well enough to show that (as I said) there are some seeds of this faculty in us. This natural foundation, however, does not exist in arts which have no relation to virtue. Consequently, as there are two kinds of speech, the extended, called rhetoric, and the concise, called dialectic (Zeno[6] described the relationship between them by saying that one was like the closed fist, and the other like the open hand), the art of disputation too will be a virtue. That means there will be even less doubt about rhetoric, which is so much more splendid and transparent.

I should like however to look at this matter more fully and more explicitly by considering the actual work of the orator. For what will he do in an encomium, unless he understands honour and shame? How can he urge a policy unless he has a grasp of expediency? How can he plead in the law courts if he knows nothing about justice? Again, does not oratory call also for courage, since we often have to speak in the face of threats of public disorder, often at the risk of offending the powerful, and sometimes even, as in the trial of Milo, with armed soldiers all around? So, if it is not virtue, oratory cannot even be complete.

But if the virtue of any animal lies in that in which it surpasses all or most other animals—for example, courage in the lion, or swiftness in the horse—and if it is absolutely certain that man excels other animals in reason and speech, why should we not accept that human virtue lies in eloquence just as much as in reason? Crassus in Cicero will then be quite right to say "Eloquence is one of the highest virtues," and Cicero himself to call it a "virtue," in his letters to Brutus and in other passages.[7]

10   'At prohoemium aliquando ac narrationem dicet malus
homo et argumenta sic ut nihil sit in iis requirendum.'
Nam et latro pugnabit acriter, virtus tamen erit fortitudo,
et tormenta sine gemitu feret malus servus, tolerantia tamen doloris laude sua non carebit. Multa fiunt eadem, sed
aliter. Sufficiant igitur haec, quia de utilitate supra tracta-
vimus.

21

1   Materiam rhetorices quidam dixerunt esse orationem: qua
in sententia ponitur apud Platonem Gorgias. Quae si ita
accipitur ut sermo quacumque de re compositus dicatur
oratio, non materia sed opus est, ut statuarii statua; nam et
oratio efficitur arte sicut statua. Sin hac appellatione verba
ipsa significari putamus, nihil haec sine rerum substantia
2   faciunt. Quidam argumenta persuasibilia: quae et ipsa in
parte sunt operis et arte fiunt et materia egent. Quidam civiles quaestiones: quorum opinio non qualitate sed modo
erravit; est enim haec materia rhetorices, sed non sola.
3   Quidam, quia virtus sit rhetorice, materiam eius totam
vitam vocant. Alii, quia non omnium virtutum materia sit
tota vita, sed pleraeque earum versentur in partibus, sicut
iustitia fortitudo continentia propriis officiis et suo fine in-
telleguntur, rhetoricen quoque dicunt in una aliqua parte

---

8 12.1.23.

9 2.16.

1 Q. here addresses the view that rhetoric cannot be an art because it has no subject peculiar to itself: Lausberg §§47–52.

2 *Gorgias* 449D: rhetoric is περὶ λόγους.

"But a bad man will sometimes produce a Prooemium and a Narrative and a set of Arguments which leave nothing to be desired."[8] Yes: a brigand will fight bravely, but courage will still be a virtue; and a bad slave will bear torture without a groan, but the tolerance of pain will still deserve its proper praise. The same things are often done in ways that make them different. Let this suffice, then, since we dealt with usefulness above.[9]

CHAPTER 21

What is the subject matter of rhetoric?

(1) Some have said that the subject matter or material[1] of rhetoric is "speech": Gorgias is given this opinion in Plato.[2] If this means that discourse composed on any subject is "speech," then it is not the material but the work itself, just as the statue is the work of the sculptor, for a speech, like a statue, is a product of art. If, on the other hand, we think that the actual words are meant, then they have no power without the underlying facts. (2) Some say "persuasive arguments." But these too form *part* of the work, are produced by art, and need material themselves. (3) Some say "political questions." The mistake here lies not in the qualification but in the limitation. This *is* material of rhetoric, but not the only material. (4) Some, on the ground that rhetoric is a virtue, make its material the whole of life. (5) Others, on the ground that life as a whole does not provide material for all virtues—most of them being involved only with parts of it (justice, courage, and self-control are defined by their special functions and ends)—say that rhetoric too must be assigned to some particular area, and they

ponendam, eique locum in ἠθικῇ negotialem adsignant, id
est πραγματικόν.

4   Ego (neque id sine auctoribus) materiam esse rhetorices iudico omnes res quaecumque ei ad dicendum subiectae erunt. Nam Socrates apud Platonem dicere Gor-
giae videtur non in verbis esse materiam sed in rebus, et
in Phaedro palam non in iudiciis modo et contionibus
sed in rebus etiam privatis ac domesticis rhetoricen esse
demonstrat: quo manifestum est hanc opinionem ipsius
5   Platonis fuisse. Et Cicero quodam loco materiam rhetorices vocat res quae subiectae sint ei, sed certas demum
putat esse subiectas: alio vero de omnibus rebus oratori
dicendum arbitratur his quidem verbis: 'quamquam vis
oratoris professioque ipsa bene dicendi hoc suscipere ac
polliceri videtur, ut omni de re quaecumque sit proposita
6   ornate ab eo copioseque dicatur'. Atque adhuc alibi: 'vero
enim oratori quae sunt in hominum vita, quandoquidem
in ea versatur orator atque ea est ei subiecta materies,
omnia quaesita audita lecta disputata tractata agitata esse
debent.'

7   Hanc autem quam nos materiam vocamus, id est res
subiectas, quidam modo infinitam, modo non propriam
rhetorices esse dixerunt, eamque artem circumcurrentem
8   vocaverunt, quod in omni materia diceret. Cum quibus
mihi minima pugna est; nam de omni materia dicere eam

---

3 Reference uncertain. The Academic Eudorus of Alexandria
(Stobaeus 2.42 Hense) divided ethics into (1) theory of value, (2)
study of impulses and emotions, (3) study of action. He does not
discuss rhetoric, but his categories of "encouragement, discour-
agement, and consolation" clearly describe deliberative rhetoric.

place it in the practical or "pragmatic" department of ethics.[3]

For my part (and I have authorities to back me) I hold that the subject matter of rhetoric is everything which is submitted to it for speaking. Socrates in Plato seems to say to Gorgias that the subject matter consists of things, not words,[4] and in the *Phaedrus*[5] he openly proves that rhetoric is concerned not only with law-courts and assemblies, but also with private and domestic affairs. This shows that this was Plato's own opinion. Cicero[6] too says in one passage that the material of rhetoric is "the things submitted to it," but he thinks that these are of certain specific kinds. In another passage, however, he thinks that the orator must speak about everything. I quote:[7] "although the name of orator and the very claim to speak well seems to imply an undertaking and a promise to speak with elegance and fluency on any subject which may be proposed." And again elsewhere:[8] "It is for the true orator to investigate, hear, read, discuss, handle, and ponder every aspect of human life, since it is in this that he has his being, and this is the matter which is put before him."

But this "material," as we call it, in other words the subject of the art, has been said by some to be either "unlimited" or "not peculiar to rhetoric"; they have called it a "runabout" art, because it speaks on every subject. I have no great quarrel with these people. They admit that it speaks about all material, while the reason they give for

4 Perhaps *Gorgias* 451D.   5 261A.
6 *De inventione* 1.7; cf. *De oratore* 1.64–67.
7 *De oratore* 1.21.
8 Ibid. 3.54.

fatentur, propriam habere materiam quia multiplicem habeat negant. Sed neque infinita est, etiamsi est multiplex,
et aliae quoque artes minores habent multiplicem materiam, velut architectonice (namque ea in omnibus quae
9 sunt aedificio utilia versatur) et caelatura, quae auro ar-
gento aere ferro opera efficit. Nam scalptura etiam lignum
ebur marmor vitrum gemmas praeter ea quae supra dixi
10 complectitur. Neque protinus non est materia rhetorices si
in eadem versatur et alius. Nam si quaeram quae sit materia statuarii, dicetur aes: si quaeram quae sit excusoris, id
est fabricae eius quam Graeci χαλκευτικήν vocant, similiter aes esse respondeant: atqui plurimum statuis differunt
11 vasa. Nec medicina ideo non erit ars quia unctio et exercitatio cum palaestrica, ciborum vero qualitas etiam cum
cocorum ei sit arte communis.

12 Quod vero de bono utili iusto disserere philosophiae
officium esse dicunt, non obstat; nam cum philosophum
dicunt, hoc accipi volunt virum bonum. Quare igitur oratorem, quem a bono viro non separo, in eadem materia
13 versari mirer?—cum praesertim primo libro iam ostende-
rim philosophos omissam hanc ab oratoribus partem occu-
passe, quae rhetorices propria semper fuisset, ut illi potius
in nostra materia versentur. Denique cum sit dialectices
materia de rebus subiectis disputare, sit autem dialectice
oratio concisa, cur non eadem perpetuae quoque materia
videatur ?

14 Solet a quibusdam et illud opponi: omnium igitur ar-

---

9 Prooemium 10–17.

saying it has no material peculiar to itself is that it possesses a multifarious material. But "multifarious" material is not necessarily "unlimited"; various minor arts have multifarious materials—architecture, for example, which operates with everything useful for building, or engraving which uses gold, silver, bronze, and iron to produce its work. Carving indeed covers wood, ivory, marble, glass, and jewels, as well as what I have just mentioned. Again, if someone else is also concerned with a particular material, it does not follow that it is not a material of rhetoric. For if I ask what the sculptor's material is, I shall be told bronze; and if I ask what is the material of the smith (I mean the craft which the Greeks call *chalkeutikē*), the answer will likewise be bronze. But there is a lot of difference between statues and bowls. Nor will medicine cease to be an art because it shares the use of unguents and exercise with gymnastics, and diet even with cookery.

As to the point that it is the business of philosophy to discuss the good, the expedient, and the just, there is no problem here. For when they speak of the philosopher, they mean by this a good man. So why should I be surprised that the orator, whom I do not regard as separate from the good man, should occupy himself with the same material—especially as I showed in Book One[9] that the philosophers took over this area, which had always belonged to rhetoric, when the orators gave it up, so that the truth is rather that *they* are busy with *our* material. And finally, as the material of dialectic is the discussion of everything submitted to it, and dialectic is an abbreviated form of rhetoric, why should not continuous speech also have the same material?

There is a further objection that is commonly made by

411

tium peritus erit orator si de omnibus ei dicendum est.
Possem hic Ciceronis respondere verbis, apud quem hoc
invenio: 'mea quidem sententia nemo esse poterit omni
laude cumulatus orator nisi erit omnium rerum magnarum
atque artium scientiam consecutus': sed mihi satis est eius

15 esse oratorem rei de qua dicet non inscium. Neque enim
omnis causas novit, et debet posse de omnibus dicere. De
quibus ergo dicet? De quibus didicit. Similiter de artibus
quoque de quibus dicendum erit interim discet, et de quibus didicerit dicet.

16   Quid ergo? non faber de fabrica melius aut de musice
musicus? Si nesciat orator quid sit de quo quaeratur, plane
melius; nam et litigator rusticus inlitteratusque de causa
sua melius quam orator qui nesciet quid in lite sit: sed ac-
cepta a musico, a fabro, sicut a litigatore, melius orator

17 quam ipse qui docuerit. Verum et faber, cum de fabrica, et
musicus, cum de musica, si quid confirmationem desidera-
verit, dicet: non erit quidem orator, sed faciet illud quasi
orator, sicut, cum vulnus imperitus deligabit, non erit me-

18 dicus, sed faciet ut medicus. An huius modi res neque in
laudem neque in deliberationem neque in iudicium veniunt? Ergo cum de faciendo portu Ostiensi deliberatum
est, non debuit dicere sententiam orator? Atqui opus erat

19 ratione architectorum. Livores et tumores in corpore cru-
ditatis an veneni signa sint non tractat orator? At est id ex

---

10 *De oratore* 1.20.

11 See also 3.8.16. Q. means the enclosed harbour *(portus)*,
two miles north of Ostia itself, planned by Caesar and constructed
under Claudius (Suetonius, *Claudius* 20). This proved unsafe, and
a secure inner harbour was not made until after Q.'s death.

12 E.g. Cicero, *Pro Cluentio* 30; below, 5.9.11.

some critics: "If an orator has to speak on all subjects, he must be a master of all arts." I could have answered this in the words of Cicero, in whom I find this passage:[10] "In my opinion no one can be an orator praiseworthy in every way, unless he has acquired knowledge of all the important things and arts." But it is enough for me that the orator should not be ignorant of the subject on which he has to speak. For he does not know all Causes, and yet he ought to be able to speak on all. On which will he speak then? On those about which he has been instructed. Likewise with the arts: he will sometimes learn about those on which he is to speak, and speak of those about which he has learned.

Well, will not a builder speak better about building and a musician better about music? Of course he will, so long as the orator does not know what the problem is. Even an illiterate rural litigant will plead his own Cause better than an orator who does not know what is in dispute. But if he is instructed by the musician or the builder—or for that matter by the litigant—the orator will plead better than the person who instructed him. Nevertheless, the builder (if building is involved) and the musician (if music is involved) will both speak if there is any point which needs confirmation. They will not of course be orators, but they will be acting as orators, just as when a layman bandages a wound he is not a doctor but he is acting as a doctor. Does this sort of thing never arise in Encomia or in Deliberations or in the courts? When the construction of the harbour at Ostia[11] was discussed, was it not an orator's duty to state his view? Yet it needed the technical knowledge of the architect. Does not the orator deal with the question whether discoloration and swelling of the body are signs of poison or of indigestion?[12] But this needs medical knowl-

ratione medicinae. Circa mensuras et numeros non versabitur? Dicamus has geometriae esse partes. Equidem omnia fere posse credo casu aliquo venire in officium oratoris: quod si non accidet, non erunt ei subiecta.

20   Ita sic quoque recte diximus materiam rhetorices esse omnis res ad dicendum ei subiectas: quod quidem probat etiam sermo communis; nam cum aliquid de quo dicamus accepimus, positam nobis esse materiam frequenter etiam

21   praefatione testamur. Gorgias quidem adeo rhetori de omnibus putavit esse dicendum ut se in auditoriis interrogari pateretur qua quisque de re vellet. Hermagoras quoque dicendo materiam esse in causa et in quaestionibus omnes

22   res subiectas erat complexus: sed quaestiones si negat ad rhetoricen pertinere, dissentit a nobis; si autem ad rhetoricen pertinent, ab hoc quoque adiuvamur: nihil est enim

23   quod non in causam aut quaestionem cadat. Aristoteles tris faciendo partes orationis, iudicialem deliberativam demonstrativam, paene[1] et ipse oratori subiecit omnia: nihil enim non in haec cadit.

24   Quaesitum a paucissimis et de instrumento est. Instrumentum voco sine quo formari materia in id quod velimus effici opus non possit. Verum hoc ego non artem credo egere, sed artificem. Neque enim scientia desiderat instru-

---

[1] plane *Ammon*

---

[13] Plato, *Gorgias* 447E; Cicero, *De inventione* 1.7; *De oratore* 1.103, 3.128; Philostratus, *Lives of the Sophists* 1.1; and see below, 12.11.21.

[14] Fr. 6c Matthes: Cicero, *De inventione* 1.8.

[15] This must mean "general" Questions (see 3.5.12).

[16] Aristotle, *Rhetoric* 1. 1358b6.

edge. Will he not be concerned sometimes with measurements and figures? We may say that these are part of geometry. Indeed, I think almost anything can come into the orator's sphere on occasion; if it does not, it will not be his subject.

We were right therefore in saying that the material of rhetoric is everything that is submitted to it for speaking. Our ordinary way of talking confirms this. For when we have taken on a subject to speak about, we often make it clear in our preliminary remarks that the theme has been proposed to us. Gorgias indeed was so sure that it was an orator's duty to speak on all subjects that he allowed the audience to put questions to him on any subject they chose.[13] Hermagoras[14] also, by saying that the material consisted of the Cause and the Questions, thus included all matters submitted to the orator. If he denies that Questions[15] belong to rhetoric, his opinion is not the same as mine; but if they do belong to rhetoric, this too supports my position. For there is nothing that does not fall either under "Cause" or under "Questions." Aristotle, with his three divisions of rhetoric[16]—Forensic, Deliberative, and Epideictic—also brought virtually everything within the orator's sphere; for there is nothing that does not come under these heads.

The "instrument" of oratory

A few scholars have also raised the question of "instrument." By this I mean "that without which the material cannot be shaped into the work we wish to produce." But, in my view, it is not the art that needs this, but the artist. Knowledge needs no "instrument," because it can be per-

mentum, quae potest esse consummata etiam si nihil faciat, sed ille opifex, ut caelator caelum et pictor penicilla.
Itaque haec in eum locum quo de oratore dicturi sumus
differamus.

fect even if it does nothing, but the artist needs one; an engraver needs his chisel, and a painter his brush. So I shall put this question aside until I come to discuss the orator himself.[17]

[17] 12.5.1.

INDEX OF PROPER NAMES

INDEX OF PROPER NAMES

INDEX OF PROPER NAMES

INDEX OF PROPER NAMES

INDEX OF PROPER NAMES

INDEX OF PROPER NAMES

Prodamus, character in a comedy by Eupolis: 1.10.18

Pyrrhus (319–272 BC), king of Epirus: 2.16.7

Pythagoras of Samos (sixth century BC), philosopher, and Pythagoreans: 1.10.12, 32; 1.12.15

Quirinalis: 1.6.31

Rome, Romans: 1.5.44, 68

Romulus, founder and first king of Rome: 2.4.19

Sabines, people of the Tiber valley and central Apennines: 1.5.56

Salii, college of priests in Rome, whose ritual was a dance: 1.6.40; 1.10.20

Sallustius Crispus, C. (86–35 BC), Roman historian: 2.5.19; 2.13.14

Sardinia, Sardinians: 1.5.8

Saturninus, L. Appuleius, trib. pleb. 103, 100; killed 99 BC: 2.16.5

Saturnus (Saturn): 1.6.36

Scipio (1) P. Cornelius Scipio Africanus (236–185 BC), the conqueror of Hannibal: 2.4.19. (2) P. Cornelius Scipio Aemilianus Africanus (c.185–129 BC), destroyer of Carthage and of Numantia; adopted son of the elder Africanus' son: 1.7.25

Servius Sulpicius Galba, accused of treacherously killing or enslaving 8000 Lusitani in 151 BC; consul 144 BC: 2.15.8

Sicily, Sicilians: 1.6.30; 1.10.48

Sisenna, L. Cornelius, praetor 78 BC, historian: 1.5.13

Socrates (469–399 BC), philosopher: 1.10.13; 1.11.7; 2.15–17, 2.21 *passim*

Sophron, of Syracuse (fifth century BC), writer of mimes: 1.10.17

Spain, Spanish: 1.5.8, 57

Stoics: 1.4.19; 2.15.20; 2.17.2

Sufenas, (?) Roman cognomen: 1.5.62

Sulpicius Gallus (or Galus), C., consul 166 BC: 1.10.47; 2.15.8 (if the same person is meant)

INDEX OF PROPER NAMES